Transcendence and the Concrete

Series Board

James Bernauer

Drucilla Cornell

Thomas R. Flynn

Kevin Hart

Richard Kearney

Jean-Luc Marion

Adriaan Peperzak

Thomas Sheehan

Hent de Vries

Merold Westphal

Michael Zimmerman

John D. Caputo, *series editor*

Perspectives in
Continental
Philosophy

JEAN WAHL

Transcendence and the Concrete
Selected Writings

Edited by Alan D. Schrift
and Ian Alexander Moore

Fordham University Press
New York ▪ 2017

Frontispiece: The volume editors thank the Mount Holyoke College Archives and Special Collections for permission to use this photograph of Jean Wahl at the 1944 Entretiens de Pontigny on the Mount Holyoke College campus.

Copyright © 2017 Fordham University Press

All rights reserved. No part of this publication may be reproduced, stored in a retrieval system, or transmitted in any form or by any means—electronic, mechanical, photocopy, recording, or any other—except for brief quotations in printed reviews, without the prior permission of the publisher.

Fordham University Press has no responsibility for the persistence or accuracy of URLs for external or third-party Internet websites referred to in this publication and does not guarantee that any content on such websites is, or will remain, accurate or appropriate.

Fordham University Press also publishes its books in a variety of electronic formats. Some content that appears in print may not be available in electronic books.

Visit us online at www.fordhampress.com.

Library of Congress Cataloging-in-Publication Data available online at catalog.loc.gov.

Printed in the United States of America

19 18 17   5 4 3 2 1

First edition

Contents

1	Existence, Experience, and Transcendence: An Introduction to Jean Wahl	*1*
2	Preface to *Toward the Concrete*	*32*
3	Commentary on a Passage from Hegel's *Phenomenology of Spirit*	*54*
4	Hegel and Kierkegaard	*90*
5	Heidegger and Kierkegaard: An Investigation into the Original Elements of Heidegger's Philosophy	*107*
6	The Problem of Choice: Existence and Transcendence in Jaspers's Philosophy	*132*
7	Subjectivity and Transcendence	*152*
	Appendix: Jean Wahl's Letter to Martin Heidegger, December 12, 1937	*213*
8	Nietzsche and the Death of God: A Note on Jaspers's *Nietzsche*	*216*
9	Poetry and Metaphysics	*220*
10	Order and Disorder in Nietzsche's Thought	*237*
11	Experience and Transcendence; or, An Ontological Journey	*256*

Acknowledgments	*277*
A Bibliography of Works by Jean Wahl	*279*
Index of Names	*287*

The endless ending of metaphysics in contemporary French philosophy began with Wahl's metaphysical experience. . . . It has been a forerunner of certain daring undertakings (which are not all unduly extreme) of current philosophy. It is fair to say that in France it has paved the way for a new kind of reader and writer in philosophy and a new sort of book.
       —**Emmanuel Levinas,**
        "Jean Wahl: Neither Having nor Being"

Existence, Experience, and Transcendence
An Introduction to Jean Wahl

IAN ALEXANDER MOORE
AND ALAN D. SCHRIFT

> There should be no permanent split between academic philosophy and existentialism. Such a split, if it were possible, would leave existentialism without a content and academic philosophy without real life.
> —*Jean Wahl*

Jean Wahl, once considered by the likes of Georges Bataille and Gilles Deleuze to be among the greatest philosophers in France, and by Emmanuel Levinas to be "the life force of the academic, extra-academic, and even, to a degree, anti-academic philosophy necessary to a great culture,"[1] has today nearly been forgotten outside France. Yet his influence on French thought can hardly be overestimated. As professor at the Sorbonne for over three decades, president of the Société Française de Philosophie (1960–74), editor of the *Revue de Métaphysique et de Morale* (1950–74), and founder and director of the Collège Philosophique, Wahl was in dialogue with some of the most prominent and well-known French philosophers and intellectuals of the twentieth century, including Bataille, Henri Bergson, Simone de Beauvoir, Michel Butor, Deleuze, Jacques Derrida, Michel Foucault, Édouard Glissant, Jean Hyppolite, Claude Lévi-Strauss, Gabriel Marcel, Jacques Maritain, Jacques Lacan, Levinas, Jean-Paul Sartre, and Simone Weil, impacting several of them greatly. Wahl, who has been called "the

---

1. Emmanuel Levinas, *Outside the Subject*, trans. Michael B. Smith (Stanford, Calif.: Stanford University Press, 1994), 67.

most influential French interpreter of contemporary philosophy,"[2] also played a significant role, in some cases almost singlehandedly, in introducing French philosophy to movements such as phenomenology, existentialism, American pragmatism and literature, and British empiricism. And Wahl was an original philosopher and poet in his own right. He was, along with Gabriel Marcel, among the first to make the case that philosophy must look to the real, to the actual rather than the ideal, and attend to the concrete data of human existence. It was his focus on existence that made it possible for him to put forward a novel account of transcendence that avoided the assumption that transcendence must take us out of this world into some otherworldly domain. Instead, Wahl understood transcendence to be itself a fundamental component of what it means to exist as a human being. It was his focus on existence and transcendence that guided his interpretations of G. W. F. Hegel and Søren Kierkegaard as well as his encounters with Martin Heidegger and Karl Jaspers, and while a sensitive and insightful reader of the work of others, his own philosophical voice comes through clearly in all of his writings, as the selections we have chosen for this volume will show. After providing a biographical sketch of Jean Wahl (Section I), we will examine his influence on some of the most important French philosophers of the twentieth century (Section II), his introduction of philosophical movements and figures into France, Great Britain, and the United States (Section III), and his own original philosophical and poetic approaches to transcendence and the concrete (Section IV).

I

Jean André Wahl was born on May 25, 1888, into a secular Jewish family in Marseille, France.[3] The family relocated to Paris, where Wahl studied at the Lycée Janson de Sailly, where his father, Edmond, was a professor of

---

2. Angèle Kremer-Marietti, "Jean Wahl the Precursor," *Analecta Husserliana* 104 (2009): 335.

3. For the biographical information in this section, we have drawn from our own archival research and a variety of sources, including: Emmanuel Levinas, Xavier Tilliette, and Paul Ricoeur, *Jean Wahl et Gabriel Marcel*, ed. Jeanne Hersch (Paris: Beauchesne, 1976), 89–90; Christopher Benfey's articles "Introduction: A Violence from Within" and "A Tale of Two Iliads," both in *Artists, Intellectuals, and World War II: The Pontigny Encounters at Mount Holyoke College, 1942–1944*, ed. Christopher Benfey and Karen Remmler (Amherst: University of Massachusetts Press, 2006), 1–13 and 207–19, respectively; Alejandro Cavallazzi Sánchez and Azucena Palavicini Sánchez, "Jean Wahl: Philosophies of Existence and the Introduction of Kierkegaard in the Non-Germanic World," in *Kierkegaard and Existentialism*, ed. Jon Stewart (Burlington,

English, occupying the post once held by Stéphane Mallarmé. Wahl did one year of *khâgne* at Lycée Louis-le-Grand (1906–07) before entering the École Normale Supérieure, where he studied from 1907 to 1910. In 1910 he passed the *agrégation* (the competitive examination for recruiting teachers) at the top of his class, followed by his longtime friend Gabriel Marcel. He received a three-year scholarship from the Thiers Foundation and taught at secondary schools in Saint-Quentin, Nantes, Tours, and Le Mans. In 1920, Wahl earned his *doctorat ès lettres* under the direction of Henri Bergson with the submission of a principal thesis on *Les philosophies pluralistes d'Angleterre et d'Amérique* (*The Pluralist Philosophies of England and America*) and a *thèse complémentaire* on "*Le rôle de l'idée de l'instant chez Descartes*" (The role of the idea of the moment in the philosophy of Descartes).

Wahl taught in the Faculty of Letters at the Universities of Besançon, Nancy (1927–29) and Lyon (1929–36) before being called to join the faculty in philosophy at the Sorbonne, where he taught the history of philosophy (his initial appointment was in the history of ancient philosophy), assuming a professor's chair in 1936. During the German invasion of 1940—in fact, one day before the Germans entered Paris on June 14—Wahl "was whisked out of the city by three of his students, all Chinese," and fled to Bayonne in the south of France, where his parents had already taken refuge.[4] When Wahl learned that the Sorbonne would reopen for the school year, he returned to Paris in September, only to be forced to retire in December as a result of the first Vichy Statute on Jews of October 3, 1940, which excluded Jews from many professions, including teaching.[5]

Vt.: Ashgate, 2011), 394–96, and the accounts of Wahl's flight from France and his time in the United States by Elizabeth Alden Green and Hamilton Basso, cited below.

For Wahl's personality, physical features, mannerisms, and teaching style, see the short "Portrait de Jean Wahl" by his former student Xavier Tilliette in *Archives de Philosophie* 37, no. 4 (October–December 1974): 529–32; as well as Maurice Patronnier de Gandillac's tribute, "Wahl," in the *Association amicale des anciens élèves de l'École Normale Supérieure* (Paris: Librairie Hachette, 1975), 38–45.

4. Elizabeth Alden Green, "Philosopher in the Toils," 7. Green, a professor of English at Mount Holyoke College, wrote this twenty-three-page typescript account of Wahl's life and escape from Europe based upon conversations with Wahl. The manuscript is housed in the Fonds Jean Wahl at IMEC, the Institut Mémoires de l'Édition Contemporaine, at the Abbaye d'Ardenne, outside of Caen. See also Barbara Wahl, "Autour de Jean Wahl: Textes, Traces, Témoignages," *Revista di Storia della Filosofia* 66, no. 3 (2001): 517–38, esp. 519.

5. As he had been doing since the 1937–38 academic year, Wahl had also committed to teaching the *agrégation* preparatory course on ancient philosophy at the École Normale Supérieure (ENS) in the spring. However, because the ENS director Jérôme

Nevertheless, from November until May 1941 Wahl met regularly with a group of fifteen students from the École Normale Supérieure in his hotel room on rue des Beaux-Arts. In fact, on the very day the Gestapo seized the area, Wahl was reading Heidegger and Friedrich Hölderlin for a small circle of students,[6] and he is reported to have joked with them that "If the Gestapo comes, it will not hurt to say that we are studying Heidegger. The Nazis at one time thought highly of him."[7]

In July 1941, perhaps because of his criticism of the collaborationist turn of *La Nouvelle Revue Française*,[8] for which he had formerly written, Wahl was arrested by the Gestapo, interrogated, and tortured at La Santé prison, where he was held for thirty-six days. Although conditions at the prison were difficult, he was allowed to keep the English edition of Shakespeare his brother had given him; he read three plays a day and translated some of the sonnets into French, and although refused access to a pencil, he managed to write several poems by means of scratching on packaging paper with a needle.[9] From La Santé, Wahl was transferred to the notorious Drancy

---

Carcopino's request for funding these courses had been denied, he regretfully released Wahl from his teaching duties at the ENS. See Jérôme Carcopino's letter of November 19, 1940, to Wahl in *Collaboration and Resistance: French Literary Life under the Nazi Occupation*, ed. Robert O. Paxton, Olivier Corpet, and Claire Paulhan, trans. Jeffrey Mehlman et al. (New York: Five Ties Publishing, 2009), 187. Originally published in French under the title *Archives de la vie littéraire sous l'occupation: À travers le désastre* (Paris: Éditions Tallandier / Éditions de l'IMEC, 2009).

6. Maurice de Gandillac, "Jean Wahl existentialiste?," *Magazine Littéraire* 320 (1994): 39. Gandillac mentions elsewhere that during this period Wahl "had the audacity to intervene with the German authorities to defend the library of [his uncle by marriage and former senior colleague at the Sorbonne Léon] Brunschvicg," who had already left Paris for the free zone in the south of France (42).

7. Hamilton Basso, "Profiles: Philosopher," *New Yorker*, May 12, 1945, 31; see Stanley Cavell, "Reflections on Wallace Stevens at Mount Holyoke," in Benfey and Remmler, *Artists, Intellectuals*, 66.

8. Basso, "Profiles," 31.

9. Green, "Philosopher in the Toils," 14. See also Riccardo Piaggio, *Tra esistenza e pensiero: Saggio su Jean Wahl* (Genoa: Il Melangolo, 2007), 29; and Marcel Raymond, "Présentation aux poèmes," in Jean Wahl, *Poèmes*, with a frontispiece and seven drawings by André Masson (Montréal: Éditions de l'Arbre, 1945), 11. Wahl was only able to decipher one of these poems, "Evening in the Walls," which Charles Guenther describes as "a terse, powerful record of prisoners speaking to each other at night through the windows of their cells, sharing in the darkness their deepest thoughts, emotions, and speculations on their fate." Charles Guenther, "Introduction" to Jean Wahl, *Voices in the Dark: Fifteen Poems of the Prison and the Camp*, trans. Charles Guenther (Kirkwood, Mo.: The Printery, 1974), 8–9. In Guenther's translation: "You are with me this evening, all my friends. / I hear your voices in the dark, I see your

internment camp. While treatment of those held at Drancy by their French guards was, in some ways, more brutal than treatment by the Germans at La Santé, Drancy did not prohibit those interned from having pencils, thus allowing Wahl to write just under one hundred poems.[10] In addition, there was a certain amount of freedom to move about and congregate, thereby allowing Wahl at one point to deliver a lecture on Bergson to three hundred men.[11]

How Wahl eventually got out of Drancy and then out of occupied France involved a series of fortuitous events and more than a little good luck. In the United States, the Rockefeller Foundation, which had set up a fund to assist "deposed scholars" in 1933, established an Emergency Program for European Scholars in 1940 that placed Wahl's name on a list of one hundred important European scholars to be assisted in leaving Europe because their lives were deemed to be threatened by the Nazis.[12] A first step in this process was an appointment in the United States, and Wahl learned of his appointment to the faculty of the New School for Social Research while still in Drancy through a French woman who served as a head nurse and happened to be the friend of a friend of one of Wahl's colleagues at the Sorbonne. During a serious outbreak of dysentery at Drancy, the fear that too many of the guards might succumb to the outbreak led to the decision to release some eight hundred of the most ill prisoners. A French doctor who was aware of Wahl's offer from the New School man-

---

faces. / My power is made of all your little powers. And as I think of you I gather strength" (15). Wahl's French, titled "Soirée dans les murs, août '41," reads: "Vous êtes avec moi ce soir, tous mes amis, / J'entends vos voix dans l'ombre et je vois vos visages. / Mon courage se fait avec tous vos courages. / C'est en pensant à vous que je me raffermis" (Wahl, *Poèmes*, 125).

10. Guenther, "Introduction," 10. See Jean Wahl, *Poèmes de circonstance (1939–1941)* (Lyon: DIA, 1944), as well as Wahl, *Poèmes*, 125–45. A selection of these poems is available in English in Wahl, *Voices in the Dark*, and in the more widely available volume edited by Howard Schwartz and Anthony Rudolf, *Voices within the Ark: The Modern Jewish Poets* (New York: Avon, 1980), 924–25. Guenther explains that he had already translated and published some of Wahl's poetry in several places, including the *New Yorker* and *Driftwood* ("Introduction," 11).

11. Basso, "Profiles," 35.

12. See the online archives of the Rockefeller Foundation, http://rockefeller100.org/exhibits/show/peace-and-conflict/refugee-scholar-program and http://www.rockarch.org/collections/rf/refugee.php. Others on this list included Georges Gurvitch, Alexandre Koyré, Claude Lévi-Strauss, and Karl Löwith. Wahl also wrote to the Emergency Committee in Aid of Displaced Foreign Scholars on February 4, 1941, from Lyon about the possibility of teaching in the United States. A facsimile of his letter is available in Paxton, Corpet, and Paulhan, *Collaboration and Resistance*, 323.

aged to get him on the list of those to be released, and Jean Wahl left Drancy sixty-four days after his initial arrival.[13]

What happened next is recounted by Elizabeth Alden Green:

> In spite of the fact that his name appeared on two lists of German enemies to be shot [Basso reports that Theodor Dannecker, a protégé of Eichmann and head of the Department of Jewish Affairs in Paris, had put his name on a list of public enemies to be shot on sight] M. Wahl stayed in Paris [after his release from Drancy] for two weeks before attempting the dash across the border to unoccupied France.[14] Only the two last days, he slept outside his ordinary hotel. . . . He boarded a train in Paris without molestation. Getting off at a small village, he made a succession of trips by car with strangers to remote houses, according to a prearranged plan. The actual crossing entailed risk because the Germans had been tightening up their border supervision. After an anxious night's delay, a man came with an empty butcher cart. M. Wahl, covered with the same kind of cloth that wrapped the sides of meat, rode a half mile toward the border in the back of the cart. The unexpected presence of Germans at the chosen crossing point forced M. Wahl and his guide to abandon the cart and dash across the open fields for nearly two miles. On the other side another car picked up M. Wahl and took him to safety.[15]

---

13. This narrative is pieced together from information in the accounts by Basso, Green, and Barbara Wahl. Maurice de Gandillac maintains that Wahl's former student, the philosopher, poet, and translator Pierre Boutang (1916–98), was ultimately responsible for both Wahl's release from the camp and his flight to America; see Gandillac, "Jean Wahl existentialiste," 39; and Salomon Malka, *Emmanuel Levinas: His Life and Legacy*, trans. Michael Kigel and Sonja M. Embree (Pittsburgh: Duquesne University Press, 2006), 150. This is supported in part by Paxton, Corpet, and Paulhan, *Collaboration and Resistance*, 324, who note that Boutang welcomed the families of Wahl and Rachel Bespaloff in Casablanca during their escape to the United States, though it is not clear that any of Wahl's family members accompanied them on the transatlantic voyage.

14. Jacques Le Rider reports that during these two weeks Wahl resumed his intellectual activities in Paris, even venturing, despite the protests of his friends, to attend one of the Saturday gatherings at the apartment of Marcel Moré, a member of the editorial board of *Esprit*, whose gatherings were frequented by former members of the College of Sociology as well as philosophers including Sartre, Beauvoir, Gandillac, and Jean Hyppolite. See Jacques Le Rider, *Nietzsche en France: De la fin du XIXe siècle au temps présent* (Paris: Presses Universitaires de France, 1999), 183.

15. Green, "Philosopher in the Toils," 18–19. Cf. Basso's remark, 36. See also Marion Kingston, "Packaged as Meat, Frenchman Jean Wahl Flees Nazi Captors in

Safety here was Wahl's brother Paul's house in Mâcon, just over the border in the French Free Zone. Eventually, Wahl was able to join his friend Rachel Bespaloff[16] and her family in Marseilles, and six months after he had left Paris, in June 1942, Wahl and Bespaloff left for Casablanca, where they spent a week before boarding "a ship from Lisbon which docked in Baltimore July 31 with nearly 600 Jewish refugees."[17] It was the last refugee ship to leave France, and it arrived in Baltimore exactly one year and one day after Wahl's initial arrest and detention at La Santé.

In the United States, Wahl settled first in New York and was associated with the École Libre des Hautes Études, which had by then been established as a unit within the New School.[18] In 1942, at the instigation of

---

Dramatic Escape," *Mount Holyoke News*, September 26, 1942, 1, col. 2/3, and 3, col. 5; and the *Smith College Associated News*, September 22, 1944, 1, col. 1.

16. For biographical information about Rachel Bespaloff, see Chapter 7, note 54. On Bespaloff and her relation to Wahl, especially as regards the latter's involvement in both Simone Weil's "L'Iliade ou le poème de la force" and Bespaloff's *De l'Iliade*, for which Wahl wrote a preface, see Benfey, "A Tale of Two Iliads," in Benfey and Remmler, *Artists, Intellectuals*.

Weil's essay was first published in *Cahiers du Sud* and can be found in a bilingual critical edition under *Simone Weil's "The Iliad or the Poem of Force": A Critical Edition*, ed. and trans. James P. Holoka (New York: Peter Lang, 2003). Bespaloff's text can be found in Rachel Bespaloff, *De l'Iliade*, preface by Jean Wahl (New York: Brentano's, 1943). Both texts are available in English (without Wahl's preface) under Simone Weil and Rachel Bespaloff, *War and the "Iliad*," trans. Mary McCarthy (New York: New York Review of Books, 2005). Wahl's preface, as well as a long review Wahl wrote of Bespaloff's *Cheminements et carrefours* (originally published in 1940 in *Revue Philosophique*), can be found in Rachel Bespaloff, *Lettres à Jean Wahl (1937–1947): Sur le fond le plus déchiqueté de l'histoire*, ed. Monique Jutrin (Paris: Éditions Claire Paulhan, 2003), 164–79 and 180–82, respectively. See also Wahl's preface to the French translation of a book by Bespaloff's daughter, Naomi Levinson, *Les chevaux de bois d'Amérique*, translated from the English by Colette Thomas (Paris: Julliard, 1954).

On Wahl and Weil, their political views regarding the Vichy regime, and the interest in Wahl by the Office of Strategic Services, see Jeffrey Mehlman, *Émigré New York: French Intellectuals in Wartime Manhattan, 1940–1944* (Baltimore: Johns Hopkins University Press, 2000), 100–102. See also the letter Weil wrote to Wahl in 1942, which Wahl published a decade later in *Deucalion* 4 ("Le diurne et le nocturne dans la nature, dans l'art et dans l'acte"), vol. 36 of *Être et penser: Cahiers de philosophie* (Neuchâtel: Éditions de la Baconnière, 1952), 253–57.

17. Green, "Philosopher in the Toils," 20; Basso sets the arrival date as July 30.

18. Founded by medieval theater scholar Gustave Cohen, philosopher Jacques Maritain (who later served as president of the school), and art historian Henri Focillon, with the strong support of Alvin Johnson, the head of the New School for Social Research, and financial support from the Rockefeller Foundation, the École Libre des Hautes Études was legally a part of the New School for Social Research and operated

Helen Elizabeth Patch, chair of the French Language and Literature Department at Mount Holyoke College, Wahl joined a committee to explore the possibility of reconstituting in the United States the ten-day discussion meetings (*décades*) that had been organized by Paul Desjardins and held at the Abbey he owned in Pontigny, France, from 1910–1914 and 1922 until the German occupation during World War II. Wahl had been a frequent attendee at the Pontigny meetings,[19] and he was joined on the committee by Helen Patch, Jacques Maritain, Gustave Cohen, Raymond de Saussure, and Pierre Guedenet, a French professor at Mount Holyoke. The first of the symposiums at Mount Holyoke took place in the summer of 1942, lasting four weeks rather than ten days. In response to his participation and facilitation of the success of this first gathering, Wahl was invited to join the faculty at Mount Holyoke, where he taught from 1942 to 1945 before returning to France after the war.[20] Following that first meeting, the next two *entretiens* were largely organized by Wahl. As Christopher Benfey has written, "Jean Wahl was uniquely positioned, by temperament and training, for his role of cultural intermediary. He was a master of the 'in-between,' a writer and thinker who instinctively worked the seams of

---

for five years, providing an opportunity for exiled French-speaking intellectuals—many of whom were Jewish—to teach, do research, and share an approximation of Francophone culture with fellow emigrés in New York City. Others associated with the École Libre include Georges Gurvitch, Roman Jakobson, Claude Lévi-Strauss, and Alexandre Koyré (who served as dean). Following its dissolution in 1946, Lévi-Strauss, Koyré, and others returned to France and decided to establish an educational institution based on many of the same principles of the École Libre, the result of which was the creation in 1947 of the École des Hautes Études en Sciences Sociales. The history of the École Libre des Hautes Études is recounted in several places—not always consistently—including Aristide R. Zolberg, "The École Libre at the New School, 1941–1946," *Social Research* (Winter 1998): 921–51; and François Chaubet and Emmanuelle Loyer, "L'École Libre des Hautes Études de New York: Exil et résistance intellectuelle (1942–1946)," *Revue Historique* 302, no. 4 (October–December 2000): 939–72.

19. Laurent Jeanpierre notes that Wahl had "been slated to organize the 1939 *décade*, on the subject of destiny" (Laurent Jeanpierre, "Pontigny-en-Amérique," trans. John Cullen in Benfey and Remmler, *Artists, Intellectuals*, 23). Wahl wrote a report of the 1939 gathering, in which he also refers to topics of previous years. See Jean Wahl, "Entretiens de 1939 à Pontigny," *La Nouvelle Revue Française* 28, no. 316 (January 1, 1940): 137–39; and "Le destin à Pontigny en 1939," in *Poésie, pensée, perception* (Paris: Calmann-Lévy, 1948), 275–79. There is a picture of Wahl with Raymond Aron and Vladimir Jankélévitch at the 1937 gathering "On the Unity of Philosophy" in Paxton, Corpet, and Paulhan, *Collaboration and Resistance*, 33.

20. It was upon Wahl's recommendation that Rachel Bespaloff was invited to join the faculty of the French Department at Mount Holyoke College in 1943, where she taught until taking her own life on April 6, 1949.

cultures, natures, and languages."[21] And as Laurent Jeanpierre points out, "Starting in 1943 . . . Wahl decided virtually alone what topics would be discussed and what invitations would be sent out."[22] Under Wahl's direction, Pontigny-en-Amérique took on a different focus, concentrating less on reproducing a French event on American soil than on seeking to be both more interdisciplinary and open to the arts and sciences, and also to be "a site of intellectual and artistic *encounter*, primarily between France and the United States."[23] Among those who participated in these *entretiens* were some of the most prominent intellectuals and artists of the day, including Hannah Arendt, Louise Bourgeois, Marc Chagall, Roman Jakobson, Susanne Langer, Claude Lévi-Strauss, Karl Löwith, André Masson, Marianne Moore, Robert Motherwell, Wallace Stevens, and Ossip Zadkine.[24]

After the war, Wahl returned to France and resumed his position at the Sorbonne. Soon thereafter, he married a former student, Marcelle Sicard, and they made their apartment a central meeting place for intellectuals and artists.[25] In addition to teaching at the Sorbonne during the next few decades, Wahl was also a visiting professor at the University of Chicago, the University of California at Berkeley, Tunis University, and Smith College. In 1946, Wahl founded both the Collège Philosophique—an organization outside the formal university system that would meet three times a week and that provided a forum and audience for controversial and noninstitutionally sanctioned thinkers to present their work[26]—which he would

---

21. Benfey, "Introduction," 5.
22. Jeanpierre, "Pontigny-en-Amérique," 25.
23. Benfey, "Introduction," 5.
24. Entretiens de Pontigny Collection, Mount Holyoke College, Archives and Special Collections, South Hadley, Mass. See in general Benfey and Remmler, *Artists, Intellectuals*, and Benfey, "Introduction."
25. In doing so, they were carrying on a tradition of Gabriel Marcel, who at his "'Friday afternoons' . . . held an open house for everyone who wanted to investigate a philosophical theme that he came up with" (Jeanette Bresson Ladegaard Knox, "Gabriel Marcel: The Silence of Truth," in Stewart, *Kierkegaard and Existentialism*, 203). Knox mentions Wahl, Levinas, Sartre, and Paul Ricoeur as attending Marcel's Friday gatherings. See also Ethan Kleinberg, *Generation Existential: Heidegger's Philosophy in France, 1927–1961* (Ithaca, N.Y.: Cornell University Press, 2005), 44: "Young intellectuals seeking material outside traditional French philosophy would come [to Marcel's] to hear discussions about Kierkegaard, Nietzsche, and even Heidegger."
26. Participants and attendees included musicians, historians, artists, psychoanalysts, philosophers, and poets. Notable figures included Raymond Aron, Georges Bataille, Yves Bonnefoy, Martin Buber, Michel Butor, Georges Canguilhem, Gilles Deleuze, Paul de Man, Jacques Derrida, Pierre Hadot, Jean Hyppolite, Eugène Ionesco, Vladimir Jankélévitch, Alexandre Kojève (for whose talk over three hundred people

direct for twenty years, and the journal *Deucalion*, which he would edit until 1957. From 1950 until his death in Paris on June 19, 1974, he was the editor of the *Revue de Métaphysique et de Morale*, and he also served as president of the Société Française de Philosophie following the death of Gaston Berger in late 1960. During this time he was awarded the distinction of Grand Officier of the Ordre National de la Légion d'Honneur, as well as the Grand Prix Littéraire de la Ville de Paris.

II

As a prolific and incredibly active philosopher, historian, and poet, Wahl's influence extended to many of the most important French philosophers of the twentieth century. Wahl was Levinas's "unforgettable friend"[27] and mentor, "one of my privileged interlocutors," Levinas

---

were in attendance), Alexandre Koyré, Jacques Lacan, Emmanuel Levinas, André Lichnerowicz, Gabriel Marcel, Louis Massignon, Maurice Merleau-Ponty, Raymond Queneau, Paul Ricoeur, Alain Robbe-Grillet, Jean-Paul Sartre, and Eric Weil. This information can be found in Raymond Aron, *Mémoires* (Paris: R. Laffont, 2003), 312; Georges Canguilhem, *Knowledge of Life*, ed. Paola Marrati and Todd Meyers, trans. Stefanos Geroulanos and Daniela Ginsburg (New York: Fordham University Press, 2008), 155n1; Annie Cohen-Solal, *Jean-Paul Sartre: A Life*, ed. Norman MacAfee, trans. Anna Cancogni (New York: The New Press, 2005), 388–89; Jacques Derrida, *The Work of Mourning*, ed. Pascale-Anne Brault and Michael Naas (Chicago: University of Chicago Press, 2001), 70; Jean-Pierre Faye, "Collège philosophique: Inlassable questionnement," in *Mots de passe 1945–1985: Petit abécédaire des modes de vie*, ed. Pascal Ory (Paris: Autrement, 1985), 72; Leo Strauss, *On Tyranny*, rev. and expanded ed. including the Strauss-Kojève correspondence, ed. Victor Gourevitch and Michael S. Roth (Chicago: University of Chicago Press, 2000), 307–8; Marie-Anne Lescourret, *Emmanuel Levinas* (Paris: Flammarion, 1994), 185–86, as well as the program reprinted in the photograph section; Nicolaus Sombart, *Pariser Lehrjahre, 1951–1954, leçons de sociologie* (Hamburg: Hoffmann und Campe, 1994), 341–42; *Le choix, le monde, l'existence*, Cahiers du Collège Philosophique (Grenoble: B. Arthaud, 1947); *L'homme, le monde, l'histoire*, Cahiers du Collège Philosophique (Grenoble: B. Arthaud, 1948); and the material on Derrida, below.

Wahl himself wrote of the Collège shortly after its inauguration: "It was in returning from America [in 1945] that I had the idea of creating in Paris a national and international center of living philosophy in which the most diverse tendencies—classical philosophy, Bergsonian philosophy, Marxist philosophy, the philosophy of existence, the philosophy of Whitehead, and, if possible, even if not right away then at least later, logical positivism, Gestalt psychology, psychoanalysis—would be represented." Preface to *Le choix, le monde*, 7.

27. Levinas, *Outside the Subject*, 85.

explained in an interview in 1984.[28] They both studied in Freiburg during the winter semester of 1928–29, where they likely met for the first time.[29] There they attended Heidegger's first lecture course after he had assumed Husserl's chair.[30] After completing his thesis on Husserl in 1930, Levinas followed Wahl's courses at the Sorbonne in the 1930s[31] and participated in what he would come to call Wahl's "famous communication,"[32] namely, his 1937 lecture "Subjectivité et transcendance" ("Subjectivity and Transcendence") and the debate that followed (see Chapter 7 in this volume). Samuel Moyn contends that "this central debate ... is undoubtedly the most

28. Emmanuel Levinas, "Reality Has Weight," in *Is It Righteous to Be? Interviews with Emmanuel Levinas*, ed. Jill Robbins (Stanford, Calif.: Stanford University Press, 2001), 160. Quote from J. Aaron Simmons, "Existential Appropriations: The Influence of Jean Wahl on Levinas's Reading of Kierkegaard," in *Kierkegaard and Levinas: Ethics, Politics, and Religion*, ed. J. Aaron Simmons and David Wood (Bloomington: Indiana University Press, 2008), 51. Indeed, Levinas would wish Wahl a happy birthday each year by referring to him as "Mon Maître" and sending chocolates and his biblical commentaries; see Barbara Wahl, "Autour de Jean Wahl," 526.

29. Samuel Moyn, *Origins of the Other: Emmanuel Levinas between Revelation and Ethics* (Ithaca, N.Y.: Cornell University Press, 2005), 177.

30. Heidegger's course is entitled *Einleitung in die Philosophie* (Introduction to philosophy) and can be found in vol. 27 of his *Gesamtausgabe*. Wahl references this course, which was not published until 1996 and is only now in the process of being translated by William McNeill for Indiana University Press, several times in his *Existence humaine et transcendance* (Neuchâtel: Éditions de la Baconnière, 1944); see the notes on 13, 14, 17–18, and 52–53. He also alludes to it in *A Short History of Existentialism*, trans. Forrest Williams and Stanley Maron (New York: Philosophical Library, 1949), 16, 20. For Levinas's participation, see Moyn, *Origins of the Other*, 49–50n79.

In 1938 and 1946, respectively, Wahl also delivered lecture courses at the Sorbonne devoted to a close reading of Heidegger's *Einleitung in die Philosophie*. See Stefanos Geroulanos, *An Atheism That Is Not Humanist Emerges in French Thought* (Stanford, Calif.: Stanford University Press, 2010), 339n79, 374n27. The 1946 version was published as *Introduction à la pensée de Heidegger: Cours donnés en Sorbonne de janvier à juin 1946* (Paris: Librairie Générale Française, 1998). While Moyn, *Origins of the Other*, contends that that it was Wahl who took and later used these notes (49–50n79, 177n28), and the published French text states that it is based on notes Wahl took while in Freiburg, Geroulanos claims that Wahl used Alexandre Koyré's transcription, which is no longer extant. See Geroulanos, *An Atheism*, 339n79. (Cf. 340n85, however, where Geroulanos submits, "It is ... rumored that Koyré brought a typescript of Heidegger's 1929 *Einleitung in die Philosophie* course.") In this he follows the testimony of Frédéric de Towarnicki, *À la rencontre de Heidegger: Souvenirs d'un messager de la Forêt Noire* (Paris: Gallimard, 1993), 251. There is at any rate no evidence for this in Wahl's citations in *Existence humaine et transcendance*, nor in his published lectures on *Einleitung in die Philosophie*.

31. Lescourret, *Emmanuel Levinas*, 188.

32. Levinas, *Outside the Subject*, 81.

precious available evidence for how Levinas's thought evolved in the long decade after 1935 . . . provid[ing], indeed, the occasion for Levinas's first use of the concept 'the other.' It constitutes, in this sense, a turning point in twentieth-century intellectual history."[33] By introducing an innovative bidirectional notion of transcendence, according to which transcendence can be *transascendence* or *transdescendence*, Wahl's lecture also became the source for Levinas's interpretation of the face as both most destitute and most high.[34]

Over the next few decades, Wahl and Levinas remained in close contact. Levinas was present at a number of important events in Wahl's life. For instance, he was one of the public respondents to Wahl's hugely influential lecture, "Petite histoire de l'existentialisme" ("A Short History of Existentialism"),[35] which the Club Maintenant had organized in light of the "unprecedented cultural success" of the first lecture in their series, Sartre's "L'existentialisme est un humanisme" ("Existentialism Is a Humanism").[36] During those long years when Levinas had more or less resigned himself to a nonacademic career, it was in large part Wahl's visits that kept Levinas abreast of developments in current philosophy. Wahl also provided avenues for publication and facilitated public philosophical appearances, such as the many lectures Wahl invited Levinas to deliver at the Collège Philosophique.[37] When Levinas was on the brink of tearing to pieces what was

---

33. Moyn, *Origins of the Other*, 182.

34. Simmons, "Existential Appropriations," 53. Moyn, *Origins of the Other*, 177, writes that, "without Wahl, Levinas's formulation of his project [in *Totality and Infinity*] would have been quite simply impossible." See Emmanuel Levinas, *Totality and Infinity: An Essay on Exteriority*, trans. Alphonso Lingis (Pittsburgh: Duquesne University Press, 1969), 35n2, where Levinas says that Wahl's *Existence humaine et transcendance*, which contains a slightly truncated version of Wahl's "famous communication," was an inspiration to him.

35. Published as Jean Wahl, *Petite histoire de "l'existentialisme," suivi de Kafka et Kierkegaard, commentaires* (Paris: Éditions Club Maintenant, 1947); English translation: Williams and Maron, *A Short History of Existentialism*, republished in part as "The Roots of Existentialism: An Introduction by Jean Wahl," in Jean-Paul Sartre, *Essays in Existentialism*, ed. Wade Baskin (New York: Citadel, 1993), 3–28.

36. See Cohen-Solal, *Jean-Paul Sartre*, 249, 260.

37. Malka, *Emmanuel Levinas*, 102, 147, 149–50. It was in Wahl's 1940 seminar that Levinas gave his first public lecture devoted to Heidegger, "L'ontologie dans le temporel." Levinas's *Le temps et l'autre* and "Le visage humain" derive from lectures Wahl invited him to deliver at the Collège Philosophique in 1946–1947 and 1961, respectively. The lectures that would become *Le temps et l'autre* were first published, along with contributions from Wahl and others, in the first publication of the Collège Philosophique, entitled *Le choix, le monde, l'existence*, ed. Jean Wahl. They then

to become his magnum opus after it had been rejected by Éditions Gallimard, it was Wahl who telephoned to tell him that he should neither despair nor worry about trying to publish it since, Wahl proclaimed, "you must defend it as a thesis" instead. Thus Levinas, already in his mid-fifties, stood before a committee comprised of Wahl, Marcel, Vladimir Jankélévitch, Paul Ricoeur, and Georges Blin, as well as an audience that included Maurice Blanchot, to defend *Totalité et infini* (*Totality and Infinity*) in 1961 as his primary thesis for the *doctorat d'état*. "We are here," Wahl said at the defense, "to evaluate a thesis about which other theses will be written."[38] As Levinas's son would later relate, "That basically marked my father's entrance into the university."[39] It is on this basis that we can better understand Levinas's dedication to Wahl (along with Wahl's wife, Marcelle) in *Totalité et infini*, and his recollection of the "forty years of friendly relations in the course of which I received so much from his unlimited generosity."[40]

---

appeared separately, with a new preface, as *Le temps et l'autre* (Montpellier: Fata Morgana, 1980). This text was in turn translated into English, together with two other essays, by Richard A. Cohen as *Time and the Other* (Pittsburgh: Duquesne University Press, 1987). Levinas's "Transcendance et hauteur" comes from Wahl's invitation to present before the Société Française de Philosophie in 1962. Wahl introduces this lecture, responds to it, and moderates the discussion that follows. See "Transcendance et hauteur," *Bulletin de la Société Française de Philosophie* 56, no. 3 (1962): 89–111. Reprinted in *Levinas*, ed. Catherine Chalier and Miguel Abensour (Paris: Herne, 1991), 97–112; as well as in Emmanuel Levinas, *Liberté et commandement* (Saint-Clément-la-Rivière: Fata Morgana, 1994), 51–100. Levinas's lecture and the subsequent discussion can be found in English as "Transcendence and Height," trans. Tina Chanter, Simon Critchley, and Nicholas Walker and revised by Adriaan Peperzak, in Emmanuel Levinas, *Basic Philosophical Writings*, ed. Adriaan T. Peperzak, Simon Critchley, and Robert Bernasconi (Bloomington: Indiana University Press, 1996), 11–31.

Levinas also published a portion of his first original philosophical monograph, *De l'existence à l'existant*, under the title "Il y a" in 1946 in the first issue of Wahl's journal *Deucalion*, and in 1957 Levinas published "La philosophie et l'idée de l'infini" in the *Revue de Métaphysique et de Morale* 66, 3 (July–September 1957): 241–53, which was under Wahl's editorship at the time. (References found in Bernhard Waldenfels, "Levinas and the Face of the Other," in Critchley and Bernasconi, *The Cambridge Companion to Levinas*, 80n7 [as well as xv–xxix].)

It is not insignificant that Wahl, to whom Levinas would dedicate *Totalité et infini*, was involved in the two texts Jacques Roland argues represent the foundations of Levinas's masterpiece, namely, *De l'existence à l'existant* and *Le temps et l'autre*. Reference to Roland's claim found in Malka, *Emmanuel Levinas*, 153.

38. Malka, *Emmanuel Levinas*, 153.
39. Ibid., 267.
40. Levinas, *Outside the Subject*, 68.

Wahl's activities with the College of Sociology from 1937 to 1939 are also noteworthy. It may seem surprising that a Sorbonne professor of philosophy in the 1930s would be so interested in the work of writers and artists such as Georges Bataille, Roger Caillois, Pierre Klossowski, and André Masson, but, as Levinas would later put it, "Jean Wahl—to whom I owe much—was on the lookout for everything that had a meaning, even outside the forms traditionally devoted to its manifestation. He thought it was necessary to give the opportunity for nonacademic discourses to be heard. For this he thus founded this Collège [Philosophique] in the Latin Quarter. It was a place where intellectual non-conformism—and even what took itself to be such—was tolerated and expected."[41] Although not one of the six signatories to the note announcing the foundation of the College of Sociology,[42] Wahl was an active participant and frequent speaker at meetings of the College, so much so that the historian Henri Dubief, a frequent attendee of these meetings, would come to speak of it as "the College of Sociology of Georges Bataille, Roger Caillois, and Jean Wahl."[43] Of particular significance is Wahl's contribution on Friedrich Nietzsche to Bataille's journal *Acéphale* (1936–39), "Nietzsche et la mort de Dieu: Note à propos du 'Nietzsche' de Jaspers" (see Chapter 8 in this volume).[44] Wahl's interest in figures such as Nietzsche and Kierkegaard at a time when they

---

41. Emmanuel Levinas, *Ethics and Infinity*, trans. Richard A. Cohen (Pittsburgh: Duquesne University Press, 1985), 55. This was a primary motivation for Wahl's founding the Collège Philosophique, namely, again in Levinas's words, "to train philosophers for the adventure of a philosophy without 'a curriculum.' . . . There, alongside the Sorbonne, in opposition to or in agreement with that institution at which Jean Wahl was, after all, a professor, philosophy opened itself to new sounds. It was there that the first echoes of *Being and Time* were heard, there that the influence of Edmund Husserl was confirmed" (Levinas, *Outside the Subject*, 85, 105). On several differences between the College of Sociology and the Collège Philosophique, cf. Faye, "Collège philosophique," 70–72.

42. This note, composed in 1937, was signed by Georges Ambrosino, Georges Bataille, Roger Caillois, Pierre Klossowski, Pierre Libra, and Jules Monnerot. It is translated and published in *The College of Sociology (1937–39)*, ed. Denis Hollier, trans. Betsy Wing (Minneapolis: University of Minnesota Press, 1998), 3–5.

43. This quote comes from Henri Dubief, *Le déclin de la Troisième République: 1929–1938*, vol. 13 of *Nouvelle histoire de la France contemporaine* (Paris: Éditions du Seuil, 1976), 141. It is referenced in Hollier, *College of Sociology*, 98.

44. Jean Wahl, "Nietzsche et la mort de Dieu: Note à propos du 'Nietzsche' de Jaspers," *Acéphale* 2 (January 1937): 22–24. For other texts, see Hollier, *College of Sociology*, 3–4, 101–2. Wahl's 1938 book of poetry, *Connaître sans connaître* (Knowing without knowing), can also be connected to the concerns of the College; see Hollier, 426–27n14.

were not admitted into the canon by mainstream philosophy contributed to Noël Laurent's comment, in a review of Wahl's *Tableau de la philosophie française* (Portrait of French philosophy) published in Bataille's journal *Critique*, that,

> More discretely than by Jean-Paul Sartre, living philosophy in France is represented by Jean Wahl. Wahl has the advantage over Sartre in possessing an almost incomparable mastery in the knowledge of the history of philosophies. Yet he is no less an original philosopher, even a poet-philosopher, one who is rather remote from the professorial tradition. . . . If the word hadn't become so muddled in the public mind, [Wahl's] thought could be characterized as existential: yet, being pragmatic, it is above all and voluntarily fluid and ungraspable. Its profound difference from Sartre's thought is perhaps expressed at a fundamental level if we distinguish, within the existential tradition, between Kierkegaard and Nietzsche, on the one hand, and the philosopher-professors of contemporary Germany (Husserl, Heidegger), on the other. Wahl is preoccupied above all with Nietzsche and Kierkegaard, Sartre with the phenomenologists.[45]

Bataille and his circle were not the only ones to compare the philosophical significance of Wahl and Sartre. Deleuze, himself one of the most important philosophers of the twentieth century, wrote that, "apart from Sartre, who remained caught none the less in the trap of the verb to be, the most important philosopher in France was Jean Wahl."[46] Sartre speaks of the "great success" that Wahl's 1932 *Vers le concret* (Toward the concrete) (see Chapter 2 in this volume) had among Sartre and his friends and fellow

---

45. Noël Laurent, review of Jean Wahl, *Tableau de la philosophie française*, *Critique* 1, nos. 3–4 (1946): 372. Le Rider, *Nietzsche en France*, 184, mistakenly attributes the quote to Bataille. Mary F. Zamberlin, *Rhizosphere: Gilles Deleuze and the "Minor" American Writings of William James, W. E. B. Du Bois, Gertrude Stein, Jean Toomer, and William Faulkner* (New York: Routledge, 2006), 53–54, perpetuates this error; drawing on various of Wahl's references to Nietzsche, Zamberlin nonetheless notes correctly that Wahl "essentially set the stage for a large scale integration of Nietzsche into French philosophy" (49). Alan D. Schrift also emphasizes Wahl's role in Nietzsche's eventual appearance within academic philosophy in France in "French Nietzscheanism," in *Poststructuralism and Critical Theory's Second Generation*, ed. Alan D. Schrift, vol. 6 of *The History of Continental Philosophy* (London: Acumen Press and Chicago: University of Chicago Press, 2010), 19–46, esp. 22, 25.

46. Gilles Deleuze, "On the Superiority of Anglo-American Literature," in Gilles Deleuze and Claire Parnet, *Dialogues II*, rev. ed., trans. Hugh Tomlinson and Barbara Habberjam (New York: Columbia University Press, 2007), 57–58.

students, a work that, he goes on to say, "embarrassed idealism by discovering in the universe paradoxes, ambiguities, conflicts, still unresolved. We learned to turn pluralism (that concept of the Right) against the optimistic, monistic idealism of our professors—in the name of a Leftist thought which was still ignorant of itself."[47] In fact, it was Wahl's book that proved inspirational during Sartre's intellectual languishing as a lycée instructor.[48] At this point, Sartre had already been reading Wahl for several years, and he would continue to do so in the future.[49] On a more personal level, Wahl had been on the jury for Sartre's and Simone de Beauvoir's *agrégation* in 1929 (and, according to Maurice de Gandillac, Wahl later told him that he had had a hard time deciding to whom to give first prize, opting ultimately for Sartre),[50] and later he tried, unsuccessfully, to have Sartre defend his as yet unpublished *L'imaginaire* (*The Imaginary*) as a doctoral thesis at the Sorbonne.[51] As with other prominent names such as Bataille, Martin Buber, Lacan, and Maurice Merleau-Ponty, Sartre too presented at Wahl's Collège Philosophique after the war.[52]

Wahl's versatility as a thinker—engaging with the history of philosophy as well as contemporary philosophers of existence, equally at home

47. Jean-Paul Sartre, *Search for a Method*, trans. Hazel E. Barnes (New York: Vintage, 1968), 19.

48. Zamberlin, *Rhizosphere*, 41. Zamberlin refers to Rhiannon Goldthorpe, "Introduction" to *La Nausée* (London: Harper Collins Academic, 1991), and cites a long passage in which Goldthorpe spells out different ways in which Wahl's book could have influenced Sartre.

49. Manuela Hackel, "Jean-Paul Sartre: Kierkegaard's Influence on His Theory of Nothingness," in Stewart, *Kierkegaard and Existentialism*, 329. For Wahl's works that Sartre definitely read, see 329n31. See also Bruce Baugh, *French Hegel: From Surrealism to Postmodernism* (New York: Routledge, 2003), 200–201n14.

50. For details, see Deirdre Bair, *Simone de Beauvoir: A Biography* (New York: Touchstone, 1990), 145–46. See also the interview with Maurice de Gandillac by Ingrid Galster, "'Ils auraient pu les mettre *ex aequo*': Entretien avec le philosophe Maurice de Gandillac sur l'agrégation de Beauvoir et d'autres sujets," *Lendemains* 94 (1999): 19–36, in which he suggests that Beauvoir and Sartre should have been awarded the first rank together. In addition to Wahl, the jury that year was presided over by André Lalande, and also included Dominique Parodi, Charles Lalo, Georges Davy, and Jean Laporte.

51. See *Witness to My Life: The Letters of Jean-Paul Sartre to Simone de Beauvoir 1926–1939*, ed. Simone de Beauvoir, trans. Lee Fahnestock and Norman MacAfee (New York: Charles Scribner's Sons, 1992), 386; *Quiet Moments in a War: The Letters of Jean-Paul Sartre to Simone de Beauvoir, 1940–1963*, ed. Simone de Beauvoir, trans. Lee Fahnestock and Norman MacAfee (New York: Charles Scribner's Sons, 1993), 102.

52. Cf. note 26, above. For various ways in which Wahl influenced Sartre's philosophy, such as the latter's notion of "bad faith," see Baugh, *French Hegel*, 95–97, 186n15.

writing poems and metaphysical treatises—led him to be an important influence on later French thinkers such as Deleuze and Derrida as well. Wahl was one of Deleuze's professors at the Sorbonne in the 1940s, and François Dosse suggests it was Wahl who encouraged Deleuze's initial interest in Hume and turned him on to the writings of other Anglo-Saxon philosophers, as well as to Bergson, Nietzsche, and American pragmatism and literature.[53] In 1972, Deleuze spoke of his "complete admiration" for Wahl, praised Wahl's success in "[tearing] down the boundaries between philosophy and poetry," and said that "it was he who was the thinker of intensities and of the critique of totality. In everything that was important before and after the war, there are signs of Jean Wahl."[54] In addition to his critiques of totality and his willingness to bridge disciplines, Wahl's emphasis on plurality, difference, and anti-ontological employments of language impacted Deleuze profoundly. Wahl's utter fluency and immersion in English[55] was not merely avocational but essential to his own thought and teaching, such that Deleuze could praise Wahl's "ability to make us think,

53. François Dosse, *Gilles Deleuze and Félix Guattari: Intersecting Lives*, trans. Deborah Glassman (New York: Columbia University Press, 2010), 110. Deleuze received his *Diplôme d'études supérieures* in 1947 for a project on Hume supervised by Jean Hyppolite and Georges Canguilhem, which eventually became Deleuze's first book, *Empirisme et subjectivité: Essai sur la nature humaine selon Hume* (Paris: Presses Universitaires de France, 1953); English translation: *Empiricism and Subjectivity: An Essay on Hume's Theory of Human Nature*, trans. Constantin V. Boundas (New York: Columbia University Press, 1991). Cf. Zamberlin, *Rhizosphere*, 10, 12, 47, 49. The latter text traces Wahl's influence on several levels: political, literary, historical, philosophical. See especially its first chapter, "France's 'Two Most Important Philosophers': Jean Wahl and Jean-Paul Sartre."

54. This citation comes from an unpublished letter quoted in Dosse, *Deleuze and Guattari*, 110. Cf. Gilles Deleuze, *Difference and Repetition*, trans. Paul Patton (New York: Columbia University Press, 1994), 311n18: "All Jean Wahl's work is a profound meditation on difference: on the possibilities within empiricism for expressing its poetic, free and wild nature; on the irreducibility of difference to the simple negative; on the *non-Hegelian* relations between affirmation and negation." On the role of difference in Deleuze and Wahl, see Angèle Kremer-Marietti, "Différence et qualité," *Revue de Métaphysique et de Morale* 75, no. 3 (July–September 1970): 339–49.

55. As the son of an English professor, he was raised to be bilingual and not only wrote books and poetry in English but also was thoroughly apprised of contemporary developments in English literature, as evinced by a collection of translations of American novelists and poets he put together in 1943. This collection initially appeared in the Algerian French resistance journal *Fontaine*, nos. 27–28 (1943) and was reprinted as *Écrivains et poètes des États-Unis d'Amérique*, ed. Max Pol Fouchet and Jean André Wahl (Paris: Fontaine, 1945). Cf. *Écrivains américains d'aujourd'hui* (Geneva: Éditions du Continent, 1944).

in French, things which were very new; he on his own account took this art of the AND, this stammering of language in itself, this minoritarian use of language, the furthest."[56] After having already contributed to those early efforts of *Acéphale* to read Nietzsche against his fascist and Nazi appropriators—something Deleuze was later to recognize[57]—Wahl continued to revitalize Nietzsche upon returning to Paris after the war. He was among the first philosophers to join the Société Française d'Études Nietzschéennes, founded in 1946 by Armand Quinot and Geneviève Bianquis, and served as its president in 1963.[58] In 1959 and 1961, Wahl gave the first lecture courses on Nietzsche ever offered by a professor of philosophy at the Sorbonne.[59] He found in Deleuze an eager collaborator in Nietzsche studies, as Deleuze became a member of the Société Française d'Études Nietzschéennes and contributed to its publications.[60] When Deleuze's *Nietzsche et la philosophie* (*Nietzsche and Philosophy*) appeared in 1962, Wahl wrote a long and favorable review in which he says that Deleuze's book belongs alongside the most important books on Nietzsche, those of Jaspers, Heidegger, Eugen Fink, and Lou Salomé.[61] They also both presented at the 1964 international Nietzsche colloquium at Royaumont,

---

56. Deleuze and Parnet, "On the Superiority of Anglo-American Literature," in Deleuze and Parnet, *Dialogues II*, 58. See Gilles Deleuze and Félix Guattari, *A Thousand Plateaus: Capitalism and Schizophrenia*, trans. Brian Massumi (Minneapolis: University of Minnesota Press, 1987), 526n32: "Jean Wahl's works contain profound reflections on this [not merely conjunctive] sense of 'and,' on the way it challenges the primacy of the verb 'to be.'"

57. Gilles Deleuze, "Nomad Thought," trans. David B. Allison, in *The New Nietzsche: Contemporary Styles of Interpretation*, ed. David B. Allison (Cambridge, Mass.: MIT Press, 1985), 145.

58. Le Rider, *Nietzsche en France*, 185.

59. Jean Wahl, *La pensée philosophique de Nietzsche des années 1885–1888* (Paris: Centre de Documentation Universitaire, 1959), and *L'avant-dernière pensée de Nietzsche* (Paris: Centre de Documentation Universitaire, 1961). Nietzsche had been the subject of lecture courses in the Department of German Language and Literature as early as 1902–03, when Professor of German Literature Henri Lichtenberger (1864–1941) taught the Sorbonne's one full-year course in German language and literature on Nietzsche.

60. Le Rider, *Nietzsche en France*, 186n1. Deleuze published "Mystère d'Ariane" in *Bulletin de la Société Française d'Études Nietzschéennes* (March 1963): 12–15. A revised version appeared as "Mystère d'Ariane selon Nietzsche" in *Critique et clinique* (Paris: Éditions de Minuit, 1993), 125–34; English translation: "The Mystery of Ariadne according to Nietzsche," in *Essays Critical and Clinical*, trans. Daniel W. Smith and Michael A. Greco (Minneapolis: University of Minnesota Press, 1997), 99–106.

61. Jean Wahl, "Nietzsche et la philosophie," *Revue de Métaphysique et de Morale* 68, no. 3 (July–September 1963): 352.

which Deleuze had organized with Wahl's input.[62] (Wahl's contribution and the discussion that followed have been translated as Chapter 10 in this volume.)

Lastly, we would like to mention a couple of significant events in Derrida's career that were connected to Wahl. Derrida got to know Wahl in 1956 at the home of Maurice de Gandillac[63] and later became his research assistant.[64] Around this time, we know he made use of Wahl's "Heidegger and Kierkegaard" (Chapter 5 in this volume) and "A Note on Some Empiricist Aspects of the Thought of Husserl" for his work on Husserl,[65] as earlier he had drawn on "Heidegger and Kierkegaard" and Wahl's *A Short History of Existentialism* for a 1948 essay on Heidegger.[66] A few years later, Wahl invited Derrida to present at one of the meetings of the Collège Philosophique, and on March 4, 1963, Derrida delivered "his first major paper in Paris,"[67] a response to Foucault's *Folie et déraison: Histoire de la folie à l'âge classique* (translated as *History of Madness*) entitled "Cogito et l'histoire de la folie" ("Cogito and the History of Madness"). Foucault was present at the event and even was encouraging when Wahl suggested that Derrida publish his response in the *Revue de Métaphysique et de Morale*, of which Wahl was at the time the editor.[68] The response appeared the following

---

62. *Nietzsche: Cahiers du Royaumont* (Paris: Éditions de Minuit, 1967). See Dosse, *Deleuze and Guattari*, 132.

63. Dominique Janicaud, *Heidegger en France*, 2 vols. (Paris: Albin Michel, 2001), 2:94.

64. Though, as Derrida states, "only in the most abstract sense." See Benoît Peeters, *Derrida: A Biography*, trans. Andrew Brown (Cambridge: Polity, 2013), 114.

65. As indicated in the "Guide to the Jacques Derrida Papers," http://www.oac.cdlib.org/findaid/ark:/13030/tf3q2nb26c/dsc/#c02-1.3.7.2.5. See Jean Wahl, "Note sur quelques aspects empiristes de la pensée de Husserl," *Revue de Métaphysique et de Morale* (January–March 1952): 17–45; English translation: "A Note on Some Empiricist Aspects of the Thought of Husserl," trans. Laurence E. Winters, in *Apriori and World: European Contributions to Husserlian Phenomenology*, ed. W. McKenna, R. M. Harlan, and L. E. Winters (The Hague: Martinus Nijhoff, 1981), 202–25. Our revised and edited version of this translation can be found online at https://www.academia.edu/16712734/Jean_Wahl_A_Note_on_Some_Empiricist_Aspects_of_the_Thought_of_Husserl.

66. See Edward Baring, *The Young Derrida and French Philosophy, 1945–1968* (Cambridge: Cambridge University Press, 2011), 73–74.

67. Peeters, *Derrida*, 131.

68. Ibid., 131–32; see also Jacques Derrida, *Writing and Difference*, trans. Alan Bass (Chicago: University of Chicago Press, 1978), 307n1. After the editor of the journal *Critique*, Michel Deguy, asked that Derrida's article "Violence and Metaphysics: An Essay on the Thought of Emmanuel Levinas" be shortened by about thirty pages for him to publish it, Derrida looked elsewhere and found that Wahl was willing to publish

year. A few years later, Wahl as president of the Société Française de Philosophie provided the introduction for one of Derrida's most famous papers, "Différance," before the January 27, 1968, meeting of the society and participated in the discussion that followed.[69]

III

Wahl's influence did not just extend to particular figures in twentieth-century French intellectual life. He was also responsible for introducing philosophers and ideas that would come to play major roles in the evolution of the French intellectual scene from the 1920s onward.

Although not as well known as some of his other works, Wahl's doctoral thesis, *Les philosophies pluralistes d'Angleterre et d'Amérique*,[70] written under Bergson and published in 1920, was one of the first in France on contemporaneous Anglo-American philosophy. This work focused in general on pluralism as a response to the English and American monisms, and in particular on William James as the great representative of pluralism. Marcel, whose work Wahl would also come to champion,[71] wrote in 1921 that Wahl's book "constitutes a precious and, to our knowledge at least, hitherto unparalleled contribution to the history of the contemporary philosophical movement across the channel and across the ocean."[72]

---

it in two parts in the *Revue de Métaphysique et de Morale,* no. 3 (July–September 1964): 322–54, and no. 4 (October–December 1964): 425–73. See Peeters, *Derrida,* 138–39.

69. Baugh, *French Hegel,* 190n20. For Wahl's introduction and the earliest appearance of Derrida's talk, which was later published in Jacques Derrida, *Margins of Philosophy,* trans. Alan Bass (Chicago: University of Chicago Press, 1982), 3–27, see the Société's *Bulletin,* 62 (1968): 73–101. Wahl's introduction, along with the discussion following Derrida's talk, has been translated by David Wood, Sarah Richmond, and Malcolm Bernard as "The Original Discussion of 'Différance' (1968)," in *Derrida and Différance,* ed. David Wood and Robert Bernasconi (Evanston, Ill.: Northwestern University Press, 1988), 83–95.

70. Jean Wahl, *Les philosophies pluralistes d'Angleterre et d'Amérique* (Paris: F. Alcan, 1920); English translation: *The Pluralist Philosophies of England and America,* trans. Fred Rothwell (London: Open Court, 1925).

71. In, for example, Jean Wahl, *Vers le concret: Études d'histoire de la philosophie contemporaine: Trois articles sur W. James, Whitehead et le "Journal Métaphysique" de Gabriel Marcel* (Paris: Vrin, 1932); see Levinas, Tilliette, and Ricoeur, *Wahl et Marcel.*

72. Gabriel Marcel, review of *Les philosophies pluralistes d'Angleterre et d'Amérique,* by Jean Wahl, *Revue Philosophique de la France et de l'Étranger* 92 (July–December 1921): 411–12. Cf. Cavallazzi Sánchez and Palavicini Sánchez, "Jean Wahl," 394. Wahl's book also received favorable reviews in the English-speaking world; see, e.g.,

Wahl was also among the first in France to draw major attention to the importance of Hegel and, in particular, Hegel's *Phenomenology of Spirit*. His 1929 book, *Le malheur de la conscience dans la philosophie de Hegel* (The unhappiness of consciousness in Hegel's philosophy) (see Chapter 3 in this volume), was hugely influential.[73] It was published four years before Alexandre Kojève began to lecture on Hegel at the École Pratique des Hautes Études, and even before Alexandre Koyré's important articles on the German philosopher. Jean Hyppolite, himself among the most prominent interpreters of Hegel and the translator of the first French translation of Hegel's *Phenomenology of Spirit* in 1941, wrote, "I should say that the first real shock came from Jean Wahl, and that reading the *Conscience malheureuse dans la philosophie de Hegel* [sic] was a sort of revelation."[74] As Bruce Baugh argues, this work had a great impact on "all those French thinkers in [the twentieth century] concerned with irreparable divisions and unbridgeable differences," from Sartre and Bataille through Derrida, Deleuze, and Foucault.[75] As the title indicates, Wahl emphasizes the role of the "unhappy consciousness" in Hegel's *Phenomenology of Spirit*, rather than the more well-known master/slave dialectic that was central to Kojève's interpretation. As the title also indicates, instead of reading the unhappy consciousness as but one stage in the development of Spirit, wherein consciousness opposes itself as finite and nugatory to an infinite other of absolute worth, Wahl looks at the unhappy consciousness throughout Hegel's philosophy, at the manifold ways in which consciousness, indeed concrete human existence, is divided against itself and therefore unhappy, stressing that "one cannot exaggerate the generality of this idea [of unhappy consciousness]."[76] For it is the unhappy consciousness that drives the movement of Spirit. Wahl also puts Hegel in dialogue with figures such as

---

Sterling P. Lamprecht's review in the *Journal of Philosophy* 18, no. 26 (December 22, 1921): 717–20.

73. Jean Wahl, *Le malheur de la conscience dans la philosophie de Hegel*, 2nd ed. (Paris: Presses Universitaires de France, 1951); first published with Rieder in 1929. A portion of the second edition of this text also has been translated into English by Christopher Fox and Leonard Lawlor as "Meditation, Negativity, and Separation," in *Hegel and Contemporary Continental Philosophy*, ed. Dennis King Keenan (Albany: State University of New York Press, 2004), 1–25.

74. Jean Hyppolite, "Discours d'introduction," *Hegel-Studien* 3 (1966): 11. Quote and translation found in Keenan, *Hegel and Contemporary Continental Philosophy*, xii.

75. Baugh, *French Hegel*, 2, 6. For Wahl's subsequent reading of Hegel, as well as influential "existentialist" ideas he deployed against the latter, see 33–42.

76. Wahl, "Meditation, Negativity, and Separation," 17; *Le malheur de la conscience*, 114.

Eckhart and Boehme, Hölderlin and Novalis, Schiller and Goethe. "Far from believing that the philosophy of Hegel is a purely rational philosophy," Wahl contends that "it is an effort toward the rationalization of a background that reason cannot attain."[77] As he puts it in the preface to this pivotal work, "Behind the philosopher, we discover the theologian, and behind the rationalist, the romantic."[78]

Wahl's next major text to introduce a significant thinker to the Francophone philosophical world was his 1938 *Études kierkegaardiennes* (Kierkegaardian studies) (see Chapters 4, 5, and 6 in this volume), which collected together his writings that were "the most important ones in the Kierkegaard enthusiasm in France,"[79] and "established him as the principal French exponent of the thought of Kierkegaard."[80] Indeed, this text and the articles that preceded it sparked philosophical interest in Kierkegaard,[81] and "French-style existentialism came into its own."[82] Bergson admired it so much that in April 1939 he championed it for the Prix Broquette, "saying everything good I could think of regarding the book (and the author)." Wahl was instead awarded the Prix Bordin in December, receiving 1,800 francs.[83]

---

77. Wahl, "Meditation, Negativity, and Separation," 12; *Le malheur de la conscience*, 108.

78. Wahl, *Le malheur de la conscience*, v.

79. Moyn, *Origins of the Other*, 172.

80. Baugh, *French Hegel*, 39. Hyppolite speaks of "the great interpreter of Kierkegaard in France, Jean Wahl." See *Figures de la pensée philosophique: Écrits de Jean Hyppolite (1931–1968)*, vol. 1 (Paris: Presses Universitaires de France, 1971), 197–98. Quote from Hélène Politis, *Kierkegaard en France au XXe siècle: Archéologie d'une réception* (Paris: Éditions Kimé, 2005), 124n31.

81. "Interrogation of Jean Wahl: Conducted by Newton P. Stallknecht," in *Philosophical Interrogations: Interrogations of Martin Buber, John Wild, Jean Wahl, Brand Blanshard, Paul Weiss, Charles Hartshorne, Paul Tillich*, ed. Sydney Rome and Beatrice Rome (New York: Holt, Rinehart and Winston, 1964), 197; Cavallazzi Sánchez and Palavicini Sánchez, "Jean Wahl," 397.

82. Hollier, *College of Sociology*, viii. Kremer-Marietti, "Jean Wahl the Precursor," 337, writes that "Jean Wahl is the founder of the French Existentialists movement." Nevertheless, Wahl rejects the term "existentialist" as characteristic of his own thought; see Wahl, *A Short History of Existentialism*, 1.

83. Henri Bergson, *Correspondances*, ed. André Robinet (Paris: Presses Universitaires de France, 2002), 1620. Quote found in Margaret Teboul, "La réception de Kierkegaard en France 1930–1960," *Revue des Sciences Philosophiques et Théologiques* 89, no. 2 (2005): 328n87. For the announcement of the prize, see the December 14, 1939, "Séance publique annuelle" of the Académie Française, p. 3, http://www.academie-francaise.fr/sites/academie-francaise.fr/files/palmares_1939.pdf. For Bergson's praise of other works by Wahl, see Bergson, *Correspondances*, 1214, 1295, 1596. Bergson's relationship with Wahl was not purely professional: Wahl was only ten years old when

This "veritable summa"[84] mainly is composed of studies written between 1931 and 1935.[85] In addition to Wahl's other writings on Kierkegaard,[86] it influenced Sartre by acquainting him with Heidegger,[87] and perhaps even first provoked his interest in Kierkegaard.[88] Levinas, as well, speaks of Wahl's studies as "the most thorough, perceptive, and philosophically

---

he first met Bergson, Wahl's mother was indirectly related to Bergson's wife, and one of Wahl's cousins was a nephew of Bergson. When Bergson died, he named in his will Wahl along with Léon Brunschvicg as "advisors to Madame Bergson" (Green, "Philosopher in the Toils," 5–6).

84. Gandillac, "Wahl," 40.

85. Politis, *Kierkegaard en France*, 109, includes an appendix (128–30) in which she catalogues the original texts of various chapters in Wahl's book and explains their differences, as well as the differences among the various editions of the book.

86. Many of Wahl's shorter writings on Kierkegaard have been compiled in Jean Wahl, *L'Un devant l'Autre*, ed. Vincent Delecroix and Frédéric Worms (Paris: Hachette Littératures, 1998). Wahl's reading of Kierkegaard has been treated quite extensively in the secondary literature. Rachel Bespaloff, for example, wrote a long review in 1939: "Notes sur les *Études kierkegaardiennes* de Jean Wahl," *Revue Philosophique de la France et de l'Étranger* 127, no. 5/6 (May–June 1939): 301–24. Adorno wrote two reviews of Wahl's book, one in English, the other in German. See Theodor Wiesengrund-Adorno, review of *Études kierkegaardiennes*, by Jean Wahl, *Journal of Philosophy* 36, no. 1 (January 5, 1939): 18–19; Theodore W. Adorno, review of *Études kierkegaardiennes*, by Jean Wahl, *Studies in Philosophy and Social Science* 8 (1939–40), no. 1–2 (1940): 232–33. On Adorno's and Max Horkheimer's relationship to Wahl, see Ernani Chaves, "'Man kann von Nietzsche nicht sprechen, ohne ihn eindeutig zur Aktualität in Beziehung zu bringen': Zur Auseinandersetzung mit der französischen Nietzsche-Rezeption in der *Zeitschrift für Sozialforschung*," in *Nietzsche und Frankreich*, ed. Clemens Pornschlegel and Martin Stingelin (Berlin: Walter de Gruyter, 2009), 209–21, as well as Peter Šajda, "Theodor W. Adorno: Kierkegaard's Triumphs and Defeats," in *Kierkegaard's Influence on Philosophy*, vol. 1, *German and Scandinavian Philosophy*, ed. Jon Stewart (Burlington, Vt.: Ashgate, 2011), 22–24. For more recent contributions on Wahl's reading of Kierkegaard, see Cavallazzi Sánchez and Palavicini Sánchez, "Jean Wahl," 393–414; Politis, *Kierkegaard en France*, 109–30; and Simmons, "Existential Appropriations," 41–66. For the debate the *Études kierkegaardiennes* provoked between Wahl and Lev Shestov and his followers such as Benjamin Fondane, see Moyn, *Origins of the Other*, 180–81. For a brief discussion of the ways in which Wahl's interpretation of Kierkegaard played into his own thought, see Ole Koppang, "Quelques pensées kierkegaardiennes dans la philosophie de Jean Wahl," *Orbis Litterarum* 10, nos. 1–2 (June 1955): 112–17.

87. Kleinberg, *Generation Existential*, 130. Kleinberg mentions Wahl's reading of the unhappy consciousness in Hegel as influential on Sartre's notion of "bad faith," and Wahl's interpretation of *Angst* in Heidegger, linked as it was to Kierkegaard's concept of anxiety, as influential on Sartre's understanding of anguish (*angoisse*).

88. See Hackel, "Jean-Paul Sartre," 327, 329–30.

acute of all accounts of Kierkegaard"[89] and named Wahl as "the most influential source"[90] on his reading of Kierkegaard. The work also influenced Beauvoir, Michel Henry, and Jacques Maritain,[91] among many others. In *Études kierkegaardiennes*, Wahl interprets Kierkegaard as "a kind of [belligerent] anti-philosopher"[92] who is concerned with singular existence over subsumable essence in order to show that, despite significant agreement on a number of points,[93] Kierkegaard is in fact an anti-Hegelian, a fact that, though commonly known today, was not widely recognized in France at the time. Wahl explains on the final page of his study that Kierkegaard is, along with Nietzsche, "the master of existential dialectic." "With him," Wahl continues, "we learn the art of contraries in life. And if spirit is not always, nor above all, synthesis, but a struggle between contraries maintained in their purity and at the same time an effort to think what surpasses them and resides above them; if spirit is conceived as the monologue in front of the reality that excites it, attracts it and never responds to it, then Kierkegaard's thought is one of those in which the character of spirit has best manifested itself."[94] Wahl continued to write as a leading voice on Kierkegaard, and he later presented a paper at the 1964 conference on Kierkegaard organized by the United Nations Educational, Scientific and Cultural Organization (UNESCO), which included talks by Sartre, Marcel, and Jaspers; an essay by Heidegger read by Jean Beaufret; and a group discussion and roundtable that included Wahl, Levinas, Marcel, and Jean Hyppolite.[95]

Wahl also worked to introduce and promote in France contemporaneous German thinkers such as Edmund Husserl, Jaspers, Nicolai Hartmann,

---

89. Emmanuel Levinas, "Existence and Ethics," trans. Jonathan Rée, in *Kierkegaard: A Critical Reader*, ed. Jonathan Rée and Jane Chamberlain (Oxford: Blackwell, 1998), 37n3.

90. Simmons, "Existential Appropriations," 51. See Moyn, *Origins of the Other*, 179–89.

91. On Beauvoir, see Ronald M. Green and Mary Jean Green, "Simone de Beauvoir: A Founding Feminist's Appreciation of Kierkegaard," in Stewart, *Kierkegaard and Existentialism*, 5; see also Baugh, *French Hegel*, 200–201n14. On Henry, see Leo Stan, "Michel Henry: The Goodness of Living Affectivity," in Stewart, *Kierkegaard and Existentialism*, 134. On Maritain, see Nathaniel Kramer, "Jacques Maritain: Kierkegaard as 'Champion of the Singular,'" in Stewart, *Kierkegaard and Existentialism*, 223.

92. Cavallazzi Sánchez and Palavicini Sánchez, "Jean Wahl," 399.

93. See Politis, *Kierkegaard en France*, 112.

94. Wahl, *Études kierkegaardiennes*, 452.

95. The proceedings were published as *Kierkegaard vivant: Colloque organisé par l'Unesco à Paris du 21 au 23 avril 1964* (Paris: Gallimard, 1966).

and especially Heidegger. Otto Pöggeler noted in 1958 that Wahl's interpretation of German philosophy was both "pathbreaking" and "a work of concrete mediation."[96] Wahl was among the first to publish on Heidegger in French and among the first to lecture on his philosophy at the Sorbonne, offering courses on Heidegger's *Einleitung in die Philosophie* (Introduction to philosophy) in 1938 and 1946. He also participated in many of the important debates on Heidegger in France—even though, in protest of Heidegger's politics, he abstained from participating in the 1955 Heidegger Colloquium at Cerisy-la-Salle.[97] Wahl's initial, rather subjectivist reading of Heidegger (see, for example, Chapters 5 and 7 in this volume) was quite influential on the humanist interpretation of Heidegger—despite Heidegger's rejection of this reading in a letter to Wahl dated December 5, 1937 (available in Chapter 7 of this volume). Motivated by this letter, Wahl's interpretation of Heidegger continued to develop over the next few decades, to the point where he eventually retracted his characterization of Heidegger as an existentialist, even though he would still read Heidegger alongside other existentialist thinkers.[98] Wahl's later engagement with Heidegger's thought, which was crucial for the development of his own philosophy, can be found in many of his books and lecture courses. These served as the first serious introduction to Heidegger for many.[99]

---

96. Otto Pöggeler, "Jean Wahls Heidegger-Deutung," *Zeitschrift für philosophische Forschung* 12, no. 3 (July–September 1958): 439.

97. As Jeanne Hersch comments in her moving introduction to Levinas, Tilliette, and Ricoeur, *Wahl et Marcel*, apropos Wahl's sometimes contradictory moral passions, "each with its inflexible and coherent requirements": "Thus with Heidegger: because Heidegger was a Nazi, Wahl refused to set foot at Cerisy, where Heidegger had been invited; but because Heidegger was a great philosopher, Wahl did not stop, in his courses, commenting on his work and exploring its depths" (9). Wahl was not the only philosopher interested in Heidegger's work who refused to attend the Cerisy colloquium: Sartre, Merleau-Ponty, and Levinas also would not attend (Kleinberg, *Generation Existential*, 201).

98. For Wahl's developing interpretation of Heidegger, especially with regard to humanism and existentialism, see Rockmore, *Heidegger and French Philosophy*, 75–76, 86. For the retraction, see Wahl, *A Short History of Existentialism*, 2; and "Interrogation of Jean Wahl," 196–97. For a 1947 text in which Wahl still speaks of "the existentialism of Heidegger," see "Note sur la philosophie de l'existence," in Wahl, *Poésie, pensée, perception*, 179.

99. For example, Kostas Axelos, Jean-Luc Marion, and Edgar Morin. See Janicaud, *Heidegger en France*, 2:11, 211, 228. For Wahl's writings on Heidegger, see Chapters 2, 5, and 7 in this volume; see also Wahl, *Petite histoire de "l'existentialisme,"* and *Vers la fin de l'ontologie: Étude sur l'introduction dans la métaphysique par Heidegger* (Paris: Société d'Édition d'Enseignement Supérieur, 1956); as well as his lecture courses on Heidegger, including "Introduction à la pensée de Heidegger" (1946), "L'idée d'être chez

Although better known for his work on Hegel, Kierkegaard, Nietzsche, Heidegger, and Jaspers, Jean Wahl was also an important early French commentator on Husserl. In fact, the motto that Wahl chose for the title of his existential manifesto—*vers le concret*—can be understood as his version of Husserl's own motto: "*zu den Sachen selbst*" ("to the things themselves"). Already in 1920, in his doctoral thesis on the pluralist philosophies of England and America, Wahl revealed what Levinas later called his "innate predilection for the concrete and his intense interest in contemporary philosophy," both of which already displayed "an anticipation of Husserl's phenomenology!"[100] And in *Vers le concret*, Wahl made a point of indicating the links he saw between Alfred North Whitehead's philosophy and Husserl's phenomenology.[101] As Matthias Girel comments in his introduction to the second edition of *Vers le concret*, although he was the youngest member of the jury that examined Sartre for the *agrégation* in 1929, Wahl appeared to be the only examiner capable of fully understanding Sartre's oral presentation on Husserl.[102]

Along with his younger colleagues Merleau-Ponty and Sartre, Wahl shared a suspicion concerning idealist tendencies in Husserl's phenomenology, and his path into Husserl's work thus follows a specific trajectory: "Putting aside everything that depends upon idealist presuppositions, we will consider this system obliquely, in order to discover there, preferably, the consequences of his few realist presuppositions."[103] He also shared with them a desire to existentialize phenomenology; Merleau-Ponty noted in the very first paragraph of his *Phenomenology of Perception* that "phenomenol-

---

Heidegger" (1951); "La pensée de Heidegger et la poésie de Hölderlin" (1952); and "Mots, mythes et réalité dans la philosophie de Heidegger" (1961). The first of these lecture courses is available in Jean Wahl, *Introduction à la pensée de Heidegger: Cours donnés en Sorbonne de janvier à juin 1946* (Paris: Librairie Générale Française, 1998). The others are available through the Centre de Documentation Universitaire.

Of these texts, only *Petite histoire de "l'existentialisme"* is available in English. For others in which Wahl analyzes Heidegger, see the following: *Philosophies of Existence: An Introduction to the Basic Thought of Kierkegaard, Heidegger, Jaspers, Marcel, Sartre*, trans. F. M. Lory (London: Routledge and Kegan Paul, 1969), originally published as *Les philosophies de l'existence* (Paris: A. Colin, 1959); and *The Philosopher's Way* (New York: Oxford University Press, 1948).

100. Levinas, Tilliette, and Ricoeur, *Wahl et Marcel*, 16; Levinas, *Outside the Subject*, 70.

101. Wahl, *Vers le concret*, 2nd augmented ed. (Paris: Vrin, 2004), 149, 157–58, 180.

102. Mathias Girel, "Avant-propos," in *Vers le concret* (2004), 7. Girel no doubt gets this information from Maurice de Gandillac, "Wahl," 39.

103. Wahl, "Note sur quelques aspects," 18; "Note on Empiricist Aspects," revised translation, 2–3 (see note 65, above).

ogy is the study of essences. . . . But phenomenology is also a philosophy which puts essences back into existence."[104] Wahl put the point this way: "Although phenomenology is thus presented to us from the start as a theory of essences, what will interest us here especially, and what seems to us the most valuable, are the consequences of the realist and empiricist postulates which we are able to discover in it."[105] More significant than his own writings on Husserl were Wahl's lecture courses on Husserl at the Sorbonne: at least five times in the 1950s and 1960s, Wahl offered semester-long courses on Husserl, addressing topics from Husserl's "First Philosophy" through his posthumous *Krisis*.[106]

Wahl's influential work on contemporary philosophy extended beyond the European continent into English-speaking countries as well. In addition to his professional activities in the United States—at the École Libre, organizing the *décades* at Mount Holyoke, teaching at several colleges and universities—Wahl's publications in English-language book collections, journals and magazines such as the *New Republic* and *Philosophy and Phenomenological Research* served to introduce continental philosophy to Great Britain and the United States. His "The Present Situation and the Present Future of French Philosophy," written and published in English in 1950, is exemplary in this regard.[107] In this essay, Wahl discusses not only German philosophers such as Heidegger but also dozens of contemporary French thinkers: idealists and spiritualists, personalists and empiricists, Catholics, communists, and existentialists. Along the way, he devotes five pages to his friend Levinas, far more than to any other philosopher mentioned. Other works include Wahl's English monograph *The Philosopher's*

---

104. Maurice Merleau-Ponty, *Phenomenology of Perception*, trans. Colin Smith (London: Routledge and Kegan Paul, 1962), vii.

105. Wahl, "Note sur aspects empiristes," 18; "Note on Empiricist Aspects," 202.

106. These courses were all subsequently published; see Jean Wahl, *Les aspects qualitatifs du réel. I. Introduction, la philosophie de l'existence; II. Début d'une étude sur Husserl; III. La philosophie de la nature de N. Hartmann* (Paris: Centre de Documentation Universitaire, 1955); *L'ouvrage posthume de Husserl: La Krisis; la crise des sciences européennes et la phénoménologie transcendantale* (Paris: Centre de Documentation Universitaire, 1957); *Husserl* (Paris: Centre de Documentation Universitaire, 1958); *Husserl, la "Philosophie première 'Erste Philosophie'"* (Paris: Centre de Documentation Universitaire, 1961); and *Husserl* (Paris: Centre de Documentation Universitaire, 1966).

107. Jean Wahl, "The Present Situation and the Present Future of French Philosophy," in *Philosophic Thought in France and the United States: Essays Representing Major Trends in Contemporary French and American Philosophy*, ed. Marvin Farber (Buffalo, N.Y.: University of Buffalo Publications in Philosophy, 1950), 35–54. The essay also contains a six-page bibliography of works by contemporary French philosophers.

Way (1948), which contains discussions of many continental thinkers and was praised by Charles Hartshorne for its "profundity" and "magnificent wealth of subtle suggestions and apt reminders."[108]

IV

Wahl's concern with the history of philosophy was by no means absent in his more original philosophical works, for Wahl believed that "philosophical problems cannot be separated from their historical background."[109] This led him to write books that were at once revolutionary and of great pedagogical utility, such as his magnum opus, *Traité de métaphysique* (Treatise on metaphysics).[110] Wahl was also always interested in examining—in fact, he said that it was the business of philosophers to examine—those "essential features of reality [that] have been left aside."[111] What distinguishes Wahl's philosophical activity, especially for his time, was his willingness to mine any source whatsoever that could help him address those marginalized and excluded features of reality: English empiricism, American pragmatism, German idealism, Greek metaphysics,[112] phenomenology and existentialism, or art and poetry. He did so not in order ultimately to subsume them under a rationalist system but for the sake of a richer, more profound, yet nevertheless inexhaustible appreciation of the concrete.

Alphonse de Waelhens characterizes Wahl's basic position well: "philosophy is comprised of chains of unresolved dialectical oppositions placed

---

108. Charles Hartshorne, review of *The Philosophers Way*, by Jean Wahl, *Philosophical Review* 57, no. 5 (September 1948): 509–11. See also "Interrogation of Jean Wahl," 179–200, an interview Wahl gave in English in 1964 in which he responds to questions from a dozen colleagues, many of them professors in England and America; Jean Wahl, "Existentialism: A Preface," *New Republic,* October 1, 1945, 442–44; Jean Wahl, "Freedom and Existence in Some Recent Philosophies," *Philosophy and Phenomenological Research* 8, no. 4 (June 1948): 538–56; Jean Wahl, "A Letter to Marvin Farber," *Philosophy and Phenomenological Research* 11, no. 3 (March 1951): 401–5; Jean Wahl, "A Question: On the Impossibility of Possibility, On the Unnecessariness of Necessity, and on the Reality of Reality," *Philosophy and Phenomenological Research* 7, no. 1 (September 1946): 159–60; and Jean Wahl, "Realism, Dialectic, and the Transcendent," *Philosophy and Phenomenological Research* 4, no. 4 (June 1944): 496–506.

109. Wahl, *The Philosopher's Way,* xi.

110. Vladimir Jankélévitch, "Mystique et dialectique chez Jean Wahl," *Revue de Métaphysique et de Morale* 58, no. 4 (October–December 1953): 423.

111. "Interrogation of Jean Wahl," 181.

112. Such as his *Étude sur le Parménide de Platon* (Paris: Rieder, 1930) and *Les Problèmes platoniciens: La République, Euthydème, Cratyle,* 4 vols. (Paris: Centre de Documentation Universitaire, 1938–39).

between two transcendences: the presence of perception at one extreme, the ecstasy of the mystery at the other."[113] Wahl's employment of dialectic is not in service of sublation but of transcendences (transascendence and transdescendence) beyond hierarchy, rational intelligibility, and "the imperfections of language"; it is in service of a "vision" of the "immediate" that is both "felt" and achieved.[114] Wahl endeavors to integrate "Hegel's feeling of the whole" and Bradley's "felt totality" into an "empirical totality" that is neither strictly rationalist (with its focus on the universal) nor strictly empiricist (with its focus on the particular), but involves a Whiteheadian "concrescence" or "the interfusion of things and their contemporaneous growth" that can only be felt.[115] Wahl's "existential dialectic," his persistent questioning and renewal, his emphasis on plurality and quality over unity and quantity, his opposition to systems and even to the preeminence of ontology, his resistance to strict binaries, his inclusion of writers and artists traditionally deemed insufficiently philosophical, and his own poetic endeavors—this is all for the sake of the transcendence of life, or rather what one might call a transcended transcendence, an immanence of "the absolute felt in a very small thing, as the poet Thomas Traherne said."[116] "An intense, felt absolute," Wahl writes, "not the absolute of the philosophers, but that of a passion or a verse."[117] (For more on Wahl's own philosophy, see Chapter 11 in this volume.)

Before concluding this introduction, Wahl's relationship to art, and especially poetry, must be mentioned. Wahl contends that art, beyond propositional truth, allows access to reality via what he calls *la vérité sentie* or "felt truth."[118] Such truth is not primordial, as *alētheia* was for Heidegger but, rather, a necessary "enlargement of the [propositional] idea of truth."[119] "There are as many visions of the world as there are great artists. And each

---

113. Alphonse de Waelhens, review of *Existence humaine et transcendance*, by Jean Wahl, *Revue Philosophique de Louvain* 44, no. 2 (1946): 328.

114. Wahl, *The Philosopher's Way*, 12–13. See also "Interrogation of Jean Wahl," 187–88.

115. Wahl, *The Philosopher's Way*, 201–2. Quotes from Newton P. Stallknecht, "Beyond the Concrete: Wahl's Dialectical Existentialism," *Review of Metaphysics* 8, no. 1 (September 1954): 144–55.

116. Wahl, *Traité de métaphysique* (Paris: Payot, 1953), 703. Quote from Levinas, *Outside the Subject*, 73.

117. Wahl, *Poésie, pensée, perception*, 253. Translation from Levinas, *Outside the Subject*, 82. Levinas mistakenly refers to p. 25.

118. Wahl, *Traité de métaphysique*, 481. Reference from "Interrogation of Jean Wahl," 185.

119. "Interrogation of Jean Wahl," 187.

vision, as we said, is irreducible. But," Wahl continues, "within the soul of the spectator that we are, there are communications between these visions."[120] Wahl spent much of his life engaging in, expressing, and facilitating such communications. There were fruitful exchanges with artists and authors such as Marc Chagall and Samuel Beckett,[121] Wallace Stevens,[122] and the members of the College of Sociology. There were extended reflections on Arthur Rimbaud and Vincent Van Gogh, in whom Wahl found "an authentic ontological quest."[123] There were translations into French of twentieth-century masters such as Hart Crane, e. e. cummings, T. S. Eliot, Robert Frost, Langston Hughes, and Wallace Stevens, as well as of earlier poets such as Thomas Traherne.[124] And there was the poetry of

120. Ibid., 184.

121. See Marc Chagall, *Illustrations for the Bible*, with text by Jean Wahl and an appreciation by Meyer Shapiro (New York: Harcourt, 1956). This is the English version of the same book, published in French by Verve in 1956. Wahl's text is actually a long poem, which Wahl translated into English with help from none other than Samuel Beckett. Wahl had already published a piece by Beckett a few years earlier entitled "Je tiens le greffe," in *Deucalion* 4 ("Le diurne et le nocturne dans la nature, dans l'art et dans l'acte"), vol. 36 of *Être et penser: Cahiers de philosophie* (Neuchâtel: Éditions de la Baconnière, October 1952), 137–40. Beckett, in a letter to Jean and Marcelle Wahl from 1969, recalls that he and Jean Wahl met in 1942. Letter available in Barbara Wahl, "Autour de Jean Wahl," 525. See also his letter to Wahl from May 8, 1951: "I remember perfectly well our few meetings in 1942. You were just about to cross over to the other zone, and I, without yet knowing it, was too. I gave you Shakespeare's sonnets." *The Letters of Samuel Beckett, Volume II: 1941–1956*, ed. George Craig et al. (Cambridge: Cambridge University Press, 2011), 252. Wahl was also among the fifteen people to receive copies of *En attendant Godot* (*Waiting for Godot*) signed by Beckett on October 27, 1952 (*The Letters of Samuel Beckett*, 341–42).

122. Wahl translated Stevens into French, and Stevens read Wahl's work. See Jennifer Anna Gosetti-Ferencei, "Immanent Transcendence in Rilke and Stevens," *German Quarterly* 83, no. 3 (Summer 2010): 277, 293n7. There was also a debate in 1943 at Mount Holyoke between Wahl and Stevens on the relation of philosophy and poetry. See Anne Luyat-Moore, "Wallace Stevens and Jean Wahl," in *Strategies of Difference in Modern Poetry: Case Studies in Poetic Composition*, ed. Pierre Lagayette (Madison, N.J.: Fairleigh Dickinson University Press, 1998), 74–86.

123. Ferdinand Alquié, "Jean Wahl," *Les Études Philosophiques* 1 (January–March 1975): 82. An example of Wahl's interpretation of the ontological significance of poetry is found in the chapter of Wahl's *Existence humaine et transcendance* entitled "Poésie et métaphysique" (see translation in Chapter 9 of this volume).

124. See Thomas Traherne, *Poèmes de la félicité: Texte anglais traduit et commenté par Jean Wahl* (Paris: Éditions du Seuil, 1951); and Fouchet and Wahl, *Écrivains et poètes*. In this collection, Wahl translates dozens of other poets as well. While he does not translate the prose, he was responsible for their selection. Authors include William Faulkner, Ernest Hemingway, Henry Miller, Gertrude Stein, and John Steinbeck.

Wahl himself, several collections of which were published in both French and English during his lifetime.[125]

It is unsurprising, although, considering his many other interests and accomplishments, no less impressive, that Wahl was so committed to poetry since he believed that "the core of poetry will always be metaphysics, and it is quite possible that the core of metaphysics is, equally, always poetry" (see Chapter 9 in this volume).[126] Wahl's poetry is distinctively philosophical in the sense that, as Wahl's student and friend Ferdinand Alquié put it, "he does not want to find the meaning of poetry philosophically, but to realize through poetry the very ambition of philosophy."[127] That is to say, Wahl's poetry and, we might add, the magnificent philosophy-poetry that was his life, is an answer to the question he poses on the penultimate page of *Traité de métaphysique*: "Will the philosopher have the strength finally to transcend transcendence itself and to fall valiantly into immanence without letting the value of his effort of transcendence be lost?"[128] Wahl did have such strength. With his work, as the essays that follow bear witness, we are able to feel the absolute in a very small thing.

---

125. See, for example, Jean Wahl, *Connaître sans connaître* (Paris: G. L. M., 1938); Wahl, *Poèmes de circonstance*; and Wahl, *Poèmes*. Also available is Jean Wahl, "Poèmes de J. Wahl," *Revue de Métaphysique et de Morale* 80, no. 3 (July–September 1975): 289–315; Jean Wahl, "On Reading the Four Quartets," *Poetry* 73, no. 6 (March 1949): 317; and the poetry collected in *In'hui* 39: *Jean Wahl, le poète* (1992).

126. Wahl, *Existence humaine et transcendance*, 97.

127. Alquié, "Jean Wahl," 82.

128. Wahl, *Traité de métaphysique*, 721. Quote found in Levinas, *Outside the Subject*, 82.

Preface to *Toward the Concrete*

Three years after his book on Hegel, and two years after his study of Plato's *Parmenides*, Jean Wahl published a work that in many ways captured the spirit of the age. As Jean-Paul Sartre noted, many years later,

> At about that time, the writers whom we loved explained to us that existence is a *scandal*. What interested us, however, was real men with their labors and their troubles. We cried out for a philosophy which would account for everything, and we did not perceive that it existed already and that it was precisely this philosophy which provoked in us this demand. At that time one book enjoyed a great success among us—Jean Wahl's *Toward the Concrete*. Yet we were disappointed by this "toward." The total concrete was what we wanted to leave behind us; the absolute concrete was what we wanted to achieve. Still the work pleased us, for it embarrassed idealism by discovering in the universe paradoxes, ambiguities, conflicts, still unresolved.[1]

In successive chapters on William James, Alfred North Whitehead, and Gabriel Marcel, Wahl argued that we see in their works a dialectic between thought and

---

Preface to *Vers le concret: Études d'histoire de la philosophie contemporaine* (Paris: Vrin, 1932), 1–26; 2nd augmented ed. (Paris: Vrin, 2004), 29–46. First published in *Recherches Philosophiques* 1 (1931–32): 1–20.

1. Jean-Paul Sartre, *Search for a Method*, trans. Hazel E. Barnes (New York: Alfred Knopf, 1963), 19.

its object that refuses to lose touch with the real. Although these three chapters had each been published previously,[2] the book was in no sense a mere collection of essays. Instead, as a review by Charles W. Morris in the *Journal of Philosophy* put it, the book gives "a cross section of certain aspects of contemporary empiricism through a sympathetic but discerning presentation of the views of an American, an English, and a French thinker of diverse backgrounds: James as psychologist, Whitehead as philosopher of the exact sciences, Marcel as dramatist."[3]

The principal enemy for James, Whitehead, and Marcel is "mental aridity [*sécheresse mentale*]," and because they each retain an attention to the body and to lived experience, their dialectics, unlike those of the neo-Kantians who then dominated academic philosophy in France, remain oriented toward the concrete.[4] The three chapters were preceded by a preface that had, in fact, been published with the title "Vers le concret" at the invitation of Alexandre Koyré as the inaugural essay in the inaugural issue of the journal he edited, *Recherches Philosophiques*.[5] In this text, Wahl makes clear that phenomenology, and, in particular, Heidegger's presentation of it, will be essential to philosophy's move toward the concrete. In fact, we might see in Wahl's observation that Heidegger presents us with a phenomenology "which goes from a theory of essences separated from existence to a theory of existence in which the essences are destroyed" the emergence of French *existential* phenomenology, which in the following decade comes to be identified with Sartre and Merleau-Ponty.

But as the author of the introduction to the second edition of *Vers le concret* notes, this is not a work of merely historical interest for those looking to understand French philosophy in the years between the two world wars. Instead, "the movement that Wahl describes has lost none of its pertinence. The possibility of an 'expanded' form of empiricism attentive to scientific work as to the qualitative aspects of experience, the critique of reductive forms of naturalism, the conquest of new philosophical territories including sensation, the body, space as it is perceived, the event—all these remain open questions."[6] We can note as well that when Wahl sees in James, Whitehead, and Marcel a tendency to replace the *Aufhebung* of the

---

2. Jean Wahl, "William James d'après sa correspondance," *Revue Philosophique de la France et de l'Étranger* 93 (May–June 1922): 381–416; 94 (September–October 1922): 298–347. "La philosophie spéculative de Whitehead," *Revue Philosophique de la France et de l'Étranger* 111 (January–June 1931): 341–78; 112 (July–December 1931): 108–43. "Le Journal métaphysique de Gabriel Marcel," *Revue de Métaphysique et de Morale* 37, no. 1 (January–March 1930): 75–112.

3. Charles W. Morris, "Review of *Vers le concret*," *Journal of Philosophy* 30, no. 26 (December 21, 1933): 714.

4. Jean Wahl, *Vers le concret* (Paris: Vrin, 1932), 13.

5. Jean Wahl, "Vers le concret," *Recherches Philosophiques* 1 (1931–32): 1–20.

6. Mathias Girel, foreword to Jean Wahl, *Vers le concret* (Paris: Vrin, 2004), 5–6.

Hegelian dialectic with an oscillation and tension between opposites—immanence and transcendence, internality and externality, permanence and fluidity, continuity and discontinuity, monism and pluralism, etc.—that can never be resolved, what he is identifying is what, almost four decades later, will come to be known as a philosophy of difference. Wahl's great heir, in this regard, will be Gilles Deleuze, and we might here recall that in the bibliography to *Difference and Repetition* in which Deleuze listed the book titles that were important in relation to the concerns of his own book, following Wahl's name, Deleuze simply noted "Passim," which Deleuze explains this way: when we place the word "passim" in the column for works, "This is because the themes of difference or repetition are really present throughout all their work."[7]

Alan D. Schrift

I

At the beginning of *The Phenomenology of Spirit*, Hegel tells us that what passes for the particular and the concrete is in reality the most abstract and the most general; what the empiricists and the realists attribute the greatest richness to is in reality the poorest thing in the world. Undoubtedly, here Hegel has formulated in the most striking way one of the profound motifs of idealist thought, a motif already brought to light by Plato, especially in the *Timaeus*. The idealist will always say that what is claimed to be concrete is only an abstraction or a fiction. In reality, Hegel's argumentation, and he was conscious of this himself, was founded essentially on language. If I write, "It's night right now," this sentence is going to be discovered to be false. For, in a couple of hours, it will be day. Is it necessary to conclude from this with Hegel that language thus reveals the nonreality of the concrete? Is the concrete only an intention destined never to be realized? Is it the case that here in language, as everywhere in Hegel, the work constituted by man flatly contradicts an indefinite aspiration present in man's purely subjective intentions? Must we not rather say that language, far from revealing the real, reveals itself, but as powerless?[8]

---

7. Gilles Deleuze, *Difference and Repetition*, trans. Paul Patton (London: Athlone Press, 1994), 334.

8. Cf. a similar argument in [Erich] Becher, *Einführung in die Philosophie* ([Munich: Duncker und Humblot,] 192[6]), and [Hans] Leisegang, *Denkformen* ([Berlin: Walter de Gruyter,] 1928), 250. In addition, see the beginning of *The Phenomenology of Spirit*, the gripping pages that Hegel has devoted in the Jena *Realphilosophie* (published by Hoffmeister in 1931) to the kingdom of names and to memory, vol. 2, 184–90.

However, some will ask, "what is this concrete that the realist claims to grasp?" They will ask this question especially if we empty the concrete of the determinations that the intelligence has woven and coiled together, determinations that are the web and very texture of the supposed concrete. If we do this, nothing remains of the concrete. But, without denying the contribution that intelligence makes, the realist will respond that it is necessary to admit that there is something to this thing to which intelligence makes the contribution. Whether one calls it the thing-in-itself or a kind of impact [*choc*], the idealists are forced to grant it.

Undoubtedly, for the critical idealist, this impact fulfills only the role of an occasion, of an invitation to investigation. There will be, the idealist will tell us—and the realist will have to recognize the depth of the idealist's response and objection—an idealist way and a realist way of reflecting on the impact. If we take the impact as a simple point of departure for a reflection that connects the impact back to the whole of the universe, we will be idealists. In fact, one of the functions of science is to bring to light this connection, this interconnection of things. And the realist or at least the partisan of realism, such as we understand him, will grant that. But he will ask whether this impact and this occasion are not realities, and he will ask whether, at the same time that they race to link up with the intellectual whole under the impulse of the scientific spirit, they are not composed with other occasions and other impacts in order to form this picture that is the sensible world.[9] Science shows us the underside of the tapestry, an underside that appears first as a continuity or a quasi-continuity of assembled weaves. But the topside also has a reality, and it is even this reality of the topside that at times, at least in a sense, explains the underside.

Some will add that perception fails in its explanation of the world and it is precisely from this failure of perception that science is born. In general, one must not make use of perception in order to explain. Perception presents, it does not explain. And it is certain that, in this area of explanation, we always go back to science before going back to anything else. What is not at issue therefore is the closing of one's eyes before the astonishing successes of science, which today has managed to specify in an admirable way the very reasons for its limits. What is at issue is simply to see that science is an instrument of analysis. Now the real is not constructed by

---

[Georg Wilhelm Friedrich Hegel, *Jenenser Realphilosophie (Natur- und Geistesphilosophie)*, 2 vols., ed. Johannes Hoffmeister (Leipzig: F. Meiner, 1931–32), 2:184–90.]

9. To speak of impact is, moreover, to continue to accept the language of the idealist. Rather than an impact, sensation will present itself for the realist as contact, participation, communion.

analysis. An instrument of analysis can decompose the real. It is hardly probable that it can show how it is made or even describe it as it is.

Some will still say to us, and this is Lachelier's[10] argument, "space is external, what is this exteriority without thought?" If these parts that are outside of one another are not contained by something other than themselves, they vanish. But who says that *partes extra partes* space is concrete space and who says that concrete space is not, rather, this sense of the body and of our body? This concrete space is precisely what the philosophers that we are going to study—James, Marcel, Whitehead—are trying to help us think about. It is a primitive voluminosity that perhaps the art of certain cubists pursues as well, although without always giving an account of it.

Now these same philosophers whom we just mentioned make us see as well the inanity of Hegel's critique, a critique that accentuates the *mine*, the *here*, the *now*, all these designative elements; these are elements that thought can get a hold of only by denaturing them.[11] These philosophers claim the rights of the immediate.

By placing our spirit or mind among things, they make us see that the impact is not only this X on which idealism reflects but also a contact, a kinship, we would readily say with Claudel, a "knowledge" of spirit and of things. By giving back to the immediate its value and its role, they make us understand better what is the point of departure of the reflection.

Already the observations that we have just presented give us a sense that these three philosophers occupy one sole current of thought. It is the

---

10. [Jules Lachelier (1832–1918) was an idealist who sought to ground idealism on a theory of induction that could resist the challenges of skepticism. He was among the most influential philosophers in France in the second half of the nineteenth century.]

11. This is what Heidegger calls the a priori of the fact, *Sein und Zeit*, 229. [Martin Heidegger, *Being and Time*, trans. John Macquarrie and Edward Robinson (New York: Harper and Row, 1962), 272, §44c. Hereafter, we will insert the reference to the English translation between square brackets along with the paragraph number after Wahl's citation. For a discussion of which edition of *Sein und Zeit* Wahl might have used, see Chapter 5, note 5.] We are going to refer to Heidegger quite often. He is profoundly conscious of many of the aspirations of contemporary thought. Moreover, the clear consciousness of this obscure background of aspirations, together with his remarkable art of translating his own observations or those of others—whether they are those of Kierkegaard, pragmatism, Dilthey, or Spengler—into abstract terms, together with his great mastery of the philosophical language that he has created, make his work an invaluable benchmark. In particular—and this is also what endows his work with its scope—he has tried to join the feeling of individual existence such as Kierkegaard had experienced it to the feeling of our existence in the middle of things such as it is brought to light in contemporary philosophy. In a later study, we propose to examine this double aspect of his thinking.

tendency of this current that we will attempt to define, and it is in this way that we are going to study them.

They start from very diverse ideas. James is originally a physiologist; Whitehead a logician and a mathematician; Gabriel Marcel started from a metaphysical reflection. Among them there are divergences and, concerning certain points, perhaps some oppositions. What is more striking, however, is the agreement—more exactly, the identity of certain of their conceptions.

We have spoken of the immediate. It is necessary to add immediately that this immediacy is not atomic. To reduce the things to atoms, to elements, to space understood through points, is inevitably to give an inadequate idea. All of what tends to destroy a real value is partial. Not only what tends to destroy the person, but also and perhaps especially what tends to destroy the things is partial.[12] At every degree of the scale, the beings tend to become spherical and form themselves into totalities. And this is one of the most fruitful teachings of phenomenology, a teaching that James has already given us, the teaching that instructs us to grasp the things with all their richness, "at their face value,"[13] in the very way in which they are known.[14]

The empiricism of these philosophers is not in any way an atomic empiricism in the usual sense of the word, precisely because it is really the affirmation of atomic forms, in the primitive sense of configurations, configurations that an artificial division disfigures, just in the same way that the divisions brought about by the nondialectician disfigure reality according to Plato. The thing that is the most opposite to analysis is less the continuous by itself than this mixture of the continuous and the discontinuous that defines a rhythm, a volume, or a person. And precisely what these philosophers grasp are blocks of duration, volumes, events. In this sense one can oppose Whitehead's realism to American neorealism, to which he is at times close, but which has wanted to be a lot more "analytic." Likewise, [Samuel] Alexander speaks to us of syntheses

---

12. Concerning the idea of the thing, see the article by [Walther R]ehm, ["Wirklichkeitsdemut und Dingmystik,"] *Logos*[: *Zeitschrift für systematische Philosophie* 19] (1930): 297–358. Undoubtedly it would be appropriate to complete his suggestions by taking inspiration from the feeling of the thing in its active obscurity such as Claudel presents it to us or in its dull and hard essence such as it appears in Cézanne.

13. [In English in the original.]

14. "As they are known as." [In English in the original.] Cf. Heidegger, *Sein und Zeit*, 34 [58, §7c]. To let what shows itself, in the way in which it shows itself, be revealed by itself.

without synthetic activity, of syntheses that we find already made in experience.[15]

In James, in Whitehead, and in Marcel, one finds the same cult of reality in its thickness, using one of James's words that Whitehead loves to quote. Thus for them relations are not something added onto the primitive datum; they are included in it; or still more exactly perhaps they translate something, a background that is nonrelational and yet unifying (if we can use this word without the idea of an act of intelligence coming to mind), a background that is included in the primitive datum. We find this idea of the nonrelational background, which has not been very clearly explained by James and Whitehead, expressed in a profound way by an anti-empiricist, by Bradley;[16] empiricism in fact would gain a lot by meditating on Bradley's philosophy.[17]

Following James, we cannot therefore define empiricism as the philosophy that expresses the whole through its parts. For this is precisely the opposite of what Whitehead wants to do in his philosophy of the organism and the opposite of what James often has done. The result is that we will encounter here in James, as we will do frequently, this movement by which a tendency completes itself with the help of its opposite. There is an explanation of the whole by its parts, but there is an unexplainability of the whole by its parts.

We will say, rather, that empiricism is defined by its affirmation of the nondeducibility of being, by its affirmation of the datum, that is, its affirmation of something immediate,[18] which is welcomed, received. Without doubt, we could distinguish two degrees of empiricism. There is the empiricism that does not pose itself as a problem, that refuses to pose itself as a problem and that first takes being as given. We could include here the

---

15. Cf. [Raymond] Ruyer, ["Le problème de la personnalité et la physique moderne,"] *Revue de Synthèse* (October 1931): 73: "The absolute unity of our conscious states is nothing but a special case of the unity through real connections." 74: "In the texture of every conscious state, there is a principle of unity, a principle that is somehow physical."

16. [F. H. Bradley (1846–1924) was the leading figure in the movement of British idealism.]

17. It is perhaps to this philosophy that we must have recourse if we are to understand how it is that Whitehead presents relations sometimes as interior to the terms and sometimes as external to them. This is because the schema of relations is simply an inadequate way to translate the real. Isn't this what Whitehead says explicitly about the relation of the subject to the predicate?

18. And something particular, at least most of the time. But Alexander allows a generality, an empirical a priori; cf. Heidegger, 111 [146, §23].

empiricism of a J. S. Mill or Spencer. But there would also be the empiricism that would have passed through and overcome rationalism. This is the empiricism of the later Fichte or of the later Schelling. This is also the empiricism of Hamann—and in certain parts of *The Critique of Pure Reason* it is the empiricism of Kant.

In Hume, who was one of Hamann's masters or at least his guide, and a decisive occasion for Kant's reflection, we discover simultaneously the empiricism of the first degree and the empiricism of the second degree. Hume penetrates his empiricism of the first degree to find that of the second degree.

This empiricism of the second degree is really what we find in Gabriel Marcel; his empiricism was influenced undoubtedly by Schelling's "meta-empirical empiricism," if we can say this. James and Whitehead see the facts in their brutality and their beauty. Gabriel Marcel and at certain moments Whitehead want to get back to the root of the fact toward this meta-empirical empiricism that we just mentioned. In all three, we discover this feeling of the given, and we discover its equivalent, in another form, in the phenomenologists' "principle of all principles."

Like James, Whitehead insists on the irreducibility of being in relation to knowledge. And we will see Gabriel Marcel's theories concerning this point. We should not therefore believe that we can enclose these philosophies under one rubric, a rubric under which we could place the Thomist philosophies, the rubric of the philosophy of being. For the philosophies we are studying deny precisely the intelligibility of being. Being for them is a feeling rather than an idea, something that rebels against reason; it is not at all the essence of reason. The being that is the essence of reason is entirely different from being such as they conceive it. The theory of being that we discover in the background of these philosophies is opposed to that of Saint Thomas as well as to that of Descartes. Neo-Thomism in France is valuable because it represents certain tendencies that are expressed to foreigners in the various forms of contemporary realism.[19]

---

19. One of the reasons for the reverberation of [Émile] Meyerson's theses is discovered as well in the realist assertion. But the psychology of the knower is perhaps one of the areas in which this assertion has the least interest. For it is the work that is important, rather than the psychology of the worker. Moreover, in this case, and paradoxically, the psychology of the worker gives us only the "already made," while the examination of the work gives us supple relations, a psychology of the "being made." With the help of schemas, which are perhaps at times a bit simplistic, subtle relations, as [Léon] Brunschvicg has shown, are what are developed, and these are essential in the area of the philosophy of the sciences.

But the realism of the philosophers we are studying is still really different from these forms. It does not seem that Thomism or Saint Thomas himself had fully taken advantage of Aristotle's teachings. Before seeking the nature of being by studying essence, Aristotle had really shown the diversity of the ideas of being; for Aristotle, the analogy of being is not grounded on the superiority of this idea, but rather on the ambiguity that belongs to the abstract notions that must be defined carefully in the particular cases.[20]

II

In realism as it is conceived by these authors, we will see that there is simultaneously immanence and transcendence. Transcendence is the idea of a beyond by means of which knowledge has a direction, toward which it directs itself, from which it draws its nourishment. Immanence is the idea of this compact density in which no element is absolutely transcendent in relation to any other.

And we will be able to rediscover this double characteristic in space and in time such as this realism conceives them. Transcendence then becomes transcendence in space and in time; and it is this exteriority of the parts in relation to one another, this distance, that looks to be ordinarily the sole characteristic of space. Its immanence is this complementary aspect that is too often passed over in silence. Immanence is this interiority of the parts in relation to one another, which means that they are no longer parts. This is what Whitehead has brought to light in his theory of volume, which is an expansion of the theory of voluminosity in James. Below the space that is the instrument for the mind of the knower and below the space that belongs to the world of description, there is a space that belongs to the vital domain.[21] This is the space that we grasp by the contact with the real that

---

20. The difference between Aristotle and Saint Thomas can be appreciated in a quite opposite way. This is how Gilson writes about Thomism: "Even his general interpretation of Aristotle's metaphysics transcends the authentic Aristotelianism" ([Étienne Gilson,] *Esprit de la philosophie médiévale* [(Paris: Vrin, 1932)], 84). [*The Spirit of Medieval Philosophy (Gifford Lectures 1931–1932)*, trans. A. H. C. Downes (New York: Charles Scribner's Sons, 1940), 80]. [Wahl misquotes Gilson by writing "philosophy" rather than "metaphysics."] This is what he says about Aristotelian philosophy: "it is precisely because they [Plato and Aristotle] were on the right road that to go further along it was progress" (ibid., 86[/83]). At least concerning the existence of this difference, we can, however, invoke his authority (cf. 53[/49–50]).

21. For Heidegger, because of the fact that it is in the world, *Dasein* has a spatial character (56, 104, 141, 299) [82, §12; 104, §22; 180, §30; 346, §60]. Space is

Bergson has spoken about, by the animal faith that Santayana has spoken about. Intimately connected to this sense of space as a concrete whole is this sense of the body that we will see so vividly in James and Whitehead. James has had the sense of this third substance that is the union of the soul and the body. And we will rediscover this sense as well in Whitehead, in the theory of the *withness of the body*,[22] and in Gabriel Marcel in the theory of "my body." What in James is still an objective observation is a much more subjective view in Whitehead and Marcel.

In relation to time, this immanence will be duration such as Bergson has described it and also as Whitehead has conceived it. All three of the philosophers that we are studying retain from Bergsonism the intuition of time as continuity. But in one way or another, they complete this feeling of continuity through a feeling of discontinuity, through the theory of drops of time in James, through the assertion of the "atomistic" character of duration in Whitehead, and through the sense of dramatic scenes that fill out this duration in Marcel.

At the same time, in Whitehead and in Marcel, the notion of time acquires a great flexibility by means of the negation of the "simple location," using Whitehead's expression. And meeting up with certain things that Bradley indicates, both Whitehead and Marcel conceive of discordant temporal series, an essential relativity of time.

Immanence and transcendence are both going to form a whole in the domain of the description of knowledge just as they formed a whole in the description of the characteristics of space and time.

This volume and this duration are in a sense in us as they are in things. In a general way, there is no barrier between us and things. We are in communion with them by means of this reception that Whitehead speaks about, by means of this sympathetic mediation that Marcel speaks about, by means of this grasp from the exterior insofar as it is exterior. This idea of a grasp from the exterior as such haunts thought and, more than anything else, haunts contemporary thought. We find this idea particularly

---

something other than a simple representation. It is felt (368) [419, §70]. There is a closeness that has nothing to do with distance (102, 119) [135, §22; 155, §26]. It is true that for Heidegger as for Spengler this spatiality has its foundation in temporality (335, 367) [384, §67; 418, §70]. For the feeling of spatiality in [Oswald] Spengler, see *Der Untergang des Abendlandes*, [vol.] 1 [(Munich: Beck, 1920)], 108, 111, 218, 229, 395, 509. [Oswald Spengler, *The Decline of the West, Complete in One Volume*, trans. Charles Francis Atkinson (New York: Alfred A. Knopf, 1932), 1:75, 77, 159, 169, 291–92, 363.]

22. [In English in the original.]

visible in Scheler's *The Nature of Sympathy*, and in certain passages in D. H. Lawrence's novels.

Are these philosophers—James, Whitehead, Marcel—realists or are they idealists? In different ways, they break the frames, realizing the wish formulated by Nicolai Hartmann, by constituting an experiential idealism like James's, an organicism like Whitehead's, a philosophy of invocation like Marcel's. For James and for Whitehead, we can speak of a pan-objectivism as well as of a pan-psychism. For both of them, we can say that the object is absolutely immanent for thought (this is the theory of context in James and the theory of the objective idea in Whitehead), and that it is absolutely transcendent to thought.

We said that Whitehead places this volume and this duration, of which he speaks to us, in us as well as in things. By telling us that the subject is a "superject," Whitehead wants us to understand, it seems, that, for the view of things that presents the object to us and the subject over against it,[23] it is necessary to substitute another view for which the object, with its dense and massive character and by means of this very character, transforms itself into the subject. Space is no more a simple form than substance is a simple subject, and perhaps the often confusing language that Whitehead uses is constructed in order to give us the idea of these relations. And perhaps this word "relation" cannot even be used anymore to refer to these masses of experiences that change into one another by means of a movement, which for intelligence is always a paradox. He has created this abstract style in part in order to render better the density of the concrete.

Another note was just heard, another note that looks to be discordant but is nevertheless essential: spirit encountering the object.[24] These ideas of the encounter and presence take on a new value. Spirit or mind discovers itself in front of the object and it can really recognize itself in the object. But it also knows that there is something in the object that cannot be assimilated or exhausted completely by spirit.

The oscillation between the two poles of transcendence and immanence leads us to understand, to some extent, the oscillation, so clear in Whitehead, between knowledge conceived as reception and knowledge conceived as "prehension." The value of Whitehead has been that he has insisted on receptivity; the care to bring this characteristic to light has too often been left to the sensualistic empiricists. Novalis has written that "there is some-

---

23. Cf. Heidegger, *Sein und Zeit*, 58 and 176 [85, §12; 220, §38], for a critique of this conception.

24. Cf. Heidegger, in whom we discover simultaneously the idea of immanence in the world and the encounter of the object (for example, 137 [176, §29]).

thing to say in favor of passivity."[25] And during the same period, Maine de Biran, whom we essentially consider to be a philosopher of effort, brought into view all of what there is in man below and above activity, the hypopsychic, if we can say this, and the hyperorganic. Perhaps this is also one of the newest characteristics of contemporary German phenomenology, that is, with Husserl in the theory of knowledge and with Scheler in the theory of morality, to have insisted on this profound receptivity of the mind. Perhaps we could discover in Bergson's theory of pure perception something analogous to this tendency found in the phenomenologists.

At the same time, Whitehead brings to light the element of "prehension," the act of the mind. Does not the poet-philosopher [Novalis], whose text on passivity we were citing, possess, more than any other, the idea of a constructive idealism? Has he not insisted more than any other on the magic of thought?

In so doing, perhaps we would be led to show how passivity and activity must always complete each other, and also we would be led to wonder whether this opposition between them that we generally see exists. The highest activities look like something that we have received. Effort is seen especially in the stages that separate the beginning from the end. Maine de Biran has made us see this in a most admirable way. Waiting is tension and tension is waiting. But when the moment comes that the phenomenologists call the moment of fulfillment and reality, effort gives way to a feeling of welcome.[26]

---

25. [Perhaps Wahl is referring to a line from Fragment 88 of Novalis's *Das allgemeine Brouillon*. See Novalis, *Schriften: Die Werke Friedrich von Hardenbergs*, ed. Paul Kluckhorn and Richard Samuel, vol. 3, *Das philosophische Werk II*, ed. Richard Samuel in collaboration with Hans-Joachim Mähl and Gerhard Schulz (Stuttgart: Kohlhammer, 1960), 256: "Passivitaet ist nicht so verächtlich, als man glaubt." Novalis, *Notes for a Romantic Encyclopaedia: Das Allgemeine Brouillon*, trans. David W. Wood (Albany: State University of New York Press, 2007), 14: "Passivity is not as contemptible as one imagines."]

Likewise, Wordsworth and Shelley have been profoundly influenced by the idea, discovered in [William] Godwin, of the passivity of the mind. Cf. [H. W.] Garrod, *The Profession of Poetry* (Oxford: [Clarendon Press], 1929), 12–13.

26. On the level of aesthetics, [Denis] Saurat has brought this idea to light in his studies of *le Moderne* in *Marsyas* (1931) and *Nouvelle Revue Française* (1931). [These articles can be found, respectively, under Denis Saurat, "De l'avenir du style moderne," *Marsyas* 122 (February 1931): 570; and Denis Saurat, "L'après-guerre: Le style 'moderne,'" *Nouvelle Revue Française* 218 (November 1931): 793–800. Cf. also Denis Saurat, *Modernes* (Paris: Denoël et Steele, 1935).]

III

We have spoken of transcendence and immanence, but it would be necessary to distinguish immanences and transcendences of diverse sorts. There is a transcendence other than the purely spatial transcendence, and there is an immanence other than this immanence of massive indistinction. This distinction is going to allow us to see the theory of mind or spirit in the doctrines that we are going to study.

The principal enemy for James, Whitehead, and Marcel is mental aridity. They cannot be happy with the lifeless world of "classical materialism." Against classical materialism, they claim the rights of the psychical but also those of secondary qualities. What is real is what appears. And if psychological experience is our most profound experience, we can no more deny the value of secondary qualities than the existence of our thought. As Alexander says, are not secondary qualities psychic kinds that come to be added onto things, transforming them, giving them flesh and life?[27]

If there is for James and Whitehead a subjective-objective domain of Berkeleyan ideas and of the phenomena found in empirico-criticism, there is also a domain of profound values that is also subjective and objective—but in a sense different from the first. The first domain is subjective insofar as it enters into the context of consciousness and objective insofar as it is taken into the context of facts. The second is subjective insofar as it is the life of feeling and objective insofar as this life of feeling is real. James in his theory of religious experience, Whitehead when he speaks of aesthetic values and also of religious values, and Marcel throughout his *Metaphysical Journal*, all three are devoted to bringing into view this second degree of the fusion of the objective and the subjective in which the identity of these two opposite qualities no longer comes from the possibility of certain facts being found in different contexts. Rather, the identity of these two opposite qualities comes from the reality of spirit.[28]

---

27. See the curious and penetrating studies by Hedwig Conrad Martius in *Jahrbuch für Philosophie* (1916 and 1923) ["Zur Ontologie und Erscheinungslehre der realen Außenwelt: Verbunden mit einer Kritik positivistischer Theorien," *Jahrbuch für Philosophie und phänomenologische Forschung* 3 (1916): 345–542; "Realontologie," *Jahrbuch für Philosophie und phänomenologische Forschung* (1923): 159–333], and see [Paul] Claudel, *Conversations dans le Loir-et-Cher*, *Commerce* (Spring 1929). [The latter is more readily available in Paul Claudel, *Conversations dans le Loir-et-Cher* (Paris: Gallimard, 1935).]

28. The feeling of creation and novelty would be located in this domain as well as the modalities of feeling of which we are going to speak. The feeling of creation and novelty is so difficult, perhaps impossible to grasp since our gaze can turn itself only

For these thinkers, there is not only a material density,[29] there is also a spiritual density. What is important for them, as James has said, is the experienced feeling of the individual. And they believe that realities respond, must respond, to the demands. Their philosophy is like a call to reality.

All three are concerned with the communication of souls. What they understand by religion is the idea of a living relation between the spirit and the universe, the idea of a relation from one person to another. James, like Marcel, thinks that there is no agreement that we can formulate in words concerning the subject of what is most internal. There is no intellectual content, no intellectual message in religious feeling when it reaches its complete depth.

Thus we can see this higher transcendence and this higher immanence that we were speaking about earlier. On the one hand, there is this being beyond being to which prayers are addressed; on the other, there is this confluence of spirits on which James reflects, this communion that Marcel speaks about. For us, these truly are "ideas," calls thrown to reality, and we do not know if what responds is only the echo of this call.

IV

The characteristics that we have distinguished in these philosophies do not keep these philosophies from having a critical and analytical aspect. It is the merit of the empirico-criticist school, which is often treated unfairly by those who hail from dialectical materialism, and it is the merit of philosophers as different as a James or a Bergson on the one hand and a Russell on the other to have revealed the false positions of certain problems and to have denounced pseudo-problems. James's article "Does Consciousness Exist?,"[30] which if we must believe Whitehead is as important as the *Discourse on Method*, and Bergson's discussion of the idea of the possible, to which perhaps Whitehead's philosophy gives too large a place, are models of these dissociations and of these necessary analyses.

Let us insist a bit on the critical aspect of the doctrines that we have been studying. James and Whitehead are antisubstantialists. In James's

---

toward the past and since novelty escapes from the grasp of consciousness. And if consciousness grasps it, novelty is transformed into something earlier.

29. [In the 2004 second edition of *Vers le concret*, what appears here is "*une densité immatérielle*," "an immaterial density"; this is almost certainly a mistaken alteration of "*une densité matérielle*," "a material density," which appeared in the 1932 first edition.]

30. [See William James, *Essays in Radical Empiricism* (New York: Longman Green and Co., 1912), 1–38.]

theory of consciousness and the ego, we see a critique of the idea of substance. There is no ego over against a non-ego, and there is no unchanging substrate of the ego. The ego is neither independent nor stable. We will discover in Whitehead, in his theory of the event, the expansion of these conceptions. The negation of "bifurcation" and the negation of the "simple location" are like the explanations and generalizations of James's theories.[31] In Marcel, the critique of the idea of substance returns somehow by particularizing itself. The idea of substance is applied specifically to thinking substance, but at the same time it contains a very general aspect since it is the separation of the sphere of discourse from another sphere which is no less real, that of invocation and of prayer. Here the more the ego is opposed to the ego, the more there are events that are properly mine, and if they are still subjective, they are no longer private.

But if the idea of substance loses its value, the feeling of substance acquires a new value. James, through his insistence on the will, through his description of the warmth and intimacy of certain states of consciousness, [and] Whitehead, through his theory of the thing, make us see that there are not only series and succession but also conglomerates that are things and persons. Marcel denies the substance that belongs to the domain of the "it"; but he does not deny the substance that belongs to the domain of the "thou." The possible occupies a large place in the philosophy of James and Whitehead, too large a place, as we said about Whitehead. It is necessary to see that beside the abstract possible—which is the double projection, as if by a mirror play, of the past into the future and of the future into the past, an illusion made by retrospection and abstraction—there is perhaps, as Bergson's philosophy itself shows, a concrete possible that is made in us. Just as for the idea of substance we would have reason to distinguish on the one hand the possible that belongs to the domain of the "it," here using Marcel's language in a case where he does not use it, and on the other hand the possible that belongs to the domain of the ego. In other words, we can distinguish on the one hand the intellectual possible, which is, as Bergson has shown, a nonbeing, the abstract δύναμις, a pure logical construction like the Aristotelian substance, and on the other hand, the real dynamism. An analysis therefore is needed, but there is something that resists analysis. Contemporary science and, moreover, all science makes us become accustomed to this double necessity. Although every science encircles the unknowable within limits that are tighter and tighter, the unknowable does not disappear.

---

31. There is something arbitrary in connecting Whitehead back solely to James. We are doing it only in order to bring to light a kinship that Whitehead himself has stressed.

By starting from the idea of the possible, we could say that there is only one modality of judgment, that of existence. The other modalities, which are no less real but not in the same sphere, are modalities of feeling. The modalities of feeling are those that we would study if we followed the path opened up by Heidegger when he studies elementary feelings like anxiety, curiosity, care. We would perhaps be led to see in anxiety and hope the source of the possible, in despair and regret that of necessity. We would see that the necessary presupposes the pseudo-idea of the possible,[32] just as regret presupposes most often a prior anxiety and indecision. We would discover, perhaps by following certain ideas of Nietzsche, the origin of the idea of cause in reproach, anger, and accusation.

V

Some will say that the rapprochements among the three philosophers we are going to study have something artificial about them. It is possible that they appear somewhat artificial, but the rapprochements were produced not just among these three particular philosophers that we have been examining. Thus we see the probability grow for the three philosophers to reveal a real trend among them and in them. If we pay attention to the connections, which extend to the expressions used, between the ideas of [Richard] Hönigswald and [Bruno] Bauch and those of Whitehead, to the affinity that there is between Whitehead's "prehension" and intentionality in the phenomenologists, to the importance that the phenomenologists give to the observation of the flux of lived experience[33] (in which appearance and reality are mixed), to their theory of receptivity, to their theory of immediacy, to their assertion of the material a priori that coincides with Whitehead's assertion of secondary qualities, to all of what in Scheler's philosophy goes toward the "mode of causal efficacy" as Whitehead conceives it, and toward the theory of the body and of the "thou" as Marcel conceives them, to the idea of immanence in being such as Hartmann formulates it, the idea of being-in-the-world that we find in Heidegger,[34] we will

---

32. Necessity presupposes the possible, moreover, in several ways. The English logicians, in particular Bradley, have shown clearly the connection between the hypothetical and the apodictic.

33. We borrow this translation [of *Erlebnis* by *vécu*] from [Georges] Gurvitch's book, *Les tendances actuelles de la philosophie allemande* [Paris: Vrin, 1930], 13.

34. There would also be reason to take account of certain tendencies of the pragmatist movement, and Heidegger has sensed this by integrating certain profound features of pragmatist thought into his meditation (*Sein und Zeit*, 61, 68 [88, §13;

see that it is not possible that we are dealing with superficial and contingent rapprochements. A kind of dialectic has carried the phenomenology of a theory of eternal objects, which is close to that of Whitehead, to a theory of existence as duration, which is analogous to what Whitehead shows us under the "mode of causal efficacy" and closer still to what Marcel's philosophy uncovers for us. Thus this dialectic has turned phenomenology, which had been originally a study of timeless essences, into an investigation of temporal existence.[35] And after having put man in contact with eternal ideas, this movement puts him in contact with a pathetic [in the literal sense] world. If, furthermore, we take account of the profound influence that Kierkegaard and the dialectical theology inspired mainly by him has had on contemporary German thought, and if we note the sometimes surprising resemblances between Kierkegaard's thought and those of the *Metaphysical Journal*, we sense that there is a general movement. Alexander, whose name we will have to quote often, or [William Ernest] Hocking could just as well, as different as they might be, serve as points of comparison.[36] In Alexander, the point of comparison would come through his profound realism, through his theory of knowledge as "co-presence," through his theory of perspectives, which is quite analogous to the negation of the "simple location" in Whitehead, through his assertion of secondary qualities, through his idea of emergence, which is quite close to Whitehead's "concrescences" and "superjects," and finally through his theory of the body. In Hocking, the point of comparison would come through his theory of religious experience. We see, therefore, a vast movement directed "toward the concrete."

We do not mean that the fact of these convergences proves in the least that there is some truth there. It is because we believe there is a truth in this regard that we have considered these convergences. We could very well have accentuated entirely different philosophies.

97, §15]). The world is a world of obstacles and tools, and spirit reacts before the world through anticipations, pre-perceptions, hypotheses. Heidegger completes the pragmatist theory through a theory of resistance, which extends those of Maine de Biran, Dilthey, and Scheler.

35. Cf. Heidegger, 117 [152, §25].

36. Perhaps one could also speak here of Freud's psychology insofar as it tries to place the individual back into the whole of his concrete situation. Historical materialism too is an attempt at concrete explanation, if it is conceived not as a negation of thought; it must be conceived as a definition of thought in terms of that upon which thought functions and which is resistant to thought; in a word, thought must be defined by work and the different modes of work.

VI

We will also note that each of these studies that we have wanted to be wholly oriented toward the real terminates in questions that imply the necessity of a dialectic. In each, we have been led to follow dialectical movements of thought. We have seen James's philosophy look like an incessant movement. We have seen Whitehead's philosophy look like a dialogue between the immutability of objects and the mutability of events. And in Marcel's philosophy, we have been able to believe that we were present at a suicide of the dialectic, but it appears that this death of the dialectic is simply false. Intelligence is always repaired in order to continue questioning. Likewise, we would have been able to follow a dialectic in contemporary German thought, which goes from a theory of essences separated from existence to a theory of existence in which the essences are destroyed; it "leaves outside of the brackets" only what, in the beginning, was put between the brackets deliberately.

But still in another sense dialectical interrogation is repaired, since all these systems imply elements that are really hard to reconcile, whether these are transcendence and immanence, receptivity and intentionality in the phenomenologists, the closed character of the event and the "prehension" of events by each other in Whitehead, this very idea of "prehension" and realism, the theory of exteriority of relations and the theory of their interiority, the ambiguous meaning of the idea of objective immortality, the feeling of permanence and the feeling of fluidity. Moreover, we will have to wonder how we can separate the objects from the events, and how we can separate the events from one another.

Some have said that all philosophy is either Aristotelian or Platonic. We see, vaguely in James, but clearly in Whitehead, an Aristotelianism and a Platonism. For Whitehead, the real is the organism; the true is the eternal object, it is the idea.

James and Whitehead insist equally on the two notions of continuity and discontinuity: stream of thought, fusion of events on the one hand; on the other, the atomic character of time. We grasp here the oscillations of the spirit, this dialectic that is explained by what overcomes it. Undoubtedly, strictly speaking, we must say that this dialectic is neither continuous nor discontinuous; rather, it lets itself be interpreted in turn and each time more profoundly by these two notions of continuity and discontinuity.

James denies consciousness, but at the same time he refuses to study what, in one way or another, is not given to consciousness.

Exteriority of relations and interiority of relations: these two assertions are found in James, the first in his metaphysical pluralism, in his theory of consciousness as a function of knowledge, the second in his metaphysical temporalism, in his theory of consciousness as life and stream of thought. Both are discovered in Whitehead, in his theory of objects and in his theory of events. They are mixed together in his idea of nature and in his idea of "prehension." And will we not rediscover them in physics itself, when the principle of indetermination shows the interiority of relations being introduced into a domain where so far their exteriority was posited at least as an ideal that might be attained? Here again we have the feeling that this succession of battling ideas is explained by what is below them, by this nonrelational ground, which they try to make explicit but which will always preserve its implicit character.

Our perception of point 0 is at point 0, Bergson says in a passage from *Matter and Memory* that is famous and that deserves to be famous.[37] But it is Bergson who also shows that as soon as memory intervenes, the question "where?" can no longer be asked. Spirit is like this voice of which the English poet speaks; it is everywhere and it is nowhere. This movement that results in the elimination of the question "where?" is indicated by the negation of the "simple location" in Whitehead and in many of the passages found in Marcel's *Metaphysical Journal*.

In addition, the realist will be necessarily led to wonder if he is not the victim of two sophisms, which we could call the sophism of retrospection and the sophism of the hypothesis. Is not the thing whose existence he asserts only the trace or the residual product of this work of the spirit, which is before everything else an *élan*, an impulse? Can the critique that the pragmatists address to the notion of truth not also be applied to the idea of reality? Besides, does not asserting realism mean that the things would be there if spirit were suppressed? Does this not make an illegitimate hypothesis intervene, like all those that we make when we wonder what would happen when a fact that was produced would not be produced?

What characterizes realism is that it is the affirmation of the interiority of terms in each other that are exterior in relation to one another. In this sense, we can interpret R. B. Perry's idea concerning the immanence of the independent. On several points, neo-realism agrees with phenomenology. We understand thus that there is a dialectic of realism. The dialectic makes realism go from a doctrine of the immanence of the object in the subject and of the subject in the object (the one that has been exposed by James in his "Does Consciousness Exist?," by Bergson in his theory of images, by

---

37. [Cf. Henri Bergson, *Matter and Memory*, trans. Nancy Margaret Paul and W. Scott Palmer (New York: Zone, 1991), 57.]

the neo-realists whose doctrine agrees with empirico-criticism and can look like a form of idealism), to a theory of the transcendence of the object in relation to the subject (as it is found in Reid and in the critical realists in America). And perhaps realism always oscillates between these two ideas. One cannot use this oscillation, in which the very life of thought is highlighted, as an objection to realism.[38]

By being aware of these difficulties, of this very hesitation, of these necessary scruples, and by deciding despite everything in favor of the assertion that there is not only a road but also a point of departure that is barely glimpsed, and an orientation in this point of departure, such a realism would be constituted not as a doctrine but as an effort. And it would claim less to resolve the problems than at first to see them clearly.

The presence of this idea of a dialectic explains why these studies are placed under the title "toward the concrete." The concrete will never be something given to the philosopher. It will be what is being pursued. Only in the absence of thought can the concrete be revealed to us. The young Hegel had the feeling of the concrete, like many of the poets. A dialectic is needed precisely because there is a realism. The real is the limit of the dialectic; the real is its origin; the real is its end, its explanation and its destruction.

We see thought run aground on the real in its attempt at idealization and run aground in particular when it attempts to generalize. Reality and particularity are united. They are one and the same obstacle for thought just as the attempt at idealization and generalization are one and the same attempt. But by running aground on this obstacle, thought takes up its forces. It is in this momentary death that thought rediscovers itself being alive.

The dialectic as we would be led to conceive it would not be the Hegelian dialectic. Movement here is not immanent to the idea. Or, if it is immanent to the idea, movement comes from what the idea tries to do in relation to something other than itself. Philosophers like Dilthey, Simmel, or [Ernst] Troeltsch had tried to ground a historical dialectic, bending the Hegelian dialectic through contact with their own conception of life. As profound as their vision of the world was—and it is necessary to think

---

38. Concerning the dialectic found in contemporary philosophy, one can consult [William Henry] Sheldon, *The Strife of Systems and Productive Duality* ([Cambridge, Mass.: Harvard University Press,] 1918); [Bernard] Bosanquet, *The Meeting of Extremes in Contemporary Philosophy* ([London: Macmillan,] 192[1]); and for Germany, [Siegfried] Marck's recent book, *Die Dialektik in der Philosophie der Gegenwart* ([Tübingen: J. C. B. Mohr,] 1929 and 1931).

here especially of Simmel—the idea of the dialectic that is outlined in philosophy today is different. The dialectic looks to be born less of the auto-transcendence of spirit than in the encounter of spirit with the object.

The dialectic would agree, rather, with Fichte's ideas during the last phase of his philosophy where being appears to him to be the limit of thought. Or it agrees with Kierkegaard's dialectic. In fact, like Kierkegaard's dialectic, the dialectic today does not suppress the oppositions but holds them before itself. It is an oscillation rather than a dialectic, an active and tense oscillation of ideas.[39]

The dialectic would result not in an idea but in a mystic agnosticism, since the consequence or, rather, the necessary presupposition of this dialectical attitude is there in mystic agnosticism, as Karl Barth and his school have become aware.

Toward the real itself, we can go only by means of the dialectic. A living thought is made of innumerable erasures. The dialogue of the soul with itself is perpetual negation. This is what Hegel was saying when he saw the essence of affirmation in the negation of the negation.

The "no" of the dialectic is opposed to the "yes" of the real, and we rediscover the idea of Hegelian negativity. The "no" of the real is opposed to the "yes" of the dialectic, and this is another negativity that we find then, a negativity that is, strictly speaking, nothingness, the element of resistance and of obscurity.

We are thus led to distinguish two negativities: the "no" of the dialectic and the "no" of negative theology—or rather the "no" of negative ontology, that is, the "no" that is relativity and the very force of relativity and relation, and the "no" that is absolute, that is, the "no" to which we would be led if we followed the impulse of the thought found in the first part of Marcel's *Metaphysical Journal*.

There is no "no" without a "yes" and no "yes" without a "no." But thought cannot stop there. In order for thought to be thought, there must be in it a "yes" without a "no" that it cannot define, and a "no" without a "yes" that it also cannot define. We always find ourselves on the path of the hypotheses found in the *Parmenides*. This "no" without a "yes," this idea that absolute nonbeing exists, is the one that Heidegger took up recently by uniting, in an extremely ingenious and attractive way, Boehme and Kierkegaard.[40] In fact,

---

39. This is what Nicolai Hartmann has become aware of in his aporetics.
40. We must add Hegel, since Heidegger does not make the distinction that we believe we have to make between two kinds of negativity.

the name of Boehme imposes itself here. In this obscure region, one can no longer speak but through myths.

For Plato and Hegel, nothingness looks especially like an alterity, and on this point Bergson's ideas are no different than those of Plato and Hegel. Jankélévitch[41] has very precisely spoken of this assertion of the plentitude of the real, which is one of the essential presuppositions of Bergsonian philosophy. But we can wonder if these conceptions do not tend to eliminate an aspect of the real, an aspect that is all the more difficult to grasp, the aspect that is the element of absolute negation. And we can wonder as well whether we can discover finally in this idea of alterity the idea of negation that these thinkers tended to reduce to the idea of alterity. Here, it is more the theologians, certain philosophers close to theology, than the philosophers in the strict sense who put us on the path. Hocking, at least in certain passages, [Friedrich] von Hügel when he speaks of absolute alterity, still more [Rudolf] Otto and Barth, and in the novelists, Lawrence who brings to light—in an obscure light—this element of absolute alterity, of negation, in human love, just as the theologians make it apparent in divine love—these thinkers have the sense of this idea.

We could emerge from this battle between the dialectic and the real only with the help of a mystical vision. There are few philosophers who have pushed as far as Marcel has the theory of religious experience. The question that we have asked ourselves is the question of knowing whether we can turn this experience into a theory. From the moment there is a theory, are we not dragged again into the movement of the dialectic? And on the other hand, we wondered whether the proposed theory would be sufficient. Would it not lead us to justify pell-mell all the diverse forms that this experience can take, while it should grant us discernment? Our study of Marcel's *Metaphysical Journal* closes with an interrogation.

We do not want to conclude this preface with a dogmatic assertion, either. Spirit is movement turning around, turning between two contrary forces. Assuredly nothing can satisfy it. And satisfaction less than anything else. Spirit knows the truths of contradictory doctrines. Materialism, provided that it be coarse, brings to spirit elements in a sense as important as those of mystical experience. It knows how to deny everything, and at times to deny itself, to swallow itself up, to place itself as if it were one thing among many. It knows as well that it is the power to overcome everything.

Translated by Leonard Lawlor

---

41. [Wahl is no doubt referring to Vladimir Jankélévitch's *Henri Bergson* (Paris: Alcan, 1931).]

3

Commentary on a Passage from Hegel's *Phenomenology of Spirit*

Jean Wahl's 1929 book, *Le malheur de la conscience dans la philosophie de Hegel*, marked a turning point in French Hegel studies and profoundly influenced subsequent philosophers such as Jean-Paul Sartre, Jean Hyppolite, Gilles Deleuze, and Jacques Derrida. Wahl's was the first major French study of Hegel's *Phenomenology of Spirit* (1807), marking a turn away from Hegel's *Science of Logic* to the affective and experiential basis of Hegel's dialectical method. For Wahl, the key chapter in the *Phenomenology* is the section on "the Unhappy Consciousness," rather than the earlier section on "master and slave," which was the central focus of Alexandre Kojève's celebrated lectures (1933–39).[1] In the following selection, Wahl's commentary reveals that the dialectical method—often reduced to the

---

"Commentaire d'un passage de la '*Phénoménologie de l'Esprit*,'" *Revue de Métaphysique et de Morale* 34 (1927): 441–71. Republished as a chapter in Jean Wahl, *Le malheur de la conscience dans la philosophie de Hegel* (Paris: Rieder, 1929), chapter 3, 158–93.

1. Alexandre Kojève, *Introduction à la lecture de Hegel. Leçons sur la Phénoménologie de l'esprit professées de 1933 à 1939 à l'École des Hautes Études*, ed. Raymond Queneau (Paris: Éditions Gallimard, 1947), partially translated in the following texts: *Introduction to the Reading of Hegel: Lectures on the "Phenomenology of Spirit,"* comp. Raymond Queneau, ed. Allan Bloom, and trans. James H. Nichols Jr. (Ithaca, N.Y.: Cornell University Press, 1980); "The Idea of Death in the Philosophy of Hegel," trans. Joseph J. Carpino, in *Hegel and Contemporary Continental Philosophy*, ed. Dennis King Keenan (Albany: State University of New York Press, 2004), 27–74; "Interpretation of the General Introduction to Chapter VII [The religion chapter of Hegel's *Phenomenology of Spirit*]," trans. Ian Alexander Moore, *Parrhesia: A Journal of Critical Philosophy* 20 (2014): 15–39.

formula of "thesis-antithesis-synthesis"—arises from divisions that consciousness produces within itself and that it then attempts to overcome and heal. Consciousness divides itself and so doubles itself, reflecting on its division and in that very process grasping itself as one. It negates all its particular and determinate aspects, which are thus reduced to nothingness, but comes to understand that this active self-negation constitutes its very being. Consciousness, then, is an unstable, contradictory, and duplicitous being for whom, as Sartre will later say, its own nothingness is in question for it. Hegel's concept (*Begriff*, translated by Wahl as "*notion*") is the synthesis of these contradictory aspects that preserves all the determinate aspects of consciousness within the unity of consciousness's negating and self-negating dialectical activity. Rather than being merely logical, then, the "concept" expresses a personal ideal of a self that has returned to itself and reconciled with itself. As Wahl points out, this "triplicity" and reconciliation of the Hegelian concept translates into a philosophical register the Christian drama of God sacrificing himself and then returning to himself and reconciling himself with finitude through the Holy Spirit.

One of the great virtues of Wahl's commentary is how it relates the chapter on "the Unhappy Consciousness" to earlier and later chapters of the *Phenomenology* ("Master and Slave," "Stoicism and Scepticism," "Culture," "Revealed Religion," "Absolute Knowing") as well as Hegel's lectures on the philosophy of religion and the philosophy of history. Each stage of the dialectic, as Wahl points out, is simultaneously that of an individual consciousness, a culture's norms and values, and a form of religion. Stoicism, for example, is both the experience of a consciousness that negates sensory reality as having no real value and instead values universal reason, as well as a cultural and religious phase coinciding with the Roman Empire. But although culture and religion give historical expression to the dialectical developments of consciousness, it is consciousness itself and its experiences that are fundamental. It is Wahl's portrayal of the drama of consciousness in all its pathos and tragedy that so marked subsequent French philosophy and Hegel interpretation.[2]

In an earlier article, Wahl had written, "The beginning of philosophy and religion is not so much wonder as non-satisfaction and the dismembered consciousness [*conscience déchirée*]."[3] Consciousness is aware of the opposition between the sensory and the intelligible, between reason and instinct, duty and inclination, which in general can be construed as the opposition between the changeable and

---

2. For a more detailed account of Wahl's influence and significance, see Bruce Baugh, *French Hegel: From Surrealism to Postmodernism* (New York: Routledge, 2003).

3. Jean Wahl, "Note sur les démarches de la pensée de Hegel," *Revue Philosophique de la France et de l'Étranger* 101 (1926): 289. Unless otherwise indicated, all translations from the French are my own.

the unchanging or between the particular and the universal. The religious expression of this consciousness is the belief in an unchangeable and infinite God set over against a changeable and finite human individual, which for Hegel is the essential experience expressed in Judaism. However, the "truth" of this experience is that the infinite and eternal God is the alienation of the infinite and eternal aspects of consciousness—to paraphrase the "young Hegelian," Ludwig Feuerbach, "man's essence outside of man"[4]—and so the conflict between infinite and finite, unchangeable and changing is a conflict within consciousness.

Consciousness is always attempting to define itself through its objects; but as soon as consciousness tries to get hold of its determinacy through the determinacy of a particular object, it discovers that it is not its object but rather transcends it, and so experiences itself as a nothing that would be something, or as a *lack* of being. Consciousness finds that it endures and persists through the vanishing nothingness of the finite determinations it produces, as restlessness and absolute negativity, the continuous movement from one determination to another, from negation to negation. This restlessness and lack are felt through negative emotions such as anxiety and despair, and as Kierkegaard had noted, all despair is ultimately over the self and its inability to reconcile its finite and infinite aspects.[5] Consciousness is both the infinite power of universal thought and the finite transitoriness of particular thoughts, both being and nothingness, but without being able to think these two together.

The whole *Phenomenology*, says Wahl, is the narrative of consciousness's attempts to overcome the lack it feels within itself and to reconcile itself with itself. Indeed, in grasping its internal oppositions and divisions, consciousness catches a glimpse of the unity of duality (difference) and unity (identity), that is, the triplicity of the concept or the concrete universal, which would be the expression of the

---

4. Ludwig Feuerbach, *The Essence of Christianity* (1841), trans. George Eliot (London: John Chapman, 1854). I am paraphrasing; Feuerbach writes: "The divine being is nothing else than the human being, or, rather the human nature purified, freed from the limits of the individual man, made objective—i.e., contemplated and revered as another, a distinct being. . . . [M]an in religion—in his relation to God—is in relation to his own nature; . . . Man—this is the mystery of religion—projects his being into objectivity, and then again makes himself an object to this projected image of himself thus converted into a subject. . . . The divine activity is not distinct from the human" (14, 24, 29).

5. Cf. Søren Kierkegaard, *The Sickness unto Death*, trans. Howard V. Hong and Edna H. Hong (Princeton, N.J.: Princeton University Press, 1983). As Wahl's lifelong friend Emmanuel Levinas has pointed out, Wahl came to Hegel from the perspective of a Kierkegaardian; see Levinas, "Jean Wahl: Neither Having nor Being," in *Outside the Subject*, trans. Michael B. Smith (Stanford, Calif.: Stanford University Press, 1994), 70.

happy consciousness.⁶ On the one hand, "the more consciousness feels its dismemberment, the better it grasps its unity"; on the other hand, "just at the moment when consciousness attains its unity, we are in the presence of a game of 'loser wins' where there is a continual reversal and incessant irony and consciousness ends up with the opposite of what it sought." Such is the experience of consciousness, and of the unhappy consciousness in particular, which is then transposed into the dialectic of Being as "the history of God" or "the unhappy consciousness of God," "the absolute unrest and inequality of absolute Spirit which creates otherness."⁷

A consciousness which is to itself its own lack and which produces that lack within itself by dividing itself and opposing itself to itself—we cannot fail to recognize here a problematic and a schema that is taken up in different ways by Sartre, by Lacan, and by Derrida. By the same token, the pathos and suffering of the unhappy consciousness is also definitive of the Hegelian dialectic for Deleuze, who for that very reason opposes it. When others such as Hyppolite later move away from consciousness and toward Being or, like Derrida, from consciousness to writing, they by no means leave behind this problematic or this schema. Rather, they take it up and transpose it into a different domain. In that, they remain entirely faithful to the spirit of Wahl's Hegel interpretation.

Bruce Baugh

I

In the pages preceding those we shall be studying here,⁸ Hegel showed how sensory consciousness, perception, and the understanding were disintegrated by the power of the dialectic. He demonstrated how the play of perception follows the play of sensation and transforms the essential into the nonessential and vice versa.⁹ Perception tries in vain to see qualities without things or things without qualities and risks exhausting itself in the play of oppositions between the immutable and the changeable; in turn, it leaves us facing empty generalities. The play of soliciting and solicited forces

---

6. See Jean Wahl, *Le malheur de la conscience dans la philosophie de Hegel* (Paris: Rieder, 1929), 154.

7. Ibid., 143.

8. [Here we will be studying] Hegel, *Werke* (Berlin: Duncker und Humblot, 1845), 2:158–65.

9. [See G. W. F. Hegel, *Phenomenology of Spirit*, trans. A. V. Miller (Oxford: Oxford University Press, 1977), 58–79, hereafter cited in this chapter as *Phenomenology*; *Phänomenologie des Geistes*, ed. E. Moldenhauer and K. Markus Michel (Frankfurt: Suhrkamp, 1986), 82–107, hereafter cited in this chapter as *Phänomenologie*; A. Consciousness I. Sense-certainty: or the "This" and "Meaning" II. Perception: or the Thing and Deception.]

[in the understanding] ceaselessly transforms the one into the other, and force and law presuppose and cancel out one another.[10] Next, Hegel introduced us into the world of consciousness and of self-consciousness,[11] but only in order to make us aware of the same struggle of tendencies, the same play of forces.[12] However, in this case, it is no longer a matter of a purely logical dialectic, but rather a historical and affective dialectic. The division into two extremes that previously made itself felt not by the two extremes but by the philosopher who contemplates them, is now going to be felt by each of these two extremes themselves (*Phänomenologie*, 141 [*Phenomenology*, 112]). Self-consciousness is going to divide [*dédoubler*] itself into two opposed terms that will ceaselessly change places with each other. In order to grasp what this doubling [*doublement*] consists in and in what way this exchange of places occurs, we need only look back to see what led up to it.

The struggle between the two consciousnesses of master and slave,[13] which change places with each other much as the two extremes of perception and then the extremes of the understanding had done, such that the slave through his labor becomes the master of the master, seems to come to an end the moment when, with Epictetus and Marcus Aurelius and with the domination of the category of "master and slave" reaching its height at the very heart of the Roman Empire, the consciousness of the master and that of the slave identify with each other in self-consciousness as [consciousness of] freedom itself. In each recognizing itself in the other, the Stoics gave us in advance an image of the notion, which is essentially a vision of the one in the other and recognition.[14] But after Stoicism, whether that of Marcus Aurelius or that of Epictetus, both of whom negated the opposition of master and slave and thereby destroyed the road along which humanity had traveled up until then—which was first the struggle to the death between individuals and then slavery—consciousness passes through

---

10. [*Phenomenology*, 79–103; A. Consciousness III. Force and the Understanding: Appearance and the Super-Sensible World.]

11. [*Phenomenology*, 104–38; B. Self-Consciousness. *Conscience de soi* is Wahl's French rendering of the German *Selbstbewusstsein*, or self-consciousness. The *de* or "of" makes it appear as though in self-consciousness, consciousness were aware of itself in the way that it is aware of an object outside of itself, which is somewhat misleading.]

12. Hegel had already made use of this expression in his essay *Ueber einige charakteristische Unterschiede der alten Dichter* [1788] ([Karl] Rosenkranz, [*Georg Wilhelm Friedrich Hegel's Leben* (Berlin: Duncker und Humblot, 1844)], 460).

13. [*Phenomenology*, 104–19; B. Self-Consciousness IV. The Truth of Self-Certainty. A. Independence and Dependence of Self-Consciousness: Lordship and Bondage.]

14. [Ibid., 110, 120–21.]

Scepticism.[15] Stoicism was the expression of a certain de facto state (*imperium*),[16] composed of separate personalities, "pure and simple legality," the Pantheon where all statues are equal and all of them are hollow.[17] In the same way that the universal was the dominant element, the extreme of individuality—but of individuality as general—came into plain view. But Stoicism, which was linked to the *imperium* at the same time that it destroyed it, remained conceptual.[18] Although self-consciousness in Stoicism is really "freedom itself" because it is a doctrine both of reflection into itself and of the effort involved, it is only "simple" freedom.

Scepticism is the "realization" of that of which Stoicism is only the concept; it is the real "experience"[19] that man has of the contradiction both of freedom and of thought. Epictetus and Marcus Aurelius had the concept of freedom. Sextus Empiricus lived this same freedom. He becomes aware of the non-essentiality of *the other* [l'autre] relative to the infinity of thought in a way that was as yet unknown to the Stoic dogmatists. Of these two famous schools, the first is only the preparation for the second.[20]

Whereas self-consciousness remained abstract in Stoicism—that is, on the one hand, separated from a world that it considered external to itself and indifferent because it is different, and on the other hand not going deeply enough into itself in order to grasp its real significance—in Scepticism, we will witness the movement of this consciousness toward the

---

15. [Ibid., 119–38; B. Self-Consciousness IV. The Truth of Self-Certainty B. Freedom of Self-Consciousness: Stoicism, Scepticism and the Unhappy Consciousness. Wahl devotes his commentary to this last section on the unhappy consciousness.]

16. [Ibid., 121. Hegel refers to Stoicism specifically in its Roman form, which he regards as world-historical, and not to its Greek form. See G. W. F. Hegel, *Lectures on the History of Philosophy*, vol. 2, *Plato and the Platonists*, trans. E. S. Haldane and Frances H. Simson (Lincoln: University of Nebraska Press, 1995), 234–35, 274–76: "the philosophy of the Stoics has more specially found its home in the Roman world" (276); hereafter cited in this chapter as *History of Philosophy* followed by volume and page number.]

17. Cf. *Phänomenologie*, 152. Cf. 360, 361, 398, 563 [*Phenomenology*, 124–25, 289–91, 321–22, 453–55]. Cf. *Philosophie der Religion*, vol. 2, 224–26 [G. W. F. Hegel, *Lectures on the Philosophy of Religion*, ed. Peter C. Hodgson, trans. R. F. Brown, P. C. Hodgson, and J. M. Stewart, with the assistance of H. S. Harris (Berkeley: University of California Press, 1988), 341–42, 344–49, 357; hereafter cited in this chapter as *Philosophy of Religion*].

18. Cf. *Philosophie der Religion*, II, 144, 145, 141, 156 [*Philosophy of Religion*, 352, 386, 419–24, 450].

19. Cf. *Phänomenologie*, 158 [*Phenomenology*, 123, 124, 128].

20. [*Phenomenology*, 123.]

concrete,[21] in the sense that consciousness will realize in itself the negation of reality which in Stoicism was merely posited as a duty (*Sollen* ["ought"]). For instead of saying that one must not concern oneself with external reality, Scepticism negates that reality.[22]

But that is not all. Sceptical consciousness ceaselessly negates itself: it is the coming to consciousness of the play of forces and of the movement of Spirit[23] itself, and of this absolute negativity that is thought.[24] This absolute negativity will only become fully aware of itself in the unhappy consciousness,[25] but it is the driving force [*ressort*] of the whole *Phenomenology*, inasmuch as the *Phenomenology* is the narration of consciousness's efforts to fill in the separations that it feels within itself. The moment of negation implicit throughout the course of this history, and which made each of these terms exist only in relation to the other and finally turned each into the other; the idea of mediation; the idea of generality;[26] the idea of time: these four ideas at the root of the Hegelian dialectic here emerge into the full light of consciousness. Just as we also know that an entire itinerary must be traversed in order to enter that luminous temple where the inner choir merges with the external church square, so it is with the whole of this winding road on which we witness vanish, one after the other, sensible certainty and the act of pointing out;[27] perception and the concrete thing; force and the understanding. Even more, this road never ends; it twists its way around the shadowless pillars of the temple where, as in the Sais of the Romantic poet,[28] consciousness will unveil itself to

---

21. [*Toward the Concrete* (*Vers le concret*) was the title of Wahl's next book and is a phrase that serves as a leitmotif of Wahl's philosophy. For more information and a translation of Wahl's preface to *Vers le concret*, see Chapter 2 in this volume.]

22. Cf. *Geschichte der Philosophie*, vol. 3, 687ff; vol. 4, 3ff. [see *History of Philosophy*, 2:328–30, 334–35, 341–43, 372].

23. [Although Wahl does not capitalize *esprit*, in this excerpt we follow Miller's decision to capitalize Spirit. In some instances, however, we have translated *esprit* as "mind" according to the context.]

24. [*Phenomenology*, 124.]

25. Cf. *Phänomenologie*, 569 [*Phenomenology*, 454–56].

26. [Wahl translates Hegel's *Allgemeinheit* as "generality"; most English translations render it as "universality." Our translation retains Wahl's terms.]

27. [*Indication*, which translates the German *Meinen*, refers to the act of pointing something out; see *Phänomenologie*, 82–92; *Phenomenology*, 58–66.]

28. [A reference to the poetic novel by Novalis (Georg Philipp Friedrich von Hardenberg [1772–1801]), *Die Lehrlinge zu Sais* (*The Novices of Sais*), an account of an inner, spiritual journey. See also *Philosophy of Religion*, 126–27: "The inscription of the temple of the goddess Neith in Sais is given in full as follows: 'I am what was, what is, and what will be; no mortal has yet lifted my veil.'"]

consciousness, and will be at one and the same time the worshipper, the priestess, and the goddess.

Consciousness had indeed been the soul of the whole movement that Hegel had followed up until this point, but it is only now that it truly presents itself as a soul and becomes aware that in explaining [external] things, it is really only carrying out a dialogue with itself.[29]

Hegel calls this infinity of consciousness (127) an absolute restlessness [*inquiétude*; *Unruhe*] (Cf. Preface, 18, 127, 156 [*Phenomenology*, Preface, 6, 12, 27; Introduction, 51; 101, 124]). As soon as it has determined a thing, consciousness becomes aware that is in fact the contrary of the thing that it has determined. There is as it were a duplicity of consciousness: consciousness is immediately the contrary of that in relation to which it had just defined itself. This reversal of consciousness[30]—along with its effort to complete itself through this very reversal—will be the essential process of the *Phenomenology*.

Consciousness ceaselessly divides itself; it is the "separation of what is simple or the doubling which opposes" (*Phänomenologie*, 15 [*Phenomenology*, 10]). The similar repels and what repels unites; this is the law of polarity which we see at work in sensation, in perception, in force, and finally in consciousness (Cf. *Phänomenologie*, 151–56 [*Phenomenology*, 99–103 ("Force and the Understanding") and 120–21]).

Consciousness is duality; not only does it exist for itself only insofar as it exists for another, and only is truly con-sciousness[31] insofar as it is recognized, but it is essentially in itself division [*dédoublement*]—the action of dividing itself, of seeing itself as separated and consequently as one—and doubling [*redoublement*], the action of seeing itself as itself, and of consequently seeing itself as two. Consciousness is ceaselessly the double and the half of itself; and it is only by becoming aware of this that it is able to become adequate to itself.[32]

Its duality is symbolized by the theme of master and slave; its still abstract unity by the theme of Stoicism; the unity of its duality and its unity—what one could call its triplicity—by what will be the theme of the *Logos*.[33]

---

29. [*Phenomenology*, 124.]
30. Cf. *Phänomenologie* II, 71 [*Phenomenology*, 55].
31. [Wahl emphasizes the *con*, or "with," of consciousness in order to emphasize its fundamentally social or communal character.]
32. Cf. *Phänomenologie*, 442, 496, 508 [*Phenomenology*, 458–59, 464–65, 466, 471–72, 475, 476, 478].
33. [*Philosophy of Religion*, 430.]

But at the same time, it must be noted that each of these themes in a way overturns itself: the slave becomes, as we saw earlier, the master of the master; and later, Stoicism, in deepening itself, becomes Scepticism and leads toward the idea of Christianity.

The two consciousnesses of master and slave are thus united; but they are united in a form that is affected by duality and which, in freeing itself from every division with respect to the exterior—because there is no longer any exterior—finds itself divided within itself—for the idea of division and duality is essential to consciousness. Is that not indeed an element of the very notion of Spirit?[34] The idea of the unhappy consciousness,[35] such as it will appear in Christianity or in Romanticism, will make us aware of one of the distinctive characteristics of Spirit. But neither Christianity strictly speaking, in its form as the unhappy consciousness and still mixed with the sensory, nor Romanticism will truly attain the notion. For although the duality of the notion is clearly seen in them, its unity has not yet been brought to light. The truly happy consciousness, the Spirit that must finally be attained, will be one and double; we can even add that it will be one, double and triple. We will then witness the return into itself of the divided consciousness [*la conscience dédoublée*] and its reconciliation with itself.[36]

This element of unity that will be the source of Spirit's joy will at first be the cause of its pain, for this unity is incomplete.

If consciousness, at first divided in the master and the slave, was later unified in the Stoic consciousness, and if that marks a first return of consciousness into itself, this was only a *false return*, so to speak: for this unification is in turn followed by an internalized division that is characteristic of the unhappy consciousness.

---

34. [Ibid., 433: "Eternal being-in-and-for-itself is what discloses itself, determines itself, divides itself, posits itself as what is differentiated from itself, but the difference is at the same time constantly sublated. Thereby actual being-in-and-for-itself constantly returns into itself—only in this way is it spirit." See also *Phenomenology*, 126, 490–93.]

35. [*La conscience malheureuse*; in German, *das Unglückliche Bewusstsein*; see *Phenomenology*, 126–38; *Phänomenologie*, 163–77. The French and German adjectives, in addition to meaning "unhappy," also mean "unfortunate" and even "cursed"; a *malheur* is a misfortune, an accident, a difficulty or even doom; *Unglück* can be translated as "misery" or "wretchedness."]

36. [Wahl makes use of a number of French words that have "double" at their core: *dédoubler, redoubler, doublement*. Consciousness divides itself and so doubles itself, but it also, in grasping its own duality or doubleness, goes back into itself and redoubles itself, such that it is both "half" and the "double" of itself. See *Phenomenology*, 10, 14, 21, 26, 40, 479–80, 488–90, 493, and passim.]

Scepticism destroyed one of the terms, the external world; but at the very moment when Scepticism cancels one term, it causes a duality to appear inside of the remaining term. From that arises its unhappiness; for the Sceptic, such as Hegel represents him, is not a Montaigne; he is more of a Pascal or an Ecclesiastes, positing the infinite essence of God on the basis of the nothingness of the creature, and unable to reconcile these two ideas.

The Sceptic is conscious of the perpetual changing of one thought into another and of his purely particular character. At the same time, he is conscious of that within himself which transcends [*dépasse*] these changes because he is the consciousness of the negativity of all contents (cf. *Philosophie der Geschichte*, 407).[37] The Sceptic is thus by turns the consciousness of the particularity and of the generality of all thought. But he does not succeed in thinking both these ideas at the same time; he only goes from the one idea to the other without taking into account his own unity,[38] which is nevertheless implicit in him and is even the primary cause of his unhappiness. For what could be more painful than the opposition at the heart of unity at which consciousness has arrived?[39]

II

It is because there is a unity of consciousness instead of the duality of master and slave, and it is also, by the same token, because there is [self-]knowledge, that there is unhappiness. The identical incessantly and repeatedly separates itself into two opposed things; duality is ceaselessly reborn outside of unity (cf. *Phänomenologie*, 126 [*Phenomenology*, 125–26]).

Moreover, in this unhappy consciousness that is born from Scepticism, we witness the perpetual movement from one idea into another, the mind not being able to hold fast the contraries; we witness a play [*jeu*] of forces in the spiritual domain analogous to the play of forces in the material domain and what will later be, in the domain of morality, the game [*jeu*] of

---

37. [See G. W. F. Hegel, *The Philosophy of History*, trans. J. Sibree (New York: Dover, 1956), 318, hereafter cited in this chapter as *Philosophy of History*; *Phenomenology*, 123.]

38. Cf. *Phänomenologie*, 361 [*Phenomenology*, 123].

39. *Philosophie der Religion*, II, 227 [see *Philosophy of Religion*, 437–38, 443–44, 447–48, 451–52, especially 437–38: consciousness "*is* the split and the contradiction—yet not a contradiction that simply falls apart, but rather one that simultaneously holds itself together. It is only through its holding together that it is split and has the contradiction within itself."].

hypocrisy.[40] Each time that consciousness believes that it has attained rest and rolled its rock up to the summit of unity, it is once again pushed back toward division and the depths.[41]

The unhappy consciousness is thus indeed *the vision of one consciousness in another* and the unity of these two consciousnesses; but it is not yet conscious of being this unity, for by becoming conscious of its unity, it will become the happy consciousness.[42]

In this progression, we will have had first two individuals, then a double consciousness which is conscious of its unity only in the sense that it incessantly moves from one of its elements to that which is opposed to it, and then a consciousness which is one and double. But what remains to be seen is how we attain a consciousness that is one and double *for itself* starting from a consciousness that is one and double *in itself*.

The fundamental traits of the unhappy consciousness can be explained by the fact that it is, although only implicitly, the single consciousness of a duality, and thereby the unity, although not fully conscious, of two contradictory terms. The duality within itself is indeed *for it*, that is, it has explicit consciousness of it. But the unity of the duality is not *for it*, that is, it does not have consciousness of the nevertheless real unity of these two moments of being. One could say that the unhappy consciousness prefigures the notion, which is also the unity of contradictories,[43] but only in the way in which the blinkered Synagogue prefigures the Church. What this Synagogue brings together are two forever irreconcilable terms in struggle with each other—and yet of such a kind that when we try to grasp the one, we end up grasping the other. This is a foreshadowing, albeit a blind one, of what the notion will be.

In the unhappy consciousness, it is as if the master and the slave had been united in a single mind,[44] in such a way that if we were to consider it as master, we would straightaway discover its dependence; and if we were to consider it as slave, we would straightaway perceive its independence. We are situated between the stage of the material hostility of individuals

---

40. [*Phenomenology*, 374–83.]
41. [Wahl is implicitly referring to Sisyphus, who was condemned to roll a rock eternally up a mountain only to have it fall back down again, a theme later made famous by Albert Camus, *Le mythe de Sisyphe: Essai sur l'absurde* (Paris: Gallimard, 1942); English translation: *The Myth of Sisyphus, and Other Essays*, trans. Justin O'Brien (New York: Knopf, 1955).]
42. *Philosophie der Religion*, II, 227 [see *Phenomenology*, 126; *Philosophy of Religion*, 452].
43. [*Phenomenology*, 126.]
44. [Ibid.]

and the stage of the unity of the mind. We are at the stage of spiritual hostility, a recollection [*rappel*] of the previous struggles among men and a summons [*appel*] toward the unity for which that prior hostility would have been necessary.

More and more, consciousness feels what is painful in Scepticism; the mind of Montaigne, if it goes deeply into itself, becomes the mind of Pascal. Pascal sees more clearly into himself and better senses—but without having full consciousness of it—his unity. And it is because consciousness then better grasps its unity that it more strongly feels [*ressent*] its dismemberment [*déchirement*]. At the same time, it knows that Stoicism was not an enlargement but, on the contrary, a diminution, a loss of consciousness.[45]

The pages dealing with the unhappy consciousness will thus contain a description of the doubling of consciousness and of its striving toward unity, such as one sees in religion. Christianity, to which Hegel makes constant but veiled allusions, will have been prepared, as we have seen, by Scepticism as consciousness of human duality, and also, as we will see, by Judaism as the contradictory consciousness both of the absolute duality of man and God and of their unmediated unity.

After the contradictions of Scepticism, it was necessary for consciousness to seek its new starting point elsewhere, in the Orient. Judaism is the becoming conscious of two ideas that were merely implicit in Scepticism; the Jew says, with respect to himself conceived now as changing and now as immutable, both "I am that which is not"; "I am that which is." "He brings together the two thoughts which Scepticism kept separate."[46] He is the thesis and the antithesis, but enclosed within a purely subjective synthesis; a juxtaposition, which remains on the same level as the thesis and the antithesis, and which does not include them within a higher unity, but only posits them in a unity on the same level as them and consequently separates them. From that stems the fact that this juxtaposition can only ever be temporary and incessantly decomposes again and again into the thesis and antithesis; arriving at one term, it constantly goes back to the other, in an endless oscillation. At the very moment when the prophet celebrates God, he is a prophet of doom [*malheur*]; the Canticles turn into Lamentations.[47] Jewish consciousness knows its contradiction. It turns out to be the deepening of Scepticism and the still incomplete unification of

---

45. *Phänomenologie*, 563 [*Phenomenology*, 454–55].
46. [See *Phenomenology*, 126: "From this experience emerges a *new form* of consciousness which brings together the two thoughts which Scepticism holds apart."]
47. [A reference to the biblical books, the Song of Solomon (or Canticle of Canticles) and the Lamentations of Jeremiah.]

that which remains separated in Scepticism. It is the religion of the sublime in which the essential and the inessential are most firmly opposed to each other, but in which they are also shown in their reciprocal necessity.[48] Judaism posits the problem, the terms of which had been posited in Greece by Stoicism and Scepticism; but it does not succeed in solving it.[49]

If that is the case, do we not glimpse here a new relation of the essence and the inessential, of the particular and the general? Consciousness is conscious of its nothingness because it is conscious of being at bottom something other than nothingness. But this "something other than nothingness," this immutable, is immediately transformed before its eyes into something that is itself a particular existence. Thus, religion will be this unity of the particular and the general which consciousness has attained precisely by seeing that it itself is this opposition and this contact of the general and the particular. Pascal's feeling is not something that, strictly speaking, leads him to religion; it is religion itself. In Pascal, it is the presence of God in man and of man in God that makes itself felt. In feeling himself as nothingness, he senses himself immutable; in feeling himself as immutable, he senses himself as nothingness. Pascal in Port-Royal[50] is an image—and more than an image—of Christ on the Mount of Olives.[51] Or rather both, in different degrees and in partially different kinds, are the immutable as affected by particularity and particularity as affected by the immutable.

For this consciousness, the two elements that constitute it not only are not the same thing; they are opposite things. We will see this consciousness know itself both as free, "immutable and equal to itself," and as "bewildering and overturning itself" in its internal oppositions,[52] and as succeeding in becoming aware—for example, in what lies at the basis of Pascal's thoughts [*pensées*][53]—of the contradiction that exists between its noncontradiction and its contradictions, between its dignity and its weakness. Precisely because consciousness seems to be gathered into those particular points that all individuals *are*, consciousness is within each individual again divided into two seemingly irreducible parts. The force of division

---

48. Cf. *Philosophie der Religion*, I, 186 [*Philosophy of Religion*, 358–59, 370, 371–74n492].

49. [See *Philosophy of Religion*, 449–51.]

50. [Port-Royal is the French town that served as a center for the Jansenist sect of Catholicism with which Pascal was affiliated.]

51. [See Luke 22:39–40.]

52. [*Phenomenology*, 126.]

53. [Wahl is implicitly referring to Pascal's major work, the *Pensées* ("thoughts"). See Blaise Pascal, *Pensées*, trans. Honor Levi (Oxford: Oxford World's Classics, 1999), especially 8–9, 16, 22, 27–28, 35–37, 40–43.]

within consciousness that we have already pointed out can only be overcome after having been brought into the light of day, along with its force of unity, in a thousand ways. Just as duality will constantly be reborn more profoundly in an always better sealed unity, the most authentic unity will be born from the most acute duality. Here, as was the case with Stoicism, there will also be a separation of the essential and the nonessential. The fundamental characteristic of human consciousness, which consists in conceiving things under the category of "domination and slavery," will again be found, and we will witness an incessant natural dichotomy. There will be a being conceived of as "simple and immutable" that will be the essence, and a multiple and changing being that will be that which is not the essence.[54] As in Stoicism, these two beings will be "essences" (if we might use this word to designate also that which is not essential) that are foreign to each other. But as the unhappy consciousness is above all the consciousness of duality and of "contradiction," contrary to Stoicism, the unhappy consciousness will place itself on the side of the "nonessential" because it will be conscious of always going from one idea to another and consequently of being changeable. But we must not forget that at the same time it is "consciousness of the immutable"; indeed, it is a "simple consciousness" and, as simple, it is "immutable." It will thus be "consciousness of its immutability as being its essence." Thus, at the same time that it becomes confused in seeing itself in its changeability, it frees itself in seeing itself in its immutability,[55] and endeavors to liberate itself from its [empirical] ego [*moi*]. It only has consciousness of its ego as something changing; the immutable appears to it as something foreign, and yet it itself is this immutable. It sees clearly that this immutable is its essence, but it separates this essence from itself and places it outside of itself.[56] Thus, at the same time that consciousness sees the immutable as its essence, it sees itself as separated from it, and at the moment when it is conscious of this immutable as its essence, it comes to oppose itself to this immutable and becomes aware of itself as changing, as not being in possession of its real self [*moi*].

One contrary only engenders itself anew in its contrary, and as a contrary, not as reconciled.[57] Thus, we are in a situation in which the essential and the inessential are both equally essential for consciousness, in which consciousness has consciousness of itself as being inessential, but is conscious that its essence is the destruction of the inessential. As soon as

54. [*Phenomenology*, 127.]
55. [Ibid., 126–27.]
56. Cf. *Phänomenologie*, 403 [*Phenomenology*, 457].
57. [*Phenomenology*, 127.]

consciousness succeeds in taking the essence into account, it sees itself as opposed to the essence. Similarly, the moment that consciousness considers itself as inessential, it discovers itself as essence. Each time, consciousness finds itself on the side that is the opposite of the side on which it had just placed itself. Consciousness ceaselessly separates itself from the nonessential, that is, separates itself from itself; it is an unhappy consciousness, contradictory, divided within itself.[58]

We are so far here from being at rest that it would be better instead to speak of a struggle in which victory is a defeat and "where the fact of having at last attained one of the contraries" is immediately transformed into the fact of being thrown back into the other.[59] It is a matter of attaining consciousness of life, of its existence and its action; we thus have to pass through "the suffering [*douleur*] of the subject of this existence and of this action, for consciousness of life is above all consciousness of the unhappiness of life."[60] In becoming conscious of its life, of its existence, of its action, consciousness becomes aware of its own nothingness and sees the essence in that which is opposed to these; but in the same way that it truly becomes conscious of its own nothingness, it becomes conscious of its being; it enters into the sphere of the immutable.[61] In humbling itself, it exalts itself because, although *for it*, the essence before which it humbles itself is not itself, and yet in reality consciousness is this essence.[62] Thus, Job or Ecclesiastes shows us how the soul, in becoming aware of its weakness, glimpses its greatness.

III

We are thus witnessing a movement analogous to the logical movement by which Hegel will go from being to nonbeing, and from both of these to their synthesis in becoming. However, in this case, it is not a matter of a synthesis but of a juxtaposition of being and nothingness in the unhappy consciousness, which will essentially be a consciousness in the process of becoming. In addition, we also see how the movement [of consciousness] takes us into the immutable, an immutable that is included within the movement, not separated from that consciousness but, rather, just that consciousness itself.

58. [Ibid., 126.]
59. [Ibid., 127.]
60. [Ibid.]
61. [Ibid.]
62. [Ibid., 135–36; *Philosophy of Religion*, 450–51.]

If this elevation above itself is itself identical to consciousness, if the destiny of consciousness is to overcome itself, by the same token its destiny is to know that in overcoming itself it remains within itself. This elevation above consciousness of life, of particular existence and action, is still consciousness. The Wisdom of Solomon had to be incarnated in a concrete being, the son of David.[63] The immutable will thus be a consciousness; that is, the immutable will then appear with all the characteristics of consciousness's weakness and changeableness. We would have thought that the immutable would destroy the particular; far from that being the case, the particular appears within the immutable itself and the immutable will appear in the particular.[64] Christianity is but the becoming conscious of this contact of the immutable and the particular.[65] And consciousness thus becomes conscious of itself as particular in the moment when it becomes immediately conscious of itself as general. We have seen this game playing itself out [*ce jeu se jouer*] between the abstract terms of the essential and the nonessential. Now it plays itself out between the more concrete terms of the immutable and the particular. But is this play not realized in history, and is Christianity not the consciousness that man acquires both of his generality and his particularity? The immutable, when it enters into consciousness, is thereby affected by individuality; and individuality, far from being destroyed, simply continues to arise from the immutable.[66]

As was previously the case when he spoke of the master and the slave, of Stoicism and Scepticism, Hegel here is not afraid of finding in history a point of support and application for his ideas and, as it were, a mnemonic rule. Even less is he afraid insofar as, for him, Christianity is a prime example, and not just an example but a revelation of the union that is achieved between the particular and the general; even less, as well, insofar as Hegel's theological studies are often the point of departure for his meditations. At the beginning of this chapter, we follow the history of the Jewish people from the time of Abraham and Moses, when it is opposed to an immutable God, up to the time when David raises himself up to the level of this immutable, and finally to that time when the immutable descends into consciousness with Christ. In a sense, Judaism could be described as an

---

63. [The Wisdom of Solomon is one of the books of the Apocrypha of the Protestant Bible, although it is canonical in Catholicism. Wahl's point is that it was also the wisdom of a particular human being, Solomon, the son of David.]

64. [*Phenomenology*, 127.]

65. On the place of this idea within Romanticism, see Erwin Kircher, *Philosophie der Romantik* [Jena: Diederichs, 1906], 190.

66. [*Phenomenology*, 127.]

inverted Stoicism;⁶⁷ or a Scepticism that has become theology, and as something that in any case definitively opens the way toward higher conceptions of religion while nevertheless remaining itself within an inferior religion. Abraham and Moses, David and Christ, can be taken as symbols of the relationship between the general and the particular.⁶⁸

In this movement, says Hegel, and in this unhappiness, consciousness will come to experience "this manifestation of particular existence as connected to the immutable and the immutable as connected to particular existence."⁶⁹ The particular consciousness undergoes the experience that it itself is the immutable consciousness—that it is its God and that its God is it itself, is a particular existence. In the same way that Christ, particular existence in general, will be united with the immutable, so too will each man be united with the immutable. What will appear as the truth of this movement will thus be the unity of that consciousness that appeared to itself as double. Christianity is born out of a reflection upon the essence of Judaism, just as absolute knowing will be born out of a reflection upon the essence of Christianity.⁷⁰ The idea of the unity of the particular and the immutable that characterizes the Christian consciousness arises from the very heart of unhappiness.

Consciousness becomes aware of this unity as a fact that "happens";⁷¹ and this unity is still imperfect because although each of the two elements is present in the other, each is present in the other as other than it. "The dominant element" within this unity itself is thus, at least at the stage we are examining, "the diversity of two characters,"⁷² and consequently, Christianity cannot be given all at once. It must be prepared by a phase

---

67. Cf. *Philosophie der Geschichte*, 412 [*Philosophy of History*, 323].

68. We could just as easily (according to the *Philosophie der Geschichte*, 217 [*Philosophy of History*, 195]) take the Brahmanic religion as the Jewish religion to be an example of the absolute opposition between the general and the particular.

69. [See *Phenomenology*, 128: "this emergence of individuality in the Unchangeable, and of the Unchangeable in individuality."]

70. [See G. W. F. Hegel, *Lectures on the History of Philosophy*, vol. 3, *Medieval and Modern Philosophy*, trans. E. S. Haldane and Frances H. Simson (Lincoln: University of Nebraska Press, 1995), 20–21: the idea of the Trinity as the reconciliation of Spirit that returns to itself from Otherness is "the principle of all speculative philosophy"; 531: "eternal life consists in the very process of [each term] continually producing the opposition [from out of itself] and continually reconciling it. To know unity in opposition and opposition in unity—that is absolute knowledge; and science is the knowledge of this unity in its whole development by means of itself."]

71. [That is, of the fact of the Incarnation as a historical event. See *Phenomenology*, 129, 458–62; *Philosophy of Religion*, 455–63.]

72. [*Phenomenology*, 128.]

that is reminiscent of the Jewish or Roman phase in which the individual is opposed to the immutable essence and the immutable is a foreign essence that condemns individuality.[73] The formless immutable is here the element of thought; but by the same token, one returns to the "starting point," to the opposition between master and slave, between the essential and the nonessential, and the movement starts over again endlessly. Jesus is not recognized as the Messiah, or if he is, it is in the form of a temporal event, which is to say that the Jewish phase always has to be gone through again and always must be overcome again and again. In a more general way, the category of master and slave is characteristic of all thought at the beginning and remains, as Hegel says, the "elementary given of all situations," but a given such that one of its terms, the particular consciousness, tends to be suppressed; it is only in the second moment—in the moment when this phase is overcome—that we have Christianity. The immutable is then conscious of taking on particularity and linking itself to it; the immutable is incarnated and at first exists in a sensory fashion, and in virtue of its sensory element, is something that "separates itself" from other sensory beings and then vanishes.[74] In the eyes of consciousness itself, everything immutable in consciousness takes on the character of particular existence; conversely, everything that is particular assumes a character of generality, but without us attaining the genuine union we seek. Every relation with the unformed immutable (the God of the Jews) is destroyed, and only the relation with the formed immutable (Christ) appears.[75]

It is only during the third moment, thanks to absolute knowing, that individuality—no longer in the form of particularity resembling the immutable, but as individuality as such; no longer as individuality in general, but as the individual—finds itself, encounters itself, at the heart of the immutable. It is no longer the Incarnation; it is eternal resurrection.[76] We now have the conscious reconciliation of particularity and generality in which particularity finds itself, and we gain the joyful consciousness, Spirit.[77]

Thus the unhappy consciousness, properly speaking, takes place between the Jewish and Roman consciousness, on the one hand, and the rational

---

73. [Ibid.]
74. Cf. [Hegels] *Theologische Jugendschriften*, ed. Herman Nohl [Tübingen: J. C. B. Mohr, 1907], 400: "Die Form wie er als einzelnes gegen einzelnes [und einzelne gegen ihn stehen] . . ." ["the form in which it is a singular thing set against singular things and singular things against itself"; see *Phenomenology*, 129; *Philosophy of Religion*, 455–56].
75. [*Phenomenology*, 129.]
76. [Ibid., 132–34, 138, 462.]
77. [Ibid., 128; *History of Philosophy*, 3:4–6, 14–16.]

consciousness, on the other;[78] but in a sense one could say that the Jewish consciousness is already essentially the unhappy consciousness.

With respect to the final reconciliation, it will be found in Spirit insofar as it is conscious of both immutability and individuality as such, that is, insofar as it retains an individualistic and Romantic element. What Hegel wants is thus to retain the individual, Christian and Romantic element. At the same time, however, he seeks to elevate this element to a higher mode in order to attain the concrete universal in religion, in order to achieve a kind of rationalization of Romanticism and Christianity, and at the same time a Christianization or Romanticization of the rational. The particular as it will come to be conceived will no longer be the enduring particular which is merely affected by the immutable; it will be profoundly transformed by the immutable and yet will retain the characteristics that are most properly its own.

We will thus have a triple approach by which particularity is linked with the immutable. We have a hierarchy of immutables, of immutables that move in accordance with the way in which consciousness approaches them; and, indeed, phenomenology cannot study an immutable that would be outside of consciousness.[79]

The first movement is a moment of pure opposition; in the second, each of the two terms takes on the aspect of the other in some way; in the third, there is fusion. (See *Phänomenologie*, 509 [*Phenomenology*, 128, 130, 461–62]). The immutable (cf. 509 [*Phenomenology*, 461], *Sein unwandelbares Wesen* ["being as immutable essence"]) is the first form under which divinity appears, but it is a divinity that is not yet a person but, rather, more truly a *Das* [a "That"].[80]

The work of reason in history will consist in bringing together the two extremes of the immutable beyond and the changeable, in making that which seemed so distant as to be unknowable into that which is so close as to be identical. Consciousness at first breaks apart into two fragments that are at the two opposite poles of the phenomenological heavens:[81] on the one side, the blinding, motionless sun; on the other, the blowing dust particles, which are also blinding. When Spirit comes to see that one is the

---

78. Hegel distinguishes between two "unhappy consciousnesses": that of the Jewish people and that of the Roman people (*Philosophie der Religion*, II, 224 [*Philosophy of Religion*, 450]).

79. [*Phenomenology*, 128.]

80. [*Philosophy of Religion*, 433.]

81. [The division within consciousness is reflected in "an actuality broken in two" (*Phenomenology*, 133).]

other, then it will come into possession of itself in its fullness. The "truth of this movement," its raison d'être, is thus, as Hegel says, the unification of this double consciousness.

Consciousness starts from a formless immutable, without essence, as abstract as the abstract thought of Stoicism, although it is more musical (cf. 162, 163, 164, 169 [*Phenomenology*, 131, 135]). It can only be united with an immutable that is in some sense concrete.

In order to immediately negate itself, consciousness must be mediated by the idea of the immutable, as we shall see (170 [*Phenomenology*, 136]).

Every movement of both the one and the other will in any case be relative; mind will never move without the immutable moving. There is no unilateral movement (161; cf. 141 [*Phenomenology*, 129, 134]). This is true to such an extent that in order to attain the immutable in its perfection, in its truth, it is necessary that the movement not just start from consciousness alone. Divine grace is present everywhere, even when consciousness makes a free act of sacrifice (172 [*Phenomenology*, 137]). Hegel already glimpsed this idea when he said that there is nothing unilateral between two lovers (cf. Nohl, [*Theologische Jugendschriften*], 381),[82] and that there is nothing unilateral between them because there is nothing dead there. He will ascribe to the universe in general what he had earlier said about love, which at that time was already the universe for him (cf. Nohl, [*Theologische Jugendschriften*], 392. The return cannot be canceled in a unilateral fashion).[83] At the same time, he knows that if one is not willing to content oneself with pure subjectivity, one must from the outset posit a unity of the subjective and the objective. The subject, in positing the object, presupposes it (*Philosophie der Religion*, II, 229ff. [*Philosophy of Religion*, 114–15]), a fundamental assertion from the phenomenological point of view according to which one cannot do without a noumenology, at least as a hypothesis.[84]

This relativity of movement, which is linked to the very idea of the Absolute, is even more essential for Hegel insofar as it is opposed to the static conception of religion according to which we cannot in any way act on God but only on ourselves, and which holds that God, being immutable in his form, does not act. The conception Hegel ends up with is that of an

---

82. [See G. W. F. Hegel, *Early Theological Writings*, trans. T. M. Knox (Philadelphia: University of Pennsylvania Press, 1971), 304.]

83. [*Philosophy of Religion*, 418, 464–67, 469.]

84. This "noumenological" point of view is more or less achieved at the end of the *Phänomenologie*, 583 [*Phenomenology*, 492–93].

unending life in which God and human consciousnesses are constituted through their reciprocal actions.

To put it in yet another way, the relation of the finite to the infinite cannot be represented by propositions of the type "I am finite; God is infinite." These determinations (finite, infinite) are only moments of the process; God also exists as finite and I also exist as infinite. God is this movement in itself and is for that reason a living God (*Philosophie der Religion*, XI, 122 [cf. *Philosophy of Religion*, 170–71, 452–53]). Henceforth, one must not regard the finite as existing in itself; it must be viewed through the act by which it is canceled [as finite], and what comes from God must be viewed through its return back into God.

A phenomenological theory is the analogue of a theory of grace according to which one cannot separate what in grace comes from God from what comes from free will.[85]

Hegel had characterized this presence of the immutable in the individual and of the individual in the immutable by using the term *erfährt* [it "experiences"]; the way in which the immutable is presented is indeed an *Erfahrung* ["experience"] of consciousness, an experience [as process] that is a test [*épreuve*] through which the divided consciousness passes in its unhappiness.[86] The revelation of the immutable is born from this very unhappiness, and the whole of the *Phenomenology* is the history of that experience. But that is not to say—and Hegel points this out—that one cannot consider this movement from the point of view of the immutable just as readily as from the standpoint of individual consciousness. This movement is not a unilateral movement, or rather, the side from which one considers it is immediately transformed into the opposite side because particular consciousness itself, as we have seen, is an immutable consciousness;[87] by the same token, that immutable consciousness is nothing other than the particular consciousness. One can then, says Hegel, divide the movement we have been discussing by now considering it from the point of view of the immutable consciousness, which also moves, however paradoxical this may seem, and which in the first moment is opposed to particularity taken as a whole (and if our interpretation is correct, this is Judaism); in the second moment, the immutable is incarnated in order to be a particular opposed to other particulars (this will be Christianity in its first

---

85. [*Phenomenology*, 133–35.]
86. [Ibid., 128; *Phänomenologie*, 165.]
87. [It is immutable insofar as it is *the same* consciousness that persists through all its changing contents; see *Phenomenology*, 127.]

form);[88] in the third moment, the immutable is united with the particular (Christianity in its developed form). However, to look at things in this way, says Hegel, would be to go beyond our current phenomenological point of view; for we must consider only the immutability of consciousness, immutability affected by contradiction, not true immutability in itself and for itself, as the latter has not yet come before us.[89] The only thing that concerns us here is to know that the determinations that we have designated as connected to the immutable "appear for consciousness," and appear to it as "connected to the immutable."

We have said that immutability remains tainted by a contradiction.[90] In the same way that the particular consciousness, examined in its relations with the immutable, presents itself as divided, and as being for itself, the immutable, for its part, considered at the moment when it has taken the form of the particular, has the dual character of being divided and of being for itself. For in considering the particular consciousness as something other than itself, the immutable likewise conceives itself as being both other than consciousness and as being for itself; and being for itself the whole of reality, as consciousness is the whole of reality for itself, it sees that it is divided in two, in the same way that [particular] consciousness had the feeling of being divided. The monistic idealism of the immutable, like the monistic idealism of consciousness, results in the conception of the essential duality of both of them. Consequently, when the immutable takes the form of particularity, it is only in the eyes of consciousness that this is a fact that happens, a natural event with which consciousness "finds" itself confronted. When, in the first moment, consciousness sees itself as opposed to the immutable, this is also for consciousness like the discovery of an external fact; and when, in the final moment, consciousness witnesses the complete reconciliation of individuality and immutability, doubtless this is for consciousness "a fact of which it is in part the cause" and which is explained by consciousness's nature as an individual being.[91] But according to what we have said about this fundamental opposition, the union with the immutable will appear to consciousness as arising in part from the immutable.[92] Consequently, an opposition persists within this unity because this unity has its origin and its motor in the two opposed terms. As a historical phenomenon, Christianity presupposes two factors: both

---

88. [Cf. *Philosophy of Religion*, 454–55.]
89. [*Phenomenology*, 128; *Philosophy of Religion*, 90.]
90. Cf. *Phänomenologie*, 409 [*Phenomenology*, 323].
91. [*Phenomenology*, 129.]
92. [Ibid.]

the individual and God have a share in the initiative. Accordingly, Christianity remains divided even at the moment of its union and remains enclosed within the domain of mere facts. There persists in it an element of that opposition that characterized Judaism, and this opposition shows itself precisely in the fact that grace essentially comes first of all from God, and not from God and consciousness. An element of mere fact and of sensory reality remains within Christianity, which is linked to the element of opposition. If the Christian God dies, this is in part because the Spirit of the Christian does not live in a complete way since it needs to be vivified by grace.[93]

Inasmuch as the immutable takes on [determinate] form, the moment of the beyond, far from vanishing, "on the contrary is strengthened."[94] In other words, Christianity does not take us to genuine immanence.[95] We could have predicted this on the basis of the above fact, namely, that an opposition persists at the heart of unity. This opposition could not fail to occur because, as we previously saw, we are here concerned only with the immutable as seen by consciousness, and such as consciousness is in its current stage of development—that is, we are concerned with an immutable tainted by contradiction. Doubtless, through the Incarnation the immutable draws near to consciousness; it becomes akin to it. But in contrast, the result of the Incarnation is that the immutable is opposed to the particular consciousness as a certain sensory, opaque, resistant, inflexible *unit* [unité].[96] Consequently, the hope of becoming one with it remains a hope, cannot be realized in the present, and can be only a sort of empty form seen from a distance; there is an element of "radical contingency" and "obstinate indifference" that arises precisely from the same fact that gives rise to hope, namely from the fact that the immutable has entered into [empirical] existence and has taken on a determinate form, and that this is a pure fact.[97] Being at one with an opposite one is an impossibility.[98] The union necessarily vanishes: it vanishes in time and is remote in space. These distances in time and space are only incomplete mediations. Consciousness here will only know a dead Messiah or Christ, dead in a distant land;[99] it will

---

93. [Ibid., 131–32; *History of Philosophy*, 3:4–6.]
94. [*Phenomenology*, 129.]
95. Cf. *Phänomenologie*, 402–3 [*Phenomenology*, 465].
96. [*Phenomenology*, 129.]
97. Cf. *Phänomenologie*, 572–73; *Philosophie der Religion*, II, 23; X, 235 [*Phenomenology*, 129, 458–62, 466, 472; *Philosophy of Religion*, 452–58, 465–67n199].
98. [*Philosophy of Religion*, 427.]
99. [*Phenomenology*, 132, 462–63.]

never be able to be united with the living individual immutable, the living Christ. This failure occurs precisely because the individual immutable has taken on the character of [empirical] reality and has thereby submitted itself to the dialectic of the "this" and the "now," which was set out in the first chapter of the *Phenomenology*. From the moment that this unit is, it is far more correct to say that it has been.[100] In drawing near to us, in lowering himself down toward us, God thus at the same time distances himself from us.[101] Consciousness has not yet rid itself of the idea of the object. We are in the presence of an as yet insufficiently profound link between sensible immediacy and generality. A beyond separated from the here-below [*un au-delà séparé de l'en-deçà*] still persists here. Once again, the third stage, in which the union [of the particular changeable with the immutable] will be realized, will only be possible when instead of having a *this* we will have a Spirit.[102] In a way, God has lowered himself too far after having remained too far above us. In both cases, he remains distant, for the terrestrial Jerusalem of long ago does not appear to be any easier to reach than the heavenly Jerusalem, and the dead God is no easier to possess than the God who was never alive.

IV

With Christianity, it is thus no longer consciousness itself as particular that consciousness strives to negate but, rather, its relationship with the formless and abstract immutable—which one could call the Law or the God of the Jews—in order to no longer agree to any relationship except with the formed immutable,[103] that is, with the Christian God, but without our being able to assert that consciousness should stop at the Christian God. Now we are no longer in the presence of the simple concept of a divided consciousness but of this consciousness itself in its concrete character—no longer having "for essence and object" the formless and abstract immutable, no longer being that division into two elements in which one strives to cancel out the other—a division which, characteristic of all concepts (the pure and simple concept being, in effect, radical division and, in essence, unhappiness), is all the more characteristic of the concept of the divided consciousness. Rather, we now stand in the presence of the fusion of the immutable element and the particular element.

100. [Ibid., 462; *Philosophy of Religion*, 455; *History of Philosophy*, 3:54.]
101. [*Phenomenology*, 460.]
102. [*History of Philosophy*, 3:57.]
103. Cf. *Phänomenologie*, 585 [*Phenomenology*, 459–60].

This fusion will not be obtained straightaway, for it is going to be necessary to internalize this relationship little by little and move from the stage of an external relationship between man and his savior to an identification of the two.

As we previously saw, at first it was not possible to conceive of an external relation with the formed immutable, as this is an alien reality, an incarnate but distant God. It is this external relation that will need to be transformed so that after the God of the Jews, and after the Christian God, we will attain Spirit.

What we have to study is the movement through which the nonessential consciousness seeks to attain this absolute identity in its second phase, that is, when it finds itself in the presence of a formed beyond [*un au-delà informé*]. We will see that there is a ternary rhythm: that of being in itself, which is pure consciousness reaching toward its beyond; that of being for itself, which is consciousness turning against the here-below [*l'en-deçà*]; and that of being in and for itself, which like the Stoic sage is in possession of itself but in a more profound manner. We will pay particular attention to the first stage of the second phase.

We will first consider consciousness as pure self-consciousness in the face of its immutable and formed God (*der gestaltete Unwandelbare* ["the formed immutable"]). We can say that as pure consciousness, it is without form in the face of the formed immutable, whereas in the first phase it was, rather, the particular [consciousness] which appeared as having form in the face of the formless immutable. The presence of the immutable exists here only insofar as it comes from consciousness; it only exists as one side and under one aspect, so to speak, because it will only be later that we will see that the attention that consciousness devotes to the immutable is simultaneously the attention that the immutable devotes to consciousness, and that these two acts join up in what we could call the intellectual love of the notion.[104] For finite consciousness knows God only insofar as God knows himself in and through that consciousness, in such a way that the theological relativism of which we have been speaking is finally revealed as a mystical monism.[105] Here, however, we must say simply that formless consciousness stands before the formed immutable, a formed immutable that does not have an authentic and complete presence. We are in the presence of a God who is

---

104. [Wahl is here implicitly referring to Spinoza's idea of the intellectual love of God (*amor intellectus dei*) as elaborated in book 5 of his *Ethics*.]

105. Cf. *Philosophie der Religion*, II, 166 [*Philosophy of Religion*, 469, 479].

revealed to consciousness but who is linked to the sensory, and for that reason is a contradictory God.

The unhappy consciousness is thus not in possession of the formed immutable such that it is in itself, but only an incomplete formed immutable. It is nevertheless true that this unhappy consciousness, which for the moment is pure and simple consciousness, is above the pure and simple thought of Stoic thought, the abstract thought that in a general way makes an abstraction of every particularity, and above Scepticism, which is restlessness [*inquiétude*] and at bottom is nothing but particularity as "contradiction without consciousness and the restless movement of this contradiction."[106] Pure and simple consciousness surpasses both this false empty generality, without particularity and without movement, and that contradictory particularity without generality and without rest. At the same time, it unites pure thought as the Stoics knew it with the real particular. It is, however, a state intermediate to the one at which consciousness will reach its end, an intermediate state in which two terms are linked without mediation, a state in which abstract thought, or thought more or less as it was conceived of by the Stoics, comes into contact with the particularity of consciousness, as a particularity more or less as it was conceived of by the Sceptics, but without consciousness being fully aware of this contact and thereby being able to transform it into a deep union. In this way, a philosophy of incarnation—or, rather, of the contact of mind and body, since we are not yet at the stage of the true Incarnation—is the logical outcome of the two ancient schools, and something similar to what Pascal's conversation with Monsieur de Saci no doubt demonstrated.[107] Everything appears to this consciousness in the form of particularity, and it is well aware of the thinking particularity, and it is well aware of the immutable in the form of particularity. But what it is not aware of is that its object, the immutable, and the immutable in the form of particularity, is none other than itself, is none other than the particularity of consciousness.[108] Consciousness is indeed the contact of the two terms, but it is not this contact for itself. The unity here is a unity of contact between two abstract terms, but not the unity of fusion which will be obtained by the synthetic action of consciousness, which conceives of this unity as real for itself as

---

106. [*Phenomenology*, 125, 436, 456; *History of Philosophy*, 2:330–31, 343, 372.]

107. [See Pascal, "Conversation of Pascal with M. De Saci on Epictetus and Montaigne" (1655), trans. O. W. Wight, in Blaise Pascal, *Thoughts, Letters, Minor Works*, ed. Charles W. Elliot (New York: P. F. Collier and Son, 1910), 392–406. Cf. *Philosophy of Religion*, 457–58.]

108. [*Phenomenology*, 131.]

a synthetic function, and conceives of this unity as being nothing other than itself, discovering that its incarnated God is its self [*moi*]; what it lacks is the consciousness for itself of its self.[109] In the final analysis, consciousness will only perceive itself, and perceive itself insofar as it perceives itself as consciousness. The spiritual content of Christianity will only be truly and completely revealed when consciousness will be revealed to itself in all its plenitude.

We can already say, at least, that there is a thinking particularity, that is, that the "this," the "mine," and the whole vague region of *Meinen* ["what I mean" / "what is mine"][110] can come to negate its particularity and succeed in attaining thought in its generality. The particularity that is *thought* vanishes; but insofar as it is *thinking*, particularity is no longer able to vanish completely.

Is this not already the foreshadowing of what Christ will be in all his truth, a Christ altogether different from that unconscious mixture of particularity and universality that was ancient Olympus, where individuality was attached to essence in a nonessential way and remained inessential?[111] Here we find a fact that has an ontological value, that attaches thought to being, to particular being itself. Here we attain the unity of being and essence. Here there is a "this" that is a general essence, the negativity of which is no longer the sterile negativity of the sensory but the fecund negativity of thought. Spirit is real. Is not Christ the thinking particularity par excellence, the particularity put to death on Golgotha—the thought that holds up and supports the world?

From this point on, the death of Christ appears on the one hand as the transposition of the dialectic of the sensory in which the sensory vanishes,[112] but on the other hand as the symbol of the intelligible in which its moments are preserved. Consciousness now finds itself in the presence of a conscious particularity. But its affective content is not explicit in the *Begriff* ["concept," "notion"];[113] the *in itself* has not become

---

109. [Ibid., 130–31, 410–16, 467, 479–80.]

110. [See ibid., A. Consciousness. I. Sense-certainty: or the "This" and "Meaning" (*Meinen*). This section has to do with the particularities ("this," "here," "now") of particular sensory consciousness, which grasps these particularities through its own particularity or what is "mine" (*mein*).]

111. Cf. *Phänomenologie*, 556, 558, 571 [*Phenomenology*, 426–30, 455–58; see also *Philosophy of History*, 318–19, 324–25; *Philosophy of Religion*, 343–49].

112. [*Phenomenology*, 132.]

113. [*Begriff* means "concept," a word Wahl translates as "notion" in order to differentiate Hegel's concept from that of Kant and the neo-Kantians, which is translated as "concept."]

for itself. Consciousness is in the presence of a beyond. Doubtless its object, just like itself, is "in itself" nothing other than a thinking particularity; Christ's apostles too are all thinking particularities. But the relation between the one and the other does not yet appear as pure thought, and thus, for the moment at least, the fact of having attained the idea of the contact of two thinking particularities only distances from consciousness the unity of these two particularities that it will succeed in attaining only later. Consciousness here is only striving toward thought, toward that thought which is, in any case, consciousness itself. It is striving and tenderness, contemplation, devoutness, devotion.[114] We have said that it is not formed and that its thought thus remains vague—a musical thought of the sort that Schleiermacher, for example, thought, having not achieved the *Begriff* or the union of objectivity and immanence that characterizes it.[115] (Here the word *Begriff* is understood in the higher sense, which we are translating as "notion.") In effect, the concept from which one starts is a pure feeling (for Hegel, aspiration always remains something conceptual),[116] and the concept at which we end up—the notion—is complete and full reason.

Thus conceived, religious feeling is a sort of internal seeking, an infinite seeking. It is not without an object, but its object, not being the object of the notion, remains something alien. There is nothing further from the notion, in a sense, than that religious feeling of the apostles before the dead Christ, which Protestantism wants to revive (cf. Nohl [*Theologische Jugendschriften*], 342),[117] a completely subjective feeling before something that is completely transcendent. The pure and simple [Christian] conscious-

---

114. On *Andacht* ["devotion"], cf. *Geschichte der Philosophie*, 90, 93 [G. W. F. Hegel, *Lectures on the History of Philosophy*, vol. 1, *Greek Philosophy to Plato*, trans. E. S. Haldane (Lincoln: University of Nebraska Press, 1995), 73–74, 76], and *Philosophie der Religion*, I, 119, 120, 168 and II, 158 ff. [*Philosophy of Religion*, 138–44, 190–91, 193–94]. In these passages (except in *Philosophie der Religion*, 120), the conception of *Andacht* differs from that of his youthful writings and the *Phenomenology*; on *Gefühl* ["feeling"], see *Philosophie der Religion*, I, 172, and particularly 78; on *Sehnsucht* ["yearning" or "longing"], see *Philosophie der Religion*, II, 103, 104 [*Phenomenology*, 131, 410, 456; *Philosophy of Religion*, 193–94, 447–52].

115. [The German theologian and philosopher Friedrich Schleiermacher (1768–1834) had a theory of religion based primarily on feeling and devotion; see Schleiermacher, *On Religion: Speeches to Its Cultured Despisers* (1799), trans. Richard Crouter (Cambridge: Cambridge University Press, 1988).]

116. Cf. *Philosophie der Geschichte*, Reclam edition (Leipzig, 1920), 207.

117. [Hegel, "The Spirit of Christianity and Its Fate," in *Early Theological Writings*, 301.]

ness is presented in its first form as the movement of an infinite *Sehnsucht* ["yearning"].[118]

We spoke of contact, but consciousness, precisely as the contact [of two things], and as the absence of the feeling of the unity of this contact, is division. We are placed before the sorrowful emotion of the disciples who are conscious of themselves, but only in their division: a division within themselves, a division with respect to their object, and who remain in a state of separation. At the same time, we find this *Gemüth* ["temperament," "sensibility"], this heart, this emotion, personified, according to what Hegel says in the *Philosophy of History* (Reclam edition, 445; cf. 524), by the German consciousness insofar as it is the vague sentiment of self without determinate content.[119] Schleiermacher's thought thus represents both the thought of the disciples at the moment of the death of Christ and the thought of the Germanic world. For Hegel, it is a matter of providing a content and an object for these too-indeterminate and divided feelings vis-à-vis a being that is wrongly considered to be completely transcendent.

But if there is not the unity of a notion, there is at least the certainty that to the internal emotion there externally corresponds the transcendent emotion, so to speak, of a God; for what else but an emotion is this God one conceives of as a particular thought?[120] The disciples have the feeling that the object of their love, of this nostalgic love that cannot attain its object except as something alien, of this *Sehnsucht* conceived by Jacobi[121] but felt by Christians throughout history, is such a pure and simple emotion, that is, a pure and simple thought that feels or senses itself as something particular. As conscious individuals, they have the assurance that their object is a conscious individual, and by the same token, that because their object thinks as a particular individual, he knows and values the souls of those who long for him.[122]

In this sense, after having separated the two terms, the feeling of their dual particularity unites them.

This recognition of one soul by another is something essential;[123] for at every stage we find this same process of recognition, which, from the

---

118. [*Phenomenology*, 131.]
119. [*Philosophy of History*, 350–52; *Philosophy of Religion*, 138–44.]
120. [*Phenomenology*, 131.]
121. [Friedrich Heinrich Jacobi (1743–1819), a Romantic philosopher who placed feeling and faith higher than reason and connected faith (or belief) with the intensity of feeling, was a frequent target of Hegel's criticism.]
122. [*Phenomenology*, 131; *Philosophy of Religion*, 474.]
123. Cf. *Phänomenologie*, 339 [*Phenomenology*, 126, 131, 457–61].

point of view of the *Phenomenology*, consists of the unity of a duality (cf. *Phänomenologie*, 140, 142 [*Phenomenology*, 126, 129]). Each of these extremes has self-knowledge that stems from this recognition by the other (*Phänomenologie*, 142, 146 [*Phenomenology*, 129, 131]). On the one hand, the pious soul feels certainty in this nostalgic state, but on the other hand, it feels that the essence is an unattainable beyond that flees at the very moment when it is grasped, or rather, has already flown.[124] It has already flown, for let us take it as the immutable that thinks of itself as a particularity; let us take Christ in his spiritual aspect. Consciousness will then immediately find itself in him because Christ is an individual, but if consciousness finds itself, then what it finds is itself as opposed to the immutable. For we have not yet achieved the union of the general and the particular in the notion. Consciousness thus cannot grasp the essence; it must be content with tentatively seeking it, and at the very moment consciousness thinks it has attained it, it is thrown back into itself. Instead of having grasped the essence, it only feels the sentiment and the sensation of its self [*moi*] as nonessential and separate.[125] It feels that it gains its own satisfaction [through yearning], but this satisfaction is just that, *its own* satisfaction, that is, the satisfaction of its self insofar as it is opposed to the immutable. Faced with the dead Christ, the disciple withdraws into himself, the mystic is always thrown back into a state of aridity, and the pious soul is thrown back into a state of despair, almost a state of impiety.[126] At the moment of union, consciousness grasps itself in its own separation, and by the same token the immutable can appear to it only as something particular or real. The two terms, the immutable and consciousness, cannot be melded together. We remain in the presence of a divided consciousness and of a beyond divided and separated from it. On the one side, there is only reality; on the other side, there is only the particular. For the same reason, when consciousness now wants to try to grasp a here-below [*un en-deçà*]—the real, individual object of Christ incarnate instead of a fleeting beyond—as we already saw, this object of the pious soul is then a *This* that is subject to the dialectic of the sensory world.[127] It will thus never be found where one seeks it; for it must be precisely a beyond even when we place it in the world of the here-below. In the first case, the beyond is experienced in feeling; in the second, it is experienced in sensation. In neither case is the beyond that union of particularity and generality that is

---

124. [*Phenomenology*, 131.]
125. [Ibid.]
126. [*Philosophy of Religion*, 486.]
127. [*Phenomenology*, 132.]

the notion. In both cases, but especially in the second case (Hegel only resorts to this allusion for the latter), we will say that consciousness never finds itself in the presence of its life unless and until its life is present to it in the form of its grave.[128] If one conceives of this presence in the way that the pious soul does, and not as the presence of the notion, then one will have to kneel before the cross or go off on Crusades. But one cannot be assured even of possessing this grave.[129] And in Hegel's mind, which grants a metaphysical importance to historical events and a historical reality to a metaphysical event (was he not in any case led to this way of doing things by his meditations concerning the way in which the religious metaphysics of Christianity was constituted?), the Crusades become the sign of a philosophical truth. If the Christians were unable to secure in a lasting fashion the holy places, if the Crusades had to remain a vain attempt, it is for the same reason as what renders sensory consciousness incapable of ever showing us a "here" without that "here" vanishing.[130] There is a Crusade of the sensory consciousness for the possession of the Here; there is a dialectic of the pious soul in its search for the grave; the two correspond to each other, and both of them achieve nothing other than the destruction of sensory consciousness and the destruction of the pious soul in the sense that we have been describing it. In effect, the pious soul is going to learn that the grave of the being of an immutable reality it considers to be real has no reality as the grave of the immutable precisely because that grave is, in the ordinary sense of the term, a reality. For no grave, no reality in the ordinary [empirical] sense of the term, can contain the immutable, the real reality [*la réalité réelle*]. Consciousness is going to find that the vanished particularity, precisely because it has vanished, is not the true particularity.[131] Because consciousness cannot be certain even of possessing the grave, it is thus going to renounce any hope of finding the immutable particularity in the domain of [empirical] reality or of trying to preserve it in time, as that would amount to holding onto that which is no longer, or of holding onto that which is not.[132] Thus, the disciple and the Crusader standing

128. [Ibid.]
129. [That is, of the grave of Christ in the Holy Land, the Holy Sepulcher. See *History of Philosophy*, 3:103–4.]
130. Cf. *Philosophie der Geschichte*, 490–500. Cf. *Geschichte der Philosophie*, I, 90–91 [*Philosophy of History*, 389–93; *History of Philosophy*, 1:73–74].
131. [*Phenomenology*, 132.]
132. [Ibid.; *History of Philosophy*, 3:54: Christ as the manifestation of the unity of the divine and the human natures "cannot be one who is past and gone . . . a mere recollection of the past" retained in memory but, rather, the living and actual reconciliation of Spirit.]

before the grave, the aristocratic Romantic, the man of the people, who all feed their imagination with the sound of bells and clouds of incense, represent a stage that must be surpassed by consciousness. By the same token, consciousness is going to become capable of finding genuine individuality, general individuality.[133]

This is the conclusion of what Hegel will a bit later call the *Kampf des Gemüths* ["struggle of sensibility"].

We will not linger over the way in which the disciple, the Crusader, the Romantic, all return back into themselves after their disappointment and feel themselves to be particular individuals; nor over the stage of desire and labor; nor over the sanctification of this labor by the communion and by grace, through which the Last Supper is like the reversal of Adam's diabolical meal; nor over the contrary aspect that then comes to light, and that leads to asceticism and repentance on account of the gratuitous character of grace and the incomplete character of the communion. For us, the most important thing is that through the development of these contradictory aspects, going from the objective to the subjective, from worshipping the world to despising the world and vice versa, religion little by little strains toward what will be its end, that is, its completion and its destruction: absolute knowing, the reconciliation of the subjective and the objective, through which the world will be transmuted into its idea.

The stage of the unhappy consciousness does not occur just once in the life of Spirit; it is found at different moments in the *Phenomenology*. Transcended, it nevertheless returns to consciousness at each new bend in the road until consciousness at last feels itself to be united with the object it sought—which is at the same time the subject, itself as reality.

Unhappiness is produced when Spirit becomes aware of itself as transcendental, consciousness without content, the perpetual changing of one idea into another, the I opposed to the Not-I, the transition from being to nonbeing and from nonbeing to being.

These pages of the *Phenomenology* thus present us with a constant struggle between discordant elements, a dismemberment [*déchirement*] of consciousness that derives from its limitations. Until the moment when consciousness achieves its unity, we are in the presence of a game of loser wins, where there is a continuous and incessant irony, and where consciousness ceaselessly ends up with the opposite of what it sought.

---

133. *Phänomenologie*, 382, 383: "where the dialectic of the sensory leads to the dialectic of the intelligible"; see also 273 [*Phenomenology*, 132 ("individuality in its genuine or universal form") and 263–65].

But there is a turning point of cosmic history where, leaving behind the varied appearances of the sensory here-below, and at the same time disengaging itself from the empty night of the supersensory beyond, consciousness will find itself in the spiritual daylight of the present.

However, first of all, it must go through this twilight [*crépuscule*] of morning that is the unhappy consciousness, where the immutable sun sees itself only through the changing colors that are opposed to it. Daylight will reign and there will be peace only when the elements are conceived of not as elements but as notions; not as being opposed but as being both opposed and united.

V

Each of the stages through which consciousness passes is a deepening—or if you prefer, an elevation—of the preceding stage. The deepening or elevation consists in the fact that we are heading toward an ever greater unity. Stoicism and Scepticism, on the one side, and Judaism, on the other: in Christianity, what had been contained within these shapes is brought into the light of consciousness. Through the same process, the abstract oppositions these had contained become concrete oppositions amenable to being transformed into a union. In unifying the oppositions between which it oscillates, Scepticism allies itself with Judaism; in its turn, Judaism, in unifying its oppositions, becomes the Christian unhappy consciousness and gives birth to the idea of the Incarnation; and the succession of [Jewish] kings gives birth to the Son of God. But Christianity, even though it might be called—in contrast with Judaism, the religion of the indeterminate beyond—the religion of the incarnate beyond, remains a religion of the beyond. In the first place, it contains a sensory element that gives rise to a new opposition. Thus, starting from the antithesis placed here at the beginning, one does not immediately proceed to a synthesis but, rather, to a contact [between two terms], which will only be able to become a synthesis through enlarging itself. This enlarging of the contact into a synthesis will itself be produced in three stages. In the first, there will be contact but without there being consciousness of this contact or of the unity of the two terms. Thus, because the particular will be grasped in a sensory form, it will vanish: the death of Christ, the Crusades, the Romantic *Sehnsucht* designate the same phenomenon, the idea that the desire for contact must be transcended. Consciousness will thus move into a sort of individualism, a self-feeling.[134] Before the dead Christ, the disciple says, I, at

---

134. *Phänomenologie*, 170 [*Phenomenology*, 132].

least, as desiring and striving, I exist; and the Crusader faced with the vanishing of his victory and the Romantic faced with what is uncertain in his feeling of infinity, say the same. This will be the intermediary between the first and second stage of the unhappy consciousness. The second stage, which Hegel will study in the pages that follow, will be the stage of labor and effort, whether that of Candide tending his garden or Faust cultivating his will as producing ever new acts, or Schlegel sketching a metaphysics of the destruction of material things—or more profoundly, of the soul who communes. In its turn, this second stage will also be unable to satisfy consciousness; for it still does not achieve, even in communion, the idea of the identity between itself and the immutable. But at the same time it becomes aware that labor and communion both presuppose the presence of the immutable, and it is in this way that it finally comes to see that labor and communion presuppose the presence of its own unity with the immutable. Consciousness sees that it divides itself in labor and communion; at the same time, it sees that its labor presupposes its communion and that both labor and communion (even though labor remains a superficial relationship between the exterior of consciousness and the exterior of reality) presuppose a grace created by the immutable, a gift coming from it.[135] The immutable offers itself to consciousness in the communion and offers consciousness the world in labor. Consciousness recognizes these benefits and humbles itself, at first in a partial and superficial way, such that in its thanks-offerings it still feels itself as a particular, but then in a complete way. It is then that we pass from the second to the third stage. For if the total renunciation of asceticism only renews the feeling of consciousness's particularity, nevertheless, can this renunciation be performed without being dictated by the immutable? In that sense, this renunciation, precisely because it is not accomplished immediately but comes about thanks to the immutable, is something positive. It is through the intervention of the priest that the immutable will influence the particular consciousness and in the final analysis destroy it.[136] We will then be in the state at the furthest remove one can imagine from Stoicism as consciousness of freedom: consciousness will have become a thing.[137] But if that is how things are, it is because of the fact of grace.

In addition, in asceticism, consciousness witnesses, without being conscious of it, the appearance of the idea of the person—and even of the idea of the general will and of reason.[138] Is not the "I think" profoundly connected

---

135. [*Phenomenology*, 132–34.]
136. [Ibid., 136.]
137. [Ibid., 137.]
138. [Ibid., 138.]

to the thought of the saints meditating in the cloister? The world is no longer separated from Spirit. But the screen of the middle term, the priest, prevents consciousness from becoming aware that it is in direct communion with God and that it has achieved the unity of objectivity and independence. Yet it knows, although in a manner that remains indirect, that as an unhappy consciousness it has attained its happiness, and that its negation of action is absolute action.

These are the three stages, the three successive and complementary aspects of the religious sentiment that Hegel describes: religious desire, labor, and communion in a sanctified world; desolation; and humiliation. These three aspects take place between the phase of absolute opposition between man and God and the phase of their absolute union. In effect, religious desire is still affected by that element of separation that gives rise to the conception of the divinity as a beyond, and although we come closer to unity in labor and the communion, this stage must still be transcended in turn and must be destroyed because it still encloses an element of particularity within itself. But desolation and humiliation bring us closer to the divinity. Through humiliations, man attains the idea of the absolute act; through desolations, he attains the idea of absolute happiness. The principle of the modern world, or rather absolute knowing, is developed in this period of unhappiness, interrupted by the appearance of Christ and then by the Reformation, both momentary interruptions: Christ's thought, Luther's thought, will only fully become clear, according to Hegel, in the Hegelian philosophy itself, in which all sensory elements will have disappeared and in which Spirit will be present as unity, mediated by the very fact that it will have traversed and preserved within itself (albeit as transcended) the different modes the *Phenomenology* strives to describe.[139]

Religion is first of all transcendence, one could say, in the sense that its content always flees and remains at a distance; if it thus remains at a distance, this is because it is a given content.[140] But when this content has been internalized, it will appear as essentially mediated. The unhappy consciousness is religion inasmuch as it remains at the moment of transcendence and is only implicitly aware that it has transcended this moment. When consciousness attains the affirmation of its unity in its very duality, what had

---

139. [See *History of Philosophy*, 3:546–47: "Philosophy is thus the true theodicy, as contrasted with art and religion . . . a reconciliation of Spirit, namely, of the Spirit which has apprehended itself in its freedom and in the richness of its reality. . . . The history of philosophy is a revelation of what has been the aim of Spirit throughout history; it is therefore the world's history in its innermost signification."]

140. Cf. *Philosophie der Religion*, II, 53 [*Philosophy of Religion*, 121].

been the source of unhappiness will become the source of its happiness, and the three stages that characterize the religion of the Incarnation will allow it to take us from its starting point, the religion of opposition, to its final destination, absolute religion.

This chapter's significance has an even more universal scope, or at least a different kind of universality, if it is true that the nature of consciousness is to divide itself prior to reassembling itself, to tear itself apart [*se déchirer*] prior to sewing itself back up into a unity that will be henceforth indissoluble, and in which both consciousness and its essence, consciousness and its object, will come to coincide. From this process stems the unhappiness not only of consciousness but also of the world in general, divided from what creates its unity by a sort of cosmic tearing [*déchirure*], an abyss [*gouffre*] that reason will fill.

It must be noted that the immutable consciousness does not remain inactive throughout this process. For at the same time that the individual consciousness becomes universal through its unhappiness, the universal becomes subject, moving through the three stages of the Kingdom of the Father, the kingdom of the Son and the kingdom of the Spirit: that is, through generality, particularization and the final unity in the subject that is an object.[141] But phenomenology must not look at things from this noumenological point of view. It can only let us catch a glimpse of its possibility, its necessity.

Translated by Bruce Baugh

---

141. *Philosophie der Religion*, II, 178 [*Philosophy of Religion*, 413–16 and 416–17n67].

4

Hegel and Kierkegaard

In 1930, a substantial review of *Le malheur de la conscience dans la philosophie de Hegel* (The unhappiness of consciousness in Hegel's philosophy) appeared in the *Revue Philosophique de la France et de l'Étranger*. Its author was Alexandre Koyré. Although now principally known as a philosopher and historian of science, Koyré's initial work was in the philosophy of religion; his thesis, on René Descartes's proofs for the existence of God, was completed in 1922—two years after Jean Wahl's own thesis on Descartes—and in 1929 he received his *doctorat d'état* for *La philosophie de Jakob Boehme* (The philosophy of Jakob Boehme).

Koyré's clear admiration for Wahl's book is coupled with an equally strong rejection of its thesis. Wahl's reading of the *Phenomenology* stresses the importance of G. W. F. Hegel's early, religious writings and he understands Hegel's dialectic as a lived experience, not a merely intellectual or formal method. In Wahl's idiom, Hegel's dialectic is an ultimately vain attempt to apprehend the concrete in thought. "But," Koyré muses, "isn't such a failure characteristic of every philosopher?"[1] What is distinctive and valuable in Hegel's philosophical work is not that it arose out of a youthful infatuation with mystery and irrationality but that the

---

"Hegel et Kierkegaard," *Verhandlungen des dritten Hegelkongresses vom 19. bis 23. April 1933 in Rom*, ed. B. Wigersma (Tübingen: J. C. B. Mohr [P. Siebeck], 1934), 235–49; republished in Jean Wahl, *Études kierkegaardiennes* (Paris: Fernand Aubier, 1938), 159–71; and republished in Jean Wahl, *Kierkegaard: L'Un devant l'Autre*, ed. Vincent Delecroix and Frédéric Worms (Paris: Hachette Littératures, 1998), 97–118.

1. Alexandre Koyré, "Review of Jean Wahl, *Le malheur de la conscience dans*

system—which Hegel had formulated as early as 1800 "in his head," if not in his written works—provided a way to overcome that infatuation. In his 1934 essay "Hegel in Jena," Koyré writes that "when Hegel descends into the arena, he is already armored from head to toe."[2] But, more strikingly, he writes in 1930 that "Hegel's greatness lies in his inhuman coldness."[3] The contrast with Wahl could not be clearer.

A more detailed account of Koyré's position is articulated in his 1931 "Note sur la langue et la terminologie hégéliennes" (Note on Hegelian language and terminology). Anticipating Jean Hyppolite's later Heideggerian claim (in *Logic and Existence*) that "language is the house of being as sense,"[4] Koyré writes that for Hegel the task of philosophical thought is to make clear, to "recognize," and thereby to explicate, "to discover in the naïve speculation of language the speculative truth of reason."[5] Against Wahl, Koyré argues that Hegel's language is not difficult because it is "imaginative and poetic" but because it is the dialectical synthesis of the temporal and the eternal; the Hegelian "concept" is the "integration of past forms in the present,"[6] of the concrete in the system. Concerning the alleged difficulty of Hegel's language, Koyré concludes his essay—only slightly in jest—by arguing that the best commentary on Hegel is "a good *historical* German dictionary."[7]

Wahl presented "Hegel and Kierkegaard" in April 1933 to the Third International Hegel Congress in Rome. Koyré was in the audience and it is clear from the themes of Wahl's essay that he was unpersuaded by his interlocutor's defense of philosophical systematization.

Even more than Hegel, Søren Kierkegaard was almost entirely unknown in France in the early 1930s. The first translations of his work into French had only appeared in the previous decade—*Diary of a Seducer* in 1929 and several fragments in 1927. Many more translations would appear during the 1930s spurred in part by Wahl, whose contemporaneous work on Kierkegaard would be gathered and published in 1938 as *Études kierkegaardiennes* (Kierkegaardian studies),

---

la philosophie de Hegel," Revue Philosophique de la France et de l'Étranger 110 (July–December 1930): 141.

2. Alexandre Koyré, "Hegel à Iéna (A propos de publications récentes)," *Revue Philosophique de la France et de l'Étranger* 118, no. 9/10 (September–October 1934): 274.

3. Koyré, "Review of *Le malheur*," 142.

4. Jean Hyppolite, *Logic and Existence*, trans. Leonard Lawlor and Amit Sen (Albany: State University of New York Press, 1997), 166.

5. Alexandre Koyré, "Note sur la langue et la terminologie hégéliennes," *Revue Philosophique de la France et de l'Étranger* 112 (July–December 1931): 424.

6. Ibid., 438–39.

7. Ibid., 439.

which established Kierkegaard's importance for successive generations of French thinkers.

As Wahl's presentation makes clear, for him Kierkegaard and Hegel are motivated by a common problem: "the attempt to grasp the concept at the heart of the phenomenon without betraying the reality of the phenomenon"; the problem of what Wahl calls "concrete reason." If Hegel ultimately sided with his mature system against the Christianity of his youth, Kierkegaard will, according to Wahl, take the side of the younger Hegel against the mature, systematic philosopher. Christ is "the unmediatable mediator," his very existence a "scandal of reason" that tempts philosophy into the original sin of "the divinization of the human."

To hold fast to this scandal is to remain faithful to what Wahl calls two "feelings": the feeling for the secret and the feeling for existence. The secret is the mark of an essential difference between the internal and the external, between an individual and the necessarily general expression of this individual in language. Here is Wahl's rejoinder to Koyré's valorization of Hegel's philosophical language. And the experience of the secret that formed "the secret of Kierkegaard's existence" leads him to "the secret of existence." And this secret is that "there is no system of existence," that the concrete is a world of "radical heterogeneities" and "qualitative differences." It is not just that Hegel's system fails, it is that every system fails. No dictionary—German or otherwise—can index or enclose the sense of existence.

The final part of Wahl's essay transposes the conflict between Hegel and Kierkegaard, and between systematization and the concrete, into the discussion of the then-emerging philosophy of existentialism. Although he focuses on the contemporaneous work of Karl Jaspers (after a passing mention of Heidegger, whose influence was only just being felt in France), Wahl returns to his 1930 monograph, *Étude sur le Parménide de Platon* (A study of Plato's *Parmenides*),[8] in order to divide the entirety of the Western philosophical tradition into the alternate hypotheses of the One: either multiple or absolute unity. Wahl's choice is clear: he sides with the world of the night, of the multiple, with Jaspers's world of problems and choices, and—in the striking final line of the essay—with a world in which irreconcilable individuality makes "the relation with the *other*" even more acutely felt. The conclusion of the essay is suspended there, leaving the elaboration of this darkling thought to explorers and partisans still to come—Wahl himself, but also Emmanuel Levinas, Georges Bataille, Maurice Blanchot, as well as Gilles Deleuze, Jacques Derrida, and Michel Foucault.

Russell Ford

---

8. Jean Wahl, *Étude sur le Parménide de Platon* (Paris: Rieder, 1930).

To study the relations between Hegel and Kierkegaard is, first of all, to note their opposition, but it will also be necessary to show the deep and complex relations between them, and perhaps even some kinships, in the midst of the dissimilarities that remain. After having shown these two complementary aspects of the question, I will press on and follow the study of the Kierkegaard-Hegel opposition in the existential [*existentielle*] philosophy of present-day Germany.

I

I will begin by attempting to follow Kierkegaard's critique of Hegel, beginning with what may seem to be its most superficial and at times even imprecise claims, in order to advance step by step into its deeper motives and essential reality.

What first attracted Kierkegaard to Hegelian philosophy was not only, to use his expression, "that severe form that should impose silence," but its attempt to grasp the concept at the heart of the phenomenon without destroying the reality of the phenomenon, its idea of concrete reason, that sense of the totality that makes known [*fait comprendre*] both the essence of the universe and the essence of the individual; is not every true individuality a totality both closed within itself and simultaneously included in a larger totality?

1

But early on, even before he definitively broke with Hegelianism, Kierkegaard felt a certain aversion toward what he calls its half-heartedness [*tiédeur*]: the Hegelian always accepts an idea "to a certain extent," but never completely. In addition, on the one hand, the Hegelian tends to reduce every question to a historical search, to a study of origins and development, and thereby causes the meaning of essential problems to vanish; and on the other hand he leads people to believe that they need only look to their times, to their place in history, in order to guide their action; how convenient that feeling of being carried, supported, by universal spirit! In this sense, Hegelianism is the philosophy of ease, and we will see that it is also made such by its overly clever conceptual operations. What's more, it is necessarily conservative. It divinizes the given; it leaves "the immense criterion of ideality" in the shadows; but wanting to preserve the given is to revolt against God. As Geismar[9] says, for Hegel every great philosophy is the incarnation of the

---

9. [Eduard Geismar (1871–1939) was a professor of theology at the University of Copenhagen. His major work, to which Wahl is probably referring, is the six-volume

spirit of an age; for Kierkegaard it is a protestation against the spirit of an age. By its eclecticism, its historicism, its fatalism, and its conservatism, the whole Hegelian philosophy appears to Kierkegaard as a philosophy of enervated and indecisive generations. It is both a symptom and a cause of weakness.

These criticisms are still too external, founded above all on the repercussions of Hegelianism in the minds [*consciences*] of the nineteenth century, but we can also add the criticisms that follow from interpretations, albeit imprecise, that Kierkegaard gives of the notions of idea, objectivity, and system. Objectivity is synonymous for him with disinterested, disinterested with absence of interest, and thus with distraction and ennui. An abstract thought is a distracted thought, one that remains external to itself. Moreover, objectivity can only produce successive approximations, never certainty; history will never give us anything but more or less probable facts; to judge religion objectively is to strip it of its absolute certainty. Kierkegaard's interpretation of the Hegelian concept of the idea is equally questionable: the idea is the identical and unchanging; the system wants the identical. It is true that Hegel claims that he has introduced movement into logic, but in doing so, Kierkegaard says, he has managed to negate movement by trying to make it into something logical; Hegel's concepts of movement and evolution have nothing to do with real movement and evolution. These two criticisms, which may seem contradictory, destroy in Kierkegaard's eyes the Hegelian conception of the idea. The concept of system appears equally worthless to him; despite all of his efforts, there is no way for Hegel to "begin" his System. The System is always tied to Hegel; it is impossible to break this link, impossible to begin.[10] Here again, one might ask whether this criticism contradicts the preceding criticism of the idea of disinterestedness. But suppose, Kierkegaard continues, that the system were able to begin, and then came to an end. In that case, it would destroy the specificity of every notion; it would transform them into each other; it would annihilate them.

Thus universality and objectivity, which had initially appeared to him as the fundamental merits of Hegelianism, now seem to him to be worthless.

Søren Kierkegaard: Hans Livsudvikling og Forfattervirksomhed (Søren Kierkegaard: His life and work) (Copenhagen: G. E. C. Gad, 1926–28).]

10. He adds that the System has no end since—because it is constituted by mediation which is only a pseudo-idea and a destruction of ideas—it has no morality and its age no longer exists.

2

Kierkegaard became aware of these different defects by becoming aware of the opposition between Hegelianism and Christianity. Hegelianism destroys the specific character of Christianity. "Every Christian concept is vaporized." Sin disappears; and this disappearance of sin is the essential sin. Similarly, faith [*croyance*][11] is interpreted only as an immediate form[12] of essentially mediated thought; it is denatured, deformed, and destroyed. Hegelianism wants to mediate everything, but Abraham—the hero of faith—does not allow himself to be mediated. To believe is to refuse every philosophical mediation, every surpassing (*weitergehen*), every justification. To justify faith is to destroy it; to explain paradox is to destroy paradox. To show that there is a "truth of Christianity," meaning that its truth is a kind of philosophical knowledge, is to blaspheme. Christianity is not a doctrine of abstract man, taught by a professor to his disciples; it is a life; it is addressed to everyone; Christ does not teach; he acts, he is.

He is eternally, and he is at a given moment of history. Christian concepts are related to the eternal, but they are also related to the historical. They are engaged, incarnated in time. Our eternal beatitude depends on our belief in a historical fact. That is the paradox. Christian concepts are not philosophical concepts at all. It is not a matter of thinking an eternal becoming through them, like [Ludwig] Feuerbach, but of thinking, paradoxically, becoming and eternity at the same time.

Against Hegel, who sees in them a superior manifestation of reason, Kierkegaard finds them to be a scandal for reason. They precipitate the rupture with immanence; they make us feel simultaneously an infinite proximity, but also and above all an infinite distance, between the finite and the infinite, between man and God. There is an abyss between man and God, ceaselessly hollowed out, ceaselessly crossed by grace, but never bridged.

Christ, the unmediatable mediator, is the one that guides us across it. Even less than Abraham, Christ cannot be mediated because the mediation that is inapplicable to faith [*croyance*] in the absolute end is even less applicable to the absolute end itself. Mediation is the enemy of the mediator. The mediator is the enemy of mediation.

Thus when Hegel wants to demonstrate the absolute character of Christianity, he only manages to negate and to relativize Christianity. The

---

11. [In most cases, we will translate *croyance* as "belief" and "*foi*" as "faith." Here, however, it seems clear that Wahl is talking about what Kierkegaard means by faith.]

12. Kierkegaard attributes to Hegel the idea that faith [*croyance*] is something immediate.

original sin of Christendom and what is opposed to Christianity is clearly visible in Hegelianism: the divinization of the human.

For Kierkegaard, this demand for the rights of religion is essentially the protestation of the individual against its subjection to the species, and the protestation of the real against its subjection to the rational.

For Hegel, the human species is redeemed by the divine; it is only a matter of abstract terms. For Kierkegaard, it is the individual, it is I who am redeemed by God. And ultimately, for Hegel the philosopher, the species is superior to the individual; but in religion, by a reversal of the values proper to it, it is the individual who becomes again superior to the species.

For Hegel, the rational and the real, the internal and the external, coincide in the mixture that is the concrete universal. For Kierkegaard, there are irreducible oppositions between them.

3

The critique of Hegelianism, which first seemed to us to be so superficial in form, has revealed to us its more essential motives; and behind these motives, behind this opposition of Christianity and Hegelianism, we now find two still more profound feelings: the feeling for the secret, and the feeling of existence.

For Hegel, the idea of a force that is not expressed, or of a purely internal feeling, are idols of the romantic imagination. Everything is public, everything is open, everything is revealed. But Kierkegaard's anti-Hegelianism is explained above all by his feeling for the secret. Hadn't his father lived enclosed within his terrible secret, in the memory of the curse that he had hurled against God and that God caused to fall back so heavily upon him? Was he himself not trained, from childhood, to present himself as other than he was, while keeping his incurable melancholy and his quiet despair to himself? Had he not seen the paternal secret and his own secret as barring him from the engagements with Regine Olsen, and a third secret, born of the other two, raising an insuperable barrier between him and her? And doesn't his very life remain inexplicable to us by the force of that secret that Kierkegaard took to his grave? He always felt like a living refutation of the identity between the internal and the external; more than all of the more or less abstract demonstrations, it was his very existence that destroyed Hegelianism.[13]

13. And so, for Kierkegaard, Hegelianism and its relations with Christianity were intimately tied to his existence; at the time of the project of the engagement, he wanted, in a desperate effort to reattach himself to Hegelianism, to escape from the secret, to adopt a philosophy where everything would be "revealable," where beings would be

Through his particular experience, Kierkegaard felt that there are irreducibly subjective elements, that the unique, the incommensurable, exists. Through the mystery that he felt in himself, he knew that there is no mediation of the individual, no mediation of existence. The secret of his existence initiated him into the secret of existence.

And ultimately this is what Hegelianism forgets: it is necessarily turned toward the past; it forgets living. It immediately translates present existence into ideal existence, thus into merely possible existence. And those who protest in the name of real existence—people like [Johann Georg] Hamann, [Friedrich Heinrich] Jacobi, Kierkegaard—are themselves translated into concepts: they become the moment of the protestation of existence.

But "to be or not to be," that is the highest question for Kierkegaard, as it was for the Danish prince. And one can be only if one *is* passionately. To be is to be devoted, pledged to an absolute end—it is to be absolutely passionate. This is quite far from the Hegelian "to a certain degree." Existence is oriented entirely toward unconditionality. The person lost in his passion has lost less than the one who loses his passion. A single partial thought, but living and existent, is worth more than the whole System. Thus Kierkegaard immerses himself in all those tremblings [*frémissements*] of purely personal life that knowledge has nothing to do with, and about which it can do nothing. What can purely theoretical knowledge make of irony, of humor, of belief, of all these concrete spiritual movements that are unknowable by intelligence? What place does it have for them? And what place can it make for sin? There is no general knowledge of profound spiritual facts; and in particular there is no general knowledge of sin. There is no sin in general.

It is therefore not a matter of being able to be delivered to the simultaneously compact and transparent world of concepts, but of existing temporally in the world of anguish, of despair, of trembling, and of hope.

There is no possible system of all these movements. There is no system of existence.

The idea of existence is united to the idea of being. Christ does not teach; he is. Subjectivist meditation encounters realist meditation. The subjectivity of a Novalis is here joined with the theory of being of a Hamann or a Jacobi. There is always a leap from thought to being. Thought only attains the possible or the past, that is to say thought being [*l'être pensé*], never

---

known and trusted and would take their place in the state, in marriage, in morality. Whence certain aspects of *The Concept of Irony*. But the effort founders. *The Concept of Irony*, itself an essentially ambiguous and secret work, does not overcome the secret. From then on Kierkegaard definitively refuses Hegelianism and breaks his engagement.

being. A fight to the death is waged between existence and thought. Existence, historical being, does not allow itself to be thought. Against mediation, Kierkegaard claims the rights of the immediate.

Nothing is less applicable to this domain of existence than the idea of the *Aufhebung*, this sublimation that suppresses and conserves at once, this synthesis in which thesis and antithesis are united in such a way that they can no longer be perceived [*aperçoive*] as separated. For Kierkegaard, the antithesis must subsist, must remain armed and active. Like a perpetual goad [*un aiguillon sans cesse nouveau*], uncertainty remains at the heart of belief; sin persists in faith.

Hegelianism wants to make things easy, to smooth over difficulties. Kierkegaard wants to make things difficult, to do nothing to blunt the terms of problems. There is no possible union of these absolute oppositions. We will no longer have syntheses but alternatives, dilemmas. We will no longer have mediations but paradox and leap, the pathos of thought, the fever of thought.

Here we are no longer in the world of homogeneity but in one of radical heterogeneities, of qualitative differences, of absolute novelties. And the absolute will no longer be what unites but, conforming to the word's origin, what is separated, and what separates. Not an amalgam, but a sword. The internal is not the external; reason is not history. The absolute makes heterogeneities appear, for it is transcendence.

II

Leap opposed to mediation, paradox opposed to synthesis, heterogeneity opposed to homogeneity, transcendence opposed to immanence, such is Kierkegaard's philosophy in contrast to Hegel's. But we have said that to study the relations of Kierkegaard and Hegel is not only to see the oppositions, it is also to see what of Hegel is preserved by Kierkegaard; it is perhaps also to see that Hegel exhibited some of the apparently most anti-Hegelian conceptions before Kierkegaard did; finally, after having studied the criticisms that Kierkegaard addresses to Hegel, one might ask if one cannot find in Hegel some anticipatory criticisms directed against Kierkegaard. Here we can only touch upon three points.

1

First, what does Kierkegaard owe to Hegel? What does Kierkegaard preserve from him? If we recall that for Kierkegaard the conceptions of life are arranged [*s'étagent*] in three different levels [*paliers*]: the aesthetic stage [*stade*], the ethical stage, and the religious stage, we can say first that the criticism of the first stage, the criticism of the Romantic aesthetic, owes quite a lot to Hegel. The definition of the ethical stage in its fullness, characterized by the coincidence of the internal and the external, and by "reduplication" sometimes conceived in a way analogous to synthesis;[14] the critique of the lower levels [*étapes*] of this stage, which sometimes seems to be inspired by certain objections that Hegel made to Kantian and Fichtean moralism—all of this is influenced by Hegelian philosophy. The critique of intellectualism with its reasons (*Gründe*) is also very similar in Kierkegaard and in Hegel. And as for the religious stage itself, the way in which one ascends to it by repentance, which simultaneously completes and destroys the ethical stage, the way that it simultaneously includes within itself both the immediacy of the ethical stage and certain enlarged and deepened aspects of ethical reduplication, and the way that it is attained by that "prepared immediacy," analogous to the mediation of the immediate in Hegel, this whole ensemble of ideas again shows quite profound analogies between Kierkegaardian and Hegelian thought.

Kierkegaard opposed subjectivity to Hegelian objectivity, but didn't Hegel show both the advent and the sorrowful apotheosis of subjectivity in Christianity? Did he not thereby pave the way for Kierkegaard?

Kierkegaardian subjectivity will be dialectical, and this is a new concept borrowed from Hegel. And the Kierkegaardian dialectic doubtless differs from the Hegelian dialectic since it does not allow the *Aufhebung*, since it is discontinuous, made of leaps and ruptures, since it is lyrical and closely tied to subjectivity and, finally, since it has neither its beginning nor its end in itself but receives its impetus from God, which is a term foreign to the dialectic, and it is never confused with this origin that is simultaneously its end. The dialectic never completely rejoins being; it is not grounded by it [*ne se fond pas avec lui*]. The presence of this reality, which provides the impulse, which exercises an attraction, but which simultaneously puts up a resistance, explains the subjectivity of the Kierkegaardian dialectic. But it is no less true that the idea of a dialectical becoming, and of a dialectical becoming linked to the idea of negativity, marked by a constant reversal of the negative into the positive, of sadness into beatitude, of nonbeing into being, certainly preserves some traits of the Hegelian dialectic (which was also influenced, like Kierkegaard's dialectic, by the dialectic present in Lutheran theology).

---

14. It is curious to note that the moral stage is described in Hegelian terms, even as Kierkegaard reproaches Hegelianism for not having a morality.

Finally we have opposed paradox on one side and synthesis on the other; these ideas are, however, closely related. In *The Concept of Irony*, Kierkegaard speaks of a "paradoxical synthesis." Once the synthetic garb is removed from Hegelianism, paradox remains. Hasn't Hegel insisted on what is paradoxical in Christ's assumption of humanity, in the idea that Christ is incarnated, that he is at a given moment of space and time (in order to annihilate, it's true, by his death and resurrection, the reality of space and time)?

2

And this leads us to our second idea: on many points Hegel, and particularly the young Hegel, the Hegel of the *Theological Writings*, has preceded Kierkegaard. Before constituting his system, Hegel was one of the most powerful theorists of irrationalism. Like Kierkegaard later, he was profoundly influenced by Hamann and the *Sturm und Drang* movement; and it is this pre-Kierkegaardian more than pre-Hegelian Hegel that we hear in a cry such as: "A thought is not the living God"[15] or in the opposition with which he broke the bread of faith away from the ice and stone of concepts or in his insistence on the indemonstrability of being. Thought being [*l'être pensé*] is only possible being; it is not being. And like Kierkegaard, he tells us, imbuing the line with all of the force that a disciple of Hamann can give it: Jesus is a being. Positive religion will be characterized for him by a link—a link that Kierkegaard will call paradox—between the contingent and the eternal; positive religion is a union of opposites, and for that reason it is an example and manifestation of living nature. And he defines what Kierkegaard will call the paradoxical synthesis: God is the being-one of two natures; faith [*croyance*] is a unity of opposites as is the object in which it believes. Finally, in many of these passages, the young Hegel's individualism resembles what Kierkegaardian individualism will be: Christ speaks to individuals, not to nations; his prayer is "the prayer of the isolated man, in doubt and uncertainty, the prayer of an individual. A people cannot pray in this way."[16]

We therefore witness this curious phenomenon: Hegel is a precursor to his own criticism and to the most violent anti-Hegelianism that has ever been formulated.

---

15. [*Hegels Theologische Jugendschriften*, ed. Herman Nohl (Tübingen: J. C. B. Mohr, 1907), 391.]
16. [Ibid., 399.]

Nevertheless, a fundamental difference remains between Kierkegaard and the young Hegel:[17] in the young Hegel there is a sense of victory, an accent of triumphant joy that is absent in Kierkegaard. This is doubtless the abyss that separates them. Kierkegaard is an unhappy consciousness.

3

And this leads us to the third point that we wanted to develop briefly and to a second spectacle that is no less curious than that of Hegel as a precursor to his own criticism; it is that of Hegel as a critic of his criticism. This is the spectacle presented to us by the pages of the *Phenomenology* on the *Unhappy Consciousness*. This internally divided consciousness, which oscillates between the idea of its immutable object and of its own mutability, and each time is destroyed on contact with this immutable thing, and for whom "the consciousness of its life, of its existence and of its action, is only sadness for the subject of this life, of this existence and of this action,"[18] isn't this already Kierkegaard's consciousness? And is there not, in the *Phenomenology*, from the characteristics of the unhappy consciousness, a kind of deduction of Christianity, as Kierkegaard will come to conceive it? The God of the unhappy consciousness is a distant and vanished [*disparu*] God, a God situated in a beyond toward which our passion always tends in vain; it can only ever kneel down upon his tomb; there is no fully present God; what is present is the empty and abstract place where he was.

But is this critique of Kierkegaard *avant la lettre* definitive? Not at all; for Kierkegaard is the unhappy consciousness precisely insofar as it refuses to be integrated into the System; it is the belief that thinks that without following the winding paths of the development prescribed by philosophy, it can, from right where it is, traverse the difficult road that will lead it directly to God. The work of Kierkegaard appears as Romanticism's revenge on the System.

I know that Käte Nadler, in her brilliant doctoral thesis, and in her fine article in *Logos* on Hamann and Hegel, which is so rich with ideas and so profound, has opposed Kierkegaard to Hegel by saying that the one, Kierkegaard, moves in the oppositions between abstract terms, while the other, Hegel, is able to unite the terms because he sees them in their

---

17. [Instead of "the young Kierkegaard and Hegel," which is what appears in the original—Trans.]

18. [Cf. G. W. F. Hegel, *Phenomenology of Spirit*, trans. A. V. Miller (Oxford: Oxford University Press, 1977), 127, para. 209.]

concrete character.¹⁹ And while Kierkegaard remains a prisoner of concepts that no breath of true love animates, Hegel is inspired, she tells us, by the experience of love. I wish I could go on at length about all the ideas of this important study in *Logos*, about what Käte Nadler says about the preservation of oppositions in Hegelianism and about the opposition of Hegelian subjectivity to Kierkegaard's unhappy subjectivity, the opposition of Hegel's fecund negativity to Kierkegaard's abstract negativity, and the opposition of Hegelianism as a system of creation to Kierkegaard's philosophy as a system of the Fall. These are penetrating insights. What I will merely note is that she recognizes that whatever Kierkegaard's subjectivity loses in generality—by being isolated, by being restrained in itself—it gains in tremendous depth. Starting from there may we not ask ourselves if in certain cases an experience, concrete in origin, might not be gradually encircled by a conceptual construction that risks stifling it? And isn't this sometimes the case with Hegel? And whether, on the other hand, an acute concrete experience might not arise from certain abstract oppositions? And isn't this sometimes the case with Kierkegaard? Doesn't abstraction succeed in placing us before limit-situations, to use Jaspers's term, and making us experience them in a very intense way? A spark flies out of the encounter between abstract terms. Such was the experience reserved for Kierkegaard.²⁰

19. [Käte Nadler (1907–?) was an Austrian Germanist and philosopher who published several works on Hegel and Hermann Hesse. The two texts by Nadler referred to here are *Der dialektische Widerspruch in Hegels Philosophie und das Paradoxon des Christentums* (The dialectical contradiction in Hegel's philosophy and the paradox of Christianity) (Leipzig: Felix Meiner, 1931) and "Hamann und Hegel: Zum Verhältnis von Dialektik und Existentialität," *Logos*, no. 20 (1931): 259–85.]

20. The relations between Hegel and Kierkegaard have been studied in an interesting way by [Hans] Reuter, *Kierkegaards religionsphilosophische Gedanken in Verhältnis zur Hegels religionsphilosophischem System* (Kierkegaard's philosophico-religious thinking in relation to Hegel's philosophico-religious system) (Leipzig: Quelle und Meyer, 1914), and by [Alfred] Baeumler, "Hegel und Kierkegaard," *Deutsche Vierteljahrsschrift für Literaturwissenschaft und Geistesgeschichte* 2 (1924): 116–30. Excellent indications can be found in [Walter] Ruttenbeck, *Kierkegaard, der Christliche Denker und sein Werk* (Kierkegaard: The Christian thinker and his work) (Berlin: Trowitzsch, 1929). One can compare the ideas of Baeumler and those of Wiesengrund-Adorno in his recent work on the Aesthetic in Kierkegaard (33 and 44) [*Kierkegaard: Konstruktion des Aesthetischen* (Tubingen: J. C. B. Mohr, 1933), translated into English by Robert Hullot-Kentor as *Kierkegaard: Construction of the Aesthetic* (Minneapolis: University of Minnesota Press, 1989)] with the theses developed by Mlle. Käte Nadler.

III

It remains now to follow the battle between Kierkegaard's thought and Hegel's thought up to the existential philosophy of today. Its influence can be found in Heidegger's criticism of the conceptions of [*das*] *Man* [the "They"]—of what is for him its objectivity and entirely intellectual curiosity devoid of any deep interest. But here[21] we will look for the influence of Kierkegaardian thought in Jaspers.[22] Always quite attuned to the depth harbored in the narrowness of a *Weltanschauung*, Jaspers has been drawn by this verification, narrow and deep, that Kierkegaard's thought provides him, as well as by its tension and force. He has considered Kierkegaard's philosophy at length. He has discerned in it the feeling of existence, as separation and aspiration toward that from which it is separated. And he wants his own philosophy to illuminate the two feelings created by their reciprocal tension: the feeling of subjectivity and the feeling of being or, as he says, the feeling of existence and the feeling of transcendence. Jaspers's *Philosophy* often seems to be a commentary, in the highest sense of the term, a profound and invaluable commentary, on the thought, on the experience of Kierkegaard.[23]

Jaspers's polemic against Hegelianism is quite close to Kierkegaard's. He reproaches Hegelian idealism, as well as positivism, its apparent opposite, for wanting to be an encyclopedia, in an even more authentic sense than positivism. Hegel thinks by means of circles, and circles of circles. In this

---

21. I have studied the relations between Heidegger and Kierkegaard in my article in *Recherches Philosophiques* (1933). [Translated as Chapter 5 in this volume.]

22. Certainly one should also note Hegel's influence on Jaspers, an essentially *vielseitig* ["versatile"] thinker. For him, as for Hegel, there is only realized existence; no form is valuable if it is isolated from its rich content; there is no true interiority without an exteriority that it appropriates. Whence arises a battle, identical in Hegel and in Jaspers, against the Romantic love for nature as against a desiccated intellectualism founded on *Gründe* ["grounds," "reasons"]. Whence arises in both of them this desire to find their support in history, to see history as a cipher [*chiffre*], and to present a phenomenology of mythologies. Additionally, one might compare Jaspers's dialectic with Hegel's. For Jaspers, as for Hegel, the dialectic is the expression of absolute restlessness, and death—as relativization of *Dasein*—is an expression of the dialectic. The dialectic ceaselessly passes from the negative to the positive, and it comprehends within itself—dominated, sublimated—the negative terms that divide it. But an essential difference remains: far from being the permanent element, the absolute is the ephemeral element, an evanescing of experience.

23. [Karl Jaspers, *Philosophie,* 3 vols. (Berlin: Springer, 1932), translated into English by E. B. Ashton as *Philosophy*, 3 vols. (Chicago: University of Chicago Press, 1969–71).]

Rundung ("curve," "rounding"),[24] everything is enclosed, everything has become stable; one attains rest in totality. Surprise, chance, sin disappear.[25] Just as he criticized Hegelianism's supposed universality, Jaspers also criticizes its objectivity; for him, as for Kierkegaard, objectivity is obtained only by forgetting our deepest interests.

Jaspers is looking for the essential reasons of the System's impossibility: if the System is impossible, that is because being is essentially torn. The world is torn into two worlds that battle against each other: the world of being as universality and the world of being as existence; and each of these two worlds is torn in turn and in conflict with itself. Initially the world of universality can be ordered in an infinity of ways according to whichever science is used; there is even a whole group of sciences, the human sciences [*sciences de l'esprit*], that elude universality in their very ground because even there they draw deeply from existence; history in particular cannot attain objectivity; what has happened is subject to radically diverse interpretations. Nowhere is the opposition more strongly marked between Hegel, one of the founders of the nineteenth-century human sciences, and the critical spirit that animates Jaspers, who is reflecting on them a century later. In addition, the world of values is no less contradictory and in conflict with itself than the scientific world; there is a perpetual conflict between religion, morality, and philosophy. And beyond the world of objects and the world of values is their source: the world of existences. But there every idea of objective truth vanishes. There is no longer agreement, strictly speaking, between minds, but only call and invocation.

To the idea of an objective and universal system, Jaspers poses the problem, the world of problems and of danger, of possibility and action. He too has destroyed knowledge in order to make room for faith [*croyance*]. The risk of faith [*croyance*] is opposed to knowledge, modesty to the publicity of the Hegelian universe, existential tension to objectivity. And the transcendence that explains the tension and very existence of existence can only be grasped by it in antinomical relations, in the flux and reflux of feelings: hope-despair, defiance-humility.

There is no total truth. What we can do is actively sink into the contemplation of one aspect, renouncing a crowd of aspects and perspectives, passionately limiting ourselves to a perspective. Such is our situation as

---

24. [Reading *Rundung* for *Ründung*.]
25. Disappear in appearance at least. For by proclaiming the powerlessness of nature, by leaving room for exceptions, Hegel, according to Jaspers, proclaims his own powerlessness. What he calls the powerlessness of nature is the victorious resistance that it opposes to him.

limited beings, as essentially sinful beings, for whom sin is the door to salvation. Deepening ourselves by passionately limiting ourselves, deepening ourselves by becoming conscious of sin, these are two lessons that Jaspers's thought inherits from Kierkegaard's, and that he has artfully united into a single great lesson, essential sin being for him our essential situation as limited beings.

One must choose between the great Hegelian day and the Romantic night; and whichever we choose, we will be blind to the other aspect, and we will sin; even if we choose the day, we choose it in the night; even if we fight for the day, we fight in the night.[26]

This is the apex of faith [*croyance*]: consciousness of sin and consciousness of failure. Everywhere we run up against failure—in knowledge that can offer us neither objectivity nor universality; in action, which will only ever show us disequilibriums and injustices.

All these failures make us affirm transcendence; they are explicated by the absolute *other*, impermeable to our reason and to our acts. These failures, they are our knocks on the door of transcendence; they show us that there is a door.

Thus two *Weltanschauungen* ["worldviews"] stand facing each other; Hegel's *Weltanschauung* of the day, and the *Weltanschauung* of the night. There are two conceptions of unity here: the infinitely multiple One of the second hypothesis of the *Parmenides* reigns in the *Weltanschauung* of the day; the One that is absolutely one of the first hypothesis reigns in the *Weltanschauung* of the night. In Kierkegaard, we are very close to the negative theology inspired by the first hypothesis, and we find in both him and Jaspers a negative theology of the individual, just as there is a negative theology of God. There are also two conceptions of contradiction here: synthesis on one side, dilemma on the other. Here there are two profound experiences, which are opposed.

The Hegelian *Weltanschauung* certainly gives us a feeling of richness and a feeling of triumph that is not given by Kierkegaard's conception or by those who are inspired by him. But we might wonder whether the sharpness of certain profound feelings does not contain, from the perspective of a certain logic of quality, at least as much as the *welthistorisch* ["world-historical"] fullness of the grandest considerations, and we might also ask whether the same view of evolution and progress does not show the whole

---

26. And reminding ourselves of the song of Zarathustra, as Jaspers certainly often reminded himself, we can add: even if we are the day, we also want to be the night.

price of the feeling of bankruptcy [*faillite*] that Jaspers presents to us; accomplished art is quite close to decadence, triumph is the beginning of failure; and perfection contains the germs of decline, but imperfection contains the germs of the life of perfection; in the failure of the still clumsy primitive, do we not sometimes feel most vividly the truest triumph?

There are some souls [*âmes*] that refuse the world of the day, of manifest triumph and of that rich rational unity offered by Hegelianism; they would feel like prisoners there. And so they choose the world of problems, ruptures, and failures where, gaze fixed toward a transcendence that only they can see, they remain a problem for themselves, they remain full of irreducible multiplicities and ruptures, but perhaps they thereby feel, in a more intense fashion, both themselves and their relation with the *other*.

Translated by Russell Ford

5

Heidegger and Kierkegaard
An Investigation into the Original Elements of Heidegger's Philosophy

It is only slightly hyperbolic to say that Jean Wahl's "Heidegger and Kierkegaard: An Investigation into the Original Elements of Heidegger's Philosophy" legitimized Søren Kierkegaard in French academia and inaugurated French existentialism as such.[1] First published in 1932/1933 in *Recherches Philosophiques*, "perhaps the most significant [journal] of its time,"[2] it was republished in 1938 as an appendix to *Études kierkegaardiennes*, which would go on to become the most important book on Kierkegaard in France. Wahl's article laid the groundwork for the anthropological, humanist reading of Martin Heidegger by showing how Heidegger's philosophy must be seen as an attempt to ontologize and secularize Kierkegaard's

---

"Heidegger et Kierkegaard: Recherche des éléments originaux de la philosophie de Heidegger" was first published in *Recherches Philosophiques* 2 (1932–33): 349–70. It was republished with minor revisions in Jean Wahl, *Études kierkegaardiennes* (Paris: Fernand Aubier, 1938), 455–76, and republished again in Jean Wahl, *Kierkegaard: L'Un devant l'Autre*, ed. Vincent Delecroix and Frédéric Worms (Paris: Hachette Littératures, 1998), 69–95.

1. As editors Vincent Delecroix and Frédéric Worms contend in Jean Wahl, *Kierkegaard: L'Un devant l'Autre* (Paris: Hachette, 1998), 69–70. For corroborating claims, see the discussion of Kierkegaard in Chapter 1 in this volume as well as Lorenzo Ramella, *Il soggetto e la differenza: La ricezione del pensiero di Heidegger nella filosofia francese* (Milan: Vita e Pensiero, 2004), 21n14.

2. Stefanos Geroulanos, *An Atheism That Is Not Humanist Emerges in French Thought* (Stanford, Calif.: Stanford University Press, 2010), 55–56.

more religiously tinged thought.³ At the same time, and thanks precisely to Heidegger's philosophy, it revealed that Kierkegaard was a serious *philosophical* thinker in his own right. It is no accident that Jean-Paul Sartre cites it approvingly in a discussion of Kierkegaard and Heidegger in *Being and Nothingness*.⁴

Beyond its historical significance, Wahl's essay also stands out for being at once a succinct, admirable overview of Heidegger's early philosophy and a penetrating critique of issues still debated by Heidegger scholars today. In just over twenty pages of French text, "Heidegger and Kierkegaard" nearly spans the gamut of matters philosophical: temporality, spatiality, freedom, possibility, authenticity, objectivism, mortality, subjectivism, idealism, realism, ontology, and truth all come in for discussion. Wahl also begins to raise questions about Heidegger's philosophy that he will develop in essays, reviews, and lecture courses over the next four decades, questions concerning its theological underpinnings, its solitary emphasis on death, its deprecation of *Lebensphilosophie*, its "scholastic" abstraction, its prioritization of the future, and its relationship to time in general. Finally, in characteristic style, we see Wahl bringing thinkers into dialogue over the most fundamental issues. In this essay alone, there are more than just passing remarks on Nietzsche, Jaspers, Bergson, and Hegel. Already in 1932–33, Wahl established for the world that Kierkegaard and Heidegger must be counted among such great philosophical thinkers.

Ian Alexander Moore

[Fritz] Heinemann,⁵ in an interesting chapter he devoted to Heidegger, wrote that this philosopher endeavored to put the acosmic self of Kierkegaard back into the world.⁶ This is indeed one of the characteristics of

---

3. See Ethan Kleinberg, *Generation Existential: Heidegger's Philosophy in France 1927–1961* (Ithaca, N.Y.: Cornell University Press, 2005), 85.
4. Jean-Paul Sartre, *Being and Nothingness*, trans. Hazel E. Barnes (New York: Washington Square, 1956), 65n18.
5. Fritz H. Heinemann, *Neue Wege der Philosophie: Geist / Leben / Existenz; Eine Einführung in die Philosophie der Gegenwart* (Leipzig: Quelle und Meyer, 1929). [See in particular the section entitled "Vom Wesen zur Existenz. Martin Heidegger," 370–91.] Cf. *Being and Time*, 13: being in the world belongs essentially to the human being. 298: The human being, as an authentic self, is not separated from his world. [Unless otherwise indicated, page numbers in footnotes and in the body of the text refer to the pagination of the later German editions of *Sein und Zeit*. This has been checked against the pagination of the first edition from 1927. Wahl either used this edition or one of the similarly paginated editions published during or before 1932–33.]
6. [In what follows, Wahl's sometimes elliptical references have been filled in. For Wahl's citations of Heidegger, I have, unless otherwise specified, used John Macquarrie and Edward Robinson's translation of Martin Heidegger, *Being and Time* (San Francisco: Harper and Row, 1962). I have nevertheless tried to preserve the distinctness

Heidegger's work; the importance of this attempt stems, at least in part, from the effort to link together two of the most profound tendencies of contemporary thought—existential subjectivism and realist objectivism—and to do so without dulling their features but, rather, by accentuating them to the extreme.[7]

In an earlier study on several tendencies in contemporary philosophy,[8] I had occasion to indicate, in passing, the points that bring Heidegger closer to the objectivism of Whitehead: the role given to the idea of "being in the world," the way of representing spatiality, the subordinate place that he

---

of Wahl's terminological renderings when he does not quote Heidegger directly. When Wahl's French translations of Heidegger's German are of interest, the French has been included either in bracketed interpolations or in footnotes.

Wahl often translates Heidegger's *Dasein* as *être humain*, especially when quoting Heidegger, or simply as *l'être*, but he also occasionally leaves *Dasein* untranslated. In what follows, I translate Wahl's *être humain* as "human being"; when Wahl uses the German *Dasein,* I follow his usage and italicize *Dasein*. But when citing from English translations of Heidegger, I follow their standard usage and leave Dasein in roman type, not italics. When Wahl uses *l'être* to refer to *Dasein* or to the human being, I render it as "the being"; otherwise, *l'être* has been translated as "being."

A final issue concerns the distinction between the French terms *existential* and *existentiel* (which appear in Heidegger as *existenzial* and *existenziell* and are translated by Macquarrie and Robinson as "existential" and "existentiell"). As Heidegger writes in *Sein und Zeit*: "Only the particular Dasein decides its existence, whether it does so by taking hold or by neglecting. The question of existence never gets straightened out except through existing itself. The understanding of oneself which leads *along this way* we call '*existentiell*.' The question of existence is one of Dasein's ontical 'affairs.' This does not require that the ontological structure of existence should be theoretically transparent. The question about that structure aims at the analysis [*Auseinanderlegung*] of what constitutes existence. The context [*Zusammenhang*] of such structures we call '*existentiality*.' Its analytic has the character of an understanding which is not existentiell, but rather *existential*" (12). Although Wahl was no doubt familiar with this distinction, as it had been discussed in Emmanuel Levinas's 1932 article "Martin Heidegger et l'ontologie," with which he was familiar, Wahl unfortunately does not distinguish these terms consistently, and he rarely appears to be following Heidegger's distinction in *Sein und Zeit*. In what follows, both terms have therefore been rendered as "existential," except where Wahl is quoting Heidegger. See Emmanuel Levinas, "Martin Heidegger et l'ontologie," *Revue Philosophique de la France et de l'Étranger* 113 (January–June 1932): 395–431; translation by the Committee of Public Safety as "Martin Heidegger and Ontology," *Diacritics* 26, no. 1 (Spring 1996): 11–32.]

7. It will, however, be necessary to indicate that, in ultimately construing spatiality on the basis of an aspect of temporality, Heidegger undoubtedly tends to lessen his "objectivism."

8. [Wahl is referring to the preface of his *Vers le concret* (Paris: Vrin, 1932); see Chapter 2 in this volume.]

accords to the sense of sight.⁹ Here, I shall endeavor above all to examine what brings him closer to Kierkegaard, what the elements that he borrows from Kierkegaard are.¹⁰ And perhaps, after having set aside what is not the most personal contribution in Heidegger's philosophy, to distinguish better his proper effort to reunite, to combine, extreme subjectivism and extreme objectivism.

I

Kierkegaard said that the more one thinks (in an objective way), the less one exists; and that in this sense the *cogito ergo sum* gives an inaccurate idea of the real situation of man. In a rather similar way, or at least in setting out on a path that goes in the same direction, Heidegger writes, "He

---

9. It is necessary to add as well: how they both conceive of the interpenetration of the present, past, and future, an interpenetration that, according to them, explains the possibility of induction (cf. *Being and Time*, 360). Heidegger, like Whitehead, would be an adversary of the idea of a "simple location." [Cf. Wahl, *Vers le concret*, 10, as well as Chapter 2 in this volume.]

10. Let us mention here Heidegger's judgment on Kierkegaard: "In the nineteenth century, Søren Kierkegaard explicitly seized upon the problem of existence as an existentiell problem, and thought it through in a penetrating fashion. But the existential problematic was so alien to him that, as regards his ontology, he remained completely dominated by Hegel and by ancient philosophy as Hegel saw it. Thus there is more to be learned philosophically from his edifying writings than from his theoretical ones—with the exception of his treatise on the concept of anxiety" (235n). See note 18 to this essay as well as the passage preceding footnote indicator 31 below. In *Cahiers du Sud* (June 1932), there appeared a very curious article by B. Fondane that indicates the profound connections between Kierkegaard and Heidegger. [Benjamin Fondane, "Sur la route de Dostoyewski: Martin Heidegger," *Cahiers du Sud* 141 (June 1932): 378–92.] See also, in the same journal (January 1933): 50. [Benjamin Fondane, "[Review] *Kierkegaard: Traité du désespoir*," *Cahiers du Sud* 147 (January 1933): 42–51.] Consult also Walter Ruttenbeck, *Kierkegaard: Der christliche Denker und sein Werk* (Berlin: Trowitsch und Sohn, 1929), 373; Theodor Wiesengrund Adorno, *Kierkegaard: Konstruktion des Ästhetischen* (Tübingen: Mohr, 1933), 77; and Erich Przywara, *Das Geheimnis Kierkegaards* (Munich: R. Oldenbourg, 1929), 23–29. [In the *Études kierkegaardiennes* version, the references to Adorno and Przywara are replaced by three others: Hans Reiner, *Phänomenologie und menschliche Existenz* (Halle: M. Niemeyer, 1931), 25 (after which Wahl writes in parentheses: "Reiner in part explains the resemblances between Heidegger and Kierkegaard by the influence Luther had on both of them"); Adolf Sternberger, *Der verstandene Tod: Eine Untersuchung zu Martin Heideggers Existenzial-Ontologie; mit einer monographischen Bibliographie Martin Heidegger* (Leipzig: Hirzel, 1934); and Gerhard Lehmann, *Die Ontologie der Gegenwart in ihren Grundgestalten* (Halle: M. Niemeyer, 1933).]

[Descartes] investigates the '*cogitare*' of the '*ego*,' at least within certain limits. On the other hand, he leaves the '*sum*' completely undiscussed" (46).

Now, if one studies the *sum* itself in its relations with thought, one will see that, quite often, it is not I who am when I think; it is another, it is others, it is the anonymous crowd that exists in me. And it is precisely here that Kierkegaard's analyses are going to be of great help to Heidegger. We find an echo not only of Kierkegaard's struggle against Hegelianism and Cartesianism, but also of his struggle against the newspapers, at the moment in which, mocked by the *Corsair*,[11] he becomes aware of the necessary solitude of the individual who wants to be himself. Kierkegaard's existential cry [*cri*] becomes the point of departure for the thinker who reflects on existence. Every reader of the newspapers, writes Heidegger, becomes interchangeable with every other. Here there is a leveling and anonymity in which the "They" [*le "On"*] reveals its dictatorship. We find our delight and pleasure in the same way others find their delight and pleasure (126, 127, 128). Each is another and no one is oneself. The being [*L'être*][12] is everywhere and nowhere (347). It is the domain of forgetfulness (391), of ease, of distraction, which Pascal called *divertissement* (cf. 172). Everything becomes as good as possible: the "They" is naturally optimistic (cf. 177).

Every secret loses its force: every decision, every responsibility, disappears; each passes off his responsibilities onto the contemporary crowd and onto universal history (391).

Here there is no "exception"; all superiority is stifled (127); the authentic is abolished.

In all these characteristics, we rediscover the characteristics of the crowd and of the press[13] as Kierkegaard described them. Following his analysis,

---

11. [The *Corsair* was a Danish satirical weekly newspaper. Following a review in December 1845 by Peder Møller of *Stages on Life's Way* to which Kierkegaard responded harshly, the *Corsair* published several articles and caricatures that ridiculed Kierkegaard's appearance, voice, and habits. The Corsair Affair is considered the greatest literary battle in Danish history.]

12. [Heidegger uses the term *Dasein* in this passage.]

13. And also the characteristics of Hegelian philosophy, as they were denounced by Kierkegaard. He reproached [Hegel] with distracting us from ourselves by drawing our attention to a multitude of things that are foreign to us, and with making the history of China more familiar to us than the problems that concern our own individual destiny. One finds a remark of the same sort at the beginning of Heidegger's work on *Being and Time*. "Dasein has had its historicality so thoroughly uprooted by tradition [*La tradition annihile à tel point l'historicité de l'être*] that it confines its interest to the multiformity of possible types, directions, and standpoints of philosophical

and here again finding himself in agreement with Kierkegaard, Heidegger sees in the domain of the "They" the negation of possibility; possibilities are restricted to what happens everyday (194, 195; cf. 391); they are leveled out, and the most proper possibilities are effaced (178). However, sometimes the inverse phenomenon is produced: everything becomes possible, but it is an imagined possibility, a simple wish, a modality of desire and vague aspiration (195). On the one hand, a loss of the possible, on the other, a loss of oneself in the possible; we rediscover here, transposed, two of the forms of despair that Kierkegaard had distinguished.

This domain of the "They" is nothing other than the domain of guilt [*péché*];[14] the call [*cri*] of conscience will call us to a consciousness [*conscience*] of this guilt (269,[15] 280).

Through the chatter of the "They," through the science of history (*Historie* as opposed to *Geschichte*),[16] temporality protects itself. From what does it protect itself? From what does it divert itself? What does it flee? Precisely that profound care [*souci*] which, for Heidegger as for Kierkegaard, characterizes existence; precisely temporality itself, in its essence. This flight from myself and from time will allow me to seize my nature and the nature of time. "From an existentiell point of view, the authenticity of Being-one's-Self has of course been closed off and thrust aside in falling; but to be thus closed off is merely the *privation* of a disclosedness that manifests itself phenomenally in the fact that Dasein's [*l'être humain*] fleeing is a fleeing *in the face of* itself" (184). Through a rhythm analogous to the Kierkegaardian rhythm, the efforts of the "They" to cover up the "I" uncover it; and the moment that will allow us to pass from the "They" to the "I" will be the moment in which we become aware of our despair. For the domain of the "They" is at bottom the domain of despair. "That kind of Being-in-the-

---

activity in the most exotic and alien of cultures; and by this very interest it seeks to veil the fact that it has no ground of its own to stand on" (21). Kierkegaard said: one understands everything; only one does not understand oneself. Heidegger speaks of this alienation of man with respect to himself, an alienation that is bound up with his understanding of the most diverse cultures (178).

14. [While *péché* can be translated as "sin," in the following pages cited by Wahl Heidegger employs the term *Schuld*, which implies "guilt," and not *Sünde*, which would be "sin." The Kierkegaardian analysis of sin should nevertheless be borne in mind. The French term *faute* has also been rendered as "guilt."]

15. [Wahl writes 169, though this is most likely a typo for 269 and has been changed accordingly.]

16. [German has two words for history: *Historie* is history as the object of study by historians, while *Geschichte* is history as it is lived by human beings or, especially in the later Heidegger, as that which is sent or destined (*geschickt*) to us by being.]

world which is tranquilized and familiar is a mode of Dasein's uncanniness, not the reverse" (189). "[Anxiety's] breath quivers perpetually through Dasein" ("What Is Metaphysics?," 93[17]). What Kierkegaard says about despair is employed here: what is, and remains, first is malaise, that foundation of malaise from which an appearance of happiness comes to stand out. Likewise, it is not only when we are aware of guilt that guilt exists; guilt asleep is the greatest guilt (286). It is when we become aware of this fact that anxiety appears. As in Kierkegaard, whom he follows quite closely here,[18] the idea of anxiety is linked, in Heidegger, to those ideas of which some appear at first blush to contradict the others: the instant, the whole, the nothing, possibility, and the individual. The instant, since anxiety presents itself to consciousness [*conscience*] only in very rare moments, and only as in instantaneous flashes ("What Is Metaphysics?," 88). The whole, since in the feeling of anxiety appearances are rent asunder, the environing world sinks into insignificance (343), and what surges forth is being in general; here, moreover, it is a matter of a lived, and not thought, totality; we find ourselves in the midst of being in its totality ("What Is Metaphysics?," 87).[19] The individual, since the being [*l'être*][20] is thus presented as an isolated possibility (188); anxiety individualizes me to the highest degree. The individual is walled up in the thought of his guilt [*faute*] (269) as he is walled up in the thought of death (263). The nothing, since anxiety is indeterminate in its essence ("What Is Metaphysics?," 88); and in this indetermination the idea of the nothing is discovered. "The 'nothing' with which anxiety brings us face to face, unveils the nullity by which Dasein, in its very *basis*, is defined" (308[21]).[22] Finally, the possible; here, everything is disrupted; nothing is stable anymore,

---

17. [I have replaced Wahl's references to an early German edition of Heidegger's "*Was ist Metaphysik?*" with references to the English translation by David Farrell Krell in *Pathmarks*, ed. William McNeill (Cambridge: Cambridge University Press, 1998), 82–96.]

18. Cf. the note on 190: "The man who has gone farthest in analyzing the phenomenon of anxiety . . . is Søren Kierkegaard."

19. In *Sein und Zeit*, Heidegger explains what he means by these ontological generalizations that do not proceed by abstraction (187, 199, 200).

20. [Wahl's citation indicates that this refers to Dasein.]

21. [Wahl cites the page number incorrectly as 300.]

22. The universality of this idea of the nothing, which is applied in the theories of conscience and guilt (273, 276, 277, 283), of the future (330), of death (266, 306, 308), of anxiety (186–89), and moreover of everything that characterizes the state of *Geworfenheit* ["thrownness"] and *Verfallen* ["falling"], in particular, *Entwurf* ["projection"] (283–87), leads Heidegger to ask about the problem of the nothing. It is this problem that he endeavors to solve in his lecture: *Was ist Metaphysik?*

everything is sliding, falling away relentlessly ("What Is Metaphysics?," 88); we are delivered from the possibilities of the nothing, and free for authentic possibilities (187, 344). These diverse ideas are gathered together when Heidegger presents us to ourselves: "in the face of this 'nothing' [of the world], Dasein [*l'être humain*] is anxious with anxiety about its ownmost potentiality-for-Being" (276).[23]

Anxiety for Heidegger will be a revelation of the greatest universality: that of the world; of the most personal individuality: that of the "I"; of the most profound possibility: that of death. It will be a passage from inauthenticity to authenticity. If it is true that Heidegger transforms Kierkegaard's thought by placing the self in the world, and that anxiety is a revelation of being in the world (186, 187, 343), it is necessary to add that "in the world" can be taken in two different senses, and that the passage between these two senses, the inauthentic and the authentic, is still made by way of an analysis of the idea of anxiety, several of whose principal traits are borrowed from Kierkegaard.[24]

Once the individual penetrates into the unfolding of anxiety, whether it be the anxiety of guilt or that of death, which at any rate come to unite in the anxiety of the nothing, no one can replace him. It is the domain in which I am unsubstitutable;[25] each human being must take his death upon himself; death, insofar as it is, is always my death (239, 240, 250). Death is the domain of what Kierkegaard called the unique. The unique isolates himself, individualizes himself, makes himself one [*s'uniciser*], in the thought of death (263). And guilt, likewise, is one of those personal concepts that are always linked to the self and that cannot, as Kierkegaard said,

---

23. One sees on 287 an effort to unite the two ideas—Kierkegaardian and Heideggerian—of the nothing and of possibility. "Uncanniness brings this entity [viz., Dasein] face to face with its . . . nullity [*Le malaise de l'être humain l'amène devant son néant*], which belongs to the possibility of its ownmost potentiality-for-Being."—It is thus that Heidegger finds himself led to define death.

24. [In the *Études kierkegaardiennes* version, Wahl adds in parentheses: "not all, cf. above, p. 211." On footnote 2 of that page, Wahl writes, "One sees that there is a great difference between the use that Kierkegaard makes of the idea of anxiety and the use that Heidegger makes of it. For Kierkegaard, it is a matter of a psychological anxiety and a nothingness that is in the mind [*esprit*]. For Heidegger, anxiety is linked to a cosmic fact, to the absolute nothingness from which existence stands out. Whence Heidegger's originality, even in his theory of anxiety, which, at first blush, appears to be completely inspired by Kierkegaard."]

25. Cf. Céline, *Journey to the End of the Night*, trans. Ralph Manheim, afterword by William T. Vollmann (New York: New Directions, 2006), 283: "A time comes when you're all alone, when you've come to the end of everything that can happen to you."

be integrated into the System.—Guilt and death cannot take on more or less; guilt is anterior to any quantification; death knows no measure; what it signifies is the possibility of the absolute impossibility of existence (262).— And they are not present at one moment, absent at another. The human being is not sometimes culpable and sometimes not culpable. However unaware one is of guilt, it is there—incapable of augmentation or diminution, an immense quality of finitude, a quality that cannot be quantified (305). The phenomenology of guilt as Kierkegaard conceived it allows for the construction of Heidegger's theory. Likewise, death is always present in me, for it is the determination of my finitude.

Guilt, for Heidegger as for Kierkegaard, is the most basic determination of existence (294). The human being as such [*par lui-même*] is culpable. This is to say that, under the constant sway of guilt, and feeling itself to be essentially limited by death, existence has, as an essential characteristic, finitude ("What Is Metaphysics?," 93, 95; *Kant and the Problem of Metaphysics*, 160, 172[26]), *Nichtigkeit*, the nothing, that the human being ought to conceive of himself as essentially finite, and to see himself in his ownmost nothingness (285, 330). Thus do we become aware of the naturally humiliated, abased, dejected character (*Geworfenheit* ["thrownness"]) of existence (394). The human being is a being that has not been brought into being by itself (284). It can never leave this state of dejection, of falling [*déchéance*], that is "facticity." Here we find the expression of three Kierkegaardian ideas: the idea of existence as an indemonstrable position that can only be indicated; the idea of existence as dissemination, separation, ex-sistence, distance;[27] and finally the idea of falling [*chute*]. Moreover, these three ideas are already united in Kierkegaard.

---

26. [Wahl's references to the first edition of *Kant und das Problem der Metaphysik* have been changed to refer to *Kant and the Problem of Metaphysics*, 5th ed., enlarged, trans. Richard Taft (Bloomington: Indiana University Press, 1997).]

27. For Heidegger, existence stands out from a basis of nothingness [*se détache sur un fond de néant*]: *ex-sistere*. Existence is transcendence in relation to this obscure *other*. For Heidegger as for Kierkegaard, it is essentially an issuing forth, an exit, an act of detaching [*se détacher*], of rising up [*s'exhausser*], of transcending. And it is transcendence because it is finitude.

In a general way, transcendence is understood by Heidegger as an act, the act by which the subject surpasses "beings [*l'étant*]" in order to go toward being [*l'être*]. But another signification is often mixed up with this one, namely, transcendence as it is identified with being-in-the-world; thus there are, it appears, at least two conceptions of transcendence in Heidegger. More precisely, one could distinguish transcendence as an opening onto the world (a realist transcendence that characterizes *Dasein*), and transcendence as surpassing *beings* (an ontological transcendence that characterizes

But being-for-death,[28] the foundation of the historicity of the being, is going to be the point of departure for our ascent toward a higher historicity. And, indeed, the human being is characterized by this dilemma in which he lives, or rather by this dilemma that constitutes him, by this "either . . . or" that consists in the alternative between the fact of being oneself and the fact of not being oneself (cf. 12). It is essentially in two possible modes of being, the mode of authenticity and the mode of nonauthenticity, of the "They" (43, 232). After that moment of anxiety, it will be a matter of man choosing himself (42, 188, 287). Anticipatory resolution, the anticipation of death, reveals to the human being the fact that he was lost in the "They," and brings him before the possibility of being himself, himself in his impassioned freedom toward death (266), and here again we find the two ideas of the choice of oneself and of passion as Kierkegaard presented them. The "They" was the region of the negation of choice; one did not know who exactly had chosen; now, the "I" withdraws from the "They," it takes itself back into itself; it takes itself up in its responsibility; it chooses the choice (268, 287). This is what manifests itself in conscience, which is the will to take heed [*prendre conscience*] of oneself as freedom in the presence of one's culpability (288). The individual thus rejects itself, plunging back into its own individual culpability, into a state of silence and anxiety (297). Yet, at the same time, it makes the decision to reiterate itself (308). It becomes what it was. It takes its "facticity" upon itself. "As future, the human being is past; the future of man consists in being his own past."[29] The human being will be what it was (326). And on the other hand, the human being can have been only insofar as he is to come. "The past is born in a certain way from the future." Hence the human being (*Dasein*) gives its reality, its *Da*, to itself (335). This act, too, can be called reiteration, repetition of oneself [*reprise de soi*], following an expression of Kierkegaard's: "We call the fact of being one's past authentically repetition of oneself" (339). A return upon the past is produced (328), whereby the self opens itself up to itself and accepts itself; it takes over its heritage (383, 385). By this act, we are brought back from out of the state

---

Sein); the first can be deepened under the influence of the second. They are rooted, respectively, in the ecstasis (of time in relation to itself), and in existence (insofar as it stands out from the nothing).

28. Being for death, a symbol of the finitude of concrete temporality, recalls, by the expression, if not by the rather different thought, the sickness unto death of which the Gospel speaks, and which for Kierkegaard is the symbol of despair.

29. [Wahl's French translation here and in the remainder of the paragraph has been rendered into English directly.]

of dispersion, maintained in the future by anticipation, and in the past by this heritage that has been accepted consciously (cf. 390), and in the present, for we are anchored in our situation (326, 383). Like the Ibsenian heroes who celebrate the "Third Empire,"[30] and on whom the Kierkegaardian idea had certainly not been without influence, we thus acquire, not by an act of theoretical contemplation, but in an act of practical comprehension, in a total life that is destiny (309, 385), the incompleteness of our complete history, this mortal totality, mortal and that will consequently always remain partial.

Under this liberating gaze, the general rules of morality disappear (288). Kierkegaard said: the ethical is suspended.

Here, there is, as in Kierkegaard, a path that makes us pass from the theory of reiteration to the theory of the instant. "That *Present* which is held in authentic temporality and which thus is *authentic* itself, we call the '*moment of vision*' [*instant, Augenblick*]" (338; cf. 410). "S. Kierkegaard," Heidegger writes, "is probably the one who has seen the *existentiell* phenomenon of the moment of vision with the most penetration; but," he adds, "this does not signify that he has been correspondingly successful in Interpreting it existentially" (338).[31] In this instant, one is no longer drawn to the past, one no longer tends toward the future; for the past and the future have become present (386). Retrospection and anticipation blend into what Heidegger calls the past to come, the *Zukunftig Gewesenes* (391).

Man will be authentic or inauthentic depending on whether he reunites in a cluster—or even in a point—his future, his present, and his past, or whether he disperses himself. There is nothing in common between the instant of dispersion and the instant of concentration, of the repetition of oneself. "[The everyday] mode of the Present is the counter-phenomenon at the opposite extreme from the *moment of vision* [*veritable instant*]" (347). Kierkegaard had likewise opposed the aesthetic instant and the religious instant.

It is no less true that time remains composed of heterogeneous "ecstases," even if the human being, in his highest state, succeeds in uniting them. The essence of time is to be in these ecstases and to have this triple structure. Just as, for Heidegger as for Kierkegaard, existence is distance, dissemination, so, for Heidegger, is time (329). Now, Kierkegaard had

---

30. [See Henrik Ibsen, *Emperor and Galilean*, in *The Oxford Ibsen*, vol. 4, *The League of Youth; Emperor and Galilean*, ed. and trans. James Walter McFarlane and Graham Orton (London: Oxford University Press, 1963), 195–459.]

31. Heidegger adds: Kierkegaard remains attached to the ordinary concept of time and determines the instant by way of the now [*maintenant*] and eternity.

shown that subjective thought is essentially temporal, and, in a more general way, that history resists the concept. Heidegger will say: being is time.

Among the three ecstases of time—the past, present, and future—the nature of the human being will show us which has precedence. The human being, from the beginning of Heidegger's book, was described as the being for whom his being is always personally at issue [*l'être pour lequel il y va toujours personnellement de son être*].[32] In this way, an idea was translated in Heidegger's language that is analogous to Kierkegaard's idea concerning the interest of subjective thought, in opposition to the disinterest of objective thought. The human being is a person, that is to say, a being who is in relation with himself (41), who has an interest (who must have an infinite interest, said Kierkegaard) in himself, a being who cares [*se soucie*].

I cannot take such interest in myself as given, but rather in myself as possible. I am turned toward my ownmost possibility. I am, for myself, to come [*Je suis pour moi à venir*] (42). At issue for my self is always my future self (ibid.).

It is thus the future that I will sense as having precedence over the present and the past (326, 327, 329). The present temporalizes itself from the future. Kierkegaard had shown this precedence of the future in religious life. Saint Paul had opposed to this world here the eternity to come ("On the Essence of Ground," 113[33]).

We should say a few words concerning Heidegger's remarkable, albeit rather obscure, theories on truth. Taking the theses of pragmatism and

---

32. In Heidegger, this idea is linked to his ontologism (cf. Levinas, ["Martin Heidegger et l'ontologie"; see note 6 above]). The human being has a relation with being; the human being understands himself in his being; the human being is an ontological being (12, 42). For Kierkegaard, man, in the infinite interest he takes in himself, reaches the transcendent. For Heidegger, the human being is defined by the double, and unique, character of his personal care and of his connection with being. He is "an ontological person."

It would be necessary to see whether these diverse ideas—personality, freedom, possibility—should not have been examined more closely.

That would have been all the more necessary since the conception of *Dasein* is for Heidegger the fundamental conception, and since life cannot be understood except by way of *Dasein* (194, 240). It is not easy to see how this idea that life can only be understood by way of *Dasein* would be justified in a detailed fashion.

33. [Wahl's references to the first edition of *Vom Wesen des Grundes* have been changed to refer to "On the Essence of Ground," trans. William McNeill, in Heidegger, *Pathmarks*, 97–135.]

those of Dilthey and Scheler, which are akin to it, as his point of departure, Heidegger shows at the same time the subjectivist presuppositions and the objectivist presuppositions of pragmatism. By studying the idea of the tool, of the utensil, he returns on the one hand to the idea of the being who is in no way a tool, and for whose sake one uses tools, and on the other to that of the reality in the midst of which this being acts. On the one hand, the idea of *Dasein*, on the other, the idea of *In der Welt Sein*, ideas that, moreover, come to coincide. In like manner, anxiety has made *Dasein* and *In der Welt Sein* present to us in all their tragic force.

Investigating the existential traits of truth, he brings to relief the idea that it is linked to the human being as projecting hypotheses toward the future, returning toward the past, encountering objects in the present and being encountered by them. Taking pragmatism, the idealism of Marburg, and realism as his point of departure, and completing each by way of the others, Heidegger shows that, within truth, there is a structure that is determined by a union of projection and retrospection, of *not yet* and *already*, of a *not yet* that in some way concerns an *already*. It is at once present, past, and future, each implicated, imbricated, in the other. It is because truth has the very structure of care that intelligence is profoundly linked to existence; and one can take this structure as a point of departure for discovering the fundamental structure of the being [*l'être*] and the "ecstases" of time.

Heidegger arrives at the idea that truth is a characteristic of reality as it reveals itself in its authenticity. An "existential" conception will be a true conception, since it will reveal the being [*l'être*] in its authenticity. Through this union of the theory of existence and the theory of truth, Heidegger comes to the idea that it is equivalent to the theory according to which subjectivity is truth.[34] There is, however, a difference, one that is rooted in the fundamental difference between Heidegger and Kierkegaard: for Heidegger, the human being is existentially open, open to the world; what is revealed to him is not only the human being, it is the human being as he is in the world. "In our ontological clarification of the proposition that 'Dasein is in the truth' we have called attention to the primordial disclosedness of this entity as the *truth of existence*" (297).

With respect to his *Analytic of Dasein* [l'être humain], Heidegger writes that the path he followed "is one which has grown upon the author in connection with his attempts to Interpret the Augustinian (i.e., Helleno-Christian)

---

34. [In the *Études kierkegaardiennes* version, Wahl specifies that this is Kierkegaard's theory.]

anthropology with regard to the foundational principles reached in the ontology of Aristotle."³⁵ One could apply this remark to his study of truth. As we said, he no doubt takes the theories of Dilthey, Scheler, and pragmatism as his point of departure, but he is above all oriented by his reflection on ancient philosophy and on the scholastic theories of truth, on the one hand, and, on the other, by a meditation similar to that of Kierkegaard, born perhaps, like that of Kierkegaard, from the word of Christ: I am the Truth. Jesus is the Truth, says Kierkegaard; Heidegger says: truth is a trait that belongs to being [*l'être*] as it reveals itself; truth is an existential. Aristotle is interpreted in light of Jesus.

If we now return to the essentially finite character of our existence in order to see what results from this finitude as it concerns truth, we again find Kierkegaard's influence. In the world of the "They," the profound relation of being [*l'être*] to *beings* [*l'étant*]³⁶ is destroyed; openness to the world becomes closure to the world. This is the effect of falling. The fact of being in error is an essential determination of being in the world (222). As the ancient idea of the truth-revelation of being finds its guarantor in the reality of divine being, as Kierkegaard had conceived it, the transcendental *Schein* ["illusion"] of the Kantian critique (*Kant and the Problem of Metaphysics*, 172) finds its confirmation in the idea of the human being's falling, an idea that is again quite close to that of Kierkegaard.

For our finite existence, it is therefore necessary to say both that the human being is in the truth and that he is in the nontruth; that he is open and that he is at the same time closed off. Kierkegaard said: subjectivity is truth, and subjectivity is error.

One could draw from this theory of truth three postulates that appear to be essential to Heidegger's thought, namely, first, that the being [*l'être*] is in the truth—an affirmation that the human being is characterized by *Seinsverständniss* ["understanding of being"], that there is an essential connection between *Dasein* and *Sein*, that there is a pre-ontological knowledge of truth, and this is the very idea of *Erschlossenheit*, of openness to the world, and of openness to oneself; for man has a knowledge of his possibilities, and a knowledge of his guilt (59, 182, 183, 189, 200, 212, 226, 270, 272, 281; "What Is Metaphysics?," 83; "On the Essence of Ground,"

---

35. [This quotation can be found in *Sein und Zeit*, 199n.]

36. [I read *l'étant* as a rendering of *das Seiende*, usually translated as "beings." Because of Wahl's terminological imprecision, it is hard to know precisely what he means, though: the human's relation to beings? the human's relation to being? the ontological difference between being and beings?]

103³⁷); in the second place, that the human being is in the nontruth (theory of falling); and finally that, from the fact that he is in the nontruth, one can conclude that he is in the truth, that inauthenticity has a possible authenticity as its foundation (189, 259, 343). It is the third postulate that will allow Heidegger to say, for example, that the fact that a lot of men do not think of death, and do not know anything of it, does not at all prove that the human being does not have a relation with death as an essential characteristic: for this nonthought of death is in reality a flight from death; it is the translation of the thought of death into the domain of falling (251). An ontological postulate, a theological postulate (insofar as the idea of falling implies, despite everything, a theory of the Fall), finally a postulate that allows one to pass from theology to ontology, and that thus reconnects the two preceding postulates. The last two postulates could be connected to Kierkegaard's thought, pervaded as it is by the idea of the Fall and for which falling is the proof of a past grandeur, the proof of an infinity for which despair is the first moment of the rhythm of grace. And anxiety, for Heidegger as for Kierkegaard, is the very possibility of passing from error to truth.

II

With regard to one of Nietzsche's *Unfashionable Observations*, Heidegger says, "The beginning of his *Observation* allows us to suppose that he understood more than he has made known to us" (396).³⁸ It should perhaps be added that the revelations of a Nietzsche or of a Kierkegaard have a more existential character than those of Heidegger, whose reflection is often a "reflection" of Kierkegaard's ideas in a penetrating, profound thinker. Here we see one of the most striking features of contemporary German philosophy; whether it be [Karl] Barth, Heidegger, or Jaspers, we are in the presence of minds whose thought has been enriched by Kierkegaard's. Nothing is more striking than this repercussion of the secret experiences of a solitary individual, who is above all not a philosopher, on a vast movement of ideas, than these attempts to translate the result of these experiences into concepts as close as possible to the concrete.

The danger of such attempts is that the "existential concepts" are perhaps inseparable from the very experiences from which they were born. Because,

---

37. [Wahl also refers to *Kant und das Problem der Metaphysik*, 276–77, the pages of which do not exist in the first edition, the only one available at the time Wahl composed his essay. These ideas can, however, be found in part 4 of *Kant and the Problem of Metaphysics*.]

38. [Translator's modification.]

once separated, they risk losing a part of their authenticity. Without going so far as to say that they thus take on a certain aspect of *Vorhandenheit* ["presence-at-hand"],[39] one might, however, wonder whether, by being integrated into a system, a part of their value does not thereby disappear.

Heidegger certainly only takes from the religious ideas of Kierkegaard the aspects that concern human things;[40] he moves within the moral world, he pulls, so to speak, the categories of the religious down onto the moral plane. As with the instant, and the repetition of oneself.[41] But if this moral world takes on a tragic grandeur in Heidegger, if one hears in him the feverish and heavy accents that move him when he describes for us the concerned man enclosed within an inexplicably finite horizon, at the heart of humbled existence here-below, it is because subsisting there, at the implicit level, is a religious sentiment.

Do not these theological background colors come to be reflected on the first layers of that picture that Heidegger paints of our existence? Is it true that the feeling of the burden of existence is so constant in our spirit that any other thought would be a flight from this thought (134, 184)? Should we not distinguish two elements, the social and the instinctive, in what Heidegger includes within the domain of the "They"? For in the recoil at the idea of death, there is not only the social, and sometimes it is the idea of death that we make recoil before us, by a sort of courage that is instinctive, it is true, rather than us recoiling before it out of cowardice.

Moreover, is death our most personal moment? Is it not, rather, the contrary? Is there not a certain dignity in not attaching more importance to

---

39. [Heidegger draws a significant ontological distinction between *Vorhandenheit* ("presence-at-hand") and *Zuhandenheit* ("readiness-to-hand"): *Vorhandenheit* is the kind of being possessed by objects, while *Zuhandenheit* is the kind of being possessed by things available for use. Heidegger's example in *Being and Time* of the former is the hammer as an object that has a certain weight versus the latter as the hammer as a tool to strike a nail.]

40. Cf. Przywara, *Das Geheimnis Kierkegaards*, 28: "The transformation of Kierkegaard's 'angst,' which is directed (toward God) in an essentially transcendent manner, into Heidegger's 'care,' which stares into the immanent." [I have translated Przywara's German directly. Wahl's footnote is omitted in the *Études kierkegaardiennes* version.]

41. This latter concept in Kierkegaard is not in fact solely religious; it receives both its value and its obscurity from the fact that it is involved in other elements: a moral element, an aesthetic element, a desire to return to the first impression, to the primitive instant, to return, with full consciousness, to the unconsciousness of happiness, an ideal unrealizable on the aesthetic level, and even on the moral level, Kierkegaard had thought, and which can be realized only beyond them, on the religious level.

our death than to that of another? Here, objectivity, which is not necessarily that of the "They," is not without merit; and subjectivity is not flawless.

Also, how is that *Verfallen* ["deterioration"] of which Heidegger speaks explained, and can one not reply with regard to this subject what he himself said of *Fallen*, of the fall into time as Hegel conceived it: is there not something obscure here?[42]

This *Verfallen*, he will say, this falling, contains nothing of a theological belief, and even the traits that serve to describe the "They" are not at all pejorative, nor must they be conceived as deprecating a human experience that itself also has its authenticity. But it is indeed difficult to agree with Heidegger that his description of the "They" does not contain a judgment, a condemnation.[43]

One could also be led to wonder whether Heidegger's position is not particularly unstable, if it is neither a matter of transforming his philosophy into a theology nor of eliminating all theology. Perhaps one could say that, through the theory of anxiety on the one hand and through theories like the eternal return and the cult of the instant on the other, modern thought is searching, as best it can, for equivalents of religious emotion and the idea of eternity, forming for itself certain idols—*idola theatri*. And this, finally, leads one to pose the problem: what would remain of this philosophy if one were to eliminate from it all theology, every religious idea?

III

Valuable elements of this philosophy will remain, and it is this that, I believe, will appear at the end of this study, where, having attempted to eliminate what could possibly be explained by his influences, I would like to discern Heidegger's genuine contribution, and what constitutes the proper value of his thought. Taking the Kierkegaardian category of existence as a point of departure, Heidegger has established in a very powerful way the difference between the ontic and the existential [*l'existentiel*], as Mr. Levinas has shown so well. He has brought to light the feeling of *In-der-Welt-Sein* and in a way that is different from realism as one typically understands it. Finally, at least in certain passages, he has brought about the connection between those two aforementioned ideas, the connection between *In der Welt Sein* and *Dasein*. Reality will be linked to existence, will take

---

42. [Cf. *Sein und Zeit*, 435.]
43. Cf. Georges Gurvitch, *Les tendances actuelles de la philosophie allemande: E. Husserl, M. Scheler, E. Lask, M. Heidegger* (Paris: Vrin, 1930), 213, 214, 232.

place in existence, as, conversely, existence will be profoundly linked to reality.

What is *Dasein* for Heidegger? Without insisting here on the existential conception as it is turned toward the possibilities of being, one could bring to light the triple direction of the duration [*durée*] as Heidegger conceives it.

In the theory of *Care*, three of the most profound sentiments come to be united, sentiments that dominate, that direct Heidegger's thought, and that characterize the human being for him: a sentiment of a sort of essential falling that belongs to the human being, which makes him always be beneath what he was, and makes his truth be in his past; a sentiment of the tension toward the future, of actively waiting; a sentiment of the presence of the self to the universe. First of all, the human being is always behind himself, discovering himself, and not creating himself, as idealism believes; he finds himself; he is given to himself. In the second place, the human being is always ahead of himself, projecting hypotheses, anticipating possibilities, up to that extreme possibility that is the possibility of impossibility, that is to say, death; he is always in the future, hooked on what is not yet, determining himself on the basis of what will come. And these two characteristics are closely united to one another; there is a constant referencing of the future to the past and of the past to the future. The human being always projects himself ahead of himself by his intelligence; by his affective disposition, he at the same time sees himself as before something that is always already [*d'ores et déjà*];[44] and this is what characterizes the word *Befindlichkeit*;[45] it signifies our moods [*humeurs*], but our moods as they are discovered by us (cf. 149). The human being "projects himself," but as "dejected"; he sees that he is "dejected," yet "projecting himself" in this "dejection." In anticipatory resolve [*résolution anticipatrice*] (*Entschlossenheit*) as in the opening of the self to the world (*Erschlossenheit*), the past is placed in the future, here by the voluntary repetition of oneself, there by the projection of hypotheses. There is an anticipation of the past, as there is

---

44. I borrow this translation from Mr. Levinas's study. [See Levinas, "Martin Heidegger et l'ontologie," 412, passim; "Martin Heidegger and Ontology," 22, passim.]

45. We may note in this regard that the table of characteristics belonging to *Erschlossenheit* does not appear fully satisfying. Speech [*Parole*] and Falling can be put on the same level as Comprehension and Affection only with difficulty. Additionally, intelligence for Heidegger always appears to be linked to the future and to existentiality, affective disposition to the past and to facticity. Moreover, of the three moments designated by *Bei, Schon*, and *Vorweg* ["in the presence of," "already," and "beforehand" or "in advance"], it is not evident why the *Bei* (mode of the present) should necessarily occupy a subordinate position.

a retrospection of the future. Moreover, the basis of sensibility and the basis of intelligence that Heidegger draws out are never separate; quite the contrary, affective disposition is knowledge, knowledge is affective disposition (142). What there will be will be a *Not Yet* projecting itself upon an *Already* (181), the *geworfene Entwurf*, the dejected projection (179, 181, 199). We thereby see the union of existentiality and facticity (179, 181, 191, 192). In the third place, finally, the human being is encountered by things, and encounters them in that existential spatiality in which he discovers that he is real among real things.[46] Thus, taking up the expressions of the *Parmenides*,[47] one could say that the human being for Heidegger is older than himself, younger than himself, and the same age as himself.[48]

---

46. Perhaps one could conceive of Heidegger's position by way of Bergsonian philosophy. The mind is preperception, and it is ultimately a vital impulse [*élan vital*]: but it is also connected to pure perception, all the while limiting it, and it is also memory. We also find in Bergsonism—with a profundity to which it does not appear that the Heideggerians, nor Heidegger himself, do complete justice—what Heidegger calls the triple ecstase of temporality. One can see, moreover, that in the theory of the work of comprehension and invention on the one hand, in that of the work of memory on the other, Bergson shows the constant returns of the past to the future and of the future to the past, on which Heidegger insists. Finally, in Bergsonian philosophy, there is at once an affirmation of the progress of duration and a nostalgia for the primitive state, which are not lacking in analogy with certain features of Heidegger's conception.

47. Julius Stenzel, in his *Metaphysik des Altertums* (Munich: R. Oldenbourg, 1931), 135, makes this same connection.

48. Can one unite these three sentiments that Heidegger has described with such vigor? In acknowledging this triple dimension of care, the expression of the triple ecstase of time, can one come to a synthesis of the future, the present, and the past, analogous to the thought of the eternal return in Nietzsche? Like Nietzsche, Heidegger wants to find an equivalent of eternity. He wants to make eternity with time. This will be anticipatory resolve, by which, uniting what has come to the future, the human being will collect himself before the present. And the idea of destiny as Heidegger conceives it is not very far from the Nietzschean love of fate. There is, however, a triple difference between Nietzsche's theory and Heidegger's, a difference that is maintained at the place in Heidegger occupied by the thought of death, of the finitude of time, and of the preeminence of the future.

We should ask ourselves whether the theory of anticipatory resolve does not involve a flight from time, if, in wanting to see himself as a complete totality, if, in making of birth and death not determinate events but, in a way, constant features of his being (through a theory of continuous creation and destruction), the human being does not seek to eliminate that very time that Heidegger had appeared to want to make his essence. Thus *In der Welt Sein* is brought back to time and time is itself seen to be concentrated in the instant. And does one not see space and time, whose existential character Heidegger so vigorously brought to light before, at risk of disappearing?

No moment of time is closed in on itself, and the third moment, the present, opens onto the world. The human being is there, he is here and there—he is open to the world by affective disposition, by that primitive science of possibilities that is intelligence. There is a "multiple location," to take up Whitehead's expression. Consciousness is always already [*toujours d'ores et déjà*] outside, at once outside and inside, itself being in the world and the world in it (62). Consciousness is always destruction of remoteness, approaching, moreover, a mysterious coincidence. What is here is what is there, says Whitehead. I am at point 0 when I see point 0, says Bergson. It is a similar idea that Heidegger expresses in one of the two aspects of his conception of *Dasein*.

We thus witness throughout Heidegger's work a constant coming and going between being and consciousness. Heidegger searches for what being is; he will be able to know it only in considering consciousness; but consciousness itself exists only insofar as it is in the world. There will be truth of the world only because there is consciousness; and consciousness will always be a relation with being, a comprehension of being. Here there is a circle, an essential circularity in the constitution of being and of consciousness.

According to the very words of Heidegger, this "existential solipsism,"[49] far from transporting an isolated subject into the vacuum of a worldless event, instead, with an extreme acuity, places it before its world as world and thereby before itself as it itself is.[50] It is because we do not ordinarily exist in a quite intense, quite profound way that we pose the problem of the existence of the world, separating it from ourselves and making it an object. We dislocate a real relation in which the two terms are given to one

---

49. [*Sein und Zeit*, 188.]

50. One sees how a rapprochement between Heidegger and Hegel could be sketched, in spite of their oppositions. The existential conception of truth can be connected with certain expressions of Hegel's. The repetition of oneself can be conceived as a synthesis of the past and the future in the instant that absorbs them (cf. Gurvitch, *Les tendances actuelles de la philosophie allemande*, 222). Hegel has laid out a conception of Christianity as a religion of subjectivity, and conversely he has made us feel the fusion of spirit and things in an objectivity that is full of content; one can say that Heidegger carries to the highest level both the feeling of subjectivity and the sense of objectivity, showing our fundamental participation in the world and at the same time our absolute isolation. It is necessary to add that Heidegger does not see this subject-object unity, as Hegel does, with the preeminence of the objective aspect but, rather, with the preeminence of the subjective aspect. It is also necessary to add that the existential point of view for Heidegger remains completely opposed to the Hegelian point of view; for it is above all a consideration of possible lived experience.

another, and then we face all the possible difficulties of bringing them back together, which can only be artificial. And we should find at the origin of the problem of truth the same sort of doubling that we find at the origin of the problem of reality. We have separated ourselves from our environment; we have separated ourselves from the object of our judgments. There is an intellectual doubling, similar to that sensible doubling that occurs when we press a finger against our eyelid, making a phantom of the object jut out alongside the object itself. For Heidegger, it will therefore not be a matter of demonstrating that there is an external world that is presented to us, and that the judgments made about it are true, but a matter of showing how the human being has a tendency, on account of his falling, to bury being into nothingness through a theory of knowledge in order then to rediscover it. "The reason for this lies in Dasein's falling and in the way in which the primary understanding of Being has been diverted to Being as presence-at-hand [*un être donné comme présentation*]" (206). The theory of knowledge and the problem of knowledge are formulations that are explained by the fall into the world of the everyday. The error of all theories of knowledge is to consider knowledge of the world as a primary mode of being-in-the-world and to conceive of this knowledge only under the mode of the subject-object doubling. One thereby prevents oneself from attaining knowledge not only of the world, but also of knowledge itself (99, 100); for it is a mode of human being that is derived from being-in-the-world (63); it is not knowledge that explains being-in-the-world, but being-in-the-world that explains knowledge. The foundation of philosophy is no longer the *cogito ergo sum*; it is the *sum cogitans*. I am in the world and, being in the world, I send forth possibilities, I have certain standpoints [*attitudes*] regarding possibilities; I am thinking.

The separation between us and the world, between our judgments and their objects, this double problem of truth and of reality, comes from the fact that we leave the authentic world for the inauthentic world. If we are authentic, we open ourselves up to ourselves and the external world opens itself up to us; we are in the real and we are true. With its pharisaic character of self-contentment and contempt for the real, epistemology is a characteristic product of our falling. Our authentic self is ontological.

"It is not that the proofs are inadequate, but that the kind of Being of the entity which does the proving and makes requests for proofs has *not been made definite enough*" (205). The error of philosophy up to now lies not in having asked too much, but in not having taken in enough (315–16), in being enclosed in the *I Think*, in not having seen that the *I Think* is *openness*, and that one cannot therefore enclose oneself therein, that the *I Think* thinks something and what it thinks is the world (321). One thus separates the being and the world, and one calls into question the existence of the world, while the term that is put in question essentially refuses to be separated from the one who questions, and it repels every question (132, 205, 206).

The *In* of *In der Welt Sein* is indeed completely different from the spatial *In* (132). Heidegger insists on the fact that his theory is profoundly distinct from realism: realism thinks that there is a desirable and possible demonstration of the existence of the external world; and above all, it represents this relation of the self and of the world as a relation that takes place between two givens (207). But the world and the self are no more the "thingly realities [*réalités chosales*]" of realism than the self is the ideal subject of idealism. The realist, like the idealist, moves within the world of the "They," in which things are parceled out and leveled out, spread out on the level of presentation. *In der Welt Sein* is an existential [*existentiel*]; it is that with regard to which the human being's being is at issue for it [*il est ce au sujet de quoi il y va pour l'être humain de son être*] (143, 153; "On the Essence of Ground," 121–24); the world is an object of care and not a mode of thought; it is a world of obstacles and tools, and more profoundly still a world that is existentially [*existentiellement*] lived. Conversely, *Dasein* is always *In der Welt Sein*. Anxiety itself is the encounter between *Dasein* as it is being-in-the-world and being-in-the-world as it presents itself to *Dasein*. Anxiety becomes a revelation of being-in-the-world (188). The existential subject and the existential object are therefore not at all concepts, are neither subjective nor objective ("On the Essence of Ground," 122); the world is neither present in a subject nor present among objects; it is more objective than any possible object (366), more subjective than any subject, more objective than any object (419; cf. Siegfried Marck, *Dialektik in der Philosophie der Gegenwart*, vol. 1 [Tübingen: J. C. B. Mohr, 1929], 161), just as Plato's Ideas are more subjective than the subjects, more objective than the objects ("On the Essence of Ground," 124–25). Idealism presents to us an empty subject, realism a thing among things; we find ourselves beyond the one and the other.[51]

---

51. One could wonder whether there is not at times in Heidegger a union, which is not entirely justified, between what one can call his realism and his ontology; from our relation to the world, Heidegger concludes our relation with being (5; "What Is Metaphysics?," 8), transposing his existential experience into a scholastic language and thus introducing his postulate according to which we are in the truth. Dogmatism and scholasticism thereby risk being introduced into his theory. Heidegger himself has, in any event, noted the difference that separates ontology and realism ("On the Essence of Ground," 368n17), but he does so above all to exclude realism from ontology, while it

There can be no metaphysical knowledge that is based on the representation of the everyday world; we could say that the intellectual world is a world forged by everyday praxis, and that the world of metaphysical theory will have to be the profoundly practical world that we rediscover beyond the intellectual world.

With much precision and force, Mr. [Raymond] Ruyer recently laid out a theory of the real that only allows for physics. Yet even if one agrees with him in placing emphasis on the physical presence of man, is it not necessary to say that, at the moment in which consciousness appears, the reality of relations that are no longer juxtapositions appears, enveloping relations appear, the world appears (cf. 64)? There is nothing that is entirely juxtaposition, from which the human being appears. And one could even say: there is nothing that is entirely juxtaposition, from which there are things.[52]

Heidegger brings us to the idea, to the feeling of an existential *Inside*, which is no more a relation of material inclusion than it is juxtaposition; it is, rather, an envelopment of a consciousness by an atmosphere, familiarity, confidence, communion of the being with what surrounds it. The world ceases to be the world of common sense in order to become again this envelopment of ourselves in what surpasses us, this rootedness in a nourishing earth, this plunge into a palpitating air; it again becomes the foundation

---

would perhaps be necessary also to exclude ontology from realism, at least if ontology is an affirmation of the idea of being that is understood in an abstract way.

Let us recall, at the end of this study, the different difficulties that we have encountered in Heidegger's philosophy along the way: the three postulates, pp. 120–21; the need for an analysis of the ideas of personality, freedom, and possibility, p. 118; the underlying theological conceptions, pp. 121–23; the place accorded to anxiety, to the theory of death, and to divertissement, pp. 121–22; the obscure points in the table of human functions, p. 124n45; the reduction of spatiality to temporality and the flight from time, pp. 109n7 and 125n46; the place of the idea of being, pp. 127–28.

[In the *Études kierkegaardiennes* version of this note, Wahl adds the following paragraph: "Cf., against the value accorded to anxiety, Nicolai Hartmann, *Zur Grundlegung der Ontologie* (Berlin: Walter de Gruyter, 1935), 197: 'making a big deal out of one's own existence [*Dasein*] is always already an uprooting. . . . To the extent that it is not vital resistance to dissolution, all anxiety about death is a supposed, self-made torment. . . . It is precisely anxiety that is the worst imaginable guide to the genuine and authentic.'" (I have translated Hartmann's German directly.)]

52. The recent article of M. Ruyer, in the *Revue de Métaphysique et de Morale* (October–December 1932) [Raymond Ruyer, "Sur une illusion dans les théories philosophiques de l'étendue," *Revue de Métaphysique et de Morale* 39, no. 4 (October–December 1932): 521–27] shows that, without accepting the lines that precede and follow it, he would gladly admit this negation of juxtaposition. And his quite striking theory certainly escapes the objection that I have attempted to make to it.

of all community (cf. 54, 55; "On the Essence of Ground," 112). We are in a world that is social, spatial, affective, intellectual (in the particular sense in which it is now necessary to conceive of intelligence), colored, shimmering (cf. 138), quite different from the pure visual and theoretical world of intelligence, a world in which there are objects—for, as words and sounds present themselves to the mind when it is faced with their elements, so do things in their depth and their immediacy—a world in which there are secondary qualities, and even tertiary qualities like the threatening and the beneficent. The revelation of the world will occur, above all, by affective dispositions.

It is there that we encounter existential space, which makes possible this opening to the world, a fundamental phenomenon of knowledge. The human being is never "just present-at-hand" in space. "To be able to say that Dasein is present-at-hand at a position in space, we must first *take* [*auffassen*] this entity in a way which is ontologically inappropriate." It extends itself in space; it reaches over it; it "is" not there (368). And if we attempt to lodge it in space, this is on account of the fallen, falling character of our intelligence (369). The time in which we move primordially is no more a homogenous time than this space is a homogenous space; this primordial time is "the time to" do something or other; and this fullness of its determinations has its measure in the force of the sun, which occupies different places in the existential space of which we have spoken.

It will therefore be necessary to rediscover the primary, authentic relations with being (168, 170), to return from quotidian being-in-the-world to being in the existential world, from the fallen, inauthentic, false being-in-the-world to the being-in-the-world that is authenticity and truth.

The more the human being sees himself in his existence, the more he will see his union with the reality of the world;[53] he will live his being-in-

---

53. In Jaspers's work, one finds an effort that is analogous in this regard to Heidegger's. Karl Jaspers, *Philosophie*, 3 vols. (Berlin: Springer, 1932), 2:422. Objectivity and subjectivity are the milieu in which is explained for me what, as existence, turns toward me, as existence (3:94). Exceeding what pertains to me, I am all the more linked with the other, since the core of my existence appropriates the fact that I am there. The more profoundly I embed myself, the more I feel I have solidarity with what is initially foreign to me (94 [Wahl has "138"]). When existence makes sure of its relation with transcendence, it finds it only in unity with the world (180). It is the fact of being oneself in the most decisive manner that is the root of our most pure love for nature. . . . Nature presents itself in its most proper core for our most proper core. (See also 1:27, on the opening of the self to the world; 2:48, 135, 145, 195, on the tension between my independence and my relation with the world; 1:82, on the inauthentic world and the authentic world.)

the-world instead of putting it in question. To the acuity of consciousness there will correspond the density of the representation—if the word[54] "representation" can still be applicable—that he will have of the world, or rather the density with which the world will present itself to him.[55] In the existential light, the pseudo-problems are destroyed, the individual and the world appear in full relief, the one becoming deeper, the other thicker.[56] The world is present to him because he is present to himself.

Translated by Ian Alexander Moore

54. [Reading *mot* (as in the *Études kierkegaardiennes* version) instead of *monde* (world).]

55. M. Ruyer likewise insists on the connection between idealism and the idea of the generality, realism, and affirmation of the individuality of all thought (*Revue de Synthèse*, 1932, 84.) [Wahl writes the wrong date. See Raymond Ruyer, "Le problème de la personnalité et la physique moderne," *Revue de Synthèse* (October 1931): 67–87.]

56. The empirico-critical philosophers and the neo-realists have attempted to establish an identity between the subjective and the objective in the domain of intellectual knowledge, and have founded their theory on the ideas of the exteriority of relations and of the sterility of consciousness. They affirm the immanence of the independent and arrive at what one has called a pan-objectivism. Heidegger's philosophy, founded rather on the interiority of relations or more exactly perhaps on the inadequation of all relational schema and on the impossibility of separating consciousness and things, makes us see at a more profound level the coincidence of subjectivism and objectivism, affirms the transcendence of the immanent, and presents a sort of pan-subjectivism.

6

The Problem of Choice
Existence and Transcendence in Jaspers's Philosophy

One of the reasons Alexandre Koyré, Henri-Charles Puech, and Albert Spaier founded the journal *Recherches Philosophiques* in 1931 was because, at the time, more established journals like the *Revue de Métaphysique et de Morale* were reluctant to publish articles characteristic of what Jean Wahl aptly named, in the lead article of the inaugural issue of *Recherches Philosophiques*, the turn "toward the concrete." It accordingly gave aspiring philosophers the opportunity to discuss and advance movements such as phenomenology and the philosophy of existence.[1] While Wahl did publish extensively in *Recherches Philosophiques* (see Chapters 2 and 5 in this volume), he was also able to introduce contemporary figures and ideas to the readers of *Revue de Métaphysique et de Morale*. Following his debut article on Hegel in the journal in 1927 (see Chapter 3 in this volume) and a review essay of Gabriel Marcel's *Metaphysical Journal* in 1930,[2] Wahl's next piece would

---

"Le problème du choix: L'existence et la transcendance dans la philosophie de Jaspers," *Revue de Métaphysique et de Morale* 41, no. 3 (July 1934): 405–44; republished in Jean Wahl, *Études kierkegaardiennes* (Paris: Fernand Aubier, 1938), 510–52.

1. Olivier Argard, "Die Resonanz der deutschen zeitgenössischen Philosophie in den französischen philosophischen Fachzeitschriften zwischen 1933 und 1945," in *Philosophie und Zeitgeist im Nationalsozialismus*, ed. Marion Heinz and Goran Gretić (Würzburg: Königshausen und Neumann, 2006), 29–32; Stefanos Geroulanos, *An Atheism That Is Not Humanist Emerges in French Thought* (Stanford, Calif.: Stanford University Press, 2010), 53–55.

2. Jean Wahl, "Le Journal Métaphysique de Gabriel Marcel," *Revue de Métaphysique et de Morale* 37, no. 1 (January–March 1930): 75–112. Republished and expanded as the final chapter of Wahl's *Vers le concret*.

be the very first devoted to Karl Jaspers in the journal's pages,[3] a piece that, incidentally, draws heavily on an article Marcel had published the year before in the second issue of *Recherches Philosophiques*.

What is most striking is just how personal and confessional—one might even say existential—Wahl's article is. In an essay concerned with the problem of choice in Jaspers, Wahl begins by acknowledging that the themes he will be discussing from Jaspers's three-volume *Philosophie* (1932) are those that impressed him most. He has *chosen* to discuss what matters to him, not what may be of the most universal applicability or of the greatest interest. And what matters to him, in his reading of Jaspers, is seeing existence from the perspective of a world rent asunder, against an obscure, heterogeneous background that is intensely felt but cannot be known. Wahl speaks of failure, of the "collapse of logic" and the need for paradox and contradiction, of the limited, fragmented, and tragic character of existence. And yet, despite this deliberately chosen horizon, Wahl has hit upon a new horizon for philosophy, one quite at odds with the idealist and rationalist strands of the contemporaneous French academy. "One could say," writes Wahl, "that Jaspers's reflection is situated in a place where some of the most eternal and most real philosophical problems are located, although not all philosophers have been aware of them."

In a line that will be echoed a few years later in "Subjectivity and Transcendence" (see Chapter 7 in this volume), Wahl writes that Pascal, Nietzsche, and Kierkegaard "appear, if this word can still be used, far more existential than does a philosopher of existence." A general philosophy of existence, however antisystematic, however existential its original intuition may be, marks the negation of a necessarily narrow, yet no less significant, existential thought. "Perhaps," Wahl continues, "existence does not let itself be seen by the glow of the lamp of love or by the glow of the lamp of the intellect, but only by the flash of a thought similar to the existential thought of Kierkegaard, Nietzsche, and some poets." Does this mean we should dispense with Jaspers, then, and head straight for the source? Were this so, then we would have all the more reason to dispense with Wahl's own commentary on Jaspers, as Wahl himself suggests in his provocative conclusion. And yet, we might ourselves conclude that as Wahl's commentary helps us to appreciate Jaspers, so do Jaspers and Wahl help us to appreciate existential thought.

Ian Alexander Moore

---

3. According to a search of the journal's pages on Jstor.org, prior to Wahl's article, Jaspers does not appear to have been mentioned at all in *Revue de Métaphysique et de Morale*.

Jaspers's philosophy is both the negation of every system and the affirmation that a system is necessary for the intensity of the life of the mind.[4] It is constructed out of two propositions that oppose one another (at the same time, as we will see, the first proposition will be the basis for the second one). Like the world that it describes, it is essentially a philosophy torn apart. It is an appeal for the consideration of existence, but also an affirmation that this existence is only possible through an unknown transcendence. Twice, but in different ways, it is a sort of self-negation. Existence is only possible through the objectivity that it negates and through the transcendence that negates it, in turn; it takes place between these two negations and its value is derived from this place.

This philosophy, as I will present it here, will be first and foremost a reflection on choice and a reflection on transcendence. There are certainly many other things to say about this philosophy and many other essential points; but it seems justifiable to me precisely to *choose* what was the most striking to me and to deliberately leave in the shadows some elements of the universe, or of the multiverse constituted by this philosophy, that could be of equal or even greater value for others.

I. The World Torn Apart

In the *Philebus*, Plato showed that the idea of the Good can only be grasped through various forms and that it is refracted into an irreducible plurality of ideas (though these ideas are harmonious). Aristotle insisted on the fact that being can be said in many ways (though these ways are analogous). Jaspers says that "if I think of a being, it will always be a distinct being but not being" (1:19/59; cf. 3:2/4). Being as a unity is reduced to the empty definition of the copula, which is an ambiguous and indeterminate mode of expression (3:2/4). But these are only very general claims. More precisely, Jaspers says that being is either being as an object, being as myself, or being in itself. "None of them is absolutely being, none of them can do without

---

4. [Wahl cites references from Karl Jaspers, *Philosophie*, 3 vols. (Berlin: Springer, 1932); his references will appear in parentheses in the body of the text followed by the page reference to the English translation: Karl Jaspers, *Philosophy*, 3 vols., trans. E. B. Ashton (Chicago: University of Chicago Press, 1969, 1970, 1971). When only one page reference appears, this is Wahl's reference to the German text, as the corresponding passage in the English text has not been located. In our translation, we provide an English translation of Wahl's French translation of Jaspers's German, which will often differ significantly from the published English translation of Jaspers's *Philosophy*.]

the other; each of them is a being within being" (l:6/48).⁵ But, he adds, we cannot find the totality of being. It is neither a common feature nor an origin of all these beings. They repel and attract one another without allowing us to contain them in a genus.

Moreover, each of these worlds is itself torn apart; it can only be seen from partial and discontinuous perspectives; neither the scientific world (1:19/59, 276/280), nor the world of values, can be unified. The scientific world is visible only in isolated fragments (1:19/59, 276/280). The world of values, or the conceptions of the world that become existences, is multiple. "The breaking up of authenticity in religious faith and philosophical faith, and of these in turn, into a multiplicity of beliefs that are on both sides, is our situation here below" (l:316/314–15). As for the world of existences, which is the basis of the two other worlds, it is irreducibly heterogeneous to itself: "If I obtain a growing assurance of existence, it is always of my own existence and of those with whom I communicate. We are each time irreplaceable and not a mere example of a genus of existence" (1:19/59).⁶ "The word or the idea of existence is only a sign indicating to us from which side it is necessary to seek this growing personal assurance in a being that is objectively neither conceivable nor verifiable" (1:19/59–60; cf. 26/66).

There is thus no generality of being: "Being is not closed in on itself as an object" (2:109/96, cf. 124/108–9). It is not an object of thought, a system or a spectacle (2:19/18–19, 1:276/280⁷). There is no system of existence (1:276/280).⁸ There is no human in general nor divinity in general (1:316/314–15). The unique God cannot become an objective transcendence for all (3:118/104, 123/108–9). The metaphysical content cannot

---

5. Here one might recall Émile Boutroux's philosophy of contingency.

6. Cf. Gabriel Marcel, *Journal Métaphysique* [(Paris: Gallimard, 1927)], 42, 64, 98. [English translation: *Metaphysical Journal*, trans. Bernard Wall (Chicago: Henry Regnery, 1952), 41–42, 63–64, 98–99; Wahl also refers to p. 418 of the French, which does not exist and has therefore been deleted.] I have tried, in these notes, to indicate points where Marcel's attempt connects with that of Jaspers. (I have also noted the connections between Jaspers and Kierkegaard that can be explained by a direct influence.) Marcel had a sense of these connections. See his article, "Situation fondamentale et situations limites chez Karl Jaspers," *Recherches Philosophiques* 2 (1932/33): 322, 326. [English translation: "The Fundamental and Ultimate Situation in Karl Jaspers," in Gabriel Marcel, *Creative Fidelity*, trans. Robert Rosthal, preface by Merold Westphal (New York: Fordham University Press, 2002), 227–28, 231. Unless otherwise noted, all of Wahl's subsequent references to Marcel will be to this article in *Recherches Philosophiques*. Page numbers to the French will be given first, followed by a slash, and then to the English translation.]

7. [Here Wahl appears to mistakenly reference 2:206.]

8. Cf. similar formulations in Kierkegaard.

be understood as an a-temporal acquisition that would happen to emerge here or there. It is not an object of knowledge, for transcendence is not universal but is always a transcendence for an existence (3:22/21). The more the world is seen truly, the more it is seen in a way that is torn apart (2:253/221). What Jaspers highlights first is the essential tearing apart of the world.[9]

But this word, this idea of being torn apart, perhaps oversimplifies the situation. If I study the relations between being in itself and being in myself, I see that the relation between these worlds is ambiguous: the world will sometimes appear as something given to me and sometimes as something made by me. "If it were entirely one or the other, it would no longer be a world" (1:77/113). It is characterized by these two ways of seeing it, by the duality of the interpretations that I can always give to it.

But this is not yet everything. At the same time as there is a rift in these different aspects of reality, there is—as difficult as this statement may be to accept, if one accepts the previous one—an encroachment of each one onto the other. Nowhere is this more clearly shown than in the work of a great artist, an existential[10] artist: the great artistic genius will seek something other than conformity to the laws of aesthetics (1:260/267). What occurs in art can be seen everywhere else; and this explains why, within each sphere, there is a struggle between content and form, and content constantly strives to break through the form. There is thus a struggle between philosophy and the form of the system; it always stands outside of the system and breaks it (1:271/276). And it is precisely because Hegel's philosophy gives us the feeling of a complete triumph over the deficiencies of experience that it is able to satisfy us (1:276/280).[11] Thus, philosophy is in a permanent state of tension, just like art and all the other great human activities.

---

9. Cf. Marcel, 344/249–50, 347/252–53. [Following the footnote indicator, Wahl added the following to the version of the essay that appeared in *Études kierkegaardiennes*: "One will encounter failure everywhere; from what is thought, one cannot deduce the thought; from the individual, one will not be able to deduce the whole; from reason, one will not be able to deduce the irrational, and the inverse operations will not be possible either."]

10. [Here and in what follows, "existential" is a translation of the French *existentiel*.]

11. On the contrast between Jaspers and Hegel, see some indications in my talk to the Congrès hégélien de Rome on Hegel and Kierkegaard (1934). [See Chapter 4 in this volume.]

II. Existence and the Problem of Choice

If what we have said about the irreducibility and encroachment of these spheres is true, the question of being will thus remain unanswered—unless it receives an existential answer based on the plenitude of existence (3:37/33–34).[12] The negations to which we have been reduced will lead to an affirmation: the absence of any rational solution, the absence of any solution using simple knowledge will allow and require the activity of my freedom (3:78/69–70). Existence and, in Jaspers's sense of the term, communication are only possible because there is something other than objects.[13] "If there were nothing indeterminate, there would be no existence for me" (2:123/108). "I must will because I do not know; not knowing is the origin of having to will" (2:191/167). The same holds for communication: "There is communication only when there is no refuge in, recourse to impersonal objectivities, such as the authority of a state or a church, of an objective metaphysics, of a definitive moral order, or of an ontological knowledge" (2:106/94).[14] To make room for belief, it is necessary to destroy knowledge.

Existence will be the real act of breaking through given reality (2:8/9). I must therefore start from existence, that is, from my own existence. "Without doing so, thought and life are lost in what is endless and non-essential" (1:25/66). "The elusive assurance of the unconditionality of the existent is what gives substance and plenitude" (1:25/66). This nonobjectifiable part of us is the center of our being.[15]

Clearly, there can be no objective or complete idea concerning this realm of existence and communication. "The circle of existential experience can never become a totality. The thought of a realm of existences, like that of a totality of which I would be a member, lacks any basis as a distinct thought" (2:420/364). Similarly, the differences between existences are not conceivable by thought, properly speaking: in order for that to be possible, it would be necessary for an existence to detach from itself (2:422/366). Thus a philosophy of existences cannot be developed in the form of a monadology. "A monadology that would seek to constitute a knowledge of being in its many

---

12. As Georges Gurvitch has pointed out, the word "existence," which Heidegger and Jaspers borrowed from the philosophy of Kierkegaard, seemed particularly useful to them to avoid the appearance of subjectivism with regard to words such as "consciousness" and "subject." It refers, for that matter, to a completely different conception.

13. Cf. Marcel, *Metaphysical Journal*, and "The Fundamental and the Ultimate Situation in Karl Jaspers."

14. [The text incorrectly cites 2:166.]

15. Marcel, *Journal Métaphysique/Metaphysical Journal*, 147/147–48, 278/287.

forms would conflate consciousness in general and existence" (2:432/374). Existences are never visible from an external point of view (1:276/280).

But we must go further. Can existence, properly speaking, even be thought philosophically? Philosophy can only be applied to past existence or to future existence; it never applies to existence in the present. "Philosophy always arrives late, in order for a reality, which is no longer, to be able to know itself and to keep itself in being through memory. Hegel compares it to the owl of Minerva which takes flight at dusk. Nietzsche calls it the spark that will light new fires" (1:268/274). Philosophy is either too late or too early, either beyond or behind (2:423/367).

My understanding cannot know this eternal instant of my existence. "It can only be illuminated in the instant and then in a memory full of doubt. I never own it like an external possession" (1:17/57–58).[16]

Existence is thus ungraspable because there is always a separation, a distance between existential reality and thought (1:47/84–85). The proposition "I am an existence" has no meaning because the being of existence is not an objective category under which I can be classified. Existence is what I am, not something that I can see or know (2:16/16, 22/21). I will only ever see aspects of myself, not my self itself (2:17/17).[17]

Existence will be a perpetual dialectic, in the Kierkegaardian sense of the term.[18] It will be the transition from one thought to the next.[19] There is thus not one attitude toward death that can be called the right one, for example. Rather, my attitude toward it changes by successive leaps, each of which marks a stage in my life: "Death changes with me" (2:229/201). I can never have a full or complete view of the *Weltanschauung* in which I stand

---

16. See our later remarks on the evanescent character of transcendence.

17. In order to satisfy the desire of those who would like a definition of existence and who would ask us to make a distinction, for instance, between existence and the consciousness of existence, this could bring us to propose a definition like this: existence is consciousness of existence inasmuch as it refuses consciousness. [Wahl added the following paragraph to the body of the text here in the version that appeared in *Études kierkegaardiennes*: "Thus, as a set of determinations, as universal thought (logically expressible), as spirit (expressible as a totality), there is something deeper behind ourselves, which is existence. Here it is no longer a question of universality or of totality but of authenticity and uniqueness. It is no longer a question of intelligibility but of unintelligibility, of a thinking unintelligibility. There is always in the one who is thinking something that goes beyond what one thinks."]

18. Marcel, 344/249–50.

19. [Wahl added the following two sentences here in the version that appeared in *Études kierkegaardiennes*: "It is in this sense that it is tied to reason. Existence seeks to understand itself but never understands itself completely."]

(2:242/211–12). "Everything that we have achieved is dead; nothing that we have finished can live. As a spectacle for others, a life can have the character of something absolute, but in itself, as real, it cannot have that character" (2:228/200). For existence will always be a continual movement [*élan*]; "being in movement is one of the essential characteristics of existence" (3:125).[20]

It will thus be an achievement, but it is an achievement that must never destroy the elements over which it triumphs. One who hopes must keep despair in oneself, in a way that dominates but does not destroy it. To forget this despair would be as bad as getting taken over by it (2:227/199).

Existence is thus directed toward transcendence in constantly antinomic relationships, in defiance and abandonment, rise and fall, the law of the day and the passion of the night (3:120/106). I constantly pass from one of these contraries to the other.

Moreover, existential consciousness will always be in an antinomic tension with itself. There will thus be a tension between subjectivity and objectivity (1:47/84, 57/93; 3:71/63), not in a union between the two, but in the passage from the one to the other. Existence cannot be fulfilled in the one or in the other; this would destroy it (2:348/306); it seeks its path through each one in turn; it must always go from one extreme to the other extreme and vice versa (2:337/295). And the objective and the subjective will never coincide perfectly. There will always be an inadequation between them, arising from a primitive break. Likewise, one would like to imagine a synthesis of the world of the day and the world of the night. The world of the day is a world of virile chosen tasks, while the world of night is one of passionate sacrifice; but this synthesis cannot be accomplished in any existence; each of these two worlds is unconditional; a synthesis of the two could not occur without betraying them both (3:113/99–100).[21]

The existent lives in a constant antinomy because it must relativize everything that appears and yet be identical with one of these appearances whose relativity is known (2:124/109). It thus knows itself both as absolute and as relative, and the tension between the consciousness of the self as absolute and the consciousness of the self as relative is what Jaspers calls the historical character of being (*Geschichtlichkeit*; 2:122/107). It is here that what I have called the problem of choice arises. One cannot accept any point of view as valid objectively, and yet one always has to hold on to some

---

20. On the deep relations between the idea of the possible and the idea of existence in Jaspers, see Marcel, 321/226–27.
21. Cf. Marcel, 345/250–51. I only have access to myself in the limit-situations of antinomies.

point of view (2:124/109). Objectively, everything is relative; existentially, I am in the absolute (2:419/364).

In historical consciousness, I am aware both of the passage of time as appearance and of eternal being; I am aware of both in one; eternity is absolutely related to this instant (2:126/110). Inasmuch as I act in time in an unconditional way or love in an unconditional way, eternity is in time. What is evanescent in the instant is yet eternal, and that is existence (1:17/58).[22]

Another way to formulate this fact that I am always in a union between the eternal and circumstances is to say that I find myself always in a *situation*.[23] I can never get out of one situation without entering into another one (2:203/178). I will not dwell here on the general theory of situations. What I want to note is that I can never be fully conscious of my situation. This idea is related to the elusiveness of existence, and to another idea of Jaspers, according to which there can only be true clarity if this clarity stands out against an obscure background. One's awareness of the rules changes both the situation and these rules. The fact that I am in situations is thus not a fact that I can consider from the outside; it is in no way an object of sight (2:203/178, 206/181).

By the fact that I exist, I am bound to circumstances; I do things that are foreign to my own substance; the heterogeneous is tied to me in an indissoluble way (3:47/42). These things are given to me through my place within the historical current of the real. This gives rise, for example, to the deep relationship between a given thinker's vision of the world and the history of different visions of the world, the relationship between philosophy and the history of philosophy. What I am, I am in an intimate union with what historically awakens me to existence.[24] I am something that only happens once (1:283/286). My character as a historical being derives precisely from the thought of this whole in which I have a place and from the thought of this One that I am. Does the whole have any other means of expression than to unite with all the different "ones"? (1:283/286)

But, alongside these changing situations that pass into one another, there exist also other situations. There exist fundamental situations (for the time being, this is how we will translate the word *Grenzsituation*, or limit-

---

22. See Marcel, 325/230. Cf. Kierkegaard's theory of the instant.
23. On the theory of situations and their inexhaustible character, see Marcel, 317/222–23, 330/235, 332/237–38.
24. Cf. Kierkegaard, *Journal*, July 4, 1840: "On the unity of the contingent and the eternal." [See Søren Kierkegaard, *Papers and Journals: A Selection*, trans. Alastair Hannay (New York: Penguin, 1996), 126–27.]

situation), which are inescapable.²⁵ "Situations like these—'I am always in situations, I cannot live without struggle and pain, I cannot avoid sin, I must die'—these are what I call limit-situations. They are like a wall we run into, a reef that we get trapped in. We cannot change them but only bring them into greater clarity, without explaining them or deducing them from something else. They are one with *Dasein* itself" (2:203/178).

These situations, more than any others, go beyond any objective insight, and this is what Jaspers meant by saying that they are not situations for consciousness in general (2:203/178–79). We can only feel them and immerse ourselves in them. "We react to limit-situations, therefore, not by following the plan of a calculated activity, thanks to which one would be able to overcome them, but by a radically different kind of activity. We become ourselves by entering into limit-situations with open eyes" (2:204/179). The feeling of limit-situations is thus linked to the feeling of existence.²⁶ To experience limit-situations and to exist are one and the same thing. As we shall see, to exist is to commit the sin of limitation, and to have the feeling of helplessness (2:204/179).²⁷

Through these given situations, we can become aware of our freedom. Without doubt, here again, we are outside of the domain of the objective: freedom exists only for freedom; because it alone can raise questions about the subject of freedom, and the fact that it questions its own existence gives us an answer to the subject of this existence (2:176/154–55).

There is freedom because I have to choose: freedom is the choice that comes from what could be called the narrowness of existence. I cannot pay attention to everything, nor expect everything, but I have to act (2:180/158, 185/162).²⁸ As Marcel says in his article on Jaspers, there are radical options.²⁹

---

25. On Jaspers's theory of limit-situations, see the beautiful pages by Marcel, 336–44/241–50.

26. [Wahl added the following paragraph here in the version that appeared in *Études kierkegaardiennes*: "But how would we know that we have truly entered into this domain of existence and of transcendence? In reality, we cannot know it; we can only be entered into it. There is a struggle here between knowing and being, and it is no longer a question of knowing but of being."]

27. Cf. the role of the idea of sin in the Kierkegaardian feeling of existence. On the relation between limit-situations and existence, see Marcel, 331/236.

28. [Wahl added the following footnote here in the version that appeared in *Études kierkegaardiennes*: "Cf. Karl Jaspers, *Psychologie der Weltanschauungen* (Berlin: Julius Springer, 1919), 278–80: to decide, to act is to limit oneself." The corresponding pagination of the more widely available second edition (1922) and its unchanged successors is 315–17.]

29. Marcel, 320/225–26.

The question that I would have to ask myself would therefore be: How should I be in order to be myself? or, as Jaspers says: What is it that unifies me? Where is the One to be found for me? (2:334/290–91).[30] I have to choose between the possibilities of existence. There are infinitely many unities; they are in conflict, but someone who knows them all does not participate in them. Instead, it is someone who identifies with one of them, who plunges passionately into the contemplation of one aspect of things, who is passionately limited to one thought. "If there were only the struggle of being against nonbeing, of the true against the false, of the good against evil, there would be one single movement in *Dasein*. But the multiplicity of existences gives rise to the pathos of a situation: existence does not fight against a lack of existence, but against existence; and this other existence has its own depth" (2:437/379).

Here we can see more clearly than ever that Hegelian idealism and positivism are unsatisfactory; they are both philosophies that serve generality and destroy the individual (2:231/202–3). It is necessary to go beyond them in order to see what will truly be a *Weltanschauung*: this is a view of the world, but a view of the world by an individual, by an individual who chooses this view. Or, rather, one does not choose it as a view among other possible views; one does not see it as a possibility among other possibilities; for this would make it relative and thereby deny its very essence. "When I know a point of view as a point of view, it is no longer my *Weltanschauung*." So, to call a *Weltanschauung* by name is to classify it among others and thus to distort it. Any label falsifies it, any abstract classification destroys its specificity (2:243/213). Since I cannot escape from the truth that is the possibility of my existence in order to observe it, I can only say that there are multiple truths (2:417/362).[31] *Weltanschauungen*, in the plural, are no longer authentic *Weltanschauungen*. They are transformed into pure potentialities (1:242/252).[32] It is impossible to know multiple truths that are mutually exclusive in their unconditionality (2:417/362), just as I cannot compare my existence with other existences or place existences alongside one another (2:420/365). Existences are not parts or members of a knowable whole (1:265/270); there is thus no universal point of view from which a *Weltanschauung* would become visible (1:245/254). The person stands, from the beginning, within a specific *Weltanschauung* (1:242/252; 2:422/366); more precisely, one is this *Weltanschauung* (1:244/254). "I

---

30. Cf. the idea of the unification of the self in Kierkegaard.
31. [Here Wahl mistakenly references 2:477.]
32. [Here Wahl mistakenly cites volume 2.]

cannot step outside of this truth. I cannot look at it, and I cannot know it. If I departed from it, I would fall into the void" (2:417/361–62). The relationship that I have with it must be a relationship of fidelity.³³

One cannot, strictly speaking, even say that this is a choice.³⁴ For example, religion and philosophy are not two possibilities placed in a row and between which I can choose. "I am only aware of the decision when I already have chosen a side, when I am already standing on one of the two sides." Religion cannot be seen from the point of view of philosophy nor philosophy from the point of view of religion. The philosopher can only see absurdity in the respect for religious authority; at the same time, the philosopher will be aware of committing a contradiction (1:308/307–8). For example, the philosopher will have to submit either to the law of the day or to the passion of the night. Each of these is unconditional; they cannot be synthesized. One must choose either one or the other, unconditionally. "It is impossible at the same time to have the life of the day and the depth of the night" (3:113/99–100).³⁵

To the extent that one is faithful to one's own point of view, it is difficult to see what the other can see clearly from another point of view. "Once they have made their decision, they can no longer see the other side as it really is" (1:308/308). There are thus never two ways set out in front of me that I could recognize and choose between. To represent things in this way is to drop existential life into the paralysis of the sphere of objectivity (3:114/100, 138/121).³⁶

It is thus not a matter of choosing but of taking up resolutely what one is. The choice consists in the fact that one sees who one is and recognizes oneself (1:300/302). Every choice presupposes a kind of a priori, which is the ground of myself. The latest goal we are aware of is never the ultimate goal. The will encounters its limits everywhere; it is encased, its clarity is surrounded by a gray zone from which the will derives its power. "If this ground that carries it were to succumb, if the finite end is taken as absolute, then mechanization intervenes" (2:158/140).³⁷ We cannot be aware of

---

33. Cf. Marcel, 331/236–37.
34. Cf. Kierkegaard, Papers X A428: "The fact that there is no choice is the expression of passion, of the immense intensity with which one chooses."
35. Cf. Kierkegaard's theory of the dilemma.
36. This shows the error of polytheism and of all philosophical doctrines comparable to it. "Multiple gods justify everything that I can be. When the one circulates in the small coin of the multiple, it is no longer unconditional" (3:122/108). In polytheism, there is no struggle within transcendence; there is no eternal decision.
37. [Wahl mistakenly references 1:158 instead of 2:158.]

this absolute background against which we will. "The will to will has neither a plan nor means. It is without ground, and without purpose, it is the being of existence" (2:162/144). How can we choose between unconditionals, if not by what we are (1:258/265)?

Perhaps there will appear to be a duality between my essential self and my self that is made by historical circumstances. And, indeed, it is necessary to think this duality (2:122/107). "In contemplative thought, I can reach the Archimedean point from which I can see and know what is. With an independence that is astonishing, albeit empty, I even face my own *Dasein* as if it were something foreign" (2:204/179). Gabriel Marcel has already noted that this contemplation has a relation to that of Valéry, but for Jaspers, as Marcel also noted, it can only be an instant. This thought must be destroyed: "The paradoxical duality of historical consciousness exists for thought alone; for existential consciousness, it is something that is essentially one" (2:122/107). I must know myself not in my independence but in my connection with circumstances. "In the limit-situation, transcending any thought that I can grasp, I first experience myself as shaken and then as one with the fate which I have taken to be mine" (2:217/191). This unity should not be conceived as something posterior to my essence.

It is here that the idea of Fate regains its value. As Kant said, it has no legitimacy for those who want to judge things from the point of view of experience and reason. But, for someone who is placed in a limit-situation, the idea of fate recovers its meaning. Its validity cannot be demonstrated as a concept, but one can live through it as an experience (2:217/191).

This also lends full value to the Nietzschean idea of the love of Fate. It signifies the indissolubility of the link that attaches me to a situation. "In action, I do not simply remain for myself an other in relation to situations into which I would have arrived from the outside. Without them, I would be nothing more than an empty representation; it is in them that I am myself" (2:217/190–91).[38]

Just as a *Weltanschauung* must be narrow in order to be deep, the same holds true for communication. By this, Jaspers means that I destroy communication when I try to establish it with as many beings as possible. "If I want to do justice to all those whom I encounter, I fill my being with superficialities. For the sake of an imaginary universal possibility, I renounce the possibility of a historical being that is unique in its limitations" (2:60/55). "The one who says that one should be not too devoted to one specific person or to one specific cause, but give one's action a broad

38. Cf. Marcel, 335/240–41.

base by loving many people and many things, is someone who is not touched by the One and takes the positivity of multiple *Dasein* as the absolute" (3:118/104).[39] I exist in a way that is all the more decisive and intense when I integrate myself in the irreducible historical character of my situation (2:213/186). As Jaspers puts it, unconditionality in historicity is the nobility of existence.

"What could at first be thought of as the limitation of my finite existence is the possibility of its fulfillment. . . . What seemed objectively to be a limitation, a shrinking, and a narrowness becomes an impenetrable depth, becomes being itself, becomes the unique reality of existence" (2:122/107, 213/187, 219/192). The depth of being is revealed by exclusivity; existential unity is, first of all, limitation (3:177/155–56 [cf. 2:213/187–88]). The objectively and quantitatively finite character of existence is existentially, qualitatively, its infinite character.[40]

Does not what we have indicated show that existence, not by choice but by its being, must close itself off from certain possibilities, limit itself, and thereby be in a state of sin? Existence lives in dilemmas and alternatives. It is thereby tied to sin.

One of the origins of Jaspers's theory is clearly his reflection on passionate *Weltanschauungen*, in particular that of a Kierkegaard. Jaspers cannot affirm their truth, but he can affirm their intensity and authenticity.

Jaspers's reflection on Kierkegaard led to the idea that the depth of a doctrine is limitation. His reflection on sin, which also stems in part from a reflection on Kierkegaard, leads him to say that sin is limitation. Depth is limitation and limitation is sin.[41] To become deeper by limiting oneself passionately and to become deeper by becoming aware of sin—these are

---

39. [Wahl incorrectly references 2:118 instead of volume 3.]

40. There still remains a difficulty, however; for Jaspers tells us that if I only think the determinate through a limitation of what is more general, I remain in objective considerations. "Finite reality is only called determinate from the point of view of the general. . . . It is only from the fact of our fundamental situation that our character appears as a characterization of something more general than itself" (2:210/185).

41. Marcel writes (348/254): "but how ignore the fact that this ineradicable guilt which is coessential with us, represents the trace or abstract vestige of original sin?" It seems, however, that on this point one can make the same reproach against Jaspers's philosophy as against Heidegger's. If what we have said is true, could one say that he has managed to free the metaphysical roots of the idea of sin, which could be called the spiritual *materia prima* (in the Leibnizian sense of the term) of the monads? It remains the case, however, that the word "sin" perhaps leads Jaspers to fall back into a conception that he surpassed, since it implies that not sinning would be to open oneself to all possibilities.

almost two different ways of expressing the same truth. These are two essential teachings drawn from Kierkegaard, and Jaspers was able to forge them into one and the same idea.

The negative is a condition for the positive, and limitation is a condition for the unconditional, just as the lack of a system is the condition for value and the will.[42] This is not a theodicy; or rather, this theodicy is presented in the form of an a-theodicy. It is the lack of a unity, a truth, and a universal good that is the condition for the value of the world. In a sense, one might say that faith only exists for the atheist.[43]

The original wound is the source of my highest possibility. If the natural is turned into the supreme standard, then one can say that the human is a sickness of nature through which nature exceeds itself (2:298/260). The human is always "fragmentary" and breaking [*en rupture*] with *Dasein*. It cannot be completed in a harmonious totality. Its goals are never reached. It is in an essentially contradictory situation; it can neither completely accommodate *Dasein* nor let it completely escape. Its world is shattered, and its own self is broken. And it is this characteristic, this fact that the human being is a broken being, that makes unconditionality possible and makes it possible to devote oneself to freely set goals as absolutes (2:296/258).[44]

We don't choose our place in this struggle because we are this place itself, and we do not know the meaning of the struggle. "No one knows ultimately what this fight is about" (2:403/351). We do not know what will result in the case of victory or what will result in the case of defeat. We do not know when the fight is bad or good (2:374/326). Even if we choose the day, we are choosing in the dark. Even when we fight for the day, we are fighting in the dark.

This is why the ultimate truth is modesty, respect for attitudes that are not one's own, respect for the other, and for the pain of sin (3:113/100).[45]

---

42. Cf. Marcel, 335/240: to experience being in what objectively would only be a limitation; and 346/251–52: the failure of theodicy changes into a call for free activity.

43. This formula is not found in Jaspers but seems to express well (or at least extend) one of its tendencies.

44. [Wahl refers to 1:296 here, but based on the preceding reference, it should be presumed to be a reference to 2:296.]

45. [Wahl added the following two paragraphs here in the version that appeared in *Études kierkegaardiennes*: "In this domain of communion, each existent will be aware of what is true for others even though it is not true for oneself. One should neither transform these truths into purely objective truths—for they would thereby immediately become erroneous—nor abandon one's own truth, but live it intensely in its very narrowness and thereby in its depth. One must be oneself, without being able to call

[. . .]⁴⁶

I have not tried to summarize all of Jaspers's work here; instead I have only considered a few aspects of it and have shed light on some of his essential ideas. Perhaps this is enough to provide a sense of its richness and to give a sense of how it connects to some of my own deepest concerns. The image of the world torn apart is the basis on which the theory of existence is developed. What is appealing to me about this is perhaps especially the assertion of the connection of existence with what surrounds and exceeds it. First of all, it is tied to its background or rather its obscure substrate, which is impermeable to the intellect but is felt to be the basis of ourselves and things. Second, existence is linked with the heterogeneous. Third, it is linked with how existence is given to itself. For Jaspers resolves the problem of choice through a completely experiential dialectic in which choice and possibility are transformed before our eyes into nonchoice and facticity.⁴⁷ What we truly choose is ultimately what is dictated to us. Fourth, and finally, the connection between existence and transcendence becomes more and more clear; there is a vision of the self, at the limit of the self, on the border of transcendence and on the border of the other. Along with this relation to the infinite other, the value of existence is tied to its own finitude. Here Jaspers makes an attempt to establish a sort of qualitative logic where the acuity of a deep feeling is preferred over the weight of broader considerations, where addition no longer has any sense, and where less is more. The same efforts are continued and deepened by

---

oneself either similar to others or different from others. For, in either case, this would be to compare oneself and thus to lose oneself.

"That is to say that there is no explanation in this domain but, rather, an invocation, a call from one existence to another existence. This is no longer an intellectual communication between individuals who can trade places (here Jaspers's thought meets up with that of Marcel), nor a struggle for existence in the ordinary sense of the word, nor a harmony, but a community, a communion between irreplaceable 'Uniques,' a struggle for existence in the highest sense of the term, a struggle in which each progression of the one is a progression of the other, and a breakup of all being in front of transcendence."]

46. [For reasons of length, we have had to excise section 3 ("Transcendence") and the material in section 4 ("The World of Ciphers") preceding Wahl's conclusion. The complete translation of Wahl's essay can be found in the *Journal of French and Francophone Philosophy* 24, no. 1 (2016).]

47. Perhaps, in volumes 1 and 2, Jaspers insists too much on the aspect of creativity and the aspect of the possibility of existence. Or, at least, as we advance in his thought, the more we realize that activity gives way to something other than itself. In a sense, but only in a sense, this could be called passivity just as possibility gives way to pure facticity. The words "action" and "passion" remain unable to capture this fact that is at the same time both given and creative.

the theory of transcendence, where choice is transformed increasingly into nonchoice, and where there is a glimmer of this unthinkable idea of something that is absolutely one but yet many. We are launched into pursuit of this idea by the very fact that we exist.

The theory of failure, of the eternally ephemeral and of the miracle, are all points of connection between Jaspers's theory and my own metaphysical concerns. They are all ideas in which we can recognize something of a contemporary spirit, with its discouragement, its desire for intensity, its need to find substitutes for the absolute, its aspiration for a reality that is as beautiful as myth and that it would create on its own, and this negative ontology that inspires it. One could say that Jaspers's reflection is situated in a place where some of the most eternal and most real philosophical problems are located, although not all philosophers have been aware of them.

But precisely after having noted so many points on which we tend to agree with Jaspers and so many reasons to be interested in his philosophy, do we not come to have some distrust of this interest? Do we not find in it the worship of some idols that we would like to forge for ourselves? The idea of the instant, this idea of the union between the present and the past in an eternal instant, is indeed a myth in Jaspers's sense of the term.[48] The same goes for the assertion that can be found in Nietzsche as well as in Kierkegaard, Heidegger, and Jaspers, that one should take upon oneself what one is. Is the idea of transcendence itself sufficiently proved by the failure of immanence? There is a place that has been set for the Other, but the existence of the Other has not been proved. And how is this transcendence characterized? We cannot say anything about it, except that possibility and choice do not exist in it.[49] But then, we are faced with a negative ontology, which is a very alluring abyss, a vertiginous abyss, but at the same time a very convenient refuge. One can also ask whether the idea of transcendence is not the product of one of these objectifications or determinations that Jaspers denounces. As for the idea of the world of ciphers, it still remains quite vague. It consists, ultimately, of saying that one is faced with the fact of the world as representing a transcendence that has not been proven and remains inaccessible. As a result, Jaspers's entire

---

48. [Wahl added the following here in the version that appeared in *Études kierkegaardiennes*: "but a myth that we can only believe in part."]

49. Besides, can it be conceived without contradiction? Transcendence is what is one's own without an other (3:15/15); and at the same time, transcendence, God, does not occur without the human (3:124/110, 164/144). It is true that there is nothing about this contradiction that is not reasonable in some sense: concerning transcendence, we cannot express ourselves without contradiction.

effort amounts to telling us that it is necessary to accept the world as a fact, just as he has already told us that it is necessary to be what one is.

It is not that this claim is illegitimate. But the poet, the lover, and the believer are also situated within this vision toward which Jaspers points the difficult path. By the very fact that the philosopher can only reach this vision by starting from a point that is situated outside of it, the philosopher acquires a greater *worth*. But is this vision intensified? This is the question that needs be asked. Pascal, Nietzsche, and Kierkegaard are able to reach more tragic depths. They appear, if this word can still be used, far more existential than does a philosopher of existence. And the very pathos which comes from this dialectic is not denied to them: the dialectic never loses its rights, and its flame reignites among such thinkers to enflame even their belief and even the flickering of this flame.

That is perhaps not the most serious defect of this fine attempt. It is perhaps in the very idea of the philosophy of existence. A philosophy of existence into which so many various givens enter, where such a vast intellect is in play, is the negation of existential thought:[50] for existential thought is narrowness and an intensity based on narrowness. There is thus perhaps a contradiction in the very idea of a philosophy of existence.

---

50. We also note that from a practical point of view, Jaspers's philosophy justifies everything. When Jaspers says that we should not betray our country, our parents, our love, because it would be to betray ourselves (2:245/214–15), it reflects a very deep tendency in Jaspers's thought. I must reconcile the self, and my concrete self, with the givens from which I am derived and somehow unify them with myself. But there is also a deep tendency within him to take the side of heretics. Have Polybius and Saint Paul (2:402/350), the one who denied Hellenism and the other who denied Judaism, demonstrated fidelity in the sense in which this word was first defined? How should we respond to the question: can I change myself or must I accept myself? (cf. 2:125/109–10). We are thus divided between these two tendencies. Jaspers will say that it is necessary to remain in a sort of tension between preservation and destruction (3:99/90–91). This is only a solution in words, which cannot be used in practice.

To say that we must remain in the religion of our forefathers, but that we have to be heretics within that religion (this is the solution that Marcel highlights and criticizes on p. 348/254 of his article), is still only a middle term at which it is difficult for the existent to stop definitively. To say that we must adopt the most *geschichtlich* ["historical"] solution is to say nothing (2:242/211); for one cannot know which solution is the most *geschichtlich*. To say that there are depths that no universal consciousness can enter is perhaps also to get out of this difficulty at too high of a cost. It is legitimate that a philosophy would have no practical consequence, but it is perhaps unjustifiable for it to seem to have one when it does not. One might reply, to be sure, that Jaspers's philosophy does not command anything, that it thus demonstrates a truly existential tolerance, and that this is its ultimate virtue.

This can be felt especially in certain passages. When Jaspers thinks that combat can have a meaning, which is otherwise unattainable for us (2:374–403/327–51), when he recommends an attitude of respectful tolerance (3:113/100), when he tries to make the philosophy of existence as open and wide as possible (3:228/201), one might wonder whether he does not reestablish himself on an intellectual plane that he had in fact exceeded. The same could be said when he talks about the idea of sin, the sin of limitation, as if to escape from sin it were necessary to be on the plane of universality.[51] Could one not say that he did not follow the movement of this dialectic that, faced with the problem of choice, led him to see the idea of choice vanish, and that, here too, it would have led him to see the idea of sin disappear,[52] so that nothing but the idea of limitation would remain? Yet, this idea too perhaps only has a meaning in relation to the idea of an abstract universality and would ultimately disappear, in turn.

This is why the entire effort of this agile, expert, penetrating, sometimes profound intellect—who is eager to approach things that he does not understand, who is open enough to negate himself and see the obscure areas that surround him, who seeks to leave nothing out of what he considers to be the tragedy of existence—still does not satisfy us. This so *vielseitig* ["many-sided"] defense of *Einseitigkeit* ["one-sidedness"] cannot be content with either the *Vielseitigkeit* ["many-sidedness"] of the dilettante or the *Einseitigkeit* of the enthusiast. Perhaps that is the fate that the philosopher has to "take upon himself." But perhaps it is also the case that the obscure ground on which we want to shed light while being respectful of its obscurity refuses even this small ray of light. Or perhaps it is the case that this light is too weak or too calm. Perhaps existence does not let itself be seen by the glow of the lamp of love or by the glow of the lamp of the intellect, but only by the flash of a thought similar to the existential thought of Kierkegaard, Nietzsche, and some poets. But this judgment about Jaspers's philosophy is certainly not a condemnation of the intuition of existence which is at its origin, which is its originary intuition. Even if, while admiring it, this judgment condemns a part of his intellectual effort (written in the margins of life and of reflection on some passion-

---

51. The theory of sin, in Kierkegaard, seems to want to escape this reproach. For Kierkegaard, existence is both the highest value and sin. And this is explained by the essential paradox of Christianity.

52. On this point, my critique rejoins the objection to Jaspers previously made by Marcel.

ate thinkers), this would be all the more reason to condemn the task of the commentator that I have taken up here in order to enrich our own thinking by contact with a thought that is so rich, and to note my esteem for it.

Translated by Scott Davidson

7

Subjectivity and Transcendence

Emmanuel Leroux[1] had been scheduled to deliver a paper at the December 4, 1937, session of the eminent Société Française de Philosophie. When it became clear that, because of his wife's illness, he would be unable to attend, the president of the society, Léon Brunschvicg, asked Jean Wahl to prepare a lecture and solicit responses in his stead. Wahl decided to discuss the connection between subjectivity and transcendence, and, despite the short notice, he managed to assemble contributions from some of the greatest philosophers of the day—far more than was typical[2]—for

---

As is normally the case with presentations at meetings of the Société Française de Philosophie, the lecture and discussion that followed were subsequently published in the society's bulletin, "Subjectivité et transcendance," *Bulletin de la Société Française de Philosophie* 37, no. 5 (October–December 1937): 161–211. This lecture, as well as the exchange and letters that follow, was reprinted, in truncated form, in Jean Wahl, *Existence humaine et transcendance* (Neuchâtel: Éditions de la Baconnière, 1944), 39–51, 113–59, and then republished in part in Wahl, *Kierkegaard: L'Un devant l'Autre*, ed. Vincent Delecroix and Frédéric Worms (Paris: Hachette Littératures, 1998), 205–20. The only addition to the book version is a footnote on page 134, which the reader will find translated in note 40 below.

    1. Emmanuel Leroux (1883–1942) was a professor of philosophy at the University of Rennes.

    2. Edward Baring, "A Secular Kierkegaard: Confessional Readings of Heidegger before 1945," *New German Critique* 42, no. 1 (February 2015): 92n82. Karl Jaspers, upon reading through the published version of the exchange, spoke in a letter to Wahl from November 4, 1938, of "the lively stimulation I felt in reading what an atypical gathering of so many smart men had to say. There is much that is remarkable here

152

what would come to be called "a turning point in twentieth-century intellectual history."³ Featuring replies and letters by Raymond Aron, Nicolas Berdyaev, Martin Heidegger, Karl Jaspers, Emmanuel Levinas, Gabriel Marcel, and many others, Wahl's "Subjectivity and Transcendence" should indeed be included among the most important debates in twentieth-century European philosophy. For not only does it mark "an indispensable moment for any account of the secularization of Kierkegaard"⁴ and "the occasion for Levinas's first use of the concept 'the other'";⁵ it also provided a crucial forum in which to discuss and shape the future of existentialism.

While revealing Jaspers's and Heidegger's debt to Kierkegaard, Wahl at the same time worries that any attempt to provide a philosophy of the insights that stem from Kierkegaard's life would threaten either to fall into abstraction or to harbor implicit theological presuppositions. This, for Wahl, is precisely what makes existential philosophy so challenging. Once it provides a general theory of existence, to what extent can it still be existential?⁶ Isn't there a danger, Wahl wonders, that what a philosophy of existence takes from an existence such as Kierkegaard's will remain tainted by what, according to Kierkegaard himself, cannot be detached from that existence, namely, its belief in God and everything that goes along with this? Aren't we perhaps better off sticking with Kierkegaard, or someone like Rimbaud, Van Gogh, or Nietzsche, someone who is perhaps, in Wahl's words, "more existential and more truly philosophical than the philosophies of existence"? Someone who, rather than merely justifying or theorizing about choice, actually chooses for himself or herself?

Such questions, as Edward Baring has recently shown, proved pivotal for the development and transnational appreciation of existentialism.⁷ Baring explains that, prior to Wahl's lecture and the translation of existentialism into France, German scholars had endeavored, if not always consistently, to distinguish among

---

[*die lebhafte Anregung, die mir die Lektüre dessen bringt, was eine ungewöhnliche Versammlung so vieler kluger Männer zu sagen hatte. Es ist viel Bemerkenswertes dabei*]." Jaspers's letter is available at the Deutsches Literaturarchiv Marbach under the access number 75.9716/3.

3. Samuel Moyn, *Origins of the Other: Emmanuel Levinas between Revelation and Ethics* (Ithaca, N.Y.: Cornell University Press, 2005), 182.

4. Baring, "A Secular Kierkegaard," 92.

5. Moyn, *Origins of the Other*, 182.

6. Kierkegaard himself raised this problem in *Concluding Unscientific Postscript*, when he argued, against Hegel, that an existential system was impossible. See Søren Kierkegaard, *Concluding Unscientific Postscript to Philosophical Crumbs*, ed. and trans. Alistair Hannay (Cambridge: Cambridge University Press, 2009), 100–106.

7. Edward Baring, "Anxiety in Translation: Naming Existentialism before Sartre," *History of European Ideas* 41, no. 4 (2015): 470–88.

1. *existentiell* analysis—an extraphilosophical examination of concrete, factual aspects of human existence, undertaken above all by dialectical theologians such as Karl Barth;
2. *Existentialphilosophie*—a philosophical analysis of the ontological structures of human existence, undertaken above all by Heidegger;
3. *Existenzphilosophie*—a nonobjectifying philosophy of human existence that remained wary of ontology, undertaken above all by Jaspers.

In French these were often unwittingly lumped together under the heading *philosophie existentielle*, leading, in fact, to many of the confusions and interesting debates in "Subjectivity and Transcendence." Moreover, Heidegger's careful distinctions in *Being and Time* between *existenzial* ("existential") and *existenziell* ("existentiell"), and even between *Dasein* ("being-there," i.e., the being of the human being) and *Sein* ("being" as such), at times collapsed, in French, into *existentiell* and *l'être*, respectively.

These conflations had key implications for the history of ideas, a fact that may be gleaned from Heidegger's epistolary response to Wahl and its immense influence following the debate. It was precisely Heidegger's rejection of the label "philosophy of existence," and indeed of any philosophy focused chiefly on "the existence of man," that contributed to the reemergence of the more encompassing term "existentialism" (despite Heidegger's eventual rejection of this as well).[8] However, it did not matter what its title was—confusion still remained about what Heidegger was up to. Was he focused solely on the question of being (*Sein*), as he indicates in his letter, or did the question of the human being take precedence? Wahl, at least in the 1930s, favored the latter, even when he granted Heidegger's predilection for being.[9] Indeed, the fact that clear distinctions between *Sein* and *Dasein* and between an understanding of structures of existence (*existenzial*) and an understanding of the particular ways in which existence is carried out (*existenziell*) were not maintained surely contributed to what would become known as the "existentialist reading of Heidegger," centered as it was on the human being and the possibility of authenticity.[10]

Wahl's "famous communication,"[11] as Levinas described it, also set the stage for further dialogue about the nature of transcendence. Kierkegaardian anxiety, Wahl

---

8. Baring, "Anxiety in Translation," 483–85.

9. Wahl also continued to read Heidegger in conjunction with other existentialist thinkers, and many of his questions remained the same over the years. See, for example, Wahl's *A Short History of Existentialism*, trans. Forrest Williams and Stanley Maron (New York: Philosophical Library, 1949), in which Berdyaev, Levinas, and Marcel also took part.

10. These confusions were compounded by Heidegger's first French translator Henry Corbin's (1903–78) choice to translate "*Dasein*" by "*réalité humaine.*" The subjectivist connotation of this translation led many of his French readers to existentialize Heidegger's primarily ontological analysis in *Being and Time*.

11. Emmanuel Levinas, *Outside the Subject*, trans. Michael B. Smith (Stanford, Calif.: Stanford University Press, 1994), 81.

tells us, emerges from the remoteness of God and the presence of evil. We do not know whether we are transcending toward God or toward the devil; whether we are on the ascent or descent; whether our transcendence is, in Wahl's words, "transascendence" or "transdescendence." As Wahl reveals in his debate with Marcel[12] and in his responses to Aron and Louis Lavelle, both transcendences have a place, but both must be secularized. Transdescendence, in particular, is not so much a matter of evil and the demonic for Wahl as it is a movement toward and immersion in the intensity and depths of concrete life. In his short lecture at the international Descartes conference in 1937, "Sur l'idée de transcendance" ("On the Idea of Transcendence") (later reprinted along with "Subjectivity and Transcendence" in Wahl's 1944 book *Existence humaine et transcendance* [*Human Existence and Transcendence*]), Wahl clarifies that: "There is a movement of transcendence directed toward immanence; when transcendence transcends itself . . . falling again into immanence." Such transdescendence would be "perhaps the greatest transcendence," even if it can never be accomplished in full.[13] The directional modes of transascendence and transdescendence would later be taken up in various ways by Levinas, Blanchot, Sartre, and the musicologist and semiologist Eero Tarasti,[14] to

---

12. Their debate about "transascendence" and "transdescendence" in "Subjectivity and Transcendence" was later taken up in a discussion following Marcel's own lecture before the Société Française de Philosophie in 1958, where Marcel says, "I am no supporter of *transdescendance*, but I am not at all sure that Jean Wahl would agree with me. I think he is terribly fond of *transdescendance*." Wahl replies, "It is probably true that Mr. Marcel and I do not agree about *transdescendance*, but it is not true that I ever use this word to mean descending from the absolute to the relative," as Georges Bénézé had suggested. Gabriel Marcel, "The Questioning of Being," in Marcel, *Tragic Wisdom and Beyond*, trans. Stephen Jolin and Peter McCormick, 45–79 (Evanston, Ill.: Northwestern University Press, 1973), 59–60.

13. "Sur l'idée de transcendance," in *Travaux du IXe Congrès International de Philosophie: Congrès Descartes* (Paris: Hermann et Cie, 1937), 8:59; *Existence humaine et transcendance* (Neuchâtel: Éditions de la Baconnière, 1944), 38. Wahl speaks directly of "transascendence" and "transdescendence" on 8:58 and 37, respectively.

14. Emmanuel Levinas, *Totality and Infinity: An Essay on Exteriority*, trans. Alphonso Lingis (Pittsburgh: Duquesne University Press, 1969), 35, and "Reality and Its Shadow," trans. Alphonso Lingis, in *The Levinas Reader*, ed. Seán Hand (Oxford: Basil Blackwell, 1989), 137; Maurice Blanchot, *L'écriture du désastre* (Paris: Gallimard, 1980), 37; English translation: *The Writing of the Disaster*, trans. Ann Smock (Lincoln: University of Nebraska Press, 1986), 19; and *L'entretien infini* (Paris: Gallimard, 1969), 580; English translation: *The Infinite Conversation*, trans. Susan Hanson (Minneapolis: University of Minnesota Press, 1992), 395 (note that both of Blanchot's English translators mistranslate *transdescendance* simply as "transcendence"); Jean-Paul Sartre, *Being and Nothingness: An Essay on Phenomenological Ontology*, trans. Hazel E. Barnes (New York: Washington Square, 1984), 529; Eero Tarasti, *Existential Semiotics* (Bloomington: Indiana University Press, 2000), 19, 44, 48. Cf. also Frantz Fanon's

name but a few, and the idea of multidirectional transcendence, especially of a transcendence transcended toward immanence, would remain a constant theme throughout Wahl's career, appearing, for instance, in his ontological autobiography (see Chapter 11 in this volume) and as the culminating thought of his magisterial *Traité de métaphysique* (Treatise on metaphysics). More than merely influencing countless thinkers—no small feat in and of itself—"Subjectivity and Transcendence" thus stands out as an essential moment in Wahl's own thought as well.

Ian Alexander Moore

Session of Saturday, December 4, 1937

Mr. Jean Wahl presents[15] *to the Société Française de Philosophie the following considerations:*

I

A.—The idea of subjectivity and the idea of transcendence are the two essential ideas that, from a philosophical point of view, characterize Kierkegaard's thought. Or rather what characterizes it is the connection between the two. The tension of subjectivity is explained by the presence of transcendence. What is most subjective, by closing in on itself, suddenly discovers the transcendent. The soul alone before God alone—one could find here the ideas of Plotinus. But the soul is much more closed in on itself, and God is much more closed in on God, than is the case for Plotinus and the mystics that followed the Neoplatonists. In Kierkegaard, we do not find this confluence of souls in God, nor this expansion, this overflowing of God into souls. Here, there is a force of negation that is much more powerful, an opposition of individualities that is much more irreducible. And this is one of the reasons for Kierkegaardian anxiety.

A second reason for this anxiety is the presence of evil. The being [*l'être*][16] is anxious because it does not know what it exists in the face of, in the face of a beneficent transcendence or a malfeasant one, in the face

---

reference to the idea of transcendence in Wahl in Fanon, *Black Skin, White Masks*, trans. Richard Philcox (New York: Grove, 1995), 117 and note 25.

15. [What follows under sections I and II is what Wahl sent to the respondents and letter writers of the present exchange. His lecture proper begins following the "Record of the Session" below.]

16. [For a discussion of the ambiguity of this term in Wahl, see Chapter 5, note 6, in this volume.]

of God or in the face of a demonic force; whether the movement it accomplishes is a movement of "transascendence" or "transdescendence."

B.—In Kierkegaard, these ideas are enveloped by an atmosphere of theology as well as of morality. One might wonder whether "transascendence" is necessarily good, "transdescendence" necessarily bad. On this point, various teachings such as those of [William] Blake, of [André] Gide in his *Dostoïevsky*, of [D. H.] Lawrence, or of John Cowper Powys would be invaluable. For them, the task is to find something elemental, something wild, "an angel or a demon—it does not matter."[17]

Moreover, one might wonder whether it is appropriate to retain the theological aspect of the ideas of subjectivity and transcendence. Transcendence is not necessarily God, nor necessarily the devil. It can simply be nature, which is no less mysterious than the God of orthodoxies or the God of heterodoxies.

II

A.—If one observes the development of philosophy in Germany, one will see that those who are most especially inspired by Kierkegaard, namely, Heidegger and Jaspers, have complemented his philosophy with the idea of "being-in-the-world," with the idea of "communication," and with the idea of "historicity" (the last two, which are present in Kierkegaard's thought, are brought to light by Jaspers).

At the same time, these two thinkers wish to remain within the world that is our own; they refuse to follow Kierkegaard when he searches for "repetition" in a beyond, after having attempted in vain to find it in this world.

B.—Have they, however, completely delivered themselves from the theological elements of Kierkegaardian thought? Both of them have attempted to secularize the idea of sin as they found it in Kierkegaard and theology, the one by making it a fall into the domain of the anonymous crowd, into the "They" [*le "On"*], the other (Jaspers), in a more profound manner, by identifying it with limitation. But this latter conception implies the idea that the good would be the totality, which a thought like Jaspers's does not appear to be able to admit.

In both of them, one finds the idea of repetition. But is not repetition, just like theories of the instant or those of the eternal return, an ersatz idea of eternity?

---

17. [Victor Hugo, in reference to Napoleon in the poem "Lui," in *Les Orientales* (Brussels: Laurent, 1832), 166; translation ours.]

Can one conceive of a philosophy similar to Heidegger's and Jaspers's whose attraction would not partly be explained by the nostalgia and religious echo it contains?

And if such a philosophy were conceivable, would it not risk vanishing into a general theory of existence, from which all particularity, all historicity, all existence would be banished?

This is perhaps the problem that "existential philosophy"[18] faces; it is exposed to the double danger of either associating itself too closely with theology, or disassociating itself too much from everything that is concretely given.

Precisely this may lead us to wonder whether existences such as those of Rimbaud or Van Gogh or Nietzsche (or Kierkegaard) are not at once more existential and more truly philosophical than the philosophies of existence. But the latter at least have the merit of allowing us to better sense the value of the former.

Record of the Session

[. . .][19]

Mr. Jean Wahl.—I would like simply to pose some questions concerning Kierkegaard and contemporary philosophy.

In order to broach this subject one might begin by opposing Kierkegaard to Hegel. I will do so very briefly.

Kierkegaard places us before the *here* and the *now*, while for Hegel, in contrast, a dialectic must reabsorb the here and the now in generalities, in more and more vast universalities. This here and this now are of course not solely the corporeal here and now. Both of them are opened up onto a subjectivity, and it is before subjectivity that Kierkegaard places us. But, for him, this subjectivity itself takes its value, its reality, from the fact that

---

18. [*Philosophie existentielle.* Unless otherwise indicated, here and in what follows, *existentiel* has been rendered as "existential." Only in Levinas's letter and Wahl's response below is the French adjective *existential* used, where they are following Heidegger's distinction in *Being and Time* between *existenzial* and *existenziell*. In this case, *existentiel* and *existential* have been translated, respectively, as "existentiell" and as "existential." For a discussion of this distinction, see Chapter 5, note 6, in this volume.]

19. [We have omitted from the translation the opening remarks of Léon Brunschvicg, then president of the Société Française de Philosophie. Among other things, Brunschvicg commemorates Henri Delacroix (1873–1937)—one of the leading psychologists in France and, at the time, the dean of the Faculty of Letters at the Sorbonne—who had died just the day before the session, and he reports on the success of the recent international Descartes congress.]

it finds itself in the presence of an *other*, of the absolute *other*, of the absolutely different, of the transcendent.

Subjectivity must not attempt, as it did in Hegel's thought, to assimilate this other to itself or, rather, to assimilate itself to this other. No. It finds itself in the presence of this other in order to collide with it. And this collision is all the more violent since in Kierkegaard's thought the other takes on an essentially paradoxical aspect. This other is in fact the eternal that has been made temporal. And it is what Kierkegaard calls the absolute protest against immanence, the fact that what is eternal became historical.

It is at this moment that it becomes necessary to break with his thought, at the moment in which we feel that our eternal beatitude depends on our relation with something historical, and that this historical something is nothing other than the eternal.

But it is necessary to live this relation. It is necessary for us to live it isolated in our thought, at once curled up upon the present, as it were, and stretched out toward our future.

We obviously cannot define this other. But we can at least say that we are conscious of it through the relation we have with it. And here we have a new paradox. This *other* is at bottom the *one* of the *Parmenides*'s first hypothesis, which has absolutely no relation to anything else; and yet this one that is without relation exists only through the relation we find we have with it.

This is indeed because the most internal relation is, for Kierkegaard, a relation with something external, and because the absolutely transcendent is revealed only by this absolutely immanent relation with the individual.

If we are indeed interested in something other than ourselves, this other can only be the absolute other, such that the intensity of our passion is a sign of our being in relation with something that can only be the eternal and the absolute. The intensity of this relation is such that, by the very fact of our entering into it, it gives us this other term, this other term that, in a sense, however, can never be given. And it is in this way that what is subjective to the highest degree must be considered as relating to what is objective to the highest degree.

But, in spite of the abstract terms in which Kierkegaard presents this, and in which I have presented it following Kierkegaard, he says that this is nothing other than a description of belief.[20] Belief is necessarily belief in another. This other, in whose existence we are infinitely interested, can only

---

20. [Here and in what follows, Wahl speaks more often of belief, *croyance*, than of faith, *foi*.]

be God. And this movement, this relation that I was describing, which is at once a going out toward the other and a passionate interiority, is again nothing other than the paradox of belief. One can say that, in a sense, it is in order to give a faithful description of the phenomenon of belief that Kierkegaard entered into the domain of paradox and contradiction.

As soon as the individual finds himself in this relation, he will, in a way, by force of this paradoxical passion that is in him and that is belief, work toward the annihilation of his thought. And it is here, on account of the presence of this subjective thinker and that transcendent object, that the phenomenon of anxiety will come to pass. We thereby see at the same time how Kierkegaard's viewpoint differs radically from mysticism, at least most of the time. For there is no fusion with the other, at least most of the time; although Kierkegaard experienced certain moments of ecstasy or near ecstasy, the other is ordinarily a sort of resistant being that stands before him and from which he is separated.

There is a second reason for Kierkegaardian anxiety, which is the presence of evil. This second reason is, in reality, connected to the first in a very profound way. From the moment that this other than I is distant from me, I will no longer communicate directly with it and I will incessantly have the feeling that I can be deceived about its essence. Whence the idea that we are never certain of being in the presence of God. And this element of incertitude subsists in belief as Kierkegaard defines it. This is a new element that completes his description of belief.

This anxiety becomes all the greater since we incessantly have the idea that God can test us and at the same time fear that we may in some way be testing God, an idea that comes up quite often in Kierkegaard. Whence certain characteristics of his thought when he finds himself in the presence of moral problems—be it the suspension of the ethical, as in *Fear and Trembling*, in which he shows how Abraham must leave the rules of morality behind in order to obey God; be it even the idea that it is necessary to plumb the depths of sin to have access to faith; be it, on the contrary, the conception of the ethical-religious.

In the synopsis,[21] I presented, in a manner with which I am perhaps not entirely satisfied, some reflections that came to mind when presented with various attitudes of Kierkegaard. I wanted to say above all that one can undoubtedly interpret in a different manner the hesitation that is produced in the individual in the face of that which exceeds him, or, in a cer-

---

21. [That is, the text reproduced at the beginning of this chapter, under sections I and II.]

tain sense, if you will, that the individual can be exceeded in two different directions: he can be exceeded from down below as from up above; by mysterious forces that rejoin what there is of the animal in the being [*l'être*] and what is perhaps not for that reason bad, as, conversely, by forces of nature recognized as superior.

And, at the same time, I wondered, why in Kierkegaard there is this will to paradox and contradiction; why? It is for an intensification of the existence of the individual. But Kierkegaard himself knows that the existence of the individual is in itself a paradox. It is not simply God who is a paradox for coming to Earth, but we ourselves are paradoxes for being, as Kierkegaard says, a union and a contradiction of the finite and the infinite.

In order to have the feeling of paradox, is it therefore really so necessary to resort to those beliefs to which Kierkegaard does? Is not our vision of what surrounds us full of realities that are extremely paradoxical, like knowledge, the person, or even things?

* * *

In the synopsis, I moved from Kierkegaard on to Heidegger and Jaspers.

One could say that Heidegger's and Jaspers's thought stands in a relation that is quite similar to Kierkegaard's thought and to Husserl's thought, and, with regard to both of them, in a contradictory relation on certain points. For Husserl separates essences from existences, and Kierkegaard separates the individual and the world, while for Heidegger it is existence that is essence, and this existence is to be [*est être*] and to be in the world.

What Heidegger and Jaspers have in a way added to Kierkegaard's thought, with all the nuances—even more, the profound differences—that it would be necessary to work out between these two philosophers, are the ideas of "being in the world," of communication, and of "*Geschichtlichkeit*" or historicity. The individual is, to a certain extent at least, bound to the world, though Heidegger always insists, in a very beautiful way, on his radical isolation.

The difficulty with speaking about transcendence in Heidegger comes from the fact that this word appears to have different meanings in his thought. He speaks first of the transcendence of the being [*l'être*] with regard to nothingness. Then he employs the word "transcendence" when it is a matter of characterizing our relationship with *being in the world*. And in the third place he employs the word "transcendence" when it is a matter of describing our life as it is always ahead of itself, projecting itself toward the future. Thus existence is transcendent from nothingness; it is transcendent in relation to the world, or the world is transcendent in relation to it; and it is transcendent in relation to itself.

But all of this only gives us a better feeling for what characterizes existence for Heidegger, and that is its finitude. The two ideas of transcendence and finitude are connected for Heidegger; what he places in the foreground is the idea of the being's forsakenness, of a sort of essential poverty that belongs to the being. It is not a philosophy of abundance, of πόρος, but, on the contrary, one could say, a philosophy of πενία, of essential destitution.

I was saying that in Heidegger the word "transcendence" has multiple usages; in Jaspers, it is by definition very difficult to elucidate the idea of transcendence. Starting from the fact that in myself there are many things that do not depend on me, Jaspers comes to the idea that I am in some way a given for myself and that consequently there are things that exceed me. I am abridging and simplifying his complex thought a lot, and I apologize for that. The transcendent is also what, in opposition to myself, I know as essentially one, unconditioned, independent, and as a reality in which possibility cannot be distinct from reality.

In Heidegger and Jaspers one finds the same connection that I had taken note of in Kierkegaard between the ideas of subjectivity and transcendence. For example, in Heidegger, it is above all in transcending toward the world that a subjectivity realizes itself, or, rather, transcendence can be revealed only through the ontological interpretation of subjectivity; it is in going back into himself that the individual discovers the other than himself.

One could connect this with the analyses Heidegger gives of certain feelings [*sentiments*][22] that place us in the presence of the world as a whole [*dans son ensemble*], not only the feeling of anxiety on which he particularly insists, but also, as he is careful to say, feelings like boredom or joy. These feelings, which connect us to what is most personal in us, make a whole—even more than a whole: the totality of the world—suddenly emerge before our mind [*esprit*], at least sometimes, in certain particular joys, in certain anxieties, certain particular boredoms; through personality, we arrive at vast, impersonal feelings.

In Jaspers, we find this same connection in phrases such as: "The more profoundly I plunge into myself, the more I come to feel solidarity with what is initially foreign to me."[23] And again: "Transcendence reveals itself in my attitude with respect to it. It is the being I can attain only through my most profound subjectivity."

---

22. [Wahl is referring here to the German *Stimmung* or *Befindlichkeit* ("attunement" or "disposition"), and not *Gefühl*, which is typically translated as "feeling."]

23. [Wahl's French has been translated directly. Cf. Karl Jaspers, *Philosophie*, 3 vols. (Berlin: Julius Springer, 1932), 3:94; *Philosophy*, 3 vols., trans. E. B. Ashton (Chicago: University of Chicago Press, 1969–71), 3:83.]

And after having brought this idea of transcendence to light, both of them, Heidegger and Jaspers, make a move that is quite analogous to that move that Kierkegaard makes in turning back, in a way, toward immanence, with the help of an idea they seem to borrow from Kierkegaard, namely, "repetition."

Repetition is the fact that the past is taken back, in a way, out of the past and made present again, reaffirmed. It is something that could be compared to the way in which Aristotle defined substance: τὸ τί ἦν εἶναι.[24] The individual must be that which it was. It is the fact of "remaining that which one was" and of reaffirming oneself in this way.

Like Kierkegaard and perhaps even more so, they give this idea of repetition a metaphysical allure, analogous to what Nietzsche gave to the eternal return; by repetition, we make a unity out of the present, the past, and the future. We reach a moment in which there is an absolute union of what Heidegger calls "the three ecstases of time."[25]

With respect to these philosophies, one might wonder—it is the first question I asked myself—whether there do not remain in their thought some elements of the beliefs from which they wanted to separate themselves and from which they do in fact separate themselves. The strongest feeling that exists in Heidegger and that colors all his work is the feeling that man is thrown into the world, "*geworfen*," and abandoned; it is this idea of the "*Geworfenheit*"[26] of man, that of finitude, of forsaken finitude, and one could almost say of accursed finitude.

Is there not something here that is explained only by memory, only by the memory of other ideas, something that is not explained by itself but by its relation to that from which Heidegger has detached himself?

In the second place, the idea of repetition, it seems to me, could call for some critiques, some objections, under its extreme metaphysical form, when it takes the form of absolute repetition, when it wishes to be the absolute unification of moments of time. What, then, does philosophy wish to accomplish? It wishes to find a *nunc stans* ["a standing now"] in our time, and the task is certainly arduous.

---

24. [Literally, "the what it was to be."]
25. [Cf. *Sein und Zeit*, 365.]
26. [We have here corrected Wahl's text: he writes *entworfen* ("projected") and *Entworfenheit* ("projectedness"), while Heidegger's German terms for this idea are *geworfen* ("thrown") and *Geworfenheit* ("thrownness"). Because of his exile during World War II, Wahl was unable to correct these mistakes when the essay was reprinted in 1944 in *Existence humaine et transcendance*.]

With respect to transcendence as they define it, it seems to me that there are still questions that arise for us since we have seen the multiplicity of meanings that it has in Heidegger; and in Jaspers, it is indeed difficult to grasp, which is of course natural since transcendence by definition cannot be completely grasped, but which is complicated by the fact that he says that I can grasp it only by uniting myself with it and that he nevertheless wants to preserve it as transcendence and as other. So it is a difficult situation for him, it seems to me, since, on the one hand, transcendence must be me in my extreme unity and, on the other, something different from me and opposed to me.

But I believe that one of the most serious reproaches one could make against Jaspers's theory is that while he tells us that all philosophy consists in a choice, in a radical selection, he contents himself with establishing a theory that tells us that all philosophy consists in a radical selection, but that is to say that he does not select. Such that, if one studies this thought in depth, one will eventually say to oneself that existence as it is defined here is in a sense the least existential of all since it sees very well, and justifies every choice, but which itself only justifies the choices of others and does not choose for itself.

This does not take anything away from the importance of Jaspers's work, but it is perhaps no longer necessary to place his philosophy within the same framework as the others; it is a general theory of philosophies, it is the work of an observer of philosophies, it is not the act of a philosopher himself choosing his symbol, his cipher [*chiffre*]. Or, if it is such an act, it loses its general value and is no longer the theory of philosophies in general.

What is perhaps at the basis of these two philosophies of Heidegger and Jaspers is a double feeling of regret and hope; a double feeling that corresponds to those two ecstases of time, to speak like Heidegger, namely, the past and the future; a double feeling that, so to speak, scans [*scande*] time; it is the double feeling of paradise lost and paradise regained that is repetition.

It was in thinking of the efforts of these philosophers that I said to myself: it is perhaps in those who are not philosophers that one could find attempts that are similar and in a sense closer to existence. And the names that by chance came to mind—by chance, but in choosing among those I admire most—are Rimbaud, Van Gogh, and Nietzsche. Now, all three, in a very strong way, also had precisely these two feelings of subjectivity and transcendence. What strikes us in the work of Van Gogh is at once the intensity of his feeling and the fact that—to borrow a phrase that, I believe, is Cézanne's—he "made the image [*faisait l'image*]." And, likewise, in Nietzsche there are, on the one hand, the superhuman and, on the other, the Eternal Return symbolizing what is most absurd, the immanent symbolizing the purely transcendent in relation to our thought.

The very fact of having chosen Rimbaud or Van Gogh or Nietzsche rather than Heidegger or Jaspers does not, moreover, go against their profound thought. For Heidegger indeed tells us that the metaphysics of human reality is not only a metaphysics about reality; it is a metaphysics necessarily coming to produce itself as reality. Now, this is perhaps what we find in someone like Rimbaud or Nietzsche. And when Heidegger, in one of his later works, speaks of [Friedrich] Hölderlin, it is perhaps initially not a very different feeling that moves him; it is the idea that art is also grasped by the individual as a relation with the transcendent. And with even more reason, one could say, Jaspers could agree with what I just laid out because he very strongly has this feeling of the value of art; moreover, he also makes reference to Van Gogh and it is above all in the individual as existence that he finds the reality of philosophy.

Mr. Léon Brunschvicg.[27]—I believe that Mr. Gabriel Marcel, who has been familiar with Wahl's thought for a long time, as Wahl has been with his thought, will indeed wish to give us the pleasure of hearing his response?

Mr. Gabriel Marcel.[28]—My response will focus on the written text[29] rather than the oral presentation of Jean Wahl's talk because the latter appears to me to be subdued in comparison with what we have read, principally on the point with which I am most concerned. I will not, however, attempt to interpret this divergence, which appears to me very appreciable.

It is obvious that my remarks will not focus on the first part of the talk. Regarding Kierkegaard, I am competent only to an extremely slight degree. I have the impression, however, that everything that has been said must be true and that it bears on an essential element in Kierkegaardian thought.

---

27. [Léon Brunschvicg (1869–1944) was Wahl's senior colleague at the Sorbonne, where at this time he was France's most influential neo-Kantian and held the Chair in the History of Modern Philosophy.]

28. [Gabriel Marcel (1889–1973) was a close friend of Wahl's. Although he preferred to be called a "neo-Socratic," Marcel was known as the leading representative of Christian existentialism; his *Metaphysical Journal,* published in 1927 (the same year as Heidegger's *Being and Time*), to which Wahl devoted a chapter in his *Vers le concret* (1932), is considered by many to be the first work of twentieth-century existential philosophy.]

29. [That is, the text reproduced at the beginning of this chapter, under sections I and II.]

Conversely, I find myself much less in agreement with the remarks that were presented thereafter.

"One might wonder," we read in the text that has been sent to us, "whether 'transascendence' is necessarily good, 'transdescendence' necessarily bad." I will admit, although this is probably not the case, that the meaning of these two terms, "transascendence" and "transdescendence," is sufficiently specified by the references that follow: Blake, Gide, . . . etc. But what in any case remains absolutely vague are the words "good" and "bad," and I think that at least in many of the poets evoked—I would say in any case in Lawrence and in Cowper Powys, and quite probably also in Gide (provided that one considers the whole of his corpus)—one sees by the same token that the notion of good and evil has not been subjected to a reflection that would be liable to elucidate it. It would therefore be necessary to begin by making explicit the meaning that these two words present in the phrase in question.

Do we mean—and I suppose we do—that what is good is what exalts our powers, or our feeling of this power? From this point of view, we might in fact be tempted to say that transdescendence can be good. This would mean, in a more precise, more graspable language, that in placing a very strong emphasis on the subterranean parts of ourselves, or, if you will, on the dark God—it is not difficult to find many analogous expressions, particularly in Lawrence—we can contribute to reinforcing in ourselves a certain immediate awareness of our existence as power.

I would say that this is not a discovery, not even a paradox, but a truism. I want to note especially that this claim makes sense only if we have begun by denaturing the notion of the good, that is to say, if we have begun by taking it in the bio-energetic sense. On the contrary, the more one is concerned here with remaining in accord with the grand spiritual tradition of humanity—here it is not a matter of Occidentalism—the more this claim will appear devoid of meaning. But I wonder whether one will not refuse to clarify rather carefully, as I have just done, this radical change in sense of the words "good" and "evil," whether one will not in a way play on the uncertainty in which one will have left it.

Generally, I would say that, in speaking of transdescendence in opposition to transascendence, one is confined, it seems to me, to recalling what Schelling understood perfectly after Boehme: that the order of powers is reversible, and I for my part think that any philosophy that fails to recognize this possibility is in a certain sense strictly obsolete. Only, I would add right away that the philosopher is obliged to take up a position with respect to this reversal, to see it as it is, that is to say, as subversion, and this is what Schelling in particular never failed to do.

I think that if a philosopher abstains from taking up a position of this sort in the presence of this reversal, he risks *betraying himself*. I believe that if there is a possible betrayal in philosophy, it is probably doing just this. And all the thoughts which, I would say, come to terms with an infrarational element make themselves culpable of precisely this. Moreover, it is the point at which I think that, between the philosophies of existence as I, for my part, conceive them and a certain rationalism, the accord is most readily established. Here I suppose that what would need to be attacked is the Nietzschean notion of transvaluation, of *Umwertung* . . . , with the confusion that it implies between a will to purification, a sincerity that is militant and always more attentive to its own requirements—which is the essential element in Nietzsche—and a sort of will to subversion of fundamental values that takes root either in an ensemble of complexes treated as postulates, or in a naturalist metaphysics.

I will not accept very readily the remark according to which transcendence is not necessarily God or the devil, but perhaps simply nature. Here, too, it seems to me that the imprecision of terms may be indicative of an uncertainty about what one is aiming for. What does this phrase mean: transcendence can simply be nature? In opposing the latter to God, it seems to me that your observation comes down to this: nature can itself be experienced as being beyond what is conceived according to certain norms. This is what attests almost without exception to the experience of all the great lyric poetry. But this is simply a given. The philosophical problem arises with this word, with this naturing and not natured nature.[30] Here it is opposed to God only because one allows oneself, but here too without making it explicit, a certain idea of God, for example as the moral order of the world, if you will, or perhaps as a person, . . . etc.

Moreover, it remains to be investigated whether, in the very breast of this naturing nature, hierarchical powers, whose order, once again, can be reversed, are not to be distinguished, to be opposed as the Romantics believed.

---

30. [Marcel here appeals to a Scholastic distinction used primarily by Spinoza between *natura naturans* (nature naturing) and *natura naturata* (nature natured): "By *Natura naturans* we must understand what is in itself and is conceived through itself, *or* such attributes of substance as express an eternal and infinite essence, that is . . . God, insofar as he is considered as a free cause. But by *Natura naturata* I understand whatever follows from the necessity of God's nature, *or* from God's attributes, that is, all the modes of God's attributes insofar as they are considered as things which are in God, and can neither be nor be conceived without God." Baruch Spinoza, *Ethics*, trans. Edwin Curley (London: Penguin, 1996), part I, prop. 29, Scholium.]

These remarks lead to the response that I for my part will give to the questions of the last paragraph. Can one conceive of a philosophy similar to Heidegger's and Jaspers's whose attraction would not partly be explained by the nostalgia and religious echo it contains? I will not speak here of attraction. The problem is rather of knowing whether a philosophy of existence can be constituted without reference to the transcendent. It certainly can in appearance, or if one wishes to consider only the formal aspect of these notions; but it remains to be asked whether an existence that is not referred to the transcendent is not thinned out or does not degenerate into pure facticity.... Would the general theory that this philosophy of existence would come down to not be a schematic of observation? One signals the danger that this philosophy of existence courts of associating itself too closely with theology. What does this mean? I perceive here only the peril—one that is, moreover, real—that the philosopher would surreptitiously make use of elements, not of theology, but of a specific theology, and that he would thereby betray himself.

Here again a very careful examination is required. Does not the idea of sin or of falling as it appears in existential philosophy translate a fundamental given that opens itself up to reflection as soon as we become fully conscious of the situation that makes us exist? This is surely Jaspers's point of view; and also, I think, Heidegger's....

It is a matter of seeing what is valid in itself in these analyses; if they are found to coincide to some degree with the affirmations of theology, then there is nothing there that should arouse our mistrust if these analyses are recognized to be accurate. After all, it is all the more necessary to wonder where these theological ideas come from. They have not fallen from the sky.

Finally, a word about the concluding remark, explaining why I cannot accept it either. The existence of Rimbaud, or of Nietzsche, or of Hölderlin, is not in itself philosophical or existential. It presents these characteristics—which are, moreover, ambiguous—only in terms of a philosophy of existence. If I am a doctor, what is it that prevents me from treating the fate of Nietzsche as a clinical case of syphilis? Nothing objectively, absolutely nothing. One is always free not to understand anything at all. But what is thus at issue is justifying this other point of view, this existential point of view. And it is philosophy and it alone that can do this by showing that in a certain respect—but it is still necessary to establish in what respect—the pathological particularities that the individuality of Nietzsche presents are devoid of significance or at least have a significance that ought to be interpreted according to the complete whole.

The conclusion of all of these remarks is that, on the one hand, one cannot do without philosophy in this domain. I think it is absolutely futile to say: after all, the philosophies of existence are much less important than these or those lives. Certainly, these lives are essential, and I will indeed go so far as to say that a philosophy of existence can probably be constituted *in concreto* only by "monographs" (I do not like this word), that is to say, only by reference to lives endowed with a certain tragic significance. Nothing appears to me to be more precise.

Only this cannot mean, once again, that the consideration of these privileged lives can be sufficient unto itself. I do not even see how one could conceive it.

Finally—it is this point that is personally closest to my heart, and concerning which we could perhaps have a useful discussion—I do not at all believe that a philosophy, an existential philosophy if you will, can take any sort of liberty with the fundamental values, or, more exactly, it can do so, assuredly, it can do so to the extent to which, as philosophy, it is, if you will, liberty in action; only, it remains to be known whether this liberty, exercised in such a way, I would say in such a self-destructive way, does not head toward its own annihilation?

Mr. Jean Wahl.—It is true that, in the second paragraph of the synopsis, in which I spoke of "transascendence" and of "transdescendence," I connected the word "transdescendence," in associating it with what Kierkegaard said, to the idea of a demonic force, and that it has consequently taken on a moral, and thereby even immoral, aspect. I would have liked to stay outside of these categories of morality and immorality. I wanted to say that, as indeed you said, there is a way to reconnect with the profound forces of being [*l'être*], and that this transdescendence is not degeneration. I did not want to say that evil is good; this is a problem that I am not going to analyze for the moment. Have I betrayed myself in saying what I said? I do not believe so. I believe, rather, that many betray philosophy who make use of questions of morals or of value in questions that are of pure knowledge.

Here it is not a matter of saying what is good or evil, and I was wrong insofar as I used the words "good" and "evil." In remaining within the domain of a sort of contemplation, whether it be sensible or artistic or metaphysical, it is a matter of seeking what, indeed, expands our knowledge and intensifies our spontaneity.

Your second objection concerned the idea of nature. You said that nature was divinized. That is possible. It depends. Do you think that the idea of divinizing necessarily presupposes the idea of a God? I mean: do you think that there is not perhaps a more primitive idea here? And it is to this primitive something that I would like to return. The word "nature" is indeed, for many reasons, perhaps not very well chosen. I had, I believe, said at the beginning "the world" or "the external world," words equally insufficient. There is no word. I mean the other who is not necessarily the God of religions or the God of heterodoxies.

You said that there cannot be philosophical reflection without transcendence. But I am struck by the fact that, in [Herbert] Spencer for example, there is transcendence and yet we do not find in him, in any case I do not find in him, this tension that I am looking for in a Kierkegaard. It thus does not depend on transcendence or nontranscendence, it also depends on one's attitude with respect to things. A philosopher with transcendence like Spencer does not appear to be very satisfying. And there can be such a philosopher or such an artist without transcendence who, by his intensity, much more gives me the impression of calling out to something profound within me.

With respect to that feeling of falling, I do not know whether we have that feeling of falling; it is a question to be studied: do we originally have the feeling of the original fall? Sometimes we have a feeling of solitude, we have a feeling of anxiety if you will; I do not know whether by nature we have the feeling of falling.

As for the artists or philosophers I mentioned at the end of my talk, I believe that it would be necessary to make a distinction between, for example, Nietzsche and Rimbaud, or Van Gogh, and it would even be necessary to make yet another distinction between Rimbaud and Van Gogh. But there is indeed a philosophical reflection in Nietzsche, I can even say in Rimbaud, and I can even say in Van Gogh if one makes reference to certain of his letters. I do not see why I would be prohibited from turning toward them as sources of philosophy. For it is indeed as sources of philosophy that I turn toward them. You told me that, on their own, they cannot be interpretations, responses. That seems obvious to me. You also told me that Nietzsche could be explained by psychoanalysis. But perhaps inasmuch as the philosophy of Heidegger touches the depths of being [*l'être*], it can also be explained by psychoanalysis.

I see that there would be many other things to say. But perhaps what you will add will lead me to clarify a bit.

Mr. Gabriel Marcel.—I would like to respond to these different points.

Regarding the first point, it seems to me that, at bottom, the essential thing would be to analyze the idea of profundity because I believe that there are terrible equivocations there. The elemental is, in a certain sense, what is profound. But, in another sense, it is not at all what is profound. In reality, we ought to make use of these tarnished metaphors with prudence, metaphors about which we are not even careful anymore.

You spoke of pure knowledge with respect to my first objection. But we are not in the order of knowledge, we are at all times in the order of evaluation. You said that the words "good" and "bad" with their moral resonance were perhaps not those that were essential [*s'imposaient*] here. It will nevertheless be necessary for you to substitute others for them, which will also be evaluative terms. Consequently, if we are in the order of evaluation (and it seems to me that if we are not then we are nowhere; because it is not a matter of explanation, we are absolutely not in the order of explanatory theory), if you introduce an evaluation, I believe that the objection I have made will reappear.

Let us move on to the second point, that is to say, to the transcendence of nature. You said, "I am not sure that nature, for example as it is found in the great lyric poetry, is divinized. Is there really the idea of a God there?" I am terribly suspicious of the word "idea." It is certain that, if we place ourselves on properly ideological terrain, we will be able to grant you all you want. What is important here is the attitude. It is difficult to deny that there is, in someone like Schelling for example, a certain attitude of adoration in the presence of nature. For me, it is enough to speak of a sort of diffuse theology. It seems to me that you employ the terms "God" and "theology" in a determinate, hyper-Christian sense. But there can be a non-Christian theology. This is all the same what is important.

It is not a question of words. The term you used there is very important. From the moment one introduces a transcendence, isn't one, to some degree, doing theology? I do not believe that the idea of transcendence can ultimately be secularized. This is perhaps the expression I would use.

On the third point, regarding existence, you evoke Spencer. This is a man who has perhaps never reflected, and who, at the very least, has probably not had any idea of what we can call transcendence. I will therefore not speak of transcendence with regard to his doctrine. We are playing here on purely verbal analogies. You cannot say that transcendence in Kierkegaard or Heidegger has anything in common with the Spencerian unknown—and perhaps precisely because Spencer always places himself on a terrain of knowledge. He is marginally an intellectual, but he remains all the same an intellectual. He is not at all elevated to something higher. Everything you said at the beginning, which is important and ought to be elaborated concerning the relations between objectivity and transcendence, is precisely the contrary of what we can see in Spencer. I will thus not accept you citing Spencer as an example; there, it seems to me, the problem does not even arise. We are not in the order of the subjective, but in the order of the infra-objective. . . .

In what concerns the feeling of falling: again a question that appears to me very ambiguous. You seem to pose this question for the sake of a potential inquiry. Can one say that every being finds in itself, in some way, this experience or this feeling? I would say: it is infinitely probable that no, one cannot; in any case, every being is not conscious of it. But that is still a matter of absolute indifference to me; it is not what interests me, and I would say that the first to recognize that a single being, a single soul in which we truly find this experience or this feeling to a certain degree of intensity and clarity counts much more than the millions of beings that all in all do not have any sort of interior life.

Conversely, it is difficult for me to subscribe to what you said about Nietzsche, Rimbaud, Van Gogh, etc. First of all, because I believe that this connection is altogether fallacious. Nietzsche is still a philosopher. That distorts everything. The problem that you raise exists in its purity only if you draw from artists who are not at all philosophers. From this point of view, if you will, Van Gogh, and I would say Rimbaud as well, are more satisfying examples. But there is still a question of interpretation. How can you ignore this? Do not they themselves furnish us with all the elements of this interpretation? It is not certain. There is a methodological problem here that we are obliged to raise. When you said, at the end: after all, the philosophy of Heidegger itself can in a certain sense be considered as a phenomenon answerable to psychoanalysis, just like the experience of Rimbaud—you were not taking into account the difference between this philosophy and a nonphilosophy: this philosophy is above all an effort to make its own postulates explicit. To the extent to which the philosophy of Heidegger harbors psychoanalytic elements, supposing that this is the case, it will recognize this. And, to me, it is only philosophy on this condition. This is why I am obliged to employ this term "explicitation [*explicitation*]" all the time. Herein lies the whole question. From the moment in which there is explicitation, there is philosophy, and from that moment alone.

You said that lives like those are philosophical ones. I agree. I do not see that there is a question here. Only, are the sources of philosophy, independently, in some way, the philosophers who interpret them and comment on them? Posing the question seems to me to be sufficient for answering it.

Mr. Jean Wahl.—I believe that you risk belittling philosophy, whereas I would like to exalt it in saying that it exists just as much in "the nonphilosophers as in the philosophers." I do not see that philosophy should simply be defined as explicitation. When the postulates are implicit, will this mean there is no philosophy? No. I would say that precisely in Rimbaud, whose postulates I moreover do not know exactly, there is not philosophy but, rather, a source of philosophy. You will tell me that I thus agree with you, since you admit that there is a source of philosophy in Rimbaud? Except that the philosopher, according to you, will be the one who reflects on what is, in another, the state of existence?

Mr. Gabriel Marcel.—Not necessarily. Because I completely believe that the greatest can be those who have been at once their own poet and their own philosopher. When you say that I make philosophy into a function of pure explicitation, you distort my thought a little. I believe that there is truly philosophy only where there is a certain interior creation that is absolutely fundamental. What I am saying is that if this creation is not accompanied by a reflection on itself, it is pre-philosophical or peri-philosophical. And here the example of Kierkegaard would be significant.

Mr. Jean Wahl.—It is no less significant in the sense that he is indeed the example of both. He is the example of a life that does not make completely explicit . . . He is the example of someone whom I can place on the same level as Nietzsche and even as Rimbaud and Van Gogh, and to whom you no doubt accord the name of philosopher.

Mr. Gabriel Marcel.—It is an unfulfilled philosophy [*une philosophie manquée*].

Mr. Jean Wahl.—He is rather a source of philosophy, but a source of philosophy appears to me to be at least as great as philosophy.

Mr. Gabriel Marcel.—"As great . . ." We cannot pose the question in these terms. Who would think to make a sort of comparison between the greatness of an artist and that of a philosopher? I do not see any sort of sense in this question. What I can say simply is that a creation that is not accompanied by a reflection is an incomplete creation, it is a creation that needs the other, which is drawn toward the other, while, in spite of everything, for me, if we remain faithful to a certain traditional notion, the philosopher is all the same αὐτάρχης ["independent," "autonomous"].

Mr. Jean Wahl.—The essence of man is precisely that in him nothing is accomplished unless there is at the same time reflection on what he accomplishes, at least on a certain level. In someone like Van Gogh or Rimbaud you cannot say that there is no reflection on what comes to pass in them. While for you it would be a matter of putting thoroughly philosophical reflections on one side, and a reflection that is not philosophical on the other?

Mr. Gabriel Marcel.—The case of Rimbaud is very discouraging. When one sees the absolutely contradictory interpretations on the evolution of Rimbaud that continue to be proposed, we are forced to conclude that one does not find in Rimbaud himself something to elucidate him; I am not saying that, from a certain perspective, it diminishes him, but it does not permit classifying him as a philosopher.

Mr. Jean Wahl.—In a great philosopher, what in part comprises his value is that he cannot be completely elucidated either.

Mr. Gabriel Marcel.—I share your opinion. It is indeed certain that to the extent to which a philosopher fits into a history, he is a sort of call to interpretations that will come after him. But, nevertheless, it is still necessary for him to have made a certain effort to interpret himself. This does not mean that this self-interpretation is sufficient.

Mr. Jean Wahl.—This appears to me to be very difficult. I indeed see that Rimbaud did not express himself in the language of the courses that are taught here, and that Heidegger comes closer to philosophical lectures. But I do not at all see that there is less profound reflection in a Rimbaud than in Heidegger. It would be a matter of studying the mode of reflection you call philosophy.

Mr. Gabriel Marcel.—I would say, at the risk of scandalizing all the Rimbaudians, that the greater an artist is, the more he is reduced to a phenomenon; to the extent to which there is the phenomenon Rimbaud, what you said applies to him, but on the condition of entirely refusing him this αὐτάρχεια ["independence," "autonomy"], that is to say, of containing within himself his own interpretation.

Mr. Léon Brunschvicg (chair)—Perhaps there are autarchic philosophers who propose to intervene to arbitrate the debate?

Mr. René Berthelot.[31]—I do not claim to arbitrate anything, I want only to present some remarks parallel to those of Mr. Wahl, which may, on certain points, agree with the scope of his conclusions, while diverging from it on other points.

I will first of all consider, as he did, Kierkegaard's work. When he tells us that, from a philosophical point of view, one can characterize Kierkegaard's thought by the ideas of subjectivity and transcendence and by their union, I agree with him. But I will at once make an objection. Another characteristic of Kierkegaard is not especially being a philosopher. In him, philosophy, artistic and literary creation, and religious feeling have not ceased to be indissolubly united and to affect one another. He was even a theater and music critic as well as a religious apologist. He himself divided his work into two groups, the first including what he called his aesthetic works; the sec-

---

31. [René Berthelot (1872–1960) worked in metaphysics and political philosophy; he also wrote on pragmatism, Goethe, and was one of the first French philosophers to work on Indian philosophy.]

ond, what he called his works of piety. He did not make a third group for the philosophical works. The books in which he more directly treated philosophical problems and defined what he calls its "categories" (the individual, anxiety, sin, repetition, and the instant) are *Philosophical Fragments* (1844), *The Concept of Anxiety* (1844), and *Repetition* (1843); yet he classified these books among his aesthetic works. One would be tempted, moreover, to classify them as religious works as well, given the space they allot to the notion of sin, and the manner in which, with respect to the notion of the instant, the author invokes the passage in which Saint Paul speaks of the transformation of our being "in the twinkling of an eye."[32]

It thus seems to me that to isolate Kierkegaard's philosophical thought is to distort his own personality, his vital and historical individuality, and almost, in a certain sense, to distort his philosophical thought itself, since one of the characteristics of the latter is not being uniquely, independently philosophical.

Yet, if we attempt to view Kierkegaard from this point of view, which I can do in only the most summary fashion, I will translate your two philosophical terms—subjectivity and transcendence—by two others that are in large part aesthetic and religious and that appear to me to indicate more intimately who he was. I would say first of all that, in him, subjectivity is Romanticism, and then that, in him, transcendence is Calvinism. And if I attempted to define, in an inevitably incomplete formula, as all formulae of this variety are, who Kierkegaard was, I would say that he was a Romantic Calvinist, and that it is by this that he is distinguished from other Romantics and other Calvinists.

In the first place, Kierkegaard (1813–55) appears to me necessarily to be a Romantic, and, to be more specific, a German Romantic. Despite claiming that, for him, his religious faith permitted him to exceed subjectivity—he thereby opposed himself to Romanticism—we nevertheless find in him all the dominant traits. This is what Georg Brandes established clearly in his study of German Romanticism, a number of chapters of which cite or take up Kierkegaard in order to show point by point that his thought and his literary conception come close to either that of [Ludwig] Tieck (with his belief in the metaphysical significance of music and humor) or that of Novalis, or that of the Schlegel brothers, . . . etc. Brandes, like Kierkegaard, was Danish, and the influence of Kierkegaard was so strong in Denmark when Brandes was writing that it was natural for him to have wanted to make his contemporaries see that Kierkegaard was

32. [1 Cor. 15:52 (KJV).]

not an isolated phenomenon, an aerolite, but rather a Danish reflection of the feelings, literary forms, and philosophical thought of the German Romantics.

I thus believe that if one takes him in his concrete individuality and in his historicity, it is indispensible to begin by realigning him with this current of German Romanticism.

Mr. Jean Wahl.—What I wanted to do was to separate him from this current in order to take him on his own.

Mr. René Berthelot.—But do you not risk distorting his physiognomy in isolating him, in abstracting him, from this current, if, taken on his own and in his concrete reality, he is inseparable from it? If I insist on this point, it is because Kierkegaard's thought appears to me to have contemporary import only to the extent to which German Romanticism does. What do we find in Kierkegaard? What we find with much more richness, creative poetic power, and philosophical profundity in the great German Romantics.

In certain respects, the thought of Kierkegaard is connected to the reaction of Schelling, in his old age, against Hegelianism. But, to interpret it more broadly, his subjectivism corresponds to an intermediary attitude between that of Fichte and that of Schelling and in which one finds something of the second Fichte and something of the first Schelling, during the period in which these two thinkers were most closely in contact with one another. Here there is a form of philosophical Romanticism that only lasted several years, and the thought of Kierkegaard as a theory of subjectivity is linked, not exclusively, but quite particularly, with that epoch of German thought.

I pass over to the second point, transcendence. As I said, it seems to me that in order to attempt to move us closer to Kierkegaard, in his concrete individuality and his historical reality, we ought once again to place him within the Calvinist current. He knows himself to be isolated not only from other men but from his God. This can be seen precisely in his violent attacks against the official Danish church. And this double isolation, as you said, is essential for him.

Now, we find this in Ibsen's Brand, and we know through Georg Brandes that this tragic persona was, for the dramaturge, inspired by the personality of Kierkegaard. He indeed presents the double mark of transcendence in Kierkegaard, the isolation vis-à-vis those close to him, and the fact of conceiving of his God as unattainable.

In certain heroes of Ibsen as in Ibsen himself, there is what one could call a Calvinism without Christianity. [Thomas Henry] Huxley (Huxley the Elder, the friend of Darwin) said of Auguste Comte that his philosophy was a Catholicism without Christianity. There has likewise been for a half-century now a certain number of thinkers and writers of whom one can say that they are linked with a Protestantism without Christianity, and, for many among them, with a Calvinism without Christianity. Up to the end, that Calvinist pessimism did not cease to mark Ibsenian theater with its stamp. Jean-Gabriel Borkman is still like Brand, and here the lasting influence of Kierkegaard's thought on the dramaturge can be seen, in the sense in which you defined it with the word "transcendence." Even when he undertook to detach himself from the Romanticism of his youth, even when he parted from traditional Protestantism, there persisted in Ibsen the moral attitude of the Calvinist. And, by reason of the more literary than philosophical nature of the spirit of Kierkegaard, it is without doubt in a dramaturge like Ibsen rather than among the philosophers that one should look for his most authentic successor: Kierkegaard is situated between Calvin and Ibsen.

One can also discern thereby which of his contemporaries the Danish writer appears to be closest to, by his feelings or his thoughts as by his literary style: it is to [Thomas] Carlyle, above all to the Carlyle of the first period. The solitary Scot of Craigenputtock was of Puritan (that is to say, Calvinist) formation and at the same time of Romantic formation (in the sense of German Romanticism, to which he owed, among other things, his "inarticulate" "song"[33] and his tormented humor, so similar to those of Kierkegaard). Kierkegaard is a sort of Danish Carlyle, a Carlyle who would have stayed with *Sartor Resartus*, who would not have suffered the social influence of Saint-Simonianism and would not have dedicated himself to historical researches.

I believe equally that from there we can draw some general conclusions concerning the use that certain philosophers today are making of the thought of Kierkegaard.

Can one make some of the central themes of this thought the point of departure for a philosophical doctrine? This is the problem you have posed for yourself.

I do not at all want to enter into the details of Heidegger's and Jaspers's doctrine. I will keep myself to an overall indication: it seems to me that these diverse philosophies open to us, above all, the reflections of a rather particular state of the soul, and that it is chimerical for this reason to claim to interpret this state of the soul as justified as a whole by a metaphysical doctrine aiming at universality. The largely aesthetic character of the thought of Kierkegaard is one of the reasons that makes an interpretation of this

---

33. [See Thomas Carlyle, *Heroes and Hero Worship*, in *The Works of Thomas Carlyle*, vol. 5 (Cambridge: Cambridge University Press, 2010), 83, 247.]

genre difficult and, to my mind, illegitimate. And this critique seems to me to fall back in many respects on the Kierkegaardians of whom you spoke, in spite of all the differences that there may be among these philosophers and their master. I believe, moreover, that, on this point, I would no longer find myself in disagreement with you.

I am thereby brought back to Schelling, by whom Kierkegaard was inspired philosophically; for Schelling does not fail to provide us with the elements for a judgment not only on Kierkegaard but on the Kierkegaardians of our times.

In a work of his first period, the *System of Transcendental Idealism*, Schelling declared—and this is a profound view—that what is at once necessary and incomprehensible in the development of spirit is the passage from "original limitation" to "derived limitation."[34] Roughly, original limitation is the necessity, for spirit, to manifest itself as a finite and individual "I." Derived limitation is, for spirit, the fact of being precisely such a finite "I," this individual "I" precisely that I am, in such an instant of time, and not some other "I," different from the former, in some other instant. Now, following Schelling, from the moment in which spirit posits the original limitation in itself, it is impossible for it not to posit the derived limitation in itself by the same spiritual act. But, conversely, the derived limitation, that is to say, the very particularity of this "I" that it is, cannot extract itself from the original limitation. What is at once necessary and incomprehensible in philosophy, according to Schelling, is therefore the passage from original limitation to derived limitation. Now, to want to interpret, by a metaphysics that has a universal value, either Kierkegaard or the particular psychological cases which Heidegger and Jaspers analyze and to which they claim to attribute a universal value, is precisely for the philosopher to attempt to make this illegitimate, incomprehensible passage from original limitation to derived limitation. And, therefore, this formula of Schelling appears to me implicitly to contain within itself the critique both of the general attitude of Kierkegaard, and of the contemporary philosophers about whom you have spoken to us.

At the end of the same work—and this is not at all Fichtean—Schelling affirms (I translate his thought metaphorically) that, upon this half-open abyss that is at each instant in us and before each of our steps, the only spiritual force that can cast a rainbow is art. Here is a thought of which Kierkegaard himself, the good Romantic that he was, did not fail to take

---

34. [Friedrich Wilhelm Joseph von Schelling, *System of Transcendental Idealism*, trans. Peter Heath (Charlottesville: University Press of Virginia, 1978), 59.]

advantage. And it is, I believe, a thought that the contemporary disciples of Kierkegaard, as well as without doubt Schelling toward the end of his life, would have done well to contemplate more.

Rousseau recounts that a Venetian woman, irritated with the way he was acting toward her, told him one day: *"Va e fa della matematica"* ["Go and do math"].[35] If philosophy could speak and address herself in Italian to her hesitant lovers, perhaps she would say to them: *"Va e fa della musica"* ["Go and make music"].

Mr. Jean Wahl.—I thank you very much for what you have brought to bear on the elements that have formed the thought of Kierkegaard.

The president proposes to Mr. Berdyaev and Mr. Landsberg to take the floor. Mr. Jean Wahl will then be able to give an overall response.

Mr. Nicolas Berdyaev.[36]—I will present two remarks.

A distinction should be made between an existential philosophy and the philosophy of existence. I think that you essentially make this distinction. For example, Kierkegaard and Nietzsche are existential philosophers. Heidegger and Jaspers are not. Theirs is a philosophy of existence. Existential philosophy is the expression of an existential experience and it gives a very high value to philosophers themselves as existing. The philosophy of existence, even though Jaspers says that existence can never be an object, makes existence an object of the philosopher's knowledge.

Another remark. There is a very great difference, I think, between transcendence and the simple supposition that there is a reality beyond, an absolute reality, God, or the world beyond. For transcendence is an existential experience; it is a movement. We can suppose that there exists a world beyond, as, for example, Spencer supposes that there is the "unknowable," and at the same time, there is no transcendence at all in Spencer's experience itself, nor in his philosophy. Nothing happens here, even though he says: there is the unknowable; absolutely nothing. It is exactly the opposite of transcendence as an existential experience.

---

35. [Rousseau writes, in book 7 of the *Confessions*: "*lascia le donne, e studia la matematica*" ("leave the ladies alone, and study mathematics"). See Jean-Jacques Rousseau, *Les Confessions / Les Rêveries du promeneur solitaire*, ed. Louis Martin-Chauffier (Paris: Gallimard, 1951), 315; *The "Confessions" and Correspondence, Including the Letters to Malesherbes*, in *The Collected Writings of Rousseau*, vol. 5, ed. Christopher Kelley, Roger D. Masters, and Peter G. Stillman, trans. Christopher Kelley (Hanover, N.H.: University Press of New England, 270).]

36. [Nicholas Berdyaev (1874–1948) was a Russian religious and political philosopher who emigrated to Paris in 1923. Like Marcel, his work is associated with Christian existentialism.]

The philosopher, in his knowledge, can pass from subjectivity to the objective, through objectification. And he can pass from subjectivity to the transcendent, through transcendence. These are two completely different paths. I think that philosophy becomes less and less existential when the philosopher passes from subjectivity to objectivity. And it remains existential if the philosopher passes from subjectivity to a transcendence. Transcendence is never an object, is never an objective world. It is something completely different. When one makes transcendence an objective world, one does precisely the opposite of what an existential philosophy does. And I think that this is the danger of Heidegger's and Jasper's philosophy, that, at bottom, it is not quite clear what they are doing: is it a movement toward objectivity, or a transcendence?

In Kierkegaard, it is completely the opposite.

One cannot—not only the philosopher, but also man—remain in subjectivity. Man is a being who surpasses himself, who transcends himself. Different roads open up here in this surpassing of oneself. Basically, Jaspers, in his little book *Vernunft und Existenz*[37] (one of the most recent books he has written), admits that existential philosophy is not possible. He says this. I think that what is interesting about Heidegger's and Jaspers's philosophy is that they are philosophers who were wounded by the existential experience of Kierkegaard and Nietzsche. Jaspers says this. This experience of Kierkegaard and of Nietzsche influenced their philosophy; but even so it is not an existential philosophy. Perhaps it would be paradoxical, but if, for example, one took the philosophy of Hegel, which is completely the opposite of Kierkegaard's philosophy and of existential philosophy as Kierkegaard understood it, one could say that it is more existential than Heidegger's and Jaspers's philosophy because Hegel lived in the dialectic. He experienced it; it was existence for him, in a certain sense. A completely different existence from the experience of transcendence, which is a catastrophic experience; it is not a development, it is not an evolution. Hegel inhabited an existence of a completely different type. But it was, all the same, a lived, experienced [*vécue*] philosophy.

Mr. Jean Wahl.—I think that I am in complete agreement with you, except that we would still have to examine the question of knowing whether Heidegger lives his philosophy. This, we do not have the right . . .

Mr. Nicolas Berdyaev.—Every important philosopher, every true philosopher does this, it is not only Heidegger; but if we say this, we must say

---

37. [Karl Jaspers, *Vernunft und Existenz* (Groningen: Wolters, 1935); *Reason and Existenz*, trans. William Earle (New York: Noonday Press, 1955).]

that in general there is no philosophy other than existential philosophy, but there is here, all the same, a certain difference.

Mr. Paul Landsberg.[38]—I do not want to come back to the problem of existential philosophy, nor to speak of Heidegger and Jaspers because I think that Berdyaev has formulated here and in his books some evident truths on this transformation of an existential philosophy into a false objectification of existence. It seems to me that this took place irrefutably, and that a tragic and fascinating fall of spirit occurred there. I do want to come back to this quite captivating dialogue that Mr. Wahl had with Mr. Gabriel Marcel, particularly to the, so to speak, burning issue that is present in this dialogue—I mean the problem of "transascendence" and "transdescendence," as I believe he put it—in any case, we think we know what he means by these terms.

I think that perhaps the problem posed by this dialogue was not posed with absolute clarity, and that here Mr. Wahl, Mr. Marcel, and the rest of us still have some work to do in order to first make clear what the problem is. Because I think that it is a problem that is not artificial, but that exists in itself. If I understand the approach that Wahl was taking, he began, not only in his talk, since I am taking the liberty to speak a little about the history of his thought [*esprit*] as well—he began with the interpretation of Kierkegaard, and he found there a certain description of a lived experience, of an existential experience of transcendence.

And here I must note that, for me, what takes precedence over everything in Kierkegaard is that he is a Christian. He is a believer, he is a Christian, and all of his philosophy, if it is philosophy, is an interpretation and a Christian pedagogy. It is an effort to direct men toward a certain realization, toward Christianity, toward a certain serious Christian, it being well understood that to be a Christian can signify no lived experience [*vécu*] other than that of becoming a Christian. If one abstracts from this, I think that Kierkegaard becomes absolutely obscure, and that one can no longer understand him. He is neither a universal philosopher in the sense that Hegel is a universal philosopher, nor a romantic. I do not want to deny what he has in common with German Romanticism, but he is not defined essentially by a romantic quality. In his work, the Christian quality is much more considerable. I think that on this point we are in agreement, Mr. Wahl and I. The lived experience [*vécue*] of transcendence by Kierkegaard, under

---

38. [Paul Landsberg (1901–44) was a German-Jewish philosopher who emigrated to France in 1933 after Hitler became Germany's chancellor. A member of the French Resistance, he was arrested in 1943 and deported to the Sachsenhausen concentration camp, where he died in April 1944.]

a rather particular form that you have distinguished nicely, is Christian transcendence, in any case *a* lived experience of Christian transcendence. And Kierkegaard's importance is, above all, that in this moment, in the middle of the nineteenth century, he is someone who authentically lived Christian transcendence and expressed it in a way that did not belong to a church or a theology. Rather, he expressed it in an immediately dialectical way, in the language of the century so to speak, with all of the richness of expression that Romanticism, poetry, etc. conveyed. You all know that this corresponds more or less to the interpretation that Kierkegaard gave to his vocation: to be a simple Christian who makes use of all the seductions of the language and thought of his century in order, as it were, to make the Christian situation and faith understood again.

Mr. Wahl has interpreted—you all know with what profundity—Kierkegaard's thought. And he finds in it, in a manner different than, for example, Jaspers and Heidegger, a certain idea of transcendence in itself that one can distinguish even from lived Christian experience, but which is, so to speak, this experience in a formalized state. (I do not know whether this expression is absolutely exact . . .) That is to say, at issue is a transcendence that, in effect, is essentially ascending, and that finds the *other* in the sacrifice of the *self* [moi] and in the sacrifice also of all there is of nature, of natural temptation, in relation to the self. As a Christian, Kierkegaard, in short, renounces the world and himself in order to give himself to his faith, in order to give himself to an ascending transcendence.

By following Kierkegaard's spiritual path, it seems to me that Mr. Wahl has found that this lived experience, which he saw under a certain form in Kierkegaard, has a much more universal sense. That is, there are other experiences that have remarkable characteristics in common with this experience: especially the characteristic of the experience of the *other*, in the strict and absolute sense that Mr. Wahl characterized it when interpreting Kierkegaard. That is, even in the sphere of the biological, of the biological as the subject of a metaphysics of life, there are some ecstasies in which the depersonalizing life takes on this character of something absolutely other, in which the self experiences the anxiety of disappearing and to which man, the self, can give himself over. Indeed, the self is between two forces . . . which, in this sense, transcend it. It is true that the self can suffer the trembling of anxiety, of feelings analogous to the approach of these two forces, one from down below and one from up above, to make use of that image, or in any case an essentially spiritual force and an essentially vital force. I think that the most fecund interpretation would be offered starting with Nietzsche and what he called Dionysus. Indeed, when he says that Dionysus is a God, he also means that here it is a matter of a transcendence, that is, that the self is as anxious, as sacrificed, as destroyed, and as transcended in uniting itself to Dionysus as it is in coming close to a spiritual God. Up to now, I think there really is an analogy from this purely descriptive point of view, and up to now, I think that everything that Mr. Wahl has said is also absolutely justifiable from a point of view that is situated, in the end, very close to Mr. Marcel. The problem Mr. Marcel touched on begins afterward and is a problem not of the philosophy of existence but of existential philosophy, to make use of Berdyaev's terms. That is, in existential philosophy man is concretely between two forces. The self is really affected by these different forces; it can grasp their difference. When in existential philosophy—I almost do not dare say it, but allow me to do so in order to be brief—one tries to follow a path very close to that of Kierkegaard, one taken by men like Kierkegaard, one indeed can recognize that there is a clash, not only between the self and an ascending transcendence, but also, in Mr. Wahl's sense, between the self and a different transcendence. If the problem of transcendence were only between the self and a single transcending "center," it would be much simpler; that which you have brought to our attention is that this problem is much more complex and that the self is situated between two forces opposed to it and to each other.

From another point of view, that is, where one is already engaged in a precise existential philosophy, one can speak, as Mr. Marcel has, of a "subversion" when a man is devoted to the dark ecstasy. Mr. Marcel already has decided on a certain direction of existence, whereas Mr. Wahl's point of view is, at first, purely descriptive, perhaps with a certain penchant for what he calls transdescendence.

Mr. Jean Wahl.—I really have nothing to say, except to thank Mr. Landsberg.

Mr. S. Marck.[39]—I have had the impression that the whole discussion, which at first seemed to accentuate a lively opposition, is, on the contrary, oriented toward goals of conciliation and agreement. This discussion is coming to a sort of negative critique of the philosophy of existence, a critique of which I entirely approve. Mr. Wahl's address has shown the evolution of the dialectics of the philosophy of existence. But in what does this dialectical evolution consist? All of the ideas discussed have converged toward the same solution, toward the recognition that the absolute, the point at which these philosophies want to locate their departure, must be taken up by a dialectical

---

39. [Siegfried Marck (1889–1957) was a German political philosopher. Both Jewish and a socialist, he moved to France after Hitler came to power and emigrated to the United States shortly before the German occupation of France.]

progression, inevitably and despite everything. The dialectical absolute is at the beginning and end of these philosophies. These philosophers begin with a definition of the absolute whose paradoxical aspect is, above all, not to offer the characteristics of a definition. We are dealing here with realities that are hidden from any definition. Indeed, subjectivity usually is defined by means of transcendence and transcendence by means of subjectivity. But this inevitable correlation—transcendence and subjectivity—can be defined for our thinking [*esprit*] only if we conceive of it beyond the play of our usual definitions. And this is why such a philosophy must end with the return to immanence. Mr. Wahl has spoken about nonphilosophies in which philosophies of existence could culminate. This remark was highly appropriate. The name of Spencer was even cited on this matter and with good reason, since the results of pseudo-dialectics necessarily lead us to a nonphilosophy.

This is why I would say that all philosophy must offer a Platonic relationship to transcendence. It will be Platonic or it will not be, or it will not exist, one could say on this occasion. And this does not mean that there are not excellent analyses in Jaspers's philosophy. But what is excellent in this philosophy is what comes from Kant. And what is excellent in Heidegger's philosophy is what comes from Husserl. But this marriage between Kant and Kierkegaard or Husserl and Kierkegaard must culminate in a nonphilosophy.

Mr. Jean Wahl.—I thank everyone who has been willing to take part in the discussion.

Mr. Marck says that he agrees with me. I, however, am afraid I do not agree with him concerning the severe judgment he directs at Heidegger and Jaspers; I have a lot of admiration for both of them. Certainly one of the starting points of their reflection is in Kierkegaard, but I think that there is a very profound elaboration and even a very particular tone in their work.

I would like to recall a comment that Mr. Berdyaev made, in thanking him. I think that the notion of transcendence would indeed need to be analyzed a little more than I have done. On this matter, it would behoove us to remember a remark that Nicolai Hartmann made, saying that one in fact must not speak of transcendence but of the "movement of that which is transcended toward that which transcends it," and which perhaps could clear up our debates. There are movements of transcendence, movements of surpassing. But transcendence should not be applied to that toward which this movement is directed. Such is Hartmann's observation, which perhaps it would be necessary to take into account.[40]

---

40. [In the *Existence humaine et transcendance* version of Wahl's talk, the following two paragraphs were added in a footnote on p. 134: "Likewise, for Heidegger, what is

Mr. Berdyaev considered the same problem as the one that Mr. Landsberg very profoundly brought to light, namely, can there be a sort of transcendence toward that which is not usually the object of transcendence, toward the object of the movement of transcendence? This is what Mr. Berdyaev had criticized; this is what Mr. Landsberg, if I understand correctly, declares to be possible. But I would not like to end by presenting a solution, because I think that the most important part of existential philosophy is, rather, to tell us that problems have value in themselves; philosophical problems cannot be completely resolved. "It is necessary," Rimbaud said, "to mold oneself into a seer [*Il faut se faire voyant*]."[41] It is necessary to mold oneself into a problem. And this is why I will not respond.

The session is ended at 6:49 P.M.

Letters with Wahl's Responses[42]

Letter from Mr. M. Heidegger[43]

Thank you very much for the kind invitation to your talk. I unfortunately cannot attend because of the work I have for the current semester.

Your critical remarks on the subject of the "philosophy of existence" ["Existenzphilosophie"] are very instructive. I however must

---

transcendent is not that toward which Dasein transcends, but is Dasein itself. Perhaps we ought to distinguish immanence and transcendence in accordance with the way in which they are presented in the theory of reality or in the theory of knowledge. In this way, Heidegger's philosophy is a philosophy of immanence, if it is seen from the perspective of the theory of reality,—and it is a theory of transcendence, if it is seen from the perspective of the theory of knowledge. Mr. Brunschvicg's theory would be a theory of immanence, from the perspective of the theory of knowledge (nevertheless putting aside the 'shock') and a theory of transcendence, from the perspective of the theory of reality, at least in a sense. Thomism is at once a theory of transcendence in the theory of knowledge and in the theory of reality.

Moreover, we indeed should have reservations about these two terms, which both retain a certain echo of their spatial origin."]

41. ["Letter to Paul Demeny (May 15, 1871)," in *Rimbaud Complete*, trans. Wyatt Mason (New York: Modern Library, 2002), 367.]

42. [Wahl's responses will follow immediately after the individual letters.]

43. [As indicated in Martin Heidegger, *Seminare, Gesamtausgabe* vol. 15, ed. Curd Ochwadt (Frankfurt am Main: Vittorio Klostermann, 1986), 410n3, Heidegger's letter to Wahl was originally written in German and then translated into French for "Subjectivity and Transcendence." The original, dated December 5, 1937, and housed in the Deutsches Literaturarchiv Marbach under call number 75.6803, differs from the French, and these differences are indicated within brackets in the text.]

repeat [also say here] that my philosophical leanings [work] cannot [can *not*] be classified as *Existenzphilosophie* ["Existenzphilosophie"], even though "Existenz" and "Kierkegaard" are at issue in *Sein und Zeit*. But, for the moment, this interpretive error will probably be difficult to set aside [stamp out, *auszurotten*].

I am in complete agreement with you when you say that the "philosophy of existence" ["Existenzphilosophie"] is exposed to the double danger of falling into either theology or ["]abstraction.["] But the question that concerns me is not the existence of man, but being as a whole and as such. And Nietzsche is not a ["]philosopher of existence["] either, since in his doctrine of the ["]will [to power"] and the ["]eternal return,["] he poses the ancient and unique question of being [*Seyn*]. But the question that alone is posed in *Sein und Zeit* is in no way taken up by Kierkegaard or Nietzsche [is as little known to Kierkegaard as it is to Nietzsche], and Jaspers misses it completely.

But perhaps these remarks [indications] are too general [rough] of a sketch to clarify what is essential.

I am pleased to be able to reproduce this letter. The fact remains that the philosophy of existence is the necessary point of departure for Heidegger, if one wants to establish a philosophy of being. I also wonder what Heidegger gives us with respect to being, properly speaking. He tells us that it is time, with its three moments, its three ecstases. But, on this point, it is very difficult to isolate his thought on the being of these "existential" elements since its three ecstases are defined in relation to *Sorge* ["care"].

Letter from Mr. E. Levinas

According to Mr. Wahl, existential philosophy includes, *in fact*, a certain number of notions of theological origin. Kierkegaard presents them as such; Heidegger and Jaspers would seek to secularize them. These notions play no less considerable a role in these philosophers, constitute the appeal of their thought, and secure its connection with the concrete.

One might wonder whether the link between theology and existential philosophy is not at once more profound and—in what concerns Heidegger—less decisive for existential philosophy than Mr. Wahl says.

More profound, on the condition that theology is not limited to the dogmatics of one positive religion or another. Dogmatics provides solutions for problems that are independent of it and appear from the simple fact of the existence of modern man. To exist is always already for him to know solitude, death and the need for salvation. When the soul is unaware of the consolation of God's presence, it has a positive experience of his absence. The discourse on God does not lose its religious essence when it appears as a "discourse on the absence of God" or even as silence with respect to God. Religiousness is never the unexpected. What thus connects existential philosophy to theology is foremost its very object, existence, taken at least as religious, if not as theological.

But, conversely, under the form that existential philosophy takes in Heidegger, it moves as far away from theology as possible. Furthermore, whatever part theology played in Heidegger's intellectual formation, one will readily admit that, for him, secularizing a notion does not amount to camouflaging its religious aspect. Secularization must signify an operation that really ends up exceeding the theological point of view. Consequently, the problem of the relationship between Heidegger's philosophy and theology depends on the sense that this secularization assumes. The point at which it occurs is, indeed, the sensitive spot of his philosophy, as it were.

In the theological attitude, things and beings [*les êtres*] are considered in a way that in Heideggerian terms we can call *ontic*. One deals with *that* which is, with "being"s ["*étant*"s][44] that serve their purpose. They are the objects of narratives. They are treated individually and belong to a drama in which we are engaged ourselves. Theology is essentially story [*histoire*] and mythology. This is why, in matters of theology, *authority* can guarantee what is true.

The great interest of Heideggerian philosophy consists in showing that at the basis of the *ontic* adventure of man there is something more than a relation of one "being" to another "being" [*d'"étant" à "étant"*], namely, the comprehension of being [*l'être*],

---

44. [Here Levinas seems to be pointing to the fact that *das Seiende* is singular in German, like *to on* in Greek, but it can sometimes function as a *singulare tantum*, that is, have a plural signification. In such cases, it is better pluralized when rendered into French (or English): étant*s* (being*s*). In contrast, *das Sein*, which is Heidegger's chief interest, as Levinas explains below, does not signify a particular being or even the sum total of all beings, but being as such and as a whole (*als solches und im Ganzen*). In this case, it cannot be plural and should appear in French (or English) as *l'être* (being) or, as some translators have done, *l'Être* (Being). "Ontic" pertains to *das Seiende*, *étants*, beings, "ontological" to *das Sein*, *l'être*, being.]

ontology. The destiny of human existence interests Heidegger only because of this ontology that it carries out. Heidegger thus breaks with theology exactly insofar as he distinguishes the ontic and the ontological (and he does this with a radicalism that is without precedent in the history of philosophy) and insofar as fundamental transcendence is carried out for him not in the passage from one "being" [*un "étant"*] to another, but from the "being" [*l'"étant"*] toward being [*l'être*].

Under these conditions, we will have to say that if Kierkegaard remains a theologian, it is not because he identified the transcendent with God rather than with nature or the devil, but because he interpreted transcendence as contact with a "being" [*un "étant"*]. If Heidegger renounces the beyond, it is not because the *beyond* would be unknowable or "more theological" than the *here-below*, but because the very distinction between the "beyond" and the "here-below" is ontic and posterior to the ontological problem. Can we claim that Heidegger derives the "fall into the domain of the anonymous crowd" from sin? Does he not, rather, look for the ontological condition of the fall, which is an ontic fact and of which original sin is a particular case (*Sein und Zeit*, 306n). It is always a matter of finding the ontological conditions for different situations of actual existence, of passing from ontic and existenti*ell* comprehension to the comprehension he calls ontological and existenti*al*. Heidegger sees this, in any case, as what is essential in his philosophical discovery. What, according to him (*Sein und Zeit*, 235n), remained foreign to Kierkegaard is the position of the problem of existence as an existenti*al* problem (in contrast with an existentiell one), in other words, the very perspective of ontology.

I would not readily accept the idea that existence is by itself a religious fact. For me, religion is of the nature of a response. And existence is first of the nature of a question.

To this question, there are responses other than religious ones; every engagement, every risk, every decision, should not necessarily be qualified as religious.

I recognize that secularization in Heidegger's work is a surpassing or, in any case, a destruction of the theological point of view.

And Mr. Levinas's observations allow us, I think, to discover the profound sense of Heidegger's reservations: the problem of being [*l'être*], which he tells us is his problem, is the problem of being transposed from the ontic domain to the existential domain (no doubt by passing through the existentiell domain). But what I do not see clearly is precisely what this existential domain is. I'm afraid that it is determined by the problem of the conditions of the possibility of existence, or a critique of existence, which poses its questions in a no more authentic and satisfying way than the critique of reason, and which, like this critique, appeals to the formal idea of "conditions of possibility." That being the case, one of the questions that would arise is how Heidegger conceives of this idea of possibility, which plays such a large role in his thought, as it does in Jaspers's, and whether he can give a definition or theory for it that would allow him to conceive it in a nonformal way.

Letter from Mr. Karl Jaspers[45]

Some weeks ago, you were gracious enough to send me your theses entitled "Subjectivity and Transcendence."[46] I will confine myself to what you said on the subject of my philosophy:

1. You write that my elucidations of limit situations also presuppose, by the concept of limitation, the idea of a totality, that of the Good and the True, but that my way of thinking cannot actually accept this totality. Now, nowhere do I claim that there is a knowledge of the totality of being; I admit only a knowledge of various "modes of encompassing" in which the knowable is revealed to me in a manner that is in each case original. Each mode of encompassing—at first, real being [*être réel*],[47] consciousness as such, spirit; then, existence[48]— encounters a limitation that is proper to it, and thus comes to the

---

45. [Jaspers's letter, like Heidegger's and perhaps other letters translated here, was originally written in German and then translated into French for publication in the *Bulletin de la Société Française de Philosophie*. As Wahl reveals in a letter to Jaspers dated April 16 (sc., 1938), it was Hans Pollnow who translated Jaspers's letter (and, we may suppose, Heidegger's and any others originally written in German). Wahl's letters to Jaspers are available at the Deutsches Literaturarchiv Marbach under access number 75.15014. Jaspers's German letter, dated January 30, 1938, began with a discussion of Descartes that was not included in the French translation, and is available under access number 75.9716/1. (Both Jaspers's original German and Pollnow's translation are forthcoming in the *Karl Jaspers Gesamtausgabe*, vol. 1/8: *Schriften zur Existenzphilosophie*, ed. Dominic Kaegi [Basel: Schwabe].) In what follows, we have translated the French, though it has been checked against the German, with two significant variations explained in the notes below.]

46. [After this sentence, the German version has: "It will be difficult for me to answer in the form of theses" ("Es wird mir schwer, thesenartig zu antworten").]

47. [The German has *Dasein*.]
48. [The German has *Existenz*.]

situation where, in another space, the barrier can be broken until tranquility becomes possible in transcendence. This tranquility, however, cannot be acquired through any possession of knowledge. Limitation thus always exists only in relation to a mode of the consciousness of being, but it is not absolute. Totality, in its turn, has several significations: perfection, concordance, achievement of a harmony that contains in itself unlimited correspondences; but totality is also given each time only in relation to a mode of encompassing. In transcendence, totality ceases to be, as well as its contrary, since, there, everything that is expressible is only an inadequate metaphor.

2. Your statement that I find myself in opposition to Kierkegaard by wanting to remain here, in this our own world, creates the opportunity for misunderstanding. It is true that I deny faith in a transcendence where this faith does not come to be manifested, assured, or confirmed in our world. However, I do not deny transcendence, and I am surprised to find myself facing the "exception" that Kierkegaard saw in himself; I also think that I face this exception as he wanted: it is not an example to emulate but only draws one's attention. It submits itself to the general principle of the "realization of oneself in the world," as to a measure that it is conscious of not fulfilling, and it does so in the constant ambiguity of either profound culpability or unprecedented election to an irreplaceable and nonrepeatable unicity.

3. I would reject as deceptive any *ersatz* idea of eternity by thoughts that secularize. The fact that, in the world, fidelity, continuity, and "repetition" are a confirmation and assurance of eternity, does not mean that we substitute them for eternity; this does not mean that eternity no longer exists, but that it sinks into oblivion [*sombre*] for me if I no longer have faith in anyone or, consequently, in myself.

4. I would not deny that the nostalgia for something lost makes itself felt in my philosophy and that an echo of religion resonates in it. However, I believe I can discern this echo in every philosophy that stands in the shadow of Plato and Kant, for whom such great nostalgia was the source of their investigations and of their vocation. Who among us would not want, in the most profound depths of his heart, for God to speak personally to him as to a child,—even if we know that the Divinity, by refusing this to us, has, in this way, precisely given us the possibility to exist, as men, in our freedom (Kant)?

5. That a "theory" of existence excludes precisely existence itself is true for the erroneous interpretations operating in the world with the

help of thoughts that clarify existence and call upon us, as if they could subsume, know, and decide something in a concrete situation. Existentialism is the death of the philosophy of existence, as it has been ever since the students of Plato. Philosophy can only awaken us.

6. As for the "dangers" of either an overly narrow attachment to theology or an overly comprehensive detachment from all "concreteness," I do not recognize them as dangers, strictly speaking. I almost could say: what you designate as dangers is exactly what I would like to achieve, at least as I conceive it. Concerning theology: what imposes itself on me as originally true remains true, even when I understand thereafter that, historically, it probably would not have entered my soul without Christianity. Concerning "concreteness": it is necessary that rationally communicated philosophy remain, as such, an open construction whose completion is, every time, the concern of the one who is thinking it. It must not contain the concrete as it is gained in the sciences or becomes communicable in the visions of poets, nor in such a way that it remains historical in its very substance and, thereby, free for anyone who is possible existence.[49] The greatest efforts of philosophical thought aim, it seems to me, to gain not an empty but a true and active unconcreteness.[50] It is in this sense, for example, that we have to give up basing postulates and commandments on an anticipation of what is yet to be decided in history. Whoever communicates through a philosophy must adopt an attitude contrary to that of a dictator, an attitude in which he almost disappears into a seeming softness and pliability, thus offering a completely free space to the one who listens; if the latter does not come to him by philosophizing from his own source, he will prefer to leave him to despair rather than to offer a substitute of some sort. Furthermore, among other concrete attitudes, we have to abandon, for example, "psychologizing," which makes the abstract imaginable and thereby precisely denatures it. Philosophy must seek to reach a degree of abstraction that, by its very form, is capable of acting upon the deepest reality. Psychology—in our day, under the form of psychoanalysis—is the doppelgänger of philosophy. As soon as one becomes attached to it, all philosophy is lost. But, for almost every manifest

---

49. [The German has *mögliche Existenz*.]
50. [In his German letter to Wahl, Jaspers writes *Unconcretheit* or "unconcreteness." However, the French translation incorrectly renders *Unconcretheit* as *concrétude* ("concreteness"), thereby obfuscating Jaspers's point. We thus translate here from Jaspers's original letter.]

form of philosophy, this psychological interpretation constitutes an erroneously drawn parallel. Indeed, the concrete actions, all real acts of the philosopher, are relevant for the comprehension and examination of his philosophical thought. For philosophy is not, as is the case for science, a truth capable of being isolated. Even in the tone, even in the decisive nuance, one can recognize who the thinker is and what is reflected in his entire life. However, psychological analysis—when psychoanalysis combats the adversary, not through substantial arguments but by psychoanalyzing him—gives only a deformed image, already falsified at its origin. And yet, this deformed image is oriented toward the truth: in philosophy, I operate with thoughts of the other so that, thanks to these thoughts, I come close to the thinker himself; the connection can be all the more profound the purer the thoughts have become as to their form. The "concrete" analyses of my philosophy are intended to be a traversal of the psychological in order to make possible existence acutely present.

7. You ask whether Rimbaud, Van Gogh, Nietzsche, Kierkegaard are not more existential and, ultimately, more philosophical than the philosophy of existence. For a philosophy to be existential is, in fact, an impossibility. Only a man, in his temporal being, is possible existence . . . I am happy to be counted among those who you say have made the value of these exceptions better felt.

8. The move to align Heidegger's name with mine, as if we were doing the same thing, exposes both of us, it seems to me, to erroneous interpretations. What we perhaps have had in common is a critical and negative attitude toward the traditional philosophy of the university, as well as a dependence upon some of Kierkegaard's thoughts. But what distinguishes us are the substantial contents that give rise to our respective philosophies.

I ask that you tolerate the insufficiency of the succinct observations I have just made. I am not completely sure that I have understood perfectly the theses that you sent me. For we enter, with every philosophical thought, into such an inextricable network of multiple possible interpretations that only a happy encounter will occasionally make us feel, for an instant and through the foreground of thought, the indubitable simplicity of truth.

I thank Karl Jaspers for the clarifications that his response provides. They are valuable for me. And what he said in points 5 and 7 marks, it seems to me, an agreement. I follow him less easily when, in point 6, he radically condemns the effort of psychoanalysis. He recognizes in point 2 that he denies faith in a transcendence that is not reassured and is not confirmed in our world. If I understand his expressions correctly, he therefore admits, with respect to this point, a difference between his thought and that of Kierkegaard according to *Fear and Trembling*. I think that what he says in paragraph 1 does not resolve the antinomy in his philosophy between the idea of limitation as good and the idea of limitation as evil, or it resolves it only with the help of distinctions that remain somewhat conceptual. Moreover, can there be a knowledge of different modes of the *Umgreifende* ["encompassing"]? Does not one find here the antinomy between breadth and narrowness that shines a light on existence? I would admit rather (and I think that he could admit this) that this is one of those essential tensions, one of those antinomies that is found in the very nature of being [*l'être*].

I do not think I discern (as he says in point 4) in Kant, and a fortiori in Plato, the nostalgia for a lost religious climate, because they still live in this climate. And their nostalgia is religious nostalgia rather than the nostalgia for the religious. Regarding what he says in point 3, the question is precisely of knowing whether one can pose the question of "eternity for myself" and at the same time truly believe in eternity. It sinks into oblivion for me, Jaspers says, but whoever believes in eternity perhaps sinks into oblivion when faced with it, but he does not see it sink into oblivion "for him."

Mr. H. Pollnow's Observations[51]

By developing certain fundamental problems related to the philosophy of existence (or, more precisely, by developing them "into questions") in his very instructive talk, Mr. Jean Wahl is entitled to expect responses meant to complement his own considerations rather than to object to them. I therefore permit myself to take up three of the numerous important questions that he has raised and to add some of my own arguments.

1. The distinction drawn by Mr. Wahl between "transascendence" and "transdescendence" seems to me to be of incontestable

---

51. [Hans Pollnow (1902–43) was a German psychiatrist best known for his description, with Franz Kramer (1878–1967), of a hyperkinetic syndrome in children (the Kramer-Pollnow syndrome) that today is regarded as attention deficit hyperactivity disorder (ADHD). He studied philosophy and psychology with Karl Jaspers from 1921 to 1923. Pollnow emigrated to Paris in 1933 after passage of a law prohibiting non-Aryans from civil service employment, joined the French army, and eventually fled to southern France during the German occupation. He was caught and arrested by the Gestapo and deported to the Mauthausen concentration camp, where he was killed.]

philosophical fecundity, since it not only differentiates the two forms under which every relation with transcendence is concretized, but also usefully recalls, in its own terms, that transcendence, conceived too often as a *given* that is congealed into a sort of objectification, ultimately signifies an existential *act* of the knowing subject. It thus is a question, as Mr. Wahl has formulated it, of knowing whether transascendence inevitably entails a movement toward good and whether transdescendence, in contrast, entails an inevitable direction toward evil.

I think that the human mind [*esprit*], by placing some phenomena above and others below according to a spatial, cosmic order of values, which it does as much in philosophical interpretations as in religious conceptions of the world, conveys, through this primordial symbolism, nothing other than a transcendental schema, so to speak, of its own "anthropological" structure. This schema, verifiable by our phenomenological consciousness, is transcendental because it links the phenomenality as much as the cognizability of the world to a certain system of not metaphorical but real directions. It is anthropological because it expresses precisely the primitive attitude of the human being toward every other being as well as toward the world in general, an attitude establishing in the rationality of man his "superiority" in relation to the rest of creation.

Thus it seems to me that the process of rationalization is originally experienced [*vécu*] as a sort of ascension toward the light, as one speaks of daybreak. Conversely, for the man who "ascends" thanks to his knowledge of the self and the universe, the return to that which remains unknown or even unknowable appears like a descent toward obscurity or, in other words, like nightfall. But, only insofar as a philosophy coordinates the good with the clarity of the rational and therefore evil with the obscurity of the irrational, which is essentially only elemental in its force and impenetrable in its structure—only to this extent is the good placed above and evil placed below on the hierarchy of vital or moral values. The proof of this is that any conception of the world that identifies the good with the irrational and thereby conceives of rationality as bad implies the necessity of a transdescendence toward the good, for example, in Goethe's "Faust" under the form of the "descent to the Mothers,"[52] or a transascendence toward evil, as is the case in the philosophy of

---

52. [See the "Finstere Galarie" in part 2, act 1 of Goethe's *Faust*.]

[Ludwig] Klages, who considers the mind [*esprit*] to be the irreconcilable enemy of the soul and of every vital and creative force. Moreover, for a thought that places good in inferior regions, it is self-evident that the pejorative and negative sense of below is erased when it is transformed into a positive sense of profundity, such as we find, for example, most explicitly in Romanticism.

2. I do not see why every philosophy of existence, eager to maintain close contact with particular and concrete facts in the historicity of life, must necessarily bear the character of a theology. It seems to me that a fundamental difference exists between theological thought and philosophical thought that has become a philosophy of religion. If both contemplate the same givens, they do so from quite distinct angles.

The certainty of the givens forming the content of religion and thus constituting the point of departure for the theologian is, for a philosophy of religion, only a result, and thus the coronation of constructive thought. Let us consider, from this perspective, the function that the proof of the existence of God plays, on the one hand, in the theological conception of the world, and, on the other hand, in the philosophical conception.

On the theological plane, the need to recover a proof for the existence of God signals a crisis of religious consciousness, which is due to the dynamism of destructive rationalization that no longer stops even in transcendence. Thus thought is tempted to search for proofs for the existence of God in order to be reassured in transcendence, proofs bearing, as a result, an *apologetic* character.

In direct contrast, on the philosophical plane, the proofs for the existence of God fill an essentially different function: they do not serve an apologetic end but participate in the fulfillment of the *constructive* effort of a philosophy of totality, by conveying thereby the audacious impulse [*élan*] of a thought sufficiently sure of itself to transcend its own limits and thus to offer proof of the unprovable.

That a concrete philosophy of existence can take a religious turn in its evolution appears to me to be an indubitable and inevitable consequence. But why should a theological turn be seen as inherent to existentialism, that is to say, a loss of confidence in thought directed and controlled by itself, such that it represents the only authentically philosophical attitude? For this religious perspective is not intended, in my opinion, to reassure a shaken faith and to bring threatened existence back to transcendence. I would find in it precisely the most perfect attempt at a real conquest of transcendence and the true foundation of a free communication between a subjectivity that believes and transcendence, under the form of a philosophy of religion.

3. The problem of existence is above all that of the possibility of realizing existence. Wherever the limits of this possibility are not felt, existence cannot become problematic in itself and cannot form the object, or better, the content, of a philosophy of existence. Existence then is expressed by forms other than those of the existing individual's reflection on existence. But the consciousness of a limited possibility of realizing existence is found at the basis of all existential thought. This is precisely where the essential difference between, on the one hand, *Rimbaud* and *Van Gogh* and, on the other hand, the philosophers of existence, such as *Kierkegaard, Nietzsche, Jaspers,* and *Heidegger,* resides. For it is only the experienced [*vécue*] limitation of an existence capable of being realized that allows for that which is problematic in the essence of existence to be recognized in a philosophy. Some people live their existence without thinking about it under the form of a philosophy of existence. The existences that these individuals realize bear an exemplary and *apodictic* character. For others, existence presents itself as an existential *problem*, thereby furnishing them with material for reflection and guiding them toward the deployment of existential thought in a philosophy of existence.

Over the course of the discussion of Mr. Wahl's presentation, a distinction between existential philosophy and the philosophy of existence was proposed. I do not see this distinction as well founded, nor do I understand how this antithesis could advance us in developing the problems other than by revealing to us that we must abandon it as soon as we have established it. This distinction was used to establish a sort of gradation of philosophers according to their value, by putting, for example, *Kierkegaard* and *Nietzsche*, existential philosophers, in a rank superior to that of *Jaspers* and *Heidegger*, simple philosophers of existence. Such an evaluation seems completely arbitrary to me, since there is no reason to suppose that a philosophy of existence cannot be just as existential as any other philosophy. Of course, I accept characterizing the philosophies of *Jaspers* and *Heidegger* as philosophies of existence. But is the term "existential philosophy" anything other than a tautology? Allow me to examine these antithetical concepts even more closely. Every true and authentic philosophy, and *Jaspers* has emphasized this, can be nothing but an existential philosophy. It is precisely this existentiality that, in essence, makes a thought philosophical. It makes all truly philosophical thought essentially existential, or it makes all existential thought become philosophy as soon as it finds a systematic form. Why then use a tautological formula to convey what constitutes the very essence of philosophy as such and therefore distinguishes it not from the philosophy of existence, for which it is just as valid, but rather from all thought that is contingent and inoffensive in relation to existence?

One could perhaps better clarify the difference that, in my opinion, exists not between so-called existential philosophy and the philosophy of existence but, rather, between philosophy as such and the philosophy of existence. Toward this end, it is necessary to take account of the fact that every philosophy deserving of the name is essentially existential in its transparency for the existence of the philosopher, which *is made clearer* [s'éclaire] in it. We must also recognize that the philosophy of existence, a philosophy that is no less existential as long as it is truly philosophy, has a double relation with existence: as philosophy, for existence *is made clearer* in it, and as thought concerning existence, for thus does it *clarify* [éclaircit] existence.

I therefore think that the antithesis breaks down since the term "existential philosophy" is entirely annihilated by its tautological nature, whereas the term "philosophy of existence" remains a framework vast enough to encompass *Kierkegaard* and *Nietzsche* as well as *Jaspers* and *Heidegger*.

I would accept many of the penetrating remarks that Mr. Pollnow has made in point 1, all the while bringing into question the idea of a transascendence toward evil, and thinking that the analysis of the ideas of good and evil, begun by Nietzsche, has never really been continued.

I did not say that every philosophy of existence must assume the character of a theology. And I attempted to see in what fashion it could free itself from every religious idea. Mr. Pollnow, on the contrary, wants to show that its separation from religious ideas would be a diminution of vitality and perhaps a symptom of death; he seeks to distinguish the function of the idea of transcendence in the religious man and in the philosopher. But, no doubt, he does not sufficiently take into consideration the fact that the function of transcendence in the philosopher is understandable because it takes place on the ebb of religious thought, at a low tide of religion. What he calls "the real conquest of transcendence and the foundation of free communication" is very often only the reverse of a movement of shaken and anxious faith.

I think that for someone like Van Gogh or Rimbaud, existence was a problem, although they exposed this problem not, above all, through their reflection, but through their work and their life. They also had an existence with limited possibilities, although one might argue that they were able to realize themselves in their work in a more complete fashion than philosophers have been able to do in their work. (Still, it remains a question. And Maine de Biran serves as an example of a philosopher who is still a problem, who remains limited and expresses himself in a work and a life that express him fully, through their very character of dissatisfaction and incompletion.)

Despite Mr. Pollnow's objections, I think that there is something useful and true about the distinction proposed by Berdyaev between existential philosophies and philosophies of existence. The cases of Nietzsche, Kierkegaard, Socrates, and perhaps Descartes and Kant are examples of philosophies that are sources of themselves—even if we can list their influences.

Letter from Miss Hersch[53]

> Regarding the idea of repetition, of theories of the instant or those of the eternal return: is it fair to see in them "ersatzes" of the idea of eternity? "Ersatz" is so strongly pejorative, suggesting that it is a matter of the same thing, but "fake," without any compensation for lost authenticity. Now, it seems to me that repetition, the instant, and the eternal return are projections or translations of eternity onto the human level. Authenticity is lost only in appearance, and only when one lets translation pass for the original. For me, I even lean toward thinking that authenticity is better saved by these attempts at translation than by the pure, divine term. For we are human beings, and therefore a crossing and a knot of forces and paths, and I do not think that one of these paths can be authentic *for us* without being tied to the others. This divine term can find its authenticity for us only by being incarnated in our life and in our body-laden thought. Moreover, we only barely know it in its purity through its irreducible resistance to this human effort of incarnation. And here, no doubt, is the function of these notions "repetition," "instant," and "eternal return." Is it the role of an ersatz?—I don't think so.

53. [Jeanne Hersch (1910–2000) was a Swiss philosopher of Polish and Jewish origin; she studied with Jaspers in the 1930s and was one of the first women to hold a professorship at a Swiss university, teaching as professor of philosophy at the University of Geneva from 1956 to 1977.]

Regarding the more or less religious character of existential philosophy: I think that neither Heidegger nor Jaspers, in any case, would deny it. Not in the least does Jaspers seek to eliminate it, and if he nevertheless strongly opposes his philosophy to all theology, it seems to me that it is above all by means of a refusal: a refusal to speak of God as if he were a given. One only ever speaks of the search for him. The "more or less" that I wrote above is, all in all, quite foolish because of the relative element that it introduces here: in a sense, this philosophy is absolutely religious since it looks for God and nothing else; in another sense, it is absolutely not religious since it refuses to speak of God as a revealed being [*étant*]. Thus, here again, there is a refusal to leave the human condition because of the certainty that there is no pious path for a man's thought and actions other the human path. But transcendence remains transcendent,— whence the sense of limit, of failure, of all the negative notions, not because of a love of tragedy, but because man is man, clearly.

The double danger of which you speak, theology or abstraction, indeed appears to me to be what threatens existential philosophy. But this observation appears to me to demonstrate its truth, its coincidence precisely with the human condition: for I think that man, no matter what he does, never definitively escapes from this double danger. There is no refuge from it, and to attempt to make oneself safe from it is to renounce the human condition. We must escape it all throughout our lives and thoughts.

That existences could be more existential and more philosophical than the philosophies of existence; on this point I am fully in agreement with you, and Jaspers is also, I know it. (How many times have I heard him emphasize: "Philosophie aber ist noch nicht Existenz: sie ist eine Möglichkeit der Existenz" ["Philosophy is not yet *Existenz*: it is a possibility of *Existenz*"].) And, no doubt, not only Rimbaud, Van Gogh, and Nietzsche, but very obscure existences. Nevertheless, existential philosophy appears to me to do more than make us feel their value: it is a call, perhaps more direct for some, different in every case, having a hold on one's fellow man in some other way. Can there be too many calls, too many types of call?

I find nothing to respond to in this strong letter, except that Jaspers's reader does not always remain at the level at which Miss Hersch would like, and that, this being the case, this philosophy—but this is perhaps the fate of all philosophy of this kind—can appear to be too difficult, through this negative theology that is at its summit, or it can appear to be too easy, through the fact that the unknown God can be reached by multiple ways, and that one can always tell oneself that, in one way or another, one reaches God in his ciphers [*chiffres*] and through historicity. It seems to me that Mrs. Bespaloff expresses a sentiment analogous to mine in the letter that she kindly wrote to me.

Letter from Mrs. Bespaloff[54]

In short, what distances me from Jaspers's philosophy is that I find it too agreeable; nothing in it offends or shocks me. All the same, it is a philosophy of defeat,—of the defeated people that we are. . . . In the end, its last word is: *dulden* ["sufferance"]. I know well—alas!—that *durch Dulden besteht die Welt* ["Sufferance sustains the world"],[55] I know it only too well. But is it necessary to make of this the first and last value?

Take the chapter on freedom in the second volume.[56] It seems that all of Jaspers's gifts—his marvelous insight, his conceptual clarity, and even the perfect probity of his mind [*esprit*]—are turned round against him. While I read these pages, I approve of everything, and do not have an objection to raise. But, when I get to the end of the chapter, I have the impression of a disaster: freedom is no longer, has never been. What has happened?

Nietzsche, even when he denies freedom, makes it present to me—and this is not a freedom caught between the conditioned necessity of *Dasein* and the unconditioned necessity of transcendence. It is the truth—I would not know how to tell you what I

---

54. [Rachel Bespaloff (1895–1949) was born to a Ukrainian Jewish family that relocated to Geneva in 1897. Initially drawn to philosophy through Lev Shestov (1866–1938), who was a friend of her father's, she published essays on Kierkegaard, Marcel, and other existentialist writers and themes. Her "Lettre sur Heidegger à M. Daniel Halévy," *Revue Philosophique de la France et de l'Étranger* 116 (July–December 1933): 321–39, is among the first in French to focus on Heidegger's *Being and Time*. A close friend of Wahl's, Bespaloff traveled with Wahl to the United States in 1942 on one of the last refugee ships to leave France, and at Wahl's recommendation she joined him on the faculty at Mount Holyoke College in 1943, where she taught French for six years. Her posthumous *Lettres à Jean Wahl (1937–1947): Sur le fond le plus déchiqueté de l'histoire*, ed. Monique Jutrin, was published in 2003 (Paris: Éditions Claire Paulhan).]
55. [Jaspers, *Philosophie*, 3:236; *Philosophy*, 3:207.]
56. [Jaspers, *Philosophie*, 2:175–200; *Philosophy*, 2:154–74.]

recognize it by. Why, then, would I agree with Jaspers, even when he confirms my own experience, instead of agreeing with the revelations of Nietzsche?

Es ist genug, daß Sein ist ["That there is being suffices"];[57] to be sure, Nietzsche did not say something different (although he avoids the word *Sein* ["being"]), but with what tone, with what accent. . . . That changes everything. The danger for existential philosophy is not, it seems to me, uniting itself too closely with the religious; it is of not discarding the ethical. Jaspers, in my opinion, is able to do so only through *poetic* transfiguration, in the broadest sense. Because, in short, what is the "cipher [*chiffre*]" if not (under a new term still charged with magic) the transmutation of the phenomenon into an appearance [*apparition*] in which the non-elucidated meaning of being is unveiled?

What I find enriching in Jaspers's philosophy is precisely what it strives to overshadow: the profundity and acuity of psychological intuition, which is perhaps, at its origin, a poetic intuition of temporality: the knowledge of man.

Letter from Mr. Löwith[58]

I think that Kierkegaard destroyed philosophical conceptions, rather than enlivening them. And as for Jaspers and Heidegger, I have always had the impression that there was a paradox here; for Jaspers's philosophy is, in the end, an ersatz religion, although Jaspers is himself essentially an antitheological philosopher of the Enlightenment, whereas, in contrast, Heidegger's philosophy is anti-Christian, although—or precisely because—he has remained essentially a theologian.[59] In Jaspers, "the echo of the religious" is

---

57. [Jaspers, *Philosophie*, 3:236; *Philosophy*, 3:207.]
58. [Karl Löwith (1897–1973) was a student of Heidegger's and is best known for his works on the history of German philosophy, Nietzsche, and the philosophy of history. Although a Protestant, his family was of Jewish descent and in 1934 he emigrated first to Italy, then Japan, before ending up in the United States from 1941 to 1952. In 1952, he returned to Germany and taught as professor of philosophy at the University of Heidelberg until his death.]
59. [Cf. Heidegger's letter to Löwith from August 19, 1921: "Zu dieser meiner Faktizität gehört—was ich kurz nenne—, daß ich 'christlicher Theo*loge*' bin." "Drei Briefe Martin Heideggers an Karl Löwith," in *Zur philosophischen Aktualität Heideggers: Symposium der Alexander von Humboldt-Stiftung vom 24.–28. April 1989 in Bonn-Bad*

no longer present except under the form of an existentialist Kantianism. In Heidegger's work, one still senses an immediate religious impulse, but one that has been perverted.

Letter from Miss Käte Nadler[60]

Käte Nadler, who from a Hegelian point of view is opposed to existential philosophy, writes to me that she is in agreement with me on the double danger to which existential philosophy is exposed, which she herself indicates in an article in *Tatwelt*.[61]

Letter from Mr. Denis de Rougemont[62]

Why do you want—or do they want—for philosophy to be purified of theology? Theology is a worthy science. It is even a less variable science than the so-called exact sciences, whose foundations are destroyed every twenty years from top to bottom.

    I do not think that transcendence can ever be "simply nature." Look at Goethe, at Tolstoy, at Nietzsche: to the extent that nature is an element of transcendence, it becomes divinity (and cannot not become it). For my part, I cannot conceive of a concrete relation to transcendence where the sentiment of the divine, of the sacred, would be lacking. But your paper usefully orients us toward a new analysis of transcendence in its relation not only to the ethical but to the powers of the imagination.

Godesberg, vol. 2, *Im Gespräch der Zeit*, ed. Dietrich Papenfuss and Otto Pöggeler (Frankfurt am Main: Klostermann, 1990), 29. English translation: "This facticity of mine includes—briefly put—the fact that I am a 'Christian the*ologian*.'" "Letter to Karl Löwith on His Philosophical Identity," in *Becoming Heidegger: On the Trail of His Early Occasional Writings, 1910–1927*, ed. Theodore Kisiel and Thomas Sheehan (Evanston, Ill.: Northwestern University Press, 2007), 106.]

    60. [Käte Nadler (1907–?) published several works on Hegel and Hermann Hesse. For further information, see chapter 4, note 19.]

    61. [Wahl is perhaps referring to Käte Nadler, "Die französische Existenzphilosophie der Gegenwart," *Die Tatwelt* 12 (September 1936): 162–66.]

    62. [Denis de Rougemont (1906–85) was a Swiss writer and cultural theorist who moved to Paris in 1930, where he was associated with the personalist movement.]

Letter from Mr. Louis Lavelle[63]

I would have asked you only whether, in the ambiguity between the divine and the demonic, or the transascendent and the transdescendent—an ambiguity that is quite at the heart of anxiety—there is a principle of distinction that precisely makes it so that there is an ambiguity there, and I would have asked whence this principle of distinction comes. For it could be the effect of prejudice or, on the contrary, a requirement of consciousness, of the very act by which it constitutes itself, in which case it would thus be a matter of searching for an ontological ground.

I quite voluntarily admit that it would have been necessary to keep separate, more than I have done in my summary, the distinction between the divine and the demonic (influenced by theological and moral conceptions) and that of the transascendent and the transdescendent. Doing so would not make the ambiguity disappear, but we would perhaps see that it would no longer appear except insofar as notions of a different origin are superimposed on investigations of a metaphysical nature.

This is more or less how I would also respond to Mr. Raymond Aron.

Letter from Mr. Raymond Aron[64]

Allow me to present to you the few following reflections:

You want to divorce the moral categories of good and evil, above and below, from existential philosophy; you speak of transcendence without attaching to this term any nuance of value. So be it, and I see well the difficulty of making the abstract notions of the ethical or of

---

63. [Louis Lavelle (1883–1951) taught at the leading Paris *lycées* (Saint-Louis, Condorcet, Louis-le-Grand, Henri-IV) from 1925 to 1940. He was named to the Chair in Modern Philosophy at the Collège de France in 1941 and taught there until his death. Lavelle authored over twenty-five books, the most important of which is the four-volume *La dialectique de l'éternal présent: De l'être* (1928), *De l'acte* (1937), *Du temps et de l'éternité* (1945), and *De l'âme humaine* (1951) ("The Dialectic of the Eternal Present: On Being," "On the Act," "On Time and Eternity," "On the Human Soul").]

64. [Raymond Aron (1905–83) was close friends with Jean-Paul Sartre and Simone de Beauvoir during the 1920s–1930s, but he eventually turned away from both existentialism and Marxism. A major figure in the introduction of German sociology, especially that of Max Weber, in France, he was professor of sociology at the Sorbonne from 1957 to 1968 before being elected to the Chair in Sociology at the Collège de France in 1970, a position he held until his death.]

religion enter into existential philosophy, such as you conceive it. But how then are you able to qualify lived experiences metaphysically? What does transcendence signify, and, *a fortiori*, what do transascendence and transdescendence signify? You say you give up these words, which signify the effort of being raised up and sinking down. But are you sure of thereby respecting lived experience? Does not transcendence disappear if nature stops being the goal of downward transcendence? Is it not by way of religious categories, if not moral ones, that these experiences are defined, are constituted? As a result, your supposed fidelity would convey an arbitrary interpretation of these existences. I will call this your aesthetic skepticism.

Indeed, which value—having abstracted from good and evil, from spirit [*esprit*] and nature, from God and the demon—do you retain in order to singularize philosophical existences? That of intensity: the most intense, most problematic existences would be the most philosophical. I confess that I see here a sort of amoralism and irrationalism whose psychological signification I grasp better than their philosophical signification. Will not the neurotic become the most philosophical, since no one is more riven than he? Is not the experience of destruction, of war, at least as intense as the experience of the philosopher who meditates on transcendence? You come to judge Rimbaud and Van Gogh to be more philosophical than the philosophers of existence. I find here that bad conscience of the philosopher (in France) who feels himself inferior to the artist or to the poet. In a sense, you may be right. If it is a question of human greatness, Rimbaud perhaps beats all of the professors of philosophy, but I am afraid that such a question is void of meaning. Why compare types or human beings? Souls are incomparable. Your hierarchy translates personal preferences and I wonder whether the very idea of such a hierarchy is not, spiritually speaking, sacrilege. (Wouldn't God refuse to give out prizes or fix ranks in this way?) In human terms, this hierarchy exceeds, in any case, the possibilities of our intelligence.

Conversely, if we take the word "philosopher" in the strict sense, it seems to me that you are clearly wrong. For to undergo the philosophical drama intensely, to undergo the problem of fate, is no doubt to reveal a philosophical temperament, a condition of all philosophy. But, to the extent that these beings do not express their drama, or express it in images or verse, they are not philosophers, or at least they are only philosophers in the eyes of the philosopher who, by reflecting on their experience, finds in it the mark of that which he, and he alone, determines to be philosophy, because he is capable of conceptually, ethically, and religiously qualifying what otherwise would remain at the level of experience.

I am afraid that your alternative is inexact and that there are ways of avoiding theology as well as abstraction. I do not see why theology, in itself, would risk compromising existential philosophy. The latter, in order to be authentic, does not need to reject everything it borrows from doctrines. We know quite well that mystical experiences are permeated by the religious thought in which they participate. Existential philosophers are rather in agreement concerning a human universe that they imagine to be renewed by the fact that they live in it intensely, whether it be the antinomies or the fundamental givens. But the more existentialist they are, the less they are philosophers: not because they are theologians, but because they are content to express a prior system, without demonstrating its validity, nor situating it through reflection within the totality of human life.

As for the philosophies of existence, they no doubt will tend toward abstraction if, like Jaspers, they retain existential categories by formalizing them and aim for the paradox of confining themselves to the level of existence and at the same time to the level of reflection. Indeed, in this case, they will speak of a decision—without specifying what it is—and will deny the truth of philosophy all the while concatenating judgments that make a claim to the truth. Abstract theory of the metaphysical situation of man, this is basically the theme of Jaspers's philosophy, but, as such, this theory is contradictory, for one does not live this theory; in fact, either one thinks the existence that one has chosen, or one thinks concrete human life as it unfolds throughout history. And, in the latter case, Jaspers's entire philosophy is only the introduction to a philosophical comprehension of human history and of the human being. In other words, one cannot confine oneself to a philosophy of existence (like Jaspers's), but one can no more confine oneself to demonstrating the alternative between theology and abstraction. For, from the moment that you did not choose the first term, you chose the second, and, since you recognize the danger of abstraction, you recognize at the same time the necessity of going beyond the abstract theory of choice toward a comprehension of the concrete man and beyond, perhaps toward a philosophy of being or, in any case, a philosophy of the human being and of being for man. With the phenomenology of existences, the path of philosophy opens up.

I do not think that one can say that I do not grant "any nuance of value" to the word "transcendence," nor that I divorce the notions of above and below from existential philosophy—of "being raised up" and "being lowered," unless one takes them in a purely moral sense (good and evil).—I very well admit that nature is the goal of downward transcendence. (I use Mr. Aron's expressions, in order better to show what I do not accept in the theses that he claims I support.)

I am not aware of having this bad conscience of the philosopher that Mr. Aron attributes to French philosophers. On the contrary, I take the word "philosopher" in a very broad sense. I have considered Rimbaud, Van Gogh, to be "sources of philosophy"; and I would like to add that the source has a purity that rivers do not have; and in the second place, that it is perhaps as a consequence of a somewhat scholarly conception of philosophy that I have not dared to call them philosophers.

Mr. Aron says that hierarchy exceeds the possibilities of our intelligence; no doubt, but for him it is a question of intelligence. For me, it is a question of an arbitrary evaluation, I mean an evaluation of which I am the only arbiter.

I reject the idea of a superiority of one who would conceptually, ethically, and religiously qualify what would remain otherwise at the level of experience. I notice that with the words "only he is capable of . . ." and "level of experience," Mr. Aron establishes a hierarchy.—Has he not warned us, however, that there is, for him, something of sacrilege here?

For me, there is even less sacrilege than sacredness here. It is not philosophy, if it is reflection, but what I called the source of philosophy (or philosophy in the sense that I would like to give to this word), or even its hard kernel, impenetrable to reflection, that is at the basis of all the great works.

And thus, I do not see the effect of an aesthetic system in what I have tried to express, but an affirmation of the will to see the transcendence at the end of the movement of transcendence [*transcendance du terme du mouvement de la transcendance*] in relation to our conceptual thought and its immanence in the intensity of experience.

I think I can bring Mr. Lavelle's letter together with Mr. Georges Bastide's letter as well.

Letter of Mr. Georges Bastide[65]

Meditating on the adventure of Kierkegaardian thought is full of lessons for the philosopher and, when you characterize this thought

---

65. [Georges Bastide (1901–69) was an influential philosopher of value in France in the 1930s through 1950s. Described as a spiritualist, personalist, and axiological idealist, his work reflected on those values he placed at the center of the human condition.]

by the connection between a tense and anxious [*angoissée*] subjectivity with an anxiety-inducing [*angoissante*] transcendence, I think that you profoundly grasp the dramatic crux of the matter. However, I had, for my part, interpreted this drama across a duality of slightly different terms.

1. Subjectivity and transcendence seem to me to be only an effect of the realist usage of the concept of existing Unity in its double application to the subject and to the object.

Applied to the subject, the concept of existing Unity gives rise to the concept of *unicity*: the subject is thought to be like a punctual unity; in space, it would be like the center of a sphere from which an infinity of rays emanates; in time, it is the instant in which the past is closed and the future is opened.

Applied to the object, the concept of existing Unity gives rise to the concept of *totality*: the object is thought to be like a synthetic unity; in space, it is the indefinitely multiple unfolding of the rays of the sphere; in time, it is the retrospective or prospective projection of the infinite multiplicity of possibilities.

The relation of the subject to the object is thus, for realist thought, the opposition between unicity and totality. It is because there is no object without subject, nor subject without object, that there is in every thought a "connection" of subjective unicity and transcending totality.

2. For realist thought, which posits the object in itself and the subject in itself, this double sense of existing Unity creates a fundamental antinomy, which this thought irremediably comes up against.

In a completely general fashion, the position of the absolute experience of one of the terms at first makes the existence of the other disappear into nothingness, for the absolute existence of unicity is the negation of the multiple, and the absolute existence of totality is, in contrast, the affirmation of it. To posit the Being of totality is to affirm the existence of the multiple and negate the existence of the unique; but to posit the Being of the One is to affirm the existence of the unique and negate that of the multiple totality. This is exactly the old Parmenidean problem.

One could follow the antinomy across the categories of space and time ("communication" and "historicity" for Jaspers), where each of the terms would still reveal its power to dissolve in relation to the other.

To establish the unicity of the center of the sphere as absolute is to destroy the sphere, which has existence only through the multiplicity of its rays; but to establish the synthetic totality of the sphere as absolute is to destroy the very existence of the center, which is only the convergence of the rays.

To establish the unicity of the instant in time as absolute is to destroy the existence of multiple anteriors and posteriors; but to affirm the existence of these multiples is to make the instant, which becomes a simple limit, disappear.

Thus, each time that the subject wants to posit itself in its unicity, totality loses existence and this subject finds itself in the face of the Nothing ("To exist," Heidegger says, "in fact comes to this: to be maintained within the nothing," *Bifur*, 1931, 15).[66]

Thus transcendence of totality could be thought only by a subject who would lose the unicity of its existence. The subjectivity of the Unique can think as an object only the transcendence of the Nothing.

3. It is from here that anxiety is born. The presence of theological and moral elements results from the constant equation of Being and of Value in all of the realist metaphysics. Being and the Good are identical there, and the judgments on the reality of this metaphysics are always judgments of value. This is why the antinomy becomes tragic and anxiety-inducing.

The subjective Unique will be able to protect its being, that is to say its value, only by opposing a nothingness [*un néant*] of totality, that is to say a Nothingness of transcendent value. Inversely, we will be able to posit the transcendent existence of the total Value only by negating the being, and thus the value of the Unique.

As a result, every gain in the value of the subjective would be a loss in value of the transcendent. The "transascendence" of the subject is a "transdescendence" of the object, and vice-versa. Man and God go back and forth making the demonic accusation without end.

---

66. [Bastide's French has been translated directly. Bastide here cites Heidegger's lecture "What Is Metaphysics?": "Da-sein heißt: Hineingehaltenheit in das Nichts [*Da-sein* means: being held out into the nothing]," trans. David Farrell Krell, in *Pathmarks*, ed. William McNeill (Cambridge: Cambridge University Press, 1998), 91. The German can be found in volume 9 of Heidegger's *Gesamtausgabe*, 115. The French translation appeared as "Qu'est-ce que la métaphysique?," trans. Henry Corbin-Petithenry with an introduction by Alexandre Koyré, *Bifur* 8 (June 1931): 5–27.]

4. This fundamental antinomy constitutes the ultimate "wall," as Dostoyevsky experienced it,[67] against which realist thought shatters. The Kierkegaardian moment is the *nec plus ultra* of this thought.

Indeed, realist thought cannot transcend the duality of the subject and the object. This is why it cannot think of something still further: every attempt at surpassing [*dépassement*], as Hegel called it, is doomed to the rebirth of the ever-same antinomy. Only the nostalgic thought of an impossible return or a negation of all thought (Dostoyevsky's "purposely go mad"[68]) can arise.

5. The realist consciousness can have, then, in the depths of its unhappiness, the revelation of its essential perversion. This is what it conveys with the idea of a fall that has radically separated it from Being.

But it could also see that, in a similar perspective, the thought of Being is irremediably off limits for it. Realist thought cannot be existential, for it bears within itself a power that dissolves all existence of which it would like to take possession.

The only thing that would remain for this "perverted" thought, then, would be to be "converted" to the idealist attitude that moves exactly in an inverse direction.

Subject and object cease being opposed to each other in order to become a relation to each other. The relational Unity, the unifying unity, escapes the antimony of the Unique and the Total; and the act of value-producing thought [*pensée valorisatrice*] coincides exactly with the genesis of the spiritual being.

I would feel distant especially from the thought of the last paragraph, at the moment when Mr. Bastide presents the idealist doctrine as a remedy. But he wanted to clarify his position in a way that makes the distance I feel between us diminish.

Second Letter from Mr. Bastide

By idealism, I do not at all mean a vision of the world that, once and for all, could provide the spirit with the rest and homeland that it seeks. I mean only the attitude of searching and the direc-

---

67. [Cf. Fyodor Dostoyevsky, *Notes from Underground* in *Notes from Underground and The Grand Inquisitor*, trans. Ralph E. Matlaw (New York: Dutton, 1960), 12–13.]
68. [Dostoyevsky, *Notes from Underground*, 28.]

tion of effort that find their point of departure and their orientation in the awakening of the primacy of the spiritual and that are at the origin of all works of the spirit.

I think that this attitude can never be reached straightaway, that it can arise only amid the lacerations of unhappy, realist consciousness, and even that the profundity of idealist thought, as it produces value, is a function of the depth of unhappiness that realist thought was able to reach. I would say even that as he writes a work where unhappiness is thought, Kierkegaard is already implicitly in the idealist attitude since there is in his action the affirmation that the thought of unhappiness is superior, by right, to the unhappiness that it thinks.

Perhaps these few hasty reflections will allow you to find my thought less distant from your own.

Letter of Mr. Raymond Lenoir[69]

The approximations that, beginning with Kierkegaard, authorize withdrawal from the world, retreating into oneself, the acquisition of convictions too fleeting not to prefer the modes proper to the fine arts and great literature over the dialectic, and sometimes even a meditation tinged with religiosity—these approximations are too current [*actuelles*] not to make us take pause concerning the nature of existential [*existencielle*] philosophy, which is supposed to propose existences for us.

The encounter with a thought that is rich in harmonics and with tendencies whose latest expression was found in the recent Congress of Paris[70] testifies to the power of an attitude that attacks

---

69. [Raymond Lenoir (1890–1972) was a sociologist and philosopher whose work was associated with Émile Durkheim and the French School of Sociology as well as two important journals: *L'Année sociologique* and the *Revue de Synthèse*. His letter, to which Wahl did not offer any response, did not appear in the version of "Subjectivité et transcendance" reprinted in *Existence humaine et transcendance*.]

70. [Lenoir is most likely referring to Wahl's presentation at the session on "Transcendance et Immanence" at the ninth International Congress of Philosophy (renamed in 1949 the World Congress of Philosophy), called the Descartes Congress in honor of the 300th anniversary of the publication of Descartes's *Discourse on Method*, which took place in Paris at the Sorbonne July 31–August 7, 1937. Wahl's contribution to the congress can be found under the title "Sur l'idée de transcendance," in *Travaux du IXe Congrès International de Philosophie: Congrès Descartes* (Paris: Hermann et Cie, 1937), 8:56–59; republished in Wahl, *Existence humaine et transcendance*, 34–38. Among the sixteen others who presented at this session were Maurice Blondel, Léon Brunschvicg,

traditional philosophy with renewed vigor. To situate this historically, the movement that was prepared by the consideration of forces in their relation with forms and that is common to Spinoza and [Hippolyte] Taine took shape in France before 1914 under the guidance of [Félix] Ravaisson and Bergson, and began with the study of Hegel and Pragmatism. It was in accord with the taste of the younger generations for the fine arts and for novelists' and dramaturges' deepening of the passions. It was postponed indefinitely during the postwar years by the necessity we faced of maintaining—at the price of our individual preferences and aptitudes—the institutions and the bodies of ideas constitutive of humanity, by going back in time, by rejoining epochs more concerned with stability, with domestic life. A thankless task, without appreciation. Today, it reunites currents from Italy, Germany, Poland, and Russia, each combining in its way the traditions of a people with historical events that gave birth to nations. The natural notions of organic growth, maternal power, blood and earth reappear. The detailed views of Nicolas Berdyaev develop. Ultimately, such contributions owe their freshness to this feeling of life that [Pierre Jean Georges] Cabanis distinguished from common sensations, that Maine de Biran spiritualized, and that seems to be and to remain for so-called primitive peoples a source of reflection and activity.

All in all, existences have perhaps made a name for themselves thanks to the convergence of literary tastes that prefer—over both classical heroes, who master their passions, and romantic heroes, who project over against themselves another, completely contrasting self—a complex or composite being, indefinable, in which good and bad powers are so anemic that they stagnate such that none shapes its character or permits it to respond with a yes or no to the question that Diderot already formulated: "Is it good; is it evil?" Artistic form is alone suitable for their presentation if there is indeed nothing here to prove or deduce. To depict them, to place side by side these accounts of sincerity or human artifice, of abandonments or of voluntary outbursts, is to unite oneself with

---

Henry Corbin, and Gabriel Marcel. This session was part of a broader section on "Analyse Réflexive et Transcendance," which included contributions by Louis Lavelle and Käte Nadler. Highlights from this section, "which gave rise to the most serious and interesting debates," can be found in Joseph Dopp, "Le Congrès Descartes," *Revue néo-scolastique de philosophie* 40, no. 56 (1937): 674–78 (quote on 674). Nicolas Berdyaev, Siegfried Marck, and Hans Pollnow also participated in the congress.]

familiar observations, with conversation, in order to constitute the statements of fact and formulas in which the majority of men will find a patterned or sham emotional life. But if the philosopher still hesitates to understand them through speculation, it is because society, strengthened by the biological differentiation of the normal and the pathological that comprises its life and death, takes as uncertain the value of that which erases any distinction between immoralism and morality. Its continuity demands it. Its martyrs have confirmed the identity of its will and of love.

For its part, the feeling of life forms the notion of life and death, of which Heraclitus will formulate a couple of fundamental concepts long after so-called primitive peoples had placed the source of all activity there.[71] It is to the sense of life that the relations of men with one another, inside and outside the group, as well as the relations of societies with animals, vegetation, minerals, land, water, the heavens, climates, and natural disruptions, owe their signification and their order. The sense of life promotes vitality, favors the preservation of the species, disciplines the drives, contains rivalries, prescribes politeness, imposes hygiene, extends land development. It dictates what must be done as well as what must be avoided, what observations we must remember as well as those we need to abandon, depending on whether they provide a consistent or a fleeting character. Where the sense of life achieves precision and understanding, it expresses itself in institutions, in titles and in laws. If it envisages an order that is needed for life, without being able to overcome all the obstacles to human expansion that nature and society accumulate, it becomes a symbol. A hierarchy is based on how close beings, acts, and ideas remain to life. Conditions and characteristics are fixed and overturned only at the price of death. The contemplated cosmos and the acting world are constituted, are fixed, until the moment they break into concepts.

Perhaps the philosopher to whom Plato and Plotinus taught to see love, dialectic, and music as so many methods is doomed to eternal returns. His desire to integrate existence, existences, in all of the topics of discussion and ideological organizations corresponds to the feeling of discomfort experienced before Aristotelian definitions brief to the point of aporia and yet so rich in metaphysical possibilities.

---

71. Raymond Lenoir, "Le sens de la vie dans les sociétés dites primitives," *Journal de Psychologie Normale et Pathologique* 31 (March–April 1934): 273–89.

But he cannot find a new path without finding before him the medieval and classical problem of individuation that the scientism and theologism of modern times have hastened to efface. He cannot go much further than Schopenhauer and Nietzsche without exposing himself to variations and to repetitions. He could not enrich the mysticism and casuistry of the original cases, without weakening the sense and the respective scope of theology and morality. His temperament makes him confident in the youth of spirit [*l'esprit*], in the inexhaustible novelty of ideas. This is his risk. Just as the sense of life has never straightforwardly animated theologies, metaphysics, or critical systems except in order to establish order, without which we would return to animality in politics and ethics.[72]

Translated by Anna Johnson and Ian Alexander Moore

Appendix: Jean Wahl's Letter to Martin Heidegger, December 12, 1937

On December 12, 1937, eight days after his lecture and debate on "Subjectivity and Transcendence," Wahl wrote to Martin Heidegger, thanking him for his epistolary contribution to the discussion and providing a more detailed response to it than the one published in the *Bulletin de la Société Française de Philosophie* and translated above. While acknowledging the importance of the question of being for Heidegger, Wahl nonetheless raises several objections to how Heidegger appears to solve it, and he defends his decision to number Heidegger among the philosophers of existence. Wahl's letter to Heidegger, translated into English and published here for the first time, is available at the Deutsches Literaturarchiv Marbach under the access number 75.6908/2.

Ian Alexander Moore

> 17 Avenue du Colonel Bonnet
> Paris, 16th Arrondissement
> 12 December [1937]

Dear Sir and colleague,

I was very happy to receive your letter and I sincerely thank you for it.

---

72. [The translators would like to thank Peg Birmingham, Michael Naas, and Elizabeth Rottenberg of DePaul University for their support and helpful comments on an earlier draft of the translation.]

I reproached myself for not sufficiently saying in those brief lines[73] how much admiration I have for your work, and for having insisted above all on critiques or reservations. At the end of my talk,[74] I had the occasion to say how important I find *Sein und Zeit*, as well as your lectures.

The question as to whether your philosophy is or is not *Existenzphilosophie* ["philosophy of existence"] matters rather little to me.—In a sense, Plato's philosophy is *Existenzphilosophie*. The death of a man who is Socrates, and his existence, is at the center.

It is difficult for me to think that what you say about death, about anxiety, cannot be reconciled with the philosophy of existence. In this sense, I do not feel I am at fault for ranking you among the philosophers of Existence.

But I recognize that it would be a grave error on the part of critics not to see, as you strongly indicate in your letter, that your question is that of being [*l'être*].

What I still see rather poorly is how you resolve it. I can well see that there is a relation between being and nothingness [*le néant*], a relation—if I understand correctly—of the transcendence of being in relation to nothingness—at the same time perhaps of the immanence of nothingness in relation to being; since all being [*tout être*] is as though shot through with nothingness—with the fact of time and of being-for-the-end [*l'être-pour-la-fin*].

The question of being is thus transposed—if I still understand correctly—into that of time and of nothingness.

As for time, I admire greatly certain things you say about the three ecstases. But, with regard to *Wiederholung* ["retrieval," "repetition"], I believe, as I indicated in my lecture,[75] that it is a will—a metaphysical will to power—an idea of the will (and, in the end, a substitute for eternity) rather than a reality.

With respect to nothingness, I must say that, being a great admirer of Boehme, I have always been drawn to the idea of affirming the being of nothingness.—But, on the other hand, the objections of Plato and the idea of the synonymy of otherness and nothingness (ideas taken up and clarified by Bergson) are very striking to me.

---

73. [That is, sections I and II of Chapter 7.]
74. [See the final paragraph of Wahl's presentation to the Société Française de Philosophie above.]
75. [Cf. p. 157, above.]

So I tell myself that the idea of nothingness is a myth. I would like to believe it. I have not, however, managed to be persuaded by your study, "What Is Metaphysics?" however great my admiration for it.

I would love to be able to meet with you one day. But all sorts of obstacles stand in the way at present.

Know, at least, dear Sir and colleague, that I am profoundly grateful to you for having written me and having clarified the direction of thought that must be followed in order to interpret your work; know also how highly I regard you among contemporary philosophers.

Yours faithfully,
Jean Wahl

[P.S.] Several years ago I wrote a study titled "Heidegger and Kierkegaard,"[76] which appeared in *Recherches Philosophiques* and which I could send to you if you would be interested. But, for the moment, I only have the proof sheets. Moreover, I am no longer satisfied with it, and one day I would like to be able to add to it and make it clearer.

Transcribed and translated by Ian Alexander Moore

---

76. [See Chapter 5, above.]

Nietzsche and the Death of God
A Note on Jaspers's Nietzsche

In 1936, Georges Bataille (1897–1962) and others organized a group of avant-garde intellectuals under the name Acéphale. Included among the members of this group were Pierre Klossowski (1905–2001), Georges Ambrosino (1912–84), Roger Caillois (1913–78), Jules Monnerot (1874–1942), and Jean Wahl. While the activities of this group were, to a large extent, secret, its public face was the journal of the same name: *Acéphale*.[1] Under Bataille's leadership, the journal published four issues between June 1936 and June 1939. A fifth issue, titled "La folie de Nietzsche" (Nietzsche's madness) was prepared but never published.[2] After the first issue, only eight pages in length, the remaining issues all focused on Nietzsche. The second issue, published in January 1937 and titled "Réparation à Nietzsche" (Repairing Nietzsche), was devoted to challenging the Nazi and right-wing political readings

---

["Nietzsche et la mort de Dieu: Note à propos du 'Nietzsche' de Jaspers," *Acéphale* 2 (January 1937): 22–23.]

1. The relationship between the secret society Acéphale and the journal *Acéphale* is not at all clear, in part because members of the society took an oath not to speak about it, an oath that was largely followed. In his biography of Bataille, Michel Surya argues that *"Acéphale* is the name of two things, which I do not see as being equal or similar." Michel Surya, *Georges Bataille: An Intellectual Biography*, trans. Krzysztof Fijalkowski and Michael Richardson (London: Verso, 2002), 237–38.

2. All of the issues of *Acéphale*, including the fifth unpublished issue, have been re-edited and published by Éditions Jean-Michel Place, 1997.

of Nietzsche. In addition to Bataille's opening essay "Nietzsche and the Fascists,"[3] the issue included a French translation of a short text by Nietzsche on Heraclitus (from *Philosophy in the Tragic Age of the Greeks*), another short piece by Bataille offering "propositions" on fascism and the death of God, short texts by Jean Rollin and Pierre Klossowski, and two reviews of recent interpretations of Nietzsche: Karl Jaspers's *Nietzsche: Einführung in das Verständnis seines Philosophierens* (Berlin: de Gruyter, 1936) (by Bataille) and Karl Löwith's *Nietzsches Philosophie der ewigen Wiederkunft des Gleichen* (Berlin: Die Runde, 1935) (by Klossowski), along with several drawings by André Masson. The following essay by Wahl also appeared in this issue.

Alan D. Schrift

I. Immanence and Will to Immanence

As others have philosophized in the presence of divinity, Nietzsche philosophized, so to speak, in the presence of the absence of divinity, and this is without doubt more terrible. Kierkegaard is "before God," Nietzsche is in front of the decomposed corpse of God. Moreover, while Kierkegaard thinks that God wants my death, Nietzsche thinks that man must again and again will the death of God. This death is not only a fact, it is the action of a will. For man to be truly great and veracious, to be a creator, God must be dead, God must be killed, he must be absent. By depriving him of God, I bring to man the immense gift that is perfect solitude, and at the same time the possibility of greatness and creation.

The anguish before death disappears. "It makes me happy," says Nietzsche, "to see that men can't think through the thought of death."[4] "Our only certainty is of value the more we are beyond ourselves,"[5] and rightly so. And it is also good that "the more our life has of fullness and value, the more we are prepared to give it up for a single pleasant feeling." Man will

---

3. Georges Bataille, *Visions of Excess: Selected Writings, 1927–1939*, ed. and trans. Allan Stoekl (Minneapolis: University of Minnesota Press, 1985), 182–96.

4. [Cf. Friedrich Nietzsche, *The Gay Science*, trans. Walter Kaufmann (New York: Vintage Books, 1974), § 278; Karl Jaspers, *Nietzsche: Einführung in das Verständnis seines Philosophierens* (Berlin: de Gruyter, 1936), 286; English translation: *Nietzsche: An Introduction to His Philosophical Activity*, trans. C. F. Wallraff and F. J. Schmitz (Tucson: University of Arizona Press, 1965), 324.]

5. [Wahl here appears to be freely translating from Jaspers's citation from Nietzsche, *The Gay Science,* §278: "Wie seltsam, dass diese einzige Sicherheit und Gemeinsamkeit fast gar Nichts über die Menschen vermag"; English translation: "How strange it is that this sole certainty and common element makes almost no impression on people."]

lean toward death without fear, each toward the death that is his own. Moreover, Nietzsche often links the idea of celebration to the idea of death. Let's give a warm welcome to death, let's make death a celebration, that will still be the best way for us to avenge the betrayal of life.

II. Will to Immanence and Will to Transcendence

Nietzsche's philosophy, Jaspers tells us, is essentially the affirmation of the world as pure immanence. What has being is this world here. But just as Kierkegaard's belief contains doubt, so does negation in Nietzsche. The absence of God is neither error nor truth. And that is why the thought of the absence of God is passion, is will, just as in Kierkegaard the thought of God is passion and will. Nietzsche lives this reality of the death of God in willing [*voulant*] it, as we have seen; and at the same time without wanting [*vouloir*] it. He wants God at the same time that he wants the death of God. And the thought of God's absence does not remove in him the creative instinct for God. This is the "*existenzielle Gottlosigkeit*" ["existential Godlessness"] referred to by Jaspers.

III. Transcendence

Nietzsche is shaken, then transfixed by the idea of this transcendence that he denies. And, Jaspers wonders, is not the seriousness of Nietzsche's self-surrender like the image of loss and self-sacrifice under the influence of transcendence?

"In opposition to positivism, to naturalism, to materialism, there is in him a universal negativity, an unlimited dissatisfaction with every aspect of being. And this surge of dissatisfaction and negation is carried out with such passion, with such will to sacrifice, that it seems to come from the same depth as the great religions and beliefs of the prophets."[6] Nietzsche's

---

6. [Jaspers, "daß er im Unterschied von allen positivistischen, naturalistischen, materialistischen Lehren, denen stets eine unbewegliche Selbstgewißheit in der Beschränkung auf ihren Gegenstand, der ihnen das eigentliche Sein ist, eignet, in seiner Negativität schlechthin *universell* ist. . . . Bei Nietzsche hingegen ist der Antrieb des Verneinens aus dem Ungenügen heraus von einer Leidenschaft und einer Opferwilligkeit, daß sie aus demselben Ursprung herzukommen scheinen, der die großen Religiösen und Propheten antrieb" (385); English translation: "is the absolute universality of his negativism, in relation to the position of all positivists, naturalists, and materialists who, with complete and unshakeable self-confidence, confine themselves to those palpable objects which they take to constitute genuine being. . . . In Nietzsche's case, on the other hand, dissatisfaction gives rise to such a passionate and self-sacrificing impulse

immorality is negation of false morality; similarly, Jaspers tells us, his negation of God is a genuine connection with being, an affirmation of the Yes, a will to substance. When it is radical, the No can, by its own force, by its frenzy, turn itself into a Yes, and turn nihilism, the nihilism of the strong and no longer the nihilism of the weak, into a philosophy that is positive. In this nihilism that transcends, that denies, being reveals itself. By the same wound he feels in himself, by his pain at god torn apart, Nietzsche reached the foundation of being: time. His eyes are fixed both on the wheel of the eternal return and on the finite-infinite line of the most distant horizon: on the superhuman. He unites in himself Ixion and Prometheus.

If necessity and the will, the past and the future come to be merged, if the highest fatalism comes, in the words of Nietzsche, to be identified with chance and creation, with the highest activity, if the absurd and incomplete world of perpetual dissatisfaction receives the seal and blessing of eternity, becomes the world full of eternal satisfaction, is this not because the identity of opposites is the transcendent expression of being insofar as it cannot be placed within any category? And don't we know that the circles and antinomies are just ways to touch sideways and in the shadows what exceeds all law, all speech, all form?

Translated by Alan D. Schrift

---

to deny that it seems to come from the source that impelled the great religious leaders and prophets" (434).]

9

Poetry and Metaphysics

Jean Wahl's "Poetry and Metaphysics" first appeared in what, under the editorship of Jean Lescure, would soon become one of the leading literary journals of the French Resistance, *Messages*.[1] After a premier issue on William Blake (to which Wahl contributed advice and several poems of his own),[2] the journal's second issue, in 1939, was devoted to the topic "Metaphysics and Poetry," and included, alongside Wahl's lead article, an important essay on the poetic instant by Gaston Bachelard, original poems by Paul Éluard, and photographs of Hans Bellmer's

"Poésie et métaphysique," in *Existence humaine et transcendance* (Neuchâtel: Éditions de la Baconnière, 1944), 78–97.

1. Wahl also published poetry in other journals associated with the French Resistance such as *Les Lettres Françaises, Les Cahiers du Rhône, Fontaine, Confluences,* and *L'Arbalète*. For information on Wahl's connection to the final three journals mentioned, see *Archives des années noires: Artistes, écrivains et éditeurs*, ed. Claire Paulhan and Olivier Corpet (Saint-Germain-la-Blanche-Herbe: Institut Mémoires de l'Édition Contemporaine, 2004), 26, 52, 72; and *Archives de la vie littéraire sous l'occupation: À travers le désastre*, ed. Robert O. Paxton, Olivier Corpet, and Claire Paulhan (Paris: Tallandier/Saint-Germain-la-Blanche-Herbe: IMEC, 2009), 198, 260. Wahl's poetry in the first two can be found in *Les Lettres Françaises* 11 (January 1, 1944): 35–36; and *Les Cahiers du Rhône* 2 (Cahier de Poésie) (April 1942): 90–94. Max-Pol Fouchet, editor of *Fontaine*, later wrote in a republication of some of the "the most remarkable poems" in the journal, including Wahl's, that "[t]he desire to express the tragedy of the period through poetry was expressed through the voice of Jean Wahl." *Poésie* 1, nos. 55–61 (September–November 1978): 15, 50.

2. *Messages* 1, no. 1 (1939). See Jean Lescure, *Poésie et liberté: Histoire de "Messages," 1939–1946* (Paris: Éditions de l'IMEC, 1998), 28.

*La Poupée.*³ Wahl played a major role in shaping this issue. Not only did he suggest possible contributors; he also served, in Lescure's words, as "the most diligent *go between* imaginable."⁴

In this foundational article, which would be reprinted during the war in Wahl's *Existence humaine et transcendance* (1944)⁵ and again in 1998 in Lescure's *Poésie et liberté: Histoire de "Messages," 1939–1946*,⁶ Wahl ventures nothing less than "perhaps to reach the idea, the essence, of poetry." Poetry, Wahl suggests, is located both at the foundation of metaphysics and at the summit toward which metaphysics strives. Through a "union of contradictories," of contrary images that self-destruct and advance us toward what is imageless and indeterminable; through a coincidence of opposites⁷—for example, passivity and activity, and consciousness and unconsciousness—poetry helps us to go beyond what is given "here below," but, in a move that resembles what Wahl elsewhere calls "transdescendence," also allows us to return to the world below in which we find ourselves, to "join immanence to transcendence."

And yet, as becomes evident over the course of the essay, poetry can only be understood through its relationship to metaphysics, while metaphysics can in turn only be understood through its relationship to poetry. Each may shed light on the other, but neither ultimately stands autonomous. What we have is a sort of unending dialectic in which "they always remain linked, living from their reciprocal deaths, each emerging at the moment when the other is destroyed but living also from their reciprocal lives."

Wahl shows, for example, how Whitehead expresses philosophically what Percy Bysshe Shelley's poetry "makes us feel" about nature "in its incessant mobility." But Shelley's poetry itself rests on certain "philosophical intuitions," which themselves derive in part from the philosopher-poet Plato.⁸ Wahl reveals similar connections with respect to the themes of memory in Alfred de Musset, immobile nature in William Wordsworth, time in Charles Baudelaire and Stéphane Mallarmé, space in William Blake, causality in Paul Claudel, and even non-knowledge in the early

---

3. *Messages* 1, no. 2 (1939). Bachelard's piece, which merits comparison with Wahl's, is available in English as Gaston Bachelard, "Poetic Instant and Metaphysical Instant," in Bachelard, *Intuition of the Instant*, trans. Eileen Rizo-Patron (Evanston, Ill.: Northwestern University Press, 2013), 58–63.
4. See Lescure, *Poésie et liberté*, 39: "Le plus diligent *go between* que l'on puisse rêver."
5. Jean Wahl, *Existence humaine et transcendance* (Neuchâtel: Éditions de la Baconnière, 1944), 78–97.
6. Lescure, *Poésie et liberté*, 383–92.
7. Jean Wahl, "On Poetry," *Chimera* 2, no. 3 (1944): 35; Jean Wahl, "La poésie comme union des contraires," in Wahl, *Poésie, pensée, perception* (Paris: Calmann-Lévy, 1948), 20.
8. Jean Wahl, "Philosophie et poésie," in *Encyclopédie française*, vol. 19, *Philosophie, Religion* (Paris: Société Nouvelle de l'Encyclopédie Française, 1957), 30–39.

poetry of G. W. F. Hegel. He also notes equivalents between two hypotheses of Plato's *Parmenides* and the work of Arthur Rimbaud, and between the great kinds of being in Plato's *Sophist* and poets such as Paul Valéry, Walt Whitman, Novalis, and Gérard de Nerval. And he explains how even the simplest, least metaphysical poem by someone like Friedrich Hölderlin may lead us to philosophical insight.

Refusing to take sides, Wahl's own work embodies the inconclusive dialectic between metaphysics and poetry. Their fusion is uncertain, but Wahl, whether in his prose or verse, never stopped striving "for the metaphysico-poetic Truth to appear."

Ian Alexander Moore

It seems to me that there is something forbidden, sacrilegious, about speaking of the relationship between poetry and metaphysics.[9] The ideas that I might have, when I try to specify them, they flee, a little in the manner as do images in a dream that we would like to keep; the more we try to fix them in place, the more quickly they escape us.

Indeed poetry, as Schelling said, is a union of the conscious and the unconscious, of the subjective and the objective. How to make conscious that which involves so many unconscious elements, and objective that which involves so many subjective elements?

I speak foremost of a certain kind of poetry, but it will allow us perhaps to reach the idea, the essence, of poetry. May it shed some light on the connections that it, as well as even the poems by the least metaphysical poets, has with metaphysics.

Until our time, one could say that poetry and metaphysics treat the same subjects, but with different techniques. Yet both poetry and metaphysics aim to be rid of all technique. The various masters that we would like to follow do not, strictly speaking, give a lesson. A Rimbaud, even for poetry a Mallarmé, a Kierkegaard for the theory of existence, do not teach some-

---

9. The task is made easier by studies of poetry. Father [Henri] Brémond relates it to mysticism. Others have further investigated this subject from the side of poetic-metaphysical relations: [Denis] Saurat, Rolland de Renéville, Claude-Louis Estève. In the same way, [Marcel] Raymond examined contemporary French poetry, and [Albert] Béguin considered German Romanticism in its connections with metaphysics. Cf. also the books and articles of [Jacques] Maritain and [Marcel] de Corte, where the question is considered with the help of Aristotelian notions, although such notions do not in fact allow Maritain to draw out new ideas, despite the real poetic sense and the valuable human sense that Maritain possesses.

I leave to the side Eastern poetry, a consideration of which is perhaps no less valuable. Yet I believe that all that it tells us is found in the poetry of the West, less frequently perhaps, but no less intensely.

thing but tutor us to draw from ourselves things difficult to express. As a result we may very often have the impression today that poetry and metaphysics are at an impasse.

At one point in time they were very deeply united. The Greek Sophists gladly relied on Homer and discovered in him the idea of a perpetual transformation of things. Before them the first philosophers were very often poets. We have Theophrastus's testimony concerning Anaximander: "And things return to that from which they left, as is manifest, for they make reparation to one another and pay for their injustice, the ones to the others, following marked time." And Theophrastus adds: "as Anaximander says in somewhat poetic terms."[10]

Parmenides formulated his metaphysics in very austere verse. The way of opinion leads to nothing: those who rely on sense rely on that which is not. It is necessary to rely only on those things that are known by the way of science. Thus this metaphysician poet warns us against the poetic realms and allows us to open our eyes only before the brilliance of the eternal sphere of being. Whereas the prosaist Heraclitus highlighted the reasonless elements of the universe, all the while insisting on the logos, on a reason that unites them in a mysterious way.

Plato is heir to these two philosophers. He harshly criticizes the poets Homer and Hesiod. However, it is Platonism that permitted, during the course of the centuries, the majority of poets' escapes toward metaphysics.

I would like to see what poetry can retain of metaphysical motifs, how poetry can give access to the metaphysical world, and how the poet departs from these metaphysical motifs in order to constitute a poetic system.[11]

Whitehead tells us that it is necessary to continuously turn to the testimony of the great poets: "Their survival is evidence that they express deep intuitions of mankind penetrating into what is universal in concrete fact."[12] He cites, to support his thesis, two examples: Wordsworth and Shelley. It is perhaps indeed with Romanticism that we best see appear the deep

---

10. [Wahl's French translation has been rendered into English directly. Cf. the translation in *The Presocratic Philosophers: A Critical History with a Selection of Texts*, 2nd ed., ed. G. S. Kirk, J. E. Raven, and M. Schofield (Cambridge: Cambridge University Press, 2007), 108: "'And the source of coming-to-be for existing things is that into which destruction, too, happens according to necessity; for they pay penalty and retribution to each other for their injustice according to the assessment of time,' as he describes it in these rather poetical terms."]

11. This is not without some danger since I risk transforming into a concept that which is essentially nonconceptual.

12. [Alfred North Whitehead, *Science and the Modern World* (New York: The Free Press, 1925), 87.]

connections between poetry and metaphysics. It has been said that Romanticism is the birth, the rebirth of wonder; it renders strange things familiar, and familiar things strange.[13] It is its essence that one discovers in a poet like Novalis when he ceaselessly places his hero before things that it seems he has always known, and which are at the same time, by a singular paradox, by an essential antinomy, things that he knows to have never before seen. An absolute newness, which is at the same time very ancient, an element radically foreign which is at the same time intimately ours, this is what Novalis's magic can bring before Henry von Ofterdingen, as before the disciples at Saïs, and before us.

If we take the problem of memory and of time, and read "Souvenir" by Musset, "Tristesse d'Olympio,"[14] and "Le lac,"[15] we find there this idea of the sacred character of memory that one conserves within one's self, and in Musset this idea (presented in another way in Shelley's "Adonaïs") that every being and every event has its resonance in Nature, is conserved within it, even though it no longer exists in us. However, the ideas of Nature and Memory are not deepened here.[16]

This is not the case in Wordsworth and Shelley, both imbued with the Platonic tradition. Wordsworth makes us feel nature in its immobility and Shelley in its incessant mobility. It is the idea of "endurance," to take this word from Whitehead, of duration, of a duration motionless and bleak, but also sometimes nourishing and consoling, which arises in us in reading Wordsworth, whereas Shelley shows us Nature in movement and in the reciprocal interpenetration of its forms. There is in him "a feeling for nature, as exhibiting entwined prehensive unities, each suffused with modal presences of others."[17] Here you have a poetic intuition (itself derived in a certain measure from philosophical intuitions), translated into the somewhat barbaric language of a contemporary philosophy.

If nature is therefore fathomed more deeply by Wordsworth and Shelley, time appears to us to be fathomed just as deeply by Novalis and Hölderlin. These sentiments of the always new and of the always old, which merge in

---

13. Shelley, and in our time Bergson, defined art as the power of lifting the veil that custom forms between us and things.

14. [From *Les rayons et les ombres*, by Victor Hugo.]

15. [From *Méditations poétiques*, by Alphonse de Lamartine.]

16. We should mention the opposition between Leconte de Lisle—"What is all that which is not eternal?" [from "L'illusion suprême"]—and Vigny—"Love that which one will never see twice" [from "La maison du berger (III)"]. The thoughts of these two poets find themselves in a certain measure reconciled by that of Novalis, or that of the eternal return in Nietzsche.

17. Whitehead [*Science and the Modern World*, 84].

Novalis, belong to an affective Platonism; it makes us go toward an instant that is at the same time eternity. What these poets noted is what a Baudelaire and a Mallarmé glimpsed in their turn. The theory of correspondences in Baudelaire, of the symbol, of this vision of ourselves as "tarnished and sad mirrors,"[18] is this not an echo of Platonism? A Platonism equally present, perhaps sharper still, in Mallarmé, where the idea appears both as the "glory of a long desire"[19] and as being "itself at last."[20]

We will be able to discover this idea of the instant in Blake. He tries to show us eternity and its presence at each instant of our life.[21] The poet will have the duty of consecrating this moment, of making a passing moment something that remains and is consecrated by the very fact that it is willed just as the Nietzschean hero wills to affirm himself by the concept of the eternal return.

By this consecration of time, this deepening of the instant, and also by the fact that poetry fills time in various ways (by a magic flight as in Shelley, or by a breathless race as is often the case in [Algernon Charles] Swinburne), poetry appears as a manipulation of time.

On the subject of space I will refer again to Blake:

> And on its verge the Sun rises and sets, the Clouds bow
> To meet the flat Earth and the Sea in such an order'd Space.
> The Starry Heavens reach no further, but here bend and set
> On all sides, and the two Poles turn on their valves of gold;
> And if he moves his dwelling-place, his heavens also move
> Where'er he goes, and all his neighbourhood bewail his loss.
> Such are the Spaces called Earth and such its dimension.
> As to that false appearance, which appears to the reasoner,
> As of a Globe rolling thro' Voidness, it is a delusion of Ulro.
> The Microscope knows not of this, nor the Telescope: they alter
> The ratio of the Spectator's Organs, but leave Objects untouch'd
> For every Space larger than a red Globule of Man's blood
> Is visionary, and is created by the Hammer of Los.
>
> ("Milton," plate 29 [31], ll. 8–20)[22]

---

18. [Charles Baudelaire, *Flowers of Evil and Other Works / Les Fleurs du Mal et Oeuvres Choisies: A Dual-Language Book*, ed. and trans. Wallace Fowlie (New York: Dover, 1992), 25; translation modified.]

19. [Stéphane Mallarmé, "Prose (*For des Esseintes*)," in *Collected Poems and Other Verse*, trans. E. H. and A. M. Blackmore (Oxford: Oxford University Press, 2006), 53.]

20. [Mallarmé, "The Tomb of Edgar Allan Poe," in *Collected Poems and Other Verse*, 71.]

21. Is this not analogous to the Kierkegaardian repetition?

22. [Wahl's French translation, omitted here, follows his citation of the English in the original. Blake's poem can be found in *The Complete Poetry and Prose of William*

Space is the son of time, the unit that measures the modification, and it is limited. True space is not the one that science considers, but the space felt by us; and its real rhythm, its real principle, are in its smallest bit, just as the principle of time was in its smallest bit: the instant.

One could find in Blake a conception of space and time that one could call concrete. In contemporary poetry we could compare it to that of Claudel, who in his *Poetic Art* sketched his own philosophy. He explained what causality is for him, the pressure of things one upon the other. He told us what knowledge is: something elementary, of which human understanding is only the last efflorescence. "Indeed, blue knows orange; indeed, the hand knows its shadow on the wall."[23] Knowledge is a com-presence, as [Samuel] Alexander deemed it, the juxtaposition firstly of subject and object, and since we are now before the idea of knowledge, leaving romantic poetry but not the poetry of wonder, I refer to [Thomas] Traherne's poem:

> My naked simple Life was I.
> That Act so strongly shin'd,
> Upon the Earth, the Sea, the Sky,
> It was the Substance of the Mind.
> The Sense its self was I.
> I felt no Dross nor Matter in my Soul,
> No Brims nor Borders, such as in a Bowl.
> We see: My Essence was *Capacity*.
> . . .
> This made me present evermore
> With whatsoere I saw.
> . . .
> There was my Sight, my Life, my Sense,
> My Substance, ev'n my Mind.
> My Spirit shin'd
> Ev'n there, not by a *transeunt* Influence.
>
> The Act was immanent, yet *there*,
> The Thing remote, yet felt ev'n *here*.
> O Joy! O Wonder and Delight!
> O sacred Mystery!
>
> ("My Spirit")[24]

Blake, rev. ed., ed. David V. Erdman, commentary by Harold Bloom, 95–144 (Berkeley: University of California Press, 1982), 127.]

23. [Paul Claudel, *Poetic Art*, trans. Renee Spodheim (New York: Philosophical Library, 1948), 41.]

24. [Wahl's French translation, omitted here, follows his citation of the English in the original. Wahl refers to its initial appearance in *Mesures* 2, no. 2 (April 15,

What can the poets say of the unknowable?[25] In 1796 Hegel dedicates a poem to Hölderlin:

> Thanks be to you, you my
> liberator, oh night!
> . . .
> sense shedding itself in intuition,
> what I call mine fading,
> I give myself to the vastness therein,
> I am in it, am everything, am only it.
> Recurring reflection becomes alien,
> it dreads before infinity, and astonished grasps
> not the depth of this intuition.
> . . .
> To the son of the initiation was the richness of the high learning
> the inexpressible feeling's depth much too holy
> than that he should value their dull signs.
> Even the thought does not seize the soul
> which outside of Time and Space lost in premonition of infinity
> forgets itself and again to consciousness now
> awakens. Whosoever would wish to speak thereof to others,
> speaks he with tongues of angels, feeling the poverty of the words;
> he dreads the holy so little contemplated,
> through words to have been made so small, that speech to him seems sin,
> and that he, shaking, closes his mouth.
> What the initiated thus himself forbade, forbade a wise
> law the poorer spirits to make known
> what he on the holy night saw, heard, felt—
>
> ("Eleusis," to Hölderlin, August 1796[26])

In this poetry one sees the pantheistic mysticism of the young Hegel assert itself. One thought that Hegel did not like this infinity that terrified his thought. Nevertheless he immerses himself in it as do Hölderlin

---

1936). A slightly different version of Traherne's poem can be found in *The Poetical Works of Thomas Traherne*, 2nd ed., ed. Bertram Dobell (London: Bertram Dobell, 1906), 42–47.]

25. It would be necessary to broach the vast subject of the link between love and metaphysics, such as it is, for example, suggested in Shelley's "Epipsychidion," or in Wagner's *Tristan* duet.

26. [G. W. F. Hegel, "Eleusis," trans. Alan W. Grose, *The Philosophical Forum* 33, no. 3 (Fall 2002): 312–17. We have here omitted Hegel's original German text and Wahl's French translation, both of which appear in Wahl's essay in *Existence humaine et transcendance*.]

and Novalis. For them, everything that they think is linked to the unthinkable, as everything visible is to the invisible, and everything that one hears to that which one cannot hear.[27]

The link between poetry and metaphysics is made on the one hand from below, on the other from above. If there is a base of metaphysics, a hypophysics, that which Nietzsche, Whitman, [D. H.] Lawrence, Boehme, Schelling wanted to lay bare, if there is a huge torpor in the depths of nature, and sometimes in the depths of us, it is there that one could find a link between poetry and metaphysics. And conversely, if there is a point toward which metaphysics tends, as the ogive toward its summit, it is there too that one could find this link, since that from which philosophy senses its power can be indicated only by something other than discourse, and this "something other" can be poetry. Thus there would be a bloc of reality and acute moments, there would be the base and the summit of the pyramid, and it is by this immense base and by this sharp summit that the communication between the one and the other of the fields that we are studying would occur.

If we return to the hypotheses that Plato examines in the *Parmenides*, first that the one is only itself and vanishes in order to become a kind of nonbeing, then that the one is the whole [*l'un est tout*], we will be able to find the equivalent of the chaos of the second hypothesis, and the equivalent of the negative theology of the first in *Illuminations* and in *Saison en enfer*.[28] The poet is the one who is conscious of all this disorder of being and of this purity of nonbeing that Valéry spoke of.

Yet between these two fields by which poetry and metaphysics could perhaps unite, there are a great number of regions of the soul where this meeting could equally occur. The human soul knows many countries, which are its countries. Blake puts forward this idea of regions through

---

27. The mystic has been opposed to the poet. The mystic has been preferred. There is perhaps an injustice there. The poet speaks and the mystic keeps silent, they tell us. Yet how many mystics have spoken, spoken at length, repeating what other mystics had said before them. And how many poets have been aware of the fact that the most precious moment of their poem is the one where it falls into silence, it is the sound that is extinguished little by little, then its empty vanished form, the memory of which again, by instants, echoes the silence, more sacred than the poem, melodious through the poem, before being absolute silence. There is a complex dialectic in the poem, a dialogue of dialogue with silence, which swallows it and gives birth to it again.

28. [*Illuminations* is a collection of prose poems by Arthur Rimbaud written between 1873 and 1875 and first published in 1886. *Une saison en enfer* (*A Season in Hell*) is an extended prose poem written and published by Rimbaud in 1873.]

which the soul passes, the self passes. It is the theory of *states*. The self has nothing real; it is the states that it crosses that are real.[29]

Poetry makes us grasp, under the most universal aspect, that which is most subjective. We may ask ourselves whether what we find at the depths of poetry are not the great types of being that Plato's reflection brought out. [Albert] Thibaudet shows that when Valéry tries to know himself he sees only nonbeing (and one could add "possibles"), and that when he creates, he sees being form before him. There is in him a nihilism of knowledge and a positivism of creation. If, then, we comprehend the whole movement of philosophical thought that goes from Parmenides to Mallarmé and Valéry, we will see that this nonbeing and these possibles that Parmenides had excluded are, on the contrary, in a sense what Mallarmé and Valéry cast their gaze upon. Nothingness, that which is absolutely not, *Igitur*'s whiteness of the page and obscurity of the night, the chance that one cannot abolish, these are some of the dominant motifs of Mallarméan poetry. The possible that was excluded from Parmenides's poem found a place in Valéry's world. In this way we find a reflection on being and nonbeing, both in the poet metaphysicians Mallarmé and Valéry, and in this metaphysician poet, Parmenides. Yet the poets arrive at completely different conclusions than the philosopher does. They indeed conceive of the possibility of a poetry of being. The poetry of Claudel, that of Whitman, could perhaps offer us an idea of it.

The idea of the Same accounts for the feeling of Unity and it is hard to exaggerate the role this feeling plays in poetry, since this idea is present in the love of nature, in the love of the other self, in the love of God, and we find it at the heart of the cult of the Night, which Rolland de Renéville wrote one of the principal chapters of his book about.[30] Novalis, Nerval, Wagner, Baudelaire have celebrated Unity under the obscure varieties of Night.

One could show the importance of the idea of the Other [*l'Autre*] as at once a call toward the other [*autrui*], toward a felt presence, and an affirmation of things and of beings that we cannot reach. In such a way that it would be necessary to strongly distinguish the alterity that calls us, toward

---

29. One could find in Nietzsche a plastic equivalent of this theory in the description of heroic, idyllic, and heroic-idyllic landscapes. Perhaps one could even say that the tragedy, the idyll, the elegy, and all the great classical genres are only attempts to translate the different states of the soul into well-defined genres that correspond to them.

30. [Rolland de Renéville, "Le sens de la nuit," in de Renéville, *L'expérience poétique, ou le feu secret du langage* (Paris: Gallimard, 1938), 59–94.]

which we pray (be it a human person or god), and the alterity that we collide with (be it the object of a negative ontology, the god of a negative theology, or another self, cruel and closed). If we now consider the Same and the Other no longer as isolated but as united, the play of the Same and the Other and the influence of the Same on the Other, won't we find the Platonic idea of participation, and all its derivatives: correspondence, symbol, image, reflections, analogies, Platonic love? Isn't it because Plato laid hands on this mechanism of the Same in the Other that it stands at the origin of this poetic Platonism?

We could, beyond the classes of the same and the other, cite the final two, which for Plato in the *Sophist* complete the hierarchy of the great kinds—movement and rest, which we have spoken of with respect to Wordsworth and Shelley.

How, for the poet, do all the kinds combine, and how do things combine themselves and oppose themselves? There will be a play of analogies and antitheses. The analogies are Baudelaire's "correspondences." As for the antitheses, Blake describes them: "The contraries are positive, the negation is not a contrary. The two contraries are positive, the one as the other."[31] And these analogies and these antitheses will perhaps come to blend in our eyes if we recall the mystical experiences of a Novalis or of a Nerval, the "Ode of the Marriage of Seasons" in Novalis,[32] the fusion of the Virgin and of Cybele in Nerval, or of Christ and Dionysus in Hölderlin, the eternal return when the "thirteenth comes again" in Nerval,[33] or when the great noon rings in Nietzsche.

---

31. [Wahl's French translation of Blake has been translated into English directly. The first two lines can be found written backward on plate 30 of Blake's "Milton," reproduced in his *Complete Poetry and Prose*, 129; book 2 of *Milton* begins with the third line cited by Wahl. Blake's original text reads: "Contraries are positive / A negation is not a Contrary / There is a place where Contraries are equally true."]

32. [According to Ludwig Tieck, who wrote an afterword to Novalis's incomplete novel *Henry of Ofterdingen*, the novel was to conclude with the poem "Die Vermählung der Jahreszeiten" ("The Marriage of Seasons"). The poem can be found in "Tiecks Bericht über die Fortsetzung," in Novalis, *Schriften*, vol. 4, ed. J. Minor (Jena: Eugen Diederichs, 1907), 249–50. It is also published in Novalis, *Werke*, ed. Gerhard Schulz (Munich: Beck, 1969), 89–90.]

33. [Gérard de Nerval, "Artemis," trans. Barbara Howes, in *An Anthology of French Poetry from Nerval to Valéry in English Translation with French Originals*, rev. ed., ed. Angel Flores (Garden City, N.Y.: Doubleday Anchor, 1962), 12–13; translation modified.]

The danger that exists in seeking these agreements between metaphysicians and poets is that the themes of poetry would then appear as conceptual. We would be wrong to consider these themes independently from the way in which they are incorporated in the works.

In this respect it would be curious to study the connections between a poet like Hölderlin and a philosopher like Hegel. One could maintain that they began from almost identical experiences. Yet what became the great philosophy of Hegel became, having been transformed by another temperament, the great poetry of Hölderlin. Therefore we must not say that the poet is an unfulfilled metaphysician, nor that the metaphysician is an unfulfilled poet, nor that idealism is a philosophy of the poet, nor that German Romanticism is a poetry of the philosopher. It is indeed very doubtful that one could go much further toward the metaphysical region by way of poetry than by way of another means of expression, such as drawing, color, or the sound of music, since metaphysics is ultimately nothing conceptual; and a few of Rembrandt's strokes, one of El Greco's colors, do not awaken thoughts less spiritually metaphysical than a poem by [Alfred de] Vigny or Coventry Patmore. Rest is better grasped in its essence, in an essence still more at rest, by Cézanne than by Wordsworth; and movement in its whirling and turbulent essence still more by Van Gogh than by Shelley.[34]

The manner in which the poet embodies his idea is something different from a philosophical system. Hölderlin, trying to ascertain the unascertainable that he has before his eyes when he composes a poem, wrote in a letter: "The storm as power and as shape, the light, its way of coming and of going, and the encounter of diverse characters of nature in one place, in such a way that all the places of the earth are reunited around a single place, and the philosophical light around my window, this is today what gives me joy."[35]

---

34. One could say, returning to Plato's idea, that the poet is at four removes from reality, whereas the painter or the sculpture is only at three. However, perhaps this distance from the real at which he finds himself allows him to better approach, in a manner at least more intelligible, its essence.

35. [Wahl's French translation of Hölderlin's letter to Casimir Ulrich Böhlendorff (approx. November 1802) has been translated into English directly. Cf. Friedrich Hölderlin, *Essays and Letters*, ed. and trans. Jeremy Adler and Charlie Louth (London: Penguin, 2009), 214: "Storms, not just in their greatest manifestation, but seen as power and figure, among the other forms of the sky, the effect of the light, shaping nationally and as principle and destiny, so that something is holy to us, the intensity of its coming and going, the characteristicness of the woods and the coincidence in one region of different characters of

It is therefore an instant that for the poet will be the essence of his reflection bathed in a light nonetheless philosophical. A little later Hölderlin wrote:

> In lovely blueness with its metal roof the steeple blossoms.
> Around it the crying of the swallows hovers, most moving
> blueness surrounds it. The sun hangs high above it and colours
> the sheets of tin, but up above in the wind silently crows
> the weathercock.[36]

Nothing in this poem is, properly speaking, metaphysical. Yet the emotion that it gives us, the fact that this instant has been separated from all the others, and lived intensely, at once so familiar and so strange, leaves us to make out the veiled face of what Hölderlin calls the philosophical light.[37]

The same Hölderlin says: "A sign we are, without meaning,"[38] and it is truly this sense of an absence of sense that his poem brings us, with the feeling that we are here without knowing why, but that in a certain way this instant is consecrated by the very fact that we live it.

"In certain semi-supernatural conditions of the spirit," Baudelaire writes, "the whole depths of life are revealed within the scene—no matter how commonplace—which one has before one's eyes. This becomes its symbol."[39] It is in this sense that every great poem is susceptible to metaphysical signification, even if it does not contain anything metaphysical. Keats's "Ode on a Grecian Urn," Hugo's "Sur une Stèle antique," even one of [André] Chénier's poems, one of [Jean] Racine's tragedies, where the sea of passions is contained in the play of rhymes and in the unity of day and of place, one of Shakespeare's dramas, one of Rilke's *Dinggedichte* ["thing poems"], kindle the worlds of metaphysical thought,

---

nature, so that all the holy places of the earth are together in one place, and the philosophic light at my window, they are now my joy."]

36. [Friedrich Hölderlin, "In lovely blueness . . . ," in Hölderlin, *Poems and Fragments*, trans. Michael Hamburger, 4th ed. (London: Anvil, 2004), 789.]

37. Every passion is a charm, Novalis said. [See Novalis, *Philosophical Writings*, trans. Margaret Mahoney Stoljar (Albany: State University of New York Press, 1997), 107 (Fragment 27).] It is the passion of Orpheus that is at the origin of the very order of his compositions. And his pain.

38. [Friedrich Hölderlin, "Mnemosyne," 2nd version, in Hölderlin, *Hyperion and Selected Poems*, ed. Eric L. Santner (New York: Continuum, 1990), 273.]

39. [Charles Baudelaire, *Intimate Journals*, trans. Christopher Isherwood, introduction by W. H. Auden (Mineola, N.Y.: Dover, 2006), "Squib" XVII, p. 45.]

awakening in their virtual hearth a blinding spark of thoughts unthought, and almost of formulas unformulable.[40]

The very description of that which is given to us in reality can enfold a philosophical meaning.

Poetry will be a union of contradictories, because that which cannot be imagined will be presented under the form of images, which, as Bergson could have shown, will often follow one another in order to destroy one another, finally giving the idea of that which is no longer an image. That which is pure quality will be presented under the form of quantity. Words will be bestowed at once with a "purer sense,"[41] and with an impurer sense, and in these two ways they will distinguish themselves from our ordinary words.

It is still by this union of things at odds with one another that the poet will be able not only to make us go toward the beyond, but once we have glimpsed this beyond make us return to the here below, and join immanence to transcendence. This is what Heidegger wanted to signify by that "belonging to the earth," which he spoke of with respect to Hölderlin.[42]

The poet will make us feel that physics is metaphysics, and what passes away, eternal.[43] Here Novalis, Rimbaud, Whitman, and Nietzsche are in agreement.

"Eternity. It is the sea fled away with the sun," Rimbaud says.[44] It is Joy's Noon, Nietzsche says. In these contradictories whose play we see, in this

---

40. Blake wrote [in "Milton," plate 28 (30), ll. 1–7]:

Some sons of Los surround the Passions with porches of iron and silver
Creating form and beauty around the dark regions of sorrow,
Giving to airy nothing a name and a habitation
Delightful: with bounds to the Infinite putting off the Indefinite
Into most holy forms of Thought (such is the power of Inspiration),
They labour incessant, with many tears and afflictions,
Creating the beautiful House for the piteous sufferer.

41. [Mallarmé, "The Tomb of Edgar Allan Poe," in *Collected Poems and Other Verse*, 71.]

42. [See Martin Heidegger, "Hölderlin and the Essence of Poetry," in Heidegger, *Elucidations of Hölderlin's Poetry*, trans. Keith Hoeller (New York: Humanity Books, 2000), 54.]

43. The poet does not call upon the same region of ourselves as does the prosaist. He agitates an inner lake that mysteriously communicates with the ocean, which the Greeks made the order of things. It is none other than what Schelling attempted to define: union of the subjective and the objective. The poet touches an extreme subjectivity and thereby joins us to the cosmos.

44. [Arthur Rimbaud, "L'éternité / Eternity," in Rimbaud, *Selected Verse*, trans. Oliver Bernard (Baltimore: Penguin, 1962), 217.]

union of transcendence and of immanence, we will likewise discover the explanation of the fact that the poet is at once subject and object, subjective and objective, conscious and unconscious, active and passive, living these contradictories in a tension, in an intensity, which is lyricism. Do we not rediscover the ancient thought of Heraclitus: "There is a harmony of opposed tensions like those of a lyre."[45] Modern poetry distinguishes itself from ancient poetry by its subjectivity, by this lyric subjectivity that evolved out of Romanticism. Without a doubt there is something essential to all poetry here. If Lucretius seemed to proceed with the most objective concepts in order to compose his poem, it is because his passion was intensified by the very contact with these concepts and expressed itself with even more personality, as the world before which he found himself was an impersonal destroyer of such passion. The flame, conscious it would die out soon, burned all the stronger in this dark world.

The poet is in some way conscious of the unconscious. "To dream and all together not to dream, to be in a state of absolute wakefulness and yet to dream."[46]

And it is Novalis again who allows us to see the union of activity and passivity. The poet is one in whom we can grasp something analogous to what we imagine to be the creative activity of the world; he is in the whole force of the word "poet," creator, and he is also the one who can write like Novalis: "One does not make, but one makes possible that it can be made."[47]

45. [Wahl's French translation of Fragment 53 (in the Diels-Kranz enumeration) has been translated directly. Cf. Charles H. Kahn, *The Art and Thought of Heraclitus: An Edition of the Fragments with Translation and Commentary* (Cambridge: Cambridge University Press, 1979), 65: "They do not comprehend how a thing agrees at variance with itself; it is an attunement turning back on itself, like that of the bow and the lyre."]

46. [Wahl's French has been translated directly. Perhaps Wahl is referring to a passage from Novalis's *Naturwissenschaftliche Studien 1798–1799*. See Novalis, *Schriften: Die Werke Friedrich von Hardenbergs*, ed. Paul Kluckhorn and Richard Samuel, vol. 3 (*Das philosophische Werk II*), ed. Richard Samuel in collaboration with Hans-Joachim Mähl and Gerhard Schulz (Stuttgart: Kohlhammer, 1960), 63: "Träumen und *Nichtträumen zugleich*—synthesirt ist die Operation des Genies—wodurch beydes sich gegenseitig verstärkt" ("Dreaming and *Not-dreaming at the same time*—the operation of genius is synthesized—whereby both are reciprocally strengthened").]

47. [Wahl cites Novalis's French sentence from Teplitz Fragment 77: "Alle Construction ist also indirect. On ne fait pas, mais on fait, qu'il se puisse faire." See Novalis, *Schriften: Die Werke Friedrich von Hardenbergs*, vol. 2 (*Das philosophische Werk I*), 609.] It is without a doubt something similar that Baudelaire wanted to make understood when he wrote: "The distillation and centralisation of the *ego*. Everything is in that." [*My Heart Laid Bare, and Other Prose Writings*, ed. Peter Quennell, trans.

In doing so, the poet will no longer know whether it is he who speaks or another. He no longer knows to whom he addresses himself, for whom he writes. It is not for another than himself, and it is not for himself.

What does he try to do when he who is not he addresses himself to a he who is not he? He tries at the same time to construct himself and to destroy himself, to preserve this moment and to deliver himself from this moment in destroying it. He is "the widower, the unconsoled,"[48] but also the one who exhorts himself to a daring attempt. He brings the unconscious toward the conscious. He destroys himself at the same time that he affirms himself by expression. He is Orpheus reviving Eurydice, but under the mask of the Maenad that kills him it is still he, he and his poetry, that we recognize.

A manipulation of time, poetry is also a manipulation of ourselves. It is our prayer and our revolt. It is our chance, which we ratify with the seal of necessity. It is our fate. The Poet is Prometheus the Rebel. Orpheus gathering an unconscious Eurydice toward the light, Pygmalion breathing life into Galatea. And he is also Ulysses returning to the country of his birth, Empedocles who unites himself with the unchained forces of nature, the Maenads who destroy the poet himself. There is a struggle of metaphysics against poetry and of poetry against metaphysics; however, they always remain linked, living from their reciprocal deaths, each emerging at the moment when the other is destroyed but living also from their reciprocal lives. It is when, at our core, metaphysics is reduced to silence that suddenly poetry raises its voice; but in this voice we hear the echo of the meditations of the vanished metaphysician.

What will be the destiny of the poet today? Hölderlin writes:

> But, my friend, we have come too late.
> [. . .]
> who wants poets at all in lean years?
> But they are, you say, like those holy ones, priests of the wine-god
> Who in holy Night roamed from one place to the next.[49]

Norman Cameron (New York: Haskell, 1975), 175.] Hugo likewise said in a passage quoted by Béguin: "It is a question of knowing to what extent the song belongs to the voice and poetry to the poet." [Wahl misquotes Béguin/Hugo slightly. Cf. Albert Béguin, *L'âme romantique et le rêve: Essai sur le romantisme allemand et la poésie française*, new ed. (Paris: José Corti, 1946; originally published 1939), 370; as well as *Œuvres de Victor Hugo*, vol. 1 (Brussels: J. P. Meline, 1836), 590.]

48. [Gérard de Nerval, "El Desdichado," in *The Penguin Book of French Poetry* (London: Penguin, 1990), 79.]

49. [Hölderlin, "Bread and Wine," in *Poems and Fragments*, 325–27. Wahl renders the famous second line, which in German reads, "wozu Dichter in dürftiger Zeit?," as "A quoi bon des poètes au temps de la détresse?" ("What good are poets in times of distress?").]

We can no longer fashion great metaphysical poems, and perhaps it is difficult to fashion great poems in our day. We are better off remaining at our place marked by the destiny of our culture as well as of ourselves, and to do what we can, *to do*, however little it may be. To the time of distress is suited perhaps not a poetry of distress but a poetry which is born of it in order to overcome it, after adapting to it. Perhaps in the coming era the fundamental intuitions in all fields will be more indistinct, more ponderous, more unformed, while the ideas that correspond to them will be finer and more subtle.

What I have said of these connections between poetry and metaphysics evokes in me the feeling that all has been done by the poets and that all remains to be done in order for the metaphysico-poetic Truth to appear.[50] I will quote a very short poem to summarize these connections between poetry and metaphysics. It is metaphysics who speaks and here is what she says:

> Poetry, big sister,
> That your song take its flight,
> I listen to you, and it is I who speaks.

We do not know what metaphysics is nor what poetry is, but the core of poetry will always be metaphysics, and it is quite possible that the core of metaphysics is, equally, always poetry.

Translated by Simone Rowen[51]

---

50. All great poetry is surrealism and at the same time realism. The error of surrealism proper, or rather its errors, is to have believed that one found the surreal through words in their freedom. It is also to have believed that it was surrealism even though it was only postsurrealism (the true one having happened with Blake or Rimbaud). Its enduring glory is to have maintained in the most violent manner this essence of poetry. It is necessary, today especially, not to forget what was, what still remains, its role despite its errors. We remain grateful to it for the truths that it has told, even though they are not novel.

51. [Translator's note: With special thanks to Jeanne Capelle, student at the École Normale Supérieure, for her generous attention and assistance early on in the process of this essay's translation.]

10

Order and Disorder in Nietzsche's Thought

In July 1964, the eminent French historian of philosophy, Martial Gueroult, opened a five-day conference on Friedrich Nietzsche at the Royaumont Abbey just north of Paris. The conference was co-organized by Gilles Deleuze, who invited presentations from both younger philosophers like Michel Foucault and Gianni Vattimo, as well as from distinguished senior philosophers, including Jean Wahl, Jean Beaufret, Karl Löwith, and Gabriel Marcel. Deleuze was then concluding a four-year position at the CNRS (Centre National de Recherche Scientifique) and preparing to assume the position of professor of philosophy at the University of Lyon. Nietzsche's *On the Genealogy of Morality* had appeared on the *agrégation de philosophie* in 1958 and 1959 (for the first time since 1929) while Deleuze was teaching future *agrégés* at the Sorbonne. In his brief opening remarks, Gueroult emphasized the centrality of the question of values in Nietzsche's philosophy and invoked the three metamorphoses from Nietzsche's *Thus Spoke Zarathustra*—the soul becoming first camel, then lion, then child—concluding that Nietzsche's philosophy, "with all its power of destruction," must ultimately be thought of as tending toward affirmation.

Wahl had recognized the centrality of the question of value for Nietzsche in his long review essay for the *Revue de Métaphysique et de Morale* of Deleuze's 1962 monograph, *Nietzsche and Philosophy*, published the year before the Royaumont conference.[1]

"Ordre et désordre dans la pensée de Nietzsche," plus the discussion that follows, originally appeared in *Nietzsche: Cahiers du Royaumont* (Paris: Éditions de Minuit, 1967), 85–102.

1. Jean Wahl, "Nietzsche et la philosophie," *Revue de Métaphysique et de Morale*, no. 3 (July–September 1963): 352–79.

The bulk of Wahl's lengthy review is a detailed and laudatory account of Deleuze's book that foregrounds the stark difference Deleuze draws between Nietzsche and Hegel. However, while acknowledging that Deleuze's book will take its place alongside the most important books on Nietzsche by Karl Jaspers, Martin Heidegger, Eugen Fink, and Lou Salomé, Wahl remains cautious regarding Deleuze's systematic elucidation of Nietzsche's thought, and he challenges Deleuze's interpretation at several points. While some of these critiques verge on being simply dismissive—Wahl archly notes that Deleuze's critique of Hegel's "work of the negative" as a manifestation of the "will to nothingness" is as "superficial" as the Marxist critique—he focuses his attention on two "difficulties," or "dangers," in Deleuze's interpretation. The crux of Deleuze's reading is the inevitably positive sense of the affirmation that conjoins will to power and eternal return, and the consequent overcoming of nihilism. Wahl worries that the various formulations of this affirmation given by Nietzsche (and Deleuze) retain negativity in various ways, and he discerns a dialectic at work in this retention. Wahl's concern is not strictly scholastic, however; he worries also about the consequences if one were to accept and follow out Nietzsche's affirmation. Where Nietzsche and Deleuze see the promise of a liberated existence in the affirmation of the superhuman, Wahl cautiously notes that such a promise must be balanced against the atrocities of the twentieth century, seeming to implicitly note at least an affinity between Nietzsche's philosophy and its most monstrous misinterpretations. And, in the notably sharp conclusion to his review, Wahl wonders whether the theory of the superhuman, "a theory that is as close as possible to the concrete," might "ultimately be founded on an essentially abstract and formal act of affirmation."[2]

Wahl's presentation at Royaumont can be read as the obverse side of his critique of Deleuze's interpretation of Nietzsche.[3] The disjointed style, the repeated invocations of the title as an alibi for what sounds like disorganization, the disavowal—the refusal even to name the superhuman—and the abrupt nonconclusion are the necessary performative correlates to the claim that the importance of Nietzsche's philosophy is to be found in the multiple expressions of the states of soul that animate him. The superhuman, the one whose affirmation conjoins the will to power and the eternal return, is the figure that Nietzsche invokes to ground and unify these expressions and, in so doing, risks resolving the imminent dialectic of order and disorder in favor of the former. In a key passage of his talk, Wahl

---

2. Ibid., 379.
3. For his part, Deleuze says of Wahl's presentation in his concluding remarks to the conference that "already Mr. Wahl had the picture of this ingenious extravagance before the illness, this mobility, this diversity, this power of metamorphosis that formed the pluralism of Nietzsche." Gilles Deleuze, "Conclusions sur la volonté de puissance et l'éternel retour," in *Nietzsche: Cahiers du Royaumont* (Paris: Éditions de Minuit, 1967), 276.

states that rejecting a dialectical Nietzsche does not yield pure disorder; that "the idea of relentless rigor . . . should be united with the idea of multiple perspectives." With such a reading, the order of the concrete would be thought as such, always stopping short of drawing these perspectives into a whole.

Wahl's auditors were quick to challenge his rejection of Nietzsche's crowning thought. Jean Beaufret's intervention challenges Wahl with a different interpretation of the eternal return, one that understands the return thermodynamically, as qualitative return to (and repetition of) a "zero state" rather than the recapitulation of what has occurred. Wahl's literal incomprehension at this point—and his ultimate attribution of this interpretation to Beaufret and, pointedly, not Nietzsche—is evidence of an important disagreement. A second significant moment in the discussion occurs when Jacob Taubes asks whether, in effect, poststructuralism might have run its course (in 1964!), and whether the time hasn't come to think Hegel *against* Nietzsche, to think system against the opposition to, and rejection of, systems. Wahl responds ingeniously by refusing the opposition and taking sides with that arch-antisystemic thinker: Heraclitus.

In Wahl's interpretation, Nietzsche is an irreducibly contradictory thinker in whom conflicting states coexist in a tension without resolution, in which order is imposed even as chaos is affirmed. The question of order in Nietzsche is the questionability of the affirmation that links the will to power and the eternal return in the figure of the superhuman. To affirm that figure is, for Wahl, to side with a dangerously militant side of Nietzsche that risks both surreptitiously reintroducing a formal theorizing analogous to the Hegelian dialectic and, more seriously, that may fall on the wrong side of the balance book of the twentieth century. The challenge of bearing these tensions, of living these "aporias," was enough to drive Nietzsche mad.

As Wahl says: it's difficult to sign "The Crucified."

Russell Ford

Have we come together to speak of Nietzsche an infinite number of times? Have we come together an infinite number of times, or is this time unique? I don't know: it's very awkward to think the eternal return. I believe that there is even a contradiction in thinking the eternal return, and I believe that contradictions are necessary for Nietzsche. Here I disagree with Henri Birault.[4] I believe that the supreme man—in order to avoid

---

4. [Henri Birault (1918–90) was a professor of philosophy at the Sorbonne, and later Paris IV, and a noted expert on Martin Heidegger, Nietzsche, and Blaise Pascal. He published only a single book during his lifetime, *Heidegger et l'expérience de la pensée* (Heidegger and the experience of thought) (Paris: Gallimard, 1978). Birault's presentation at Royaumont—to which Wahl is referring—was entitled "De la béatitude chez

saying the superhuman [*Surhomme, Übermensch*]—is the one who thinks contradictions: perhaps he doesn't seek their synthesis, even though Nietzsche sometimes uses the word "synthesis" (just as he sometimes uses the word "dialectic"). Well then, it is necessary for us to think that we have come together here this one time and for an infinite number of times, and yet this is difficult to think. But Nietzsche loved impossibilities, the crucifixions of the understanding.

Order and Disorder . . . These words can have many meanings, and my whole title, "Order and Disorder in Nietzsche's Thought," is both intentionally and unintentionally ambiguous. There is order and disorder in Nietzsche's thought, and there is order and disorder in the world, according to Nietzsche's thinking. Both are true, and yet this isn't shocking, since man is closely linked to the world.

The idea of order, the inception of the idea of order, is the idea of command, and unfortunately Nietzsche loves the idea of command, of a given order, a great deal, and this is the first sense of the word "order." An order that I give myself, and an order that I give to others, so that there is a hierarchy (*Rangordnung*). This is the first meaning.

There is an order in the world, probably in the sense that there is vegetative life, animal [*animale*] life, and then this indeterminate beast [*bête*], who will perhaps be determined on the basis of the superhuman, if there is a superhuman, or if there is a supreme man (since one might say that the superhuman is of secondary importance; but the fact that an idea is of secondary importance does not mean that it becomes less important).

Then there is Eternal Return. This idea of eternal return poses so many problems that I can't help but stop on it for a moment. It is truly paradoxical that Nietzsche, a former professor of philology, thought that the idea that there is nothing new was new: isn't this contradictory? When he thinks this idea, and has an inkling [*se rappel un peu*] that he used to be a professor of philology, he cites the Pythagoreans. The eternal return has multiple meanings: a hammer [*marteau*—slang for "crazy"] for some, exaltation, or a reason for exaltation for others. The eternal return is a criterion. Do we accept it? I don't know if Nietzsche liked the word "criterion." Do we accept the idea of the eternal return, do we bear it? Or is it unbearable? Nietzsche's effort consists in going to the extreme, to the limit, and seeing

---

Nietzsche"; English translation: "Beatitude in Nietzsche," trans. Alphonso Lingis, in *The New Nietzsche*, ed. David B. Allison (New York: Dell, 1977), 219–31. This essay was republished in a posthumous collection of Birault's work, *De l'Etre, du divine et des dieux* (On Being, the divine, and the gods) (Paris: Cerf, 2005).]

what one can bear; for most people the idea of eternal return is one of the most unbearable ideas, but it is bearable for some [*certains*].

In essence, it is an idea that exalts the moment, since the mix of stupidities and reasonable things, and unreasonable but ultimately correct [*justes*] things that I am going to say today, will be produced anew an infinite number of times. Thus, this moment is in some way sacralized (a word Nietzsche would perhaps dislike). The idea of eternal return is the idea of the thunderbolt: Nietzsche uses the word for lightning, "*Blitz*." Man, as he wills him, is a man who will have lightning, and who will himself be lightning. The Greeks envisaged God under the aspect of thunder, and there is ultimately a profound connection between these different ideas. And that Man can be made by what succeeds him, by what we can only glimpse, that also gives us an order, and a more profound idea of order. Nietzsche often uses the words "form" and "structure" (to designate a work stamped by a form). Man, the higher man—if I may say this in order to avoid the superhuman—will be the one who will impose a form and a structure, a *Gestalt*. But on what will he impose a "Gestalt"?

This brings me to the second part of my subject: it is on chaos that man will impose form, and he must also preserve this chaos. "Man must have chaos in himself in order to be able to give birth to a dancing star."[5] The disorder in us must be preserved, and this disorder is made of contradictions. But it must give birth to a work. Order and disorder are thus closely linked.

This is a first attempt to respond to the question: does Nietzsche form a whole [*est-ce que Nietzsche forme un ensemble*]? Yes and no. He describes himself as a kind of scribbling [*griffonnage*]: "Overall, I often feel like I'm the result of the scribbling that some unknown power traces on a piece of paper in order to test a new nib."[6] This is in a letter to Overbeck, and when the latter replies to him that his sister [i.e., Nietzsche's sister Elisabeth] is planning to make an exposé of his philosophy, he responds (and this will be my alibi): "that will be a beautiful muddle [*salade*]."[7] Conversely, though,

---

5. *Thus Spoke Zarathustra*, Prologue, §5.

6. [Nietzsche, letter to Heinrich Köselitz (aka Peter Gast), end of August 1881, in *Nietzsche Briefwechsel. Kritische Gesamtausgabe*, ed. Giorgio Colli and Mazzino Montinari (Berlin: Walter de Gruyter, 1981), (hereafter *KGB*), Abt. 3, Bd. 1, 122: "ich selber als Ganzes komme mir so oft wie der Krikelkrakel vor, den eine unbekannte Macht über's Papier zieht, um eine *neue Feder* zu probiren." As the following sentence indicates, Wahl mistakenly identifies this letter as being to Overbeck.]

7. Carl Albrecht Bernoulli, *Franz Overbeck und Friedrich Nietzsche: Eine Freundschaft* (Jena: Diederichs, 1908), 2:437. [Bernoulli does attribute this remark to Nietzsche, but he does not cite a source, noting only that it is from "the time of the Lou-affair (1882/83)." The remark Bernoulli quotes does not appear in *KGB*.]

like Kierkegaard he thinks that "everything is miraculously, marvelously arranged" and that his work is a kind of happy accident [*hazard heureux*]. He is constantly suspicious of himself. He takes sides against himself. We will find analogous formulas later in André Gide. He takes sides with what does him harm, and I would say that he goes to the limit, he brushes against the limit, he knows that he risks a great deal, and each time that he speaks—I'm taking this citation from Schlechta[8] although I don't like the edition, I will explain why—a gentle voice arises at the same time as a firmer one.

There are many floors, many houses, in Nietzsche's thought. On the one hand, he is related to some Christian thinkers whether he wants to be or not, and in a sense he does want to be. He likes Pascal a lot, he says: "his blood courses in mine";[9] he likes the Jansenists a lot.[10] On the other hand, he likes Mme. Guyon.[11] And he also likes the libertines; and one of his last utterances, "*écrasez l'infâme*" ["crush the infamy"] is taken from Voltaire.[12] Thus, as Shaeffner has nicely put it in his introduction to the letters to Peter Gast, Nietzsche's thought, Nietzsche's soul is a battlefield between his own thoughts.[13] The books that best show this contradictory aspect of Nietzsche's thought are, above all, the very beautiful book of Lou Salomé, but also Jaspers's book, and Schaeffner's introduction. Similar ideas can also be found in Klossowski, Bataille, and Heidegger.[14]

---

8. [Wahl refers here and in what follows to Karl Schlechta (1904–85). Schlechta's edition of Nietzsche's *Werke in Drei Bänden* (Munich: Carl Hanser Verlag, 1954–56) was widely used prior to the appearance of the Colli-Montinari *Kritische Gesamtausgabe* (Berlin: Walter de Gruyter, 1967–), which rendered Schlechta's edition obsolete.]

9. [Cf. Friedrich Nietzsche, *Kritische Studienausgabe*, ed. Giorgio Colli and Mazzino Montinari (Berlin: Walter de Gruyter, 1980), 9: 12[52]. Hereafter *KSA*.]

10. [Jansenism was a French Catholic theological movement centered at Port-Royal that counted Pascal among its adherents. Nietzsche mentions Port-Royal, as well as Pascal and Mme. Guyon (see next note), in §192 of *Dawn*, which is probably the passage that Wahl has in mind here.]

11. [Mme. Guyon (Jeanne-Marie Bouvier de la Motte-Guyon) (1648–1717) was a French mystic and advocate of quietism.]

12. [Nietzsche mentions "Voltaire's *écrasez*" in §7 of "On the Utility and Liability of History for Life," and also utters these words in his own voice in *Human, All Too Human*, §463, in response to Rousseau. Wahl's reference here, however, is most likely to the concluding words of §8 of the final section of *Ecce Homo*, "Why I Am a Destiny."]

13. [*Lettres à Peter Gast*, trans. Louise Servicien, with an introduction and notes by André Schaeffner (Monaco: Éditions du Rocher, 1957).]

14. [Lou Salomé, *Friedrich Nietzsche in seinen Werken* (Vienna: Carl Konegen, 1894); French translation: *Friedrich Nietzsche à travers ses oeuvres*, trans. J. Benoist-Méchin, with an introduction by Olivier Mannoni (1932; repr., Paris: Grasset, 1992); English translation: *Nietzsche*, ed. and trans. Siegfried Mandel (Champaign: University

Every great work is made of contradictions. Even Mozart's "Don Juan" has something contradictory about it. The good European is the one in the north who loves the south, and the one in the south who loves the north. I want to say a word against Bertram, who thinks that Nietzsche is a kind of traitor.[15] I don't know to what, exactly. But I want to say that I don't like Bertram's book on Nietzsche, and I think that he falsifies a great deal. In reality there is a synthesis of states in Nietzsche: states that would be irreconcilable for many men, even great men, that perhaps should be united, not reconciled. There are many "modi vivendi" between mutually negating states, either because one extreme coincides with the other, or because they must both be preserved in their tension.

It would be necessary to study the "no" in Nietzsche, all the more so as Nietzsche is a "yea-sayer." But yes can have multiple meanings, and so can no, and I believe that each exists only through the other. Besides, Nietzsche did not detest the idea of dialectic, and it is little by little that he comes to detest it. But there is a dialectic in him, and at a certain point he may even recognize it. Obviously one must avoid—here I agree with Henri Birault—one must avoid at all costs making Nietzsche into a dialectician, but the idea of a relentless rigor should be united with the idea of multiple perspectives; the idea of elevation should be united with the idea of inward penetration.

---

of Illinois Press, 2001). Karl Jaspers, *Nietzsche: Einführung in das Verständnis seines Philosophierens* (Berlin: Walter de Gruyter, 1936); French translation, with a preface by Wahl: *Nietzsche: Introduction à sa philosophie*, trans. Henri Niel (Paris: Gallimard, 1950); English translation: *Nietzsche: An Introduction to the Understanding of His Philosophical Activity*, trans. Charles F. Wallraff and Frederick J. Schmitz (Tucson: University of Arizona Press, 1965). Pierre Klossowski, *Un si funeste désir* (Paris: Gallimard, 1963); English translation: *Such a Deathly Desire*, trans. Russell Ford (Albany: State University of New York Press, 2007), includes two essays on Nietzsche, "On Some Fundamental Themes of Nietzsche's *Gaya Scienza*" and "Nietzsche, Polytheism, and Parody." Georges Bataille, *Sur Nietzsche* (Paris: Gallimard, 1945); English translation: *On Nietzsche*, trans. Stuart Kendall (Albany: State University of New York Press, 2015). Martin Heidegger, *Nietzsche*, 2 vols. (Pfullingen: Verlag Günther Neske, 1961); French translation by Pierre Klossowski (Paris: Gallimard, 1971); English translation in four volumes by David Farrell Krell et al. (New York: Harper and Row, 1979–87).]

15. [Ernst Bertram, *Nietzsche: Versuch einer Mythologie* (Berlin: Bondi, 1918); 10th ed. (Bonn: Bouvier, 1989); French translation (from the 7th edition, 1929): *Nietzsche: Essai de mythologie*, trans. Robert Pitrou (Paris: Les Éditions Rieder, 1932); English translation: *Nietzsche: Attempt at a Mythology*, trans. Robert E. Norton (Urbana: University of Illinois Press, 2009). The Pitrou translation has been republished with a preface by Pierre Hadot (1990; repr., Paris: Éditions du Félin, 2007]).]

We can apply one of Nietzsche's passages on Schopenhauer to Nietzsche himself: "Everything that he later assimilated, everything that he learned in life, in books, and in all the realms of knowledge, were little more than color and means of expression for him."[16] On occasion, he uses Buddhist or Christian mythology for the same purpose. For him there can be only one single unique task, and a hundred thousand ways of accomplishing it, a unique content, and innumerable hieroglyphs for expressing it. *Disorder*, in this sense: in the last works the contents of one book slip and glide one into another. It doesn't matter to Nietzsche whether a passage is in *Ecce Homo* or in the *Anti-Christ*, whether it remains a fragment of the *Will to Power* or belongs to an independent pamphlet. This is very curious, an author who allows a text from one of his books to slip into another, remaining somehow indifferent to this displacement . . .

"Reveries of a psychologist": as you know this is one of the titles of what is also called the "Will to Power" . . . Under this benign title, Nietzsche said, "is hidden a very bold and precise exposition of my philosophically heterodox principles, such that this work can serve both as initiation and invitation to the exchange, to the transmutation of values, and the definitive version of the first book is already almost written"[17] (this first book being, I believe, *The Anti-Christ*). Schlechta says that the idea of a work that would contain all of Nietzsche's notes is worthless. Certainly an order would be introduced into it, like the order introduced into the Will to Power, that is not exactly Nietzsche's. It's true that we have his multiple notebooks, but we don't know whether these are a selection made for a particular work, or whether they might not contain some materials for the works that appeared in the last months of his conscious life. Despite everything, he thought that he had to write a work, his fundamental work. I believe that this fundamental work, in his mind, was definitely a work entitled "Will to Power," whatever its subtitles. If it was not called "Will to Power," "Will to Power" was certainly in the subtitle, and "Transvaluation of Values" in the title. For Schlechta, these notes are remnants, and there is nothing new in them. I believe that he is wrong. Schlechta is not a philos-

---

16. [Cf. Friedrich Nietzsche, *Schopenhauer as Educator*, §7 in *Unfashionable Observations*, trans. Richard T. Gray (Stanford, Calif.: Stanford University Press, 1995), 240.]

17. [Nietzsche, letter to Heinrich Köselitz, September 12, 1888 (*KGB* 3, 5, 417): "Unter diesem harmlosen Titel verbirgt sich eine sehr kühn und präcis hingeworfne Zusammenfassung meiner wesentlichsten philosophischen *Heterodoxien*: so daß die Schrift als *einweihend* und *appetitmachend* für meine *Umwerthung der Werthe* (deren erstes Buch beinahe in der Ausarbeitung fertig ist) dienen kann."]

opher, and he is not a good connoisseur of philosophy. He is a dilettante poet. He has taken on a task that is too difficult for him; but perhaps it is too difficult for anyone. For Schlechta, the fragments are the scraps that were not placed in the three works known as the works of the Breakdown, the scraps that did not find a place in those three works. Others, on the contrary, claim that those three works come from these notes; the question remains open.[18] For the past, I don't know, three, four, five years, I have been trying to take Schlechta's edition and to see . . . it is difficult to keep at this work: I have consulted the notebooks, and I have asked myself how could Nietzsche's thought be reconstituted, if one only had the first or second of these notebooks. If everything were well organized [*ensemble*], that would be the proof of an *order* in Nietzsche . . .

Nevertheless there is an order; Nietzsche told us so (in his plans—which Schlechta has set aside[19]). First there is Nihilism, but nihilism is already a motley [*bigarrée*] thought, if I may say; we go from passive and bad nihilism to an active nihilism, which is the highest possibility, perhaps of Being. Thus, when Nietzsche says I am a nihilist, he means at least two things: I belong to the age of Baudelaire, of Bourget,[20] of Wagner. But I believe that this first "nihil" must be surpassed by an extreme nihilism, which then becomes the goal, the end, the achievement of thought and of the world. In this world without any meaning, man gives meaning.

The first book is devoted to nihilism; the second then was to be devoted to the genealogy of values. Just like the word "nihilism," this genealogy poses many problems. If art is the product of the need to wear a mask, if truth is the product of curiosity, of mistrust, etc., then mistrust is not so

---

18. [Following the appearance of the Colli-Montinari edition, many Nietzsche scholars no longer believe this question remains an open one. Mazzino Montinari's "Nietzsche's Unpublished Writings from 1885 to 1888; or, Textual Criticism and the Will to Power," in *Reading Nietzsche*, trans. Greg Whitlock (Urbana: University of Illinois Press, 2003), 80–102, makes a persuasive argument for the conclusion that Nietzsche eventually gave up any plan for completing a *magnum opus* with either the title "The Will to Power" or "Attempt at a Transvaluation of All Values." For a review of Montinari's argument and a discussion of Nietzsche's unpublished writings, see Alan D. Schrift, "Nietzsche's *Nachlass*," in *A Companion to Friedrich Nietzsche*, ed. Paul Bishop (London: Camden House, 2012), 405–28.]

19. [Wahl might be referring to the plan for a book titled *The Will to Power* found in *KSA* 13: 9[164]. It should be noted that the *KSA* contains many other plans for this work that do not share this structure.]

20. [Paul Bourget (1852–1935) was a French novelist and critic whose works, and in particular his *Essais de psychologie contemporaine* (Paris: Lemerre, 1883), were well known to Nietzsche.]

bad. Inversely, if one can make a genealogy of truth, if one can make a genealogy of goodness, then values collapse. Let us allow the good to collapse since Nietzsche tells us, in an earlier work, that we must go "beyond Good and Evil." But can't this mean several very different things: either that the ideas of good and evil are stripped of their meaning; or that we should be bad, malicious, wicked; or even that morality was founded by wise men, that slave morality is not so bad, after all, since there are masters only because there is slave morality? Nietzsche has three responses to the subject of the Good and of the True.

The question becomes still more complicated since he criticizes the idea of "fact" and yet begins many passages with "the fact is that." He does not want the fact, and nevertheless according to him there are many facts. In every case, there is the fact that we live in a decadent age, an age of nihilism; there is the fact that the search for truth arises from certain instincts not all of which are valuable. This is one of the greatest difficulties. All of the great classical ideas: the true, the beautiful, the good, pose problems for Nietzsche, but the True is particularly problematic. If one says that nothing is true, one finds oneself in the difficulty—I am ashamed to say it—of claiming that it is true that nothing is true. Human thought is inconceivable without the "it is true that," and Nietzsche cannot express himself without the "it is true that." There is always the "it is true that," and in essence there is always the "it is good that." But "good" can be taken in many ways. That is why I say that there is a certain disorder in Nietzsche's thought.

Nietzsche says that, for several weeks, he lost his mind. In a letter to Peter Gast, he writes, "All of this has clearly demonstrated my instability, and that a storm could easily plunge me into darkness. I have soared quite high, but have always brushed up against danger, and have never obtained any response to the question: where will I go?"[21] Sometimes he cries, or laughs, without any reason: "I am so farcical, and my writing so buffoonish that, in the street, I am sometimes overcome by giggling for half an hour."[22] He wants to write in his own blood. I have likened him to

---

21. [Nietzsche, letter to Heinrich Köselitz, May 20, 1887 (*KGB* 3, 5, 80): "sie hat mir allzu sehr deutlich gemacht, daß ich ohne Halt bin und leicht durch einen Sturm über Nacht fortgeblasen werden kann. Verklettert, sehr hoch, aber in der beständigen Nähe der Gefahr—und ohne eine Antwort auf die Frage 'wohin'?"]

22. [Nietzsche, letter to Heinrich Köselitz, November 25, 1888 (*KGB* 3, 5, 489): "ich mache so viele dumme Possen mit mir selber und habe solche Privat-Hanswurst-Einfälle, daß ich mitunter eine halbe Stunde auf offner Straße *grinse*" (*Lettres à Peter Gast*, 2:348).]

Lequier[23] throwing himself into the sea: he throws himself into the abyss of contradictions. Nietzsche would have also been able to say: I throw myself into the sea. He is nonetheless aware of the greatness of his work, if any human work can attain greatness.

Let us consider the moment when Nietzsche speaks: it is the moment of what he calls the decline of Europe, a decline due to the triumph of the "herd." But the importance given to the herd is balanced by the problem of the formation of elites. It is a matter of knowing what kind of elites they will be. Their elements are personal value and bodily courage, he says. Appraisals become more physical, nourishments more carnal. It is the end [*C'en est fini*] of the time of cowardice, with the "mandarins" at the summit, as Auguste Comte dreamed. The barbarian is affirmed in each of us: the savage beast; but this is precisely why the philosopher has such a great task.—It is a bit obscure: what is the task of the philosopher? To persuade the barbarians to be less barbaric? or more barbaric? Some of the consequences of Nietzscheanism are not good, if the word "good" still has any meaning. It is also a fact, and I should have said this regarding order, that there are two Orders that he particularly appreciates, and I will not pursue this point . . . : the Jesuit Order, and the Prussian Officer Corps. These are two of the models he gives us. We must decide whether we can follow him. Perhaps this is a point of departure for him; however, I don't want to compare these two very different orders.

In any event, our world is first of all an impoverished world; but to say that it is an impoverished world is precisely to say that we have in mind the contrary of poverty, that is to say, richness. And perhaps this richness can best be conceived in a time of poverty; this richness will be fashioned of tensions, and these tensions will doubtless be made of contradictions. We live in a time of *barbarity*, but we must *order* this barbarity. Barbarity/ elite, poverty/richness are linked together as contraries or contradictions.

The idea of eternity, too: there are two eternities, if one can "count" eternity. There is the eternity of the eternal return; and if he accepts the eternal return, one of the reasons is that he finds there, in our time, the closest

---

23. [Jules Lequier (Lequyer) (1814–62) was an itinerant intellectual who died (possibly a suicide) after swimming into the ocean off the coast of Brittany. The philosopher Charles Renouvier (1815–1903) corresponded with Lequier and published several of his unfinished works posthumously. Through these works, Lequier's theory of freedom influenced William James and the French existentialists. In 1948, Wahl edited a collection entitled *Jules Lequier* (Geneva: Éditions des Trois Collines). Jean Grenier published Lequier's *Oeuvres complètes* (Neuchâtel: Éditions de la Baconnière, 1952) shortly after.]

possible equivalent to eternity. However, as Mr. Heimsoeth[24] has shown quite clearly, there is also the eternity of lightning flashes [*des eclairs*], the eternity of moments in which Nietzsche touches something that is beyond time, eternity as *instant*. One must simultaneously conceive of eternal return and this eternity of lightning flashes, of lightning flashes that do or do not return. One must simultaneously conceive of the eternity of eternal return and the eternity of the moment of the discovery of eternal return. Again, this is one of the difficulties of the eternal return, and there are many, and my lecture is very disordered, but my title is my alibi!

Must we imagine that in each age there is someone who conceives the eternal return? To conceive the eternal return is in a certain sense to deny it. If there is a conception of eternal return, whatever returns eternally must be changed by this conception. We must say then that there is eternally someone who thinks the eternal return; but this someone, in Nietzsche's case, is someone who thinks they have discovered it. And if one juxtaposes the two ideas of eternal return and superhuman (admitting that the superhuman is of secondary importance in the final Nietzsche), the idea of superhuman tells us that Man must be overcome, and the idea of eternal return tells us that nothing can be overcome. Here again, then, there is a contradiction at the heart of Nietzsche's thought. Heidegger would perhaps disagree with me because, if I understand him correctly, the two ideas go together for him. They do for me as well, but not in the same way. According to Heidegger, the eternal return is Being and the will to power is essence. I am not sure, here, whether Heidegger has not applied non-Nietzschean categories to Nietzsche. Nietzsche is sometimes "for" being, but he is most often "against" being, and I believe he is also most often against essence. As for myself, I see myself before this contradiction between the eternal return and the superhuman, between the idea that Man must be overcome, and the idea that Man has been overcome an infinite number of times. I don't know how Nietzsche thought this; it is at the limit of thought, it is at the limit between thought and madness.

Man is a beast, but he is a very particular kind of beast: particular because there is in him a multitude of contradictions. This man is the one who conceives of values, these values that one must transvalue. It's unclear how art should be understood. By a need for mask and dissimulation? But in art

---

24. [Heinz Heimsoeth (1886–1975) was a German professor of philosophy at Cologne where, after joining the Nazi party in 1933, he served as dean until 1944. He published *Metaphysische Voraussetzungen und Antriebe in Nietzsches "Immoralismus"* (Metaphysical conditions and drives in Nietzsche's "Immoralism") (Mainz: Steiner, 1955), among other works.]

there is a kind of sublimation of this need. Nietzsche's problem is to simultaneously see and surpass the genealogy. We always find ourselves before the same problem. Nietzsche wants to define the type Man, what he calls the type Man, even though Man is always ill defined. Nietzsche often asks: what is noble? And I believe that what is noble, according to him, is to hold contradictory things simultaneously in one's mind, and to take one's time, to take time for leisure. There is therefore a war of thoughts in the noble man, but there will also be time left for something that we might call meditation.

We must now place some tasks before ourselves, but these tasks can only be measured and determined as a function of the superhuman or the supreme man—which we do not know. This is the whole question of values according to Nietzsche. He has popularized, perhaps almost in spite of himself, the term "value"; and I don't like this term and this idea any more than Heidegger does. The reason is that the idea of value is born only in ages where there is no value. For Plato, *agathon* ["good"] is not a value. For Plato, Being and what will later be called "value" absolutely coincide. It is in Kant's successors, and in philosophers like Rickert,[25] that the idea of value acquired its importance. It acquires its importance when there is devaluation. When there is no devaluation, there is no value. Couldn't we then criticize Nietzsche from this perspective? Perhaps he has used the word "value" too much; for him everything is value: art, science, great actions.

There is a difficult *order* in which one goes from "you ought" to "I will," and from "I will" to "I am." The "I will" are the heroes, the Stoics, but higher than the heroes, higher than the Stoics, are the Greek gods. Nietzsche wants to constitute a Hellenic classicism, but his "value judgments" of great personalities are highly variable. According to Nietzsche, the greatest personalities are Socrates and Jesus: it is certain that he has a love for Socrates, even though he has above all expressed his hatred for Socrates. And it is even more certain that he has a love for Jesus, to whom he opposes Christianity, and to whom he opposes Saint Paul. There is a remarkable parallel to be drawn here between Nietzsche and Kierkegaard. Both of them want to return across the centuries to Jesus, as Kierkegaard puts it. Ultimately Nietzsche even identifies with Jesus, signing "The Crucified." That's difficult, signing "The Crucified"!

We find ourselves again before a contradiction: here is a man who, I believe for good reason, is against History, or at least against the predominance

---

25. [Heinrich Rickert (1863–1936) was a professor of philosophy first at Freiberg (1894–1915) and then at Heidelberg (1915–32). He was one of the most prominent members of the Southwest School of Neo-Kantianism. Heidegger wrote his *Habilitationsschrift* (on Duns Scotus and Thomas of Erfurt) under Rickert at Freiburg in 1915.]

given to History in the second half of the nineteenth century. But each time that he has a value before him, he wants to give the history of it. I believe that Nietzsche's madness is not due solely to physiological factors, but to the effect of aporias in his thought. Who could hold such contradictions? He criticizes science, and nonetheless wants to go to the University of Vienna to take some science courses in order to prove the eternal return: this idea is childish, in the bad sense of the word, puerile without being childish. He found himself in labyrinths . . .

We should not flee temptations. How can we follow the indications of art and science, when we know so well whence they come, and their beginnings aren't beautiful. It is not ultimately contradictory to say that the will to truth has a bad beginning; and that it can have an end that is, I won't say good, but approvable. The world of science is a world made by man, the world of art is a world made by man; therefore, science and art are less important than the man who makes them. Must we say yes to science? To which science? Must we despite everything say no, in order to go behind the works of man, toward his fundamental will? Everything is constantly put back into question: the Beautiful and the True go together in a certain way, but it is also the case that the more we see of the True, the less there is of the Beautiful; the Beautiful vanishes. Inversely, the world that can be qualified as beautiful is the product of an error. It is only by a certain blunting [*engourdissement*] of taste that the Beautiful and the Precious are presented to the will to simplicity. And more than the True, one must appreciate the constructive force, the simplifying, informing, force.

Perhaps I'll stop there, reserving what's left—there is no conclusion—for the discussion, since it is the hour of Eternity, that is to say, Noon.

Discussion

> MR. DEMONBYNES:[26] I would like to ask Mr. Wahl to clarify a phrase that I have perhaps misunderstood: the eternal return is the equivalent of Eternity. My conception of eternity, as a European, living in a Judeo-Christian tradition, implies the ideas of creation, of a future life, of an eternal life: all things foreign to Nietzsche . . .
>
> MR. WAHL: But, for a Christian, eternity is not ours, it is first that of God.

---

26. [Jean Gaudefroy-Demonbynes (1898–1984) was the author of *Le romantisme dans la musique européenne* (with Jean Chantavoire) (Paris: Albin Michel, 1955) and one of the translators of *Mein Kampf* into French (1934).]

MR. DEMONBYNES: You also said that eternal return was an idea that exalts the instant. Personally, despite everything, I continue to find this idea hopeless [*désespérante*]. For if we cannot perfect ourselves, if we must find ourselves again . . .

MR. WAHL: But we have the joy of finding ourselves again an infinite number of times, I suppose!

MR. DEMONBYNES: If we must find ourselves again exactly as in the present moment, then it is useless for me to speak, useless for me to make an effort to perfect myself, to better myself, or even to improve my understanding of Nietzsche. If I cannot perfect myself in a new life, if this life is not new, if it is exactly the same, what is the good of anything?

MR. WAHL: I believe that the idea of eternal return is at once hopeless and exalting. It depends on the individual. I said that it was a criterion: can we bear this idea? Note that I believe that it is unthinkable; I believe that Nietzsche is wrong. To put it plainly: I believe that Nietzsche is wrong on this question as on many others. The eternal return is not a thinkable idea; I'm therefore unconcerned with its consequences.

MR. DEMONBYNES: Aren't there doctors, chemists, and even economists who admit this idea today?

MR. BEAUFRET:[27] On this very specific point, one must not forget that, at the time, thermodynamics was an important part of contemporary physics. Nietzsche talks about it in his recently translated letters to Peter Gast. In 1881, he impatiently awaited Robert Mayer's *Mechanik der Wärme*.[28] This is what he is thinking about when he says that "mechanism and Platonism are conjoined in the affirmation of eternal return."[29] Or: "the principle of the conservation of energy requires eternal return."[30]

---

27. [Jean Beaufret (1907–82) was a French philosopher best known for his work on Heidegger.]

28. [From a letter to Peter Gast dated April 16, 1881 (*Lettres à Peter Gast*, 2:62). Julius Robert von Mayer (1814–78) was a German physician and physicist now credited with having first formulated the principle of the conservation of energy, known as the first law of thermodynamics. His *Die Mechanik der Wärme* (The mechanics of heat) was first published in 1867.]

29. [Nietzsche, *Kritische Gesamtausgabe* VII 4/2: 34[260] (this fragment does not appear in the *Studienausgabe*): "Die beiden extremsten Denkweisen—die mechanistische und die platonische—kommen überein in der *ewigen Wiederkunft*: beide als Ideale."]

30. [Nietzsche, *KSA* 12: 5[54]: "Der Satz vom Bestehen der Energie fordert die *ewige Wiederkehr*."]

MR. WAHL: Yes, but he is wrong.

MR. BEAUFRET: Is he necessarily wrong to ask if the study of Mechanics could help him think what he was trying to think?

MR. WAHL: Yes, he is wrong: he is leaning on a scientific fact determined in time. His error was wanting to take university courses.

MR. BEAUFRET: There remains above all the difficulty of specifying the meaning of eternal return. I believe this is due to the thought oscillating between two ideas: the perpetual recommencement of what has been; and the perpetual return to equality, the return to the zero point of will to power, regardless of the magnitude of its conquests. I'm of the opinion that Nietzsche never clearly distinguished these two ideas.

MR. WAHL: I don't agree; I don't call it zero . . . I call it overcoming.

MR. BEAUFRET: But in order for overcoming to coincide with the endless return of the Identical, it is certainly necessary that the experience make no contribution, so to speak.

MR. WAHL: This is not proven. Your dilemma is: on the one hand, relive the same experiences; on the other hand, return to zero. I don't understand the second term.

MR. BEAUFRET: The second term is like this: since the will is will to power, the idea of eternal return is implicit in that interpretation of the will as will to power, insofar as every conquest adds nothing, and in which the will, from all its conquests, returns identical to what it was previously. It is in this sense that the circle of eternal return ceaselessly turns back upon itself, otherwise this return would be that of identical events.

MR. WAHL: It is Mr. Beaufret who says this!

MR. BEAUFRET: There is at least a late text of Nietzsche's that certainly seems to speak in this way: "I am telling you to free yourselves from eternal flux: flux does not cease to flow back into itself, and it is always anew [*à nouveau*] that you enter into this flux that is always the same, insofar as it is always the same to you yourselves."[31]

MR. WAHL: It doesn't matter, the important thing for me is that I don't understand this return to zero. The will to power is the will for more will. It is also the will to dominate, it is the will for more power.

---

31. Nietzsche, *Werke* (Leipzig: Alfred Kröner Verlag, 1964), 12:369. [*KSA* 10: 5[1]160: "Ich lehre euch die Erlösung vom ewigen Flusse: der Fluß fließt immer wieder in sich zurück, und immer wieder steigt ihr in den gleichen Fluß, als die Gleichen."]

MR. X:[32] Isn't the chief problem that of identity apropos of the return: it is an eternal return of the "Same." But what is this "same?" There is a difference here in Nietzsche: we are acquainted with an ontological identity, and yet Nietzsche says that identical cases are regulatory fictions imposed by the will to power. How then can one speak of a return of the "Same?" what is the "Same?" Isn't there a contradiction between the ontological identity of the return, and the pragmatic identity that the will to power employs to dominate chaos? This is a first question.

MR. WAHL: It may be better to strike the "same"; perhaps there is no "same."

MR. BEAUFRET: It is ambiguous. "The same," does that mean similar [*pareil*]? should we say similar? should we say equal? But if we translate it as "equal," then equal to what? That, to me, seems to be the difficulty.

MR. X: On the other hand, apropos of Nietzsche and Hegel, the discussion has so far focused on the theme of the negative or contradiction. Isn't there another theme, *appearance*, in Nietzsche and Hegel? Isn't it rather on that terrain that Nietzsche is opposed to Hegel, in the sense that he refuses to make of appearance something that would be surpassed, mediated, drawn toward an absolute knowledge? Isn't there a density of appearance in Nietzsche? Something that would protect us from the *truth*, and that would give us *art so that we do not perish from the truth*?[33] Ultimately, would there not be two types of ontology: one that makes being into a translucent and rational logos, in the Hegelian fashion; and another that, on the contrary, would present an enigmatic being, always in need of interpretation?

MR. WAHL: There are certainly oppositions between Nietzsche and Hegel. But, even in Hegel, there is a cycle: everything comes from the absolute and returns to the absolute, and at the end one finds again what was at the beginning.

MR. BEAUFRET: Philosophy as a cycle of cycles and the eternal return as a circle of circles—these are perhaps not unrelated.

---

32. [The individual making this comment is identified only as Mr. X.]
33. [See *KSA* 13: 16[40]: "wir haben die Kunst, damit wir nicht an der Wahrheit zu Grunde gehn."]

MR. TAUBES:[34] Mr. Wahl likes contradictory thought; so do I. He likes perspectives; so do I . . .

MR. WAHL: Less, less . . .

MR. TAUBES: But the question that I want to pose is this: Mr. Wahl has told us that contradictory thought leads to madness in Nietzsche, and not only in Nietzsche. We are the inheritors of a reaction against systems; Kierkegaard and Nietzsche react against systems, in particular against the Hegelian system. Hasn't the moment come to reverse this movement, to think Hegel *against* Nietzsche, *against* Kierkegaard? Without a certain systematic coherence, the richness of perspectives collapses and becomes pathology . . .

MR. WAHL: There may be different solutions, many ways out. For example, the idea of the coincidence of contraries: war and peace, noise and silence are one. Heraclitus said so a long time ago. I like Heraclitus better than Hegel, and Nietzsche likes Heraclitus better than Hegel. (There are fewer pages, it is easier to read, it takes less time, but these aren't the only reasons.) Hegel is an admirable philosopher, but must we accept the System? Shouldn't we hold on to the "here," the "now," the "mine"? Because if you deny Hegel, you have to deny him from the beginning.

MR. GUEROULT:[35] You have said that you feel there is a contradiction between the idea of eternal return, implying that there is nothing new, and the fact of finding precisely this idea new. But I don't see the contradiction, because in the cycle of the eternal return there are discoveries. And these discoveries, in the cycle, will be made again. There was a time when some people tried to combine the eternal return and Christianity: the difficulty, then, was to admit the infinity of Christ an infinite number of times; Christ would be incarnated and would have brought an infinite number of new truths an infinite number of times. And this idea was renounced not because it made novelty impossible but because it ruined the Christian religion. We shouldn't confuse novelty in

---

34. [Jacob Taubes (1923–87) was a sociologist of religion and scholar of Judaism who taught widely in the United States and Europe but published only a single book during his lifetime, *Abendländische Eschatologie* (Berlin: Matthes und Seitz, 1947); English translation: *Occidental Eschatology*, trans. David Ratmoko (Stanford, Calif.: Stanford University Press, 2009).]

35. [Martial Gueroult (1891–1976) was a noted French historian of philosophy; he delivered the opening remarks and presided over the 1964 Royaumont conference.]

itself with novelty for man in the circle. There is no novelty in itself, but there is novelty for the one that is in the circle.

MR. WAHL: Yes, a lightning flash, and unity is found again. That is also possible.

MR. BIRAULT:[36] At the beginning of his lecture, Mr. Wahl, coming back to the concept of the will, seemed to regret apropos of the notion of order that the idea of *Befehl* ["command"] should be so dominant in Nietzsche's determination of will. It is a fact that this idea of command is essential for Nietzsche. But ultimately I believe that Nietzsche simply wants to show by this fact the difference that separates the will from desire. And this discovery of a specific order of the will, as fundamentally distinct from desire, shouldn't surprise us, or should surprise us less if we simply refer ourselves to Kant: for ultimately the Kantian willing is equally an "imperium," and the will in Kant is equally "mastery," "command," and "legislation." Perhaps Nietzsche doesn't like the Kantian imperative, but the image that he forms of the will becomes clear only if one refers to the Kantian will.

MR. WAHL: Yes, but it is very different, because according to Kant, one commands oneself; while in Nietzsche, it is essentially others.

MR. BIRAULT: It is oneself and others in both cases.

MR. HEIMSOETH: There is an asceticism in Nietzsche: the will to power is the will *to form* desires, the chaos of desires, to give them a form, to give a form to oneself. A command that is addressed to others is something completely different.

MR. TAUBES: I don't think that Birault is right. Kant continues to attach the will to the faculty of desire.

MR. BIRAULT: Initially, yes. But he distinguishes between a lower faculty and a higher faculty of desire, and he separates them more and more. Nietzsche proceeds in an analogous manner.

MR. GUEROULT: A last word, Mr. Wahl?

MR. WAHL: The hour of noon has passed, eternity has not arrived, or is surpassed, is there, and is not there . . . These are the last words.

Translated by Russell Ford

---

36. [For information on Henri Birault and Heinz Heimsoeth, who speaks below, see notes 4 and 24, above.]

11

Experience and Transcendence; or, An Ontological Journey

The following selection, whose title here brings together the two titles under which it was published, is more of a philosophical-poetic autobiography than an encyclopedia entry, even though it first appeared in 1957 in a volume of the *Encyclopédie Française* devoted to philosophy and religion. This revolutionary encyclopedia did not presume to order and record every facet of knowledge but, rather, to teach and inspire through a bold and creative synthesis of the most disparate domains.[1] Jean Wahl, surely among the greatest synthesizers of philosophy and himself a recognized poet, was no doubt fit for the task. In addition to a "Brève introduction aux philosophies françaises de l'existence" ("Brief introduction to the French philosophies of existence") and an article on "Philosophie et poésie" ("Philosophy and poetry"), Wahl wrote an entry under the heading "Experience and

---

"Experience and Transcendence; or, An Ontological Journey" was first published as "Expérience et transcendance," part 2 of the section "Les philosophies de l'existence," in *Encyclopédie française*, vol. 19, devoted to philosophy and religion, directed by Gaston Berger (Paris: Société Nouvelle de L'Encyclopédie Française, 1957), 19.12-9–19.12-14. It was republished, without the first four sections, as "Itinéraire ontologique," in *Les philosophes français d'aujourd'hui par eux-mêmes: Autobiographie de la philosophie française contemporaine*, ed. Gérard Deledalle and Denis Huisman (Paris: Centre de Documentation Universitaire, 1963), 52–66.

1. See Anatole de Monzie and Lucien Febvre's prefaces to volume 1 and Gaston Berger's preface to volume 19 of *Encyclopédie française*, as well as Charles Van Doren, "The Idea of an Encyclopedia," *American Behavioral Scientist* 6, no. 1 (September 1962): 23–26.

Transcendence" that not only touches on many of his philosophical, poetic, and artistic influences—Henri Bergson, Edmund Husserl, Martin Heidegger, G. W. F. Hegel, William James, Søren Kierkegaard, Friedrich Nietzsche, Plato, and Alfred North Whitehead, Paul Claudel, Novalis, and Paul Valéry, Paul Cézanne and Vincent Van Gogh—but also brings them together in such a way as to present his own unique concerns with a radical empiricism, with relativity, negativity, and facticity, with the concrete, with surpassing dichotomies, with "the silences of the dialectic," with transcending transcendence, and especially with the preeminence of poetry. Indeed, in this text, which was later abridged and reprinted in 1963 under the title "An Ontological Journey" in a collection of autobiographies from many of the leading French philosophers of the preceding three decades, Wahl does more than just state the importance of poetry for philosophy; he demonstrates how it is crucial to his personal philosophical quest by interspersing his wide-ranging discussions with several poems of his own.[2]

Ian Alexander Moore

Two Remarks

One of the merits of phenomenology is to have allowed us to become more clearly aware of the fact that all our judgments, the entire domain of relations that constitute our conscious lives, are founded on a prerelational, prepredicative domain. At a time when attempts to explain things on the basis of historical conditions, class, race, and psychological complexes are proliferating, phenomenology has thereby shown that our concern should be less with explanation than with beholding the rootedness of our affirmations and our lives in a foundation that is itself life and that preexists affirmation.

A vision like that of William James, when he formulated his radical empiricism, had for its part the merit of revealing a reality that contains within itself both the terms and the relations. Classical empiricism presents

---

2. Some of Wahl's poetry published in "Experience and Transcendence" had appeared previously in various places and under different forms. See, for example, *Les cahiers du Rhône* 2 (Cahier de Poésie) (Neuchâtel: Éditions de la Baconnière, 1942), 92–93; Jean Wahl, "Note sur l'espace et remarque sur le temps," *Revue de Métaphysique et de Morale* 46, no. 3 (July 1939): 418 (written in 1937 and republished in Jean Wahl, *Existence humaine et transcendance* [Neuchâtel: Éditions de la Baconnière, 1944], 67); and Jean Wahl, *Poèmes*, with a frontispiece and seven drawings by André Masson and an introduction by Marcel Raymond (Montreal: Éditions de l'Arbre, 1945), 19–20, 170, 177–78, 180–81, and 190. The last text is a collection of old and new poems by Wahl, dating back at least to Wahl's 1938 collection *Connaître sans connaître*. See also Wahl, *Existence humaine et transcendance*, 23.

us with flat things that are exterior to one another and exterior to ourselves. It is easy for rationalism to be right when it comes to this latter sort of empiricism; but there is a higher empiricism that James and Bergson had a feeling for and that links up with Schelling's idea of transcendental empiricism. When opposed to rationalism, empiricism has too often appeared to be a facile theory; yet it is not necessarily a theory that is less profound or even less rigorous [*difficile*] than rationalism.

The Great Philosophical Ideas and Their Metamorphoses

If, in light of these remarks, we run through the great philosophical ideas, we will be led to wonder whether it is not necessary to replace the classical conceptions of substance, essence, form, and being with new affirmations. Instead of substance as conceived by classical philosophers, we will have felt substances that can no longer be expressed in distinct attributes but rather gleam at the heart of appearances and are as ineffable as classical substance was effable. Essences as one ordinarily represents them will be replaced with qualitative, affective essences like those we have an idea of thanks to poets and novelists such as Marcel Proust and Virginia Woolf. As opposed to forming forms, we will have formed forms, forms formed by the condensation and efflorescence of the very matter in forms. And finally, being will be being in the world as Husserl and, afterward, Heidegger claimed.

In classical philosophies, it is of course the case that not everything can be reduced to substance, form, essence, and being. There is a whole domain of accidents and matter. There are relations and negations. Here again we will have to perform the same operation, and just as we had retained an affective substance and an affective essence, we will be led to see a matter, a force that is both blind and real and that we will have to enter into communion with just as much as with substance and essence.

Relations will appear to us to be felt before they are known. Negations will be translations, into the intellectual realm, of our regrets, refusals, and flights. And, behind those ideas that complemented the intelligible ideas in classical philosophy, we will see appear the three general characteristics of our world: relativity, negativity, and facticity. The last is the idea of the accident made absolute, so to speak. There is neither being nor nothingness, only negativity and positivity; there is neither substance nor accident, only facticity.

Many ideas that were distinguished will have to be united. It is Plato himself, in the *Philebus*, who had formulated the notion of an essence that has come to be [*essence devenue*],³ in which being and becoming are joined together; it is Descartes himself who, in his theory of the soul and body, had strongly registered that third substance that cannot be reduced to the other two.

Toward the Concrete

There has been talk of a return toward the concrete; and indeed every act of mediation can be explained by something immediate that is prior to it. In claiming that this immediate something is the concrete, we mean that what is given to us primordially is an *ensemble* ["whole"]. There is in fact no word that could be satisfying here, since ideas like synthesis and even *ensemble* presuppose primordially separate elements that would then be gathered together. For us, in contrast, what there is first of all is an undecomposed totality that we cannot even legitimately call a totality. Every synthesis is a re-synthesis and re-accomplishment of this "totality" that is given first. And rather than a composition, we would say that this "totality" is position itself and thus facticity.

Time and Space

The idea of matter, like the transcendentals in Scholasticism, has an analogical unity and a double function: it indicates the independence of the real in relation to our mind, as well as the energy that is the essence of the real.

Attentive to the progression of science, Whitehead replaces the idea of "fact" as the classical empiricists and rationalists conceived it with that of spatio-temporal events that exert influence upon one another. Generally speaking, science leads us to new ideas. Many scientific concepts that are also everyday concepts like space and time are called into question. "Cause" and "measurement" take on new forms.

To no degree are space and time assemblages of terms such as points or instants. Nor are they forms either. Perhaps our first task would be to discover whence they derive. For space, [we would need to investigate] the ideas of "containing," on the one hand, and "distance," on the other,

---

3. [In Ancient Greek, *gegenêmenên ousian*. See Plato, *Statesman, Philebus, Ion*, trans. Harold N. Fowler and W.R.M. Lamb (Cambridge, Mass.: Harvard University Press, 1975), 27B.]

[investigate] these ideas themselves before they are reduced to more profound elements, to a primordial feeling of the *in* and to an affective, spatio-temporal distance. For time, [investigate] the three series of "time reckoned according to the after," "time reckoned according to the before," and "time reckoned according to the at-the-same-time"—these three kinds of time that later are more or less put together in the schematic time of common sense and then of science.

Originary space and time are those of the myths, of the Great Time; they are also the everyday time of works and days; they are the time of the occasion and the propitious moment.

Aristotelian time, time as the number of movement, is but a link in the slow constitution of our ordinary time.

A double operation would allow us to discover, at the origin of scientific space, a qualitative space that is completely different from it, and to affirm that, in contemporary science, space ceases to be that purely quantitative space under the aspect of which it had so often appeared; such that the very reflection on the current state of science would permit us to reach something similar to what was at the origin of science itself.

While the classical empiricists started with points and instants, isn't it necessary to begin instead with felt totalities like steps and phrases? I walk, therefore I am, said Gassendi; such walking is not made from a succession of points, except for an abstract understanding; I think, therefore I am, says Descartes; in a passage from a conversation with Burman, it is reported that Descartes said that a thought remains; as a discourse decomposes into phrases and not, strictly speaking, words, thought will decompose into small thoughts, but not ones that are indivisible, as a Leibnizian would be inclined to believe. Yet, under these steps, under these phrases, under these thoughts, on the one hand, we would certainly discover a sort of ongoing basis, a sort of a deep basis that allows the phrases and steps to communicate with one another, and on the other hand, our thought becomes aware of the walk in a sort of total instantaneity, in a sort of flash of lightning that illuminates the entire landscape.

Science and Philosophy

The teaching of Léon Brunschvicg had the merit of showing that in science there is an activity of relating; these relations become incessantly subtler; and the universe is but an always-incomplete ensemble of this network of relations. However, while in Brunschvicg and at the same time in Valéry, a vision of things reduced entirely to relations was made explicit, another vision developed in a more obscure fashion in Whitehead and

Claudel, who allowed us to conceive of events more opaquely, with more density, as implicated and entangled in one another.

In their respective domains, each of these visions is true. It is true that, from the point of view of science, the world is nothing but relations. It is true, or more exactly it is real, that, from the point of view of our intimate communication with it, the world is that density which Claudel helps us perceive.

Our ordinary vision moves between these two extremes; and, perhaps like every compromise, it is less true than these two extremes. But we cannot really abide in either of the two extremes. They are the limits toward which we must go. But if we place ourselves in these limits themselves, we will doubtlessly destroy ourselves, ourselves and our vision.

While acknowledging that science gives us a truth, and even gives us the truth, in the sense that for us every truth is propositional, and that the more precise a proposition is the more truth there is, we will find ourselves on the same path as the one we knew already, namely, the path of the qualitative, of the prepredicative, of secondary qualities that are more truly primary than the primary qualities, which are the products of abstraction.

We can only understand the value of science—that is to say, to declare that this value is at the same time universal in its domain and in a sense particular in relation to reality—if we incorporate the idea that there are levels of reality. Starting from the world of our sensations, but with the help of instruments that we add to our senses, so to speak, thereby transforming us into beings situated at a level of the real that is not our own level, science constitutes its world. And this world is the structure of the real itself, insofar as it is made of extremely fine and subtle relations. The distinctive feature of scientific activity, which is one of the highest activities of the mind and which constitutes one of its most essential superstructures, is to allow us to reach what in the real appears to us as infrastructure.

Just as [George] Berkeley rehabilitated secondary qualities, many great philosophers have rehabilitated the idea of appearance. We are thinking of Nietzsche, William James, and Husserl. The first resumes the tradition of the Sophists, which had been interrupted by the concatenation of the great classical philosophers, and celebrates the beautiful appearance. The second teaches us to see things as they appear to us in our knowledge, "as they are known as."[4] The third invites us to grasp the essence in appearances themselves as well as in its opposition to them. Thanks to these three

---

4. [In English in the original.]

philosophers, we can see that, at the heart of becoming, essences shine with an ambiguous, yet certain, radiance.

Works, Things

Meditating on the work and on the thing will permit us to see how we can surpass the alternative between subjectivity and objectivity, between the internal and the external. A painting we are marveling at does not lie there before us like an external object; we are not merely in front of the painting. The communication between the painting and us is not a simple presence of the one to the other. We are beyond the alternative between the "in front of" and the "in."

The rehabilitation of secondary qualities and appearances leads us to the rehabilitation of the thing. The world as it is given to us is made not of ideas and sensations, but of things. Here again Berkeley is a precursor. Nietzsche, when he shows us the thing as near and far, and Husserl, when he shows us the multiplicity of perspectives and, behind them, the more elusive central core, both allow us to perceive what this phenomenology of the thing would be. Moreover, in his *Phenomenology*, Hegel had shown in a very profound way the contradictory, but real, moment, which is that of things. Yet philosophy is undoubtedly almost always impotent when faced with the reality of the thing. Thus, after some hesitation, we gladly give the floor to poetry, a poetry which could help us to distinguish between the thing that is an instrument under man's power and the real thing in its often rebellious existence.

> Nous avons trop longtemps erré trop loin des choses.
> Voici mur et plafond, encrier, parchemin.
> Nous sommes prisonniers des œuvres de nos mains
> Et ce n'est pas cela que j'appelle les choses.

> Car une chose vraie est une âme vivante
> Qui se dissout pourtant au sein de l'univers.
> L'herbe est. Je ne vois plus qu'un monde entier tout vert.
> Je ne vois plus partout qu'unité palpitante.

> Pourtant la chose est là, sombre rayonnement
> Pensant en elle-même, excitant ma pensée,
> Miroitante d'aspect et sur elle fermée,
> Dialogue entre nous irritant et charmant.

> Toute chose se ferme à la façon d'un cercle,
> Et toute chose s'ouvre et devient arc-en-ciel.
> Toute chose est substance et terme essentiel,
> Est ouverte et pourtant close sous en couvercle.

> For too long have we wandered too far from things.
> Here is a wall and a ceiling, an inkwell and parchment.
> We are prisoners of the works of our hands
> And this is not what I mean by things.
>
> For a true thing is a living soul
> Which yet dissolves in the bosom of the universe.
> The grass is. I no longer see but a world all green.
> Everywhere I see now but a pulsing unity.
>
> Yet the thing is there, dark radiance
> Thinking in itself, exciting my thought,
> Shimmering in appearance and closed in on itself,
> Dialogue between us arousing and charming.
>
> Each thing is closed up in the manner of a circle,
> And each thing opens up and becomes a rainbow.
> Each thing is substance and an essential term,
> Is open and yet closed under its lid.

or again:

> Qu'y a-t-il donc, disons, dans le concept de chose,
> Qui m'arrête, qui m'ouvre,
> Chose, maison fermée
> Maison qui s'ouvre,
> Chose informe formée
> Et qui toi même lentement formes l'idée de forme.
> Et toutes les idées
> Et nos sens même peut-être,
> Nos sens fenêtres
> Dorées obscures sur l'Autre
> Lui-même la plus grande chose et certains disent une personne.
>
> What, we ask, is there in the concept of the thing,
> Which stops me, which opens me up,
> Thing, a closed house
> A house which opens itself up,
> Thing formless formed
> And which you yourself slowly form the idea of form.
> And all the ideas
> And even our senses perhaps,
> Our senses windows
> Gilded and dark onto the Other
> Itself the greatest thing and some say a person.

Plato said that the eye is solar, is in the form of the sun. Analogously, but inverted, we shall say that

> La chose fait l'esprit; la lumière fait l'œil
> Et les goûts font la bouche et les sons font l'oreille.
> Ainsi cela qui dort éveille ce qui veille.
> Le monde crée en moi le lieu de son accueil.
>
> The thing makes the mind; light makes the eye
> And tastes make the mouth and sounds make the ear.
> Thus what sleeps awakens what is awake.
> The world creates in me the place of its reception.

Because beyond things, those mute persons, and beyond persons, those speaking and thinking things, beyond bodies, those intermediaries between things and persons, there is the horizon of the world.

The World

The world, it has been said, is the horizon of horizons. The Heideggerian expression "being in the world" must be taken above all as referring to the inseparability of the self and the world.

There is no need for a path from the self to the world.

It is to this idea of the external world that we should henceforth devote ourselves in order to critique the idea of externality and to separate the idea of world from it. The idea of the external world implies the existence of an object that is situated, so to speak, face to face with a subject, and idea that, under the influence of philosophical conceptions, has taken shape slowly over time. The idea of world, which for a long time has been put into the background of philosophers' reflections, must instead come to the forefront of such reflection. Now this idea of world, if we try to fathom it deeply, will lead us to surpass the distinction between the external and the internal. The world presents itself first of all as something external, to which we are, so to speak, internal; that is to say, the idea of externality is bound to vanish when it comes into contact with the idea of world.

If we think that it is thus possible to start from the idea of world, it is because it is not, properly speaking, an idea. It is a fundamental given. We thereby implicitly reaffirm a certain realism, but one quite different from ordinary realism; and we would be willing to say with Heidegger that the value of that experience by which we feel we are in the world has been underestimated and that this is why philosophical understanding has raised so many problems.

We do not wish to deny that there is some value in the very problems that the understanding raises. As soon as the understanding intervenes, a dialectic takes shape. Nor do we wish to reject the value of this dialectic. The two forms of English and American realism—neo-realism and critical realism—have had the merit of representing this sort of dialectic through their very development. There is thus a tension within realism that is added to the tension between realism and idealism.

Yet in contrast to Hegel and those who follow him, we think that a dialectic can never suffice unto itself, that it can never encompass all of reality, including itself. It is justified only by the reality of a term that, through the difficulties it causes us, motivates the steps of the dialectic. It is because the real—if we may use this word—is both identical to our thought and different from it that the dialectic is set in motion.

But do these very words of the identical and the different mean anything independent from the mind? It is here that the idealist thesis—we would readily say the idealist danger—makes its appearance once again. And at the same time, we must wonder whether similar concepts can ever be equal to the reality that they presume to translate. Moreover, questions arise about the relations between the real taken as a term or the dialectic at its origin and the dialectic itself; what sort of relation is this that exists between them? Doesn't the real enclose, if not the dialectic, then at least the origin of the dialectic?

Taking these questions as our point of departure, we will come to see that philosophy does not provide a response but consists in the intense, taut, existential [*existentielle*] manner of living these questions. Torn between affirming the irreducible term and affirming the turbulent movement of the mind that must in any event certainly not be separated from the very movement of things, we must take the act of questioning upon ourselves and internalize it, all the while knowing that every response will, in its turn, be the origin of a new series of questions.

Realism and Idealism

The problem of realism arose perhaps most clearly from the moment in which, under the double influence of [F. H.] Bradley and [Bertrand] Russell—negative in the case of the former, positive in that of the latter—the English and American neo-realists connected the question of realism to the problem of the independence of terms with respect to their relations; and from the moment in which the plays and counterplays of the philosophical schools showed that there is a sort of dialectic of realism, somehow doubling and splitting itself in the affirmation of the independence of the real in relation to our thought, and of the identity of the real and our thought—an identity that makes it impossible to speak any longer of an independence of the one in relation to the other.

Let us note that idealism has also taken quite diverse forms. We believe that it is above all at its most extreme form that it reveals its complete value. We find this extreme form in the magical idealism of Novalis; we would then need to trace this romantic idealism back to its sources, which are undoubtedly in alchemical philosophy and in certain thinkers of the Middle Ages such as Albert the Great. This idealism implies, so to speak, the conception of ideas or great images formed within the interior of the imagination that will come to be conceived as either God's or Nature's.

James and Bergson have indicated how an idealism taken to the extreme and a realism likewise taken to the extreme can coincide. The philosophy of Berkeley (which in its last phase is oriented to the magical idealism we just described) is itself an indication that a certain extremely daring form of idealism does not take anything away from the reality of the world.

Dialectic and Tension

Whenever we take up any of the big philosophical problems, we will always be led to see a succession of theses and antitheses, and thus a dialectic. After the period in which there was an insistence on the universal presence of continuity, the discontinuous came to predominate. Even this awakens us to the idea that neither the one nor the other of these two concepts can suffice to exhaust the real. Both are necessary. And perhaps it then becomes necessary to take note of the fact that both need to be surpassed. This is because none of our concepts will be adequate to the entirety of the real, nor even perhaps to any part of it. With a movement that Plato's *Parmenides* and Hegel's *Logic* give us an idea of, we must accept the two contraries, and then negate both of them. As a matter of fact, precisely because he was not systematic, Plato gives us a more profound lesson here than does Hegel.

Faced with the problem of the finite and the infinite, with that of the continuous and the discontinuous, with that of terms and relations, we are in each case led to wonder how we can explain the oscillation of the mind that goes from one solution to the other; but we will also have to see whether there are no means, as there seemed to be for realism and idealism, of grounding the two opposed terms and, behind the oppositions, of discovering identities, whether because each of the terms, pushed to the extreme, turns into the other, or because a fundamental identity between them reveals itself. In certain cases, finally, we will doubtlessly come to discover neither of these identities and will thus remain in a tension that preserves the irreducible value of each of these contraries.

The will to subjectivity and the will to objectivity were never manifested so well and with so much intensity as in painting at the end of the nineteenth century. Van Gogh's interrogation makes his sun waver. He plumbs depths much more profound than those of classical song. It is this intensity—a product of the felt chasm between the subject that sinks down and the object that is raised up—that constitutes the truth of the modern soul. But at the same time a new objectivity is born. Cézanne would like to be the painter of a nature that is truly nature, without the painter, in which the forms find balance and situate themselves of their own accord. While Van Gogh is himself absorbed in such yellow. After the truth-subject that sinks down and the object that is raised up, it is the truth-object that Kierkegaard then had identified with the subject. Here we have a privileged example of those tensions we alluded to. Existence is made of such tensions.

Existence and Transcendence

If contemporary philosophers often prefer the word "existence" to the word "soul," it is because the soul was too often considered to be a permanent substance, was too clearly separated from the body, too clearly separated from the world. The union of soul and body, of soul and world—this is what is meant by the idea of existence. To use an expression of Heidegger's, existence appears to be outside of itself naturally, to be in the midst of things, as both Husserl and Heidegger said.

But at the same time as existence is in the world, it is always at a certain distance from it. In such a way that we are here in the presence of a dialectic that is immanent to experience and that makes it such that existence is both fusion and distance.

That is to say, existence is thereby linked to what is other than existence. Just as the aspect of substance in the idea of the soul vanishes in the idea of existence, that which was overly particularized in the idea of God vanishes and is raised up, is in a sense departicularized, in the idea of transcendence.

To be sure, it would be necessary to distinguish different directions of the idea of transcendence: a transcendence that is, so to speak, flat, which is that of the being in the world that we spoke about and which is the condition for intentionality; and a transcendence toward the heights, which would be classical transcendence. We indeed leave aside for the moment what we could call trans-descendence, which we can get an idea of from the sense of things we alluded to earlier.

Because we think that the dialectic starts from a point with which its relations are in any case very difficult to determine, we have to wonder whether it does not head toward a limiting point that would be either the same or different, and that would be situated beyond it like the other is situated below it; it is therefore the question of transcendence that poses itself to us; and after what we have said we are now ready to understand that this question concerning transcendence receives as few definitive responses as does the question concerning what we would call the term of origin. We have to understand at least that existence, as it has been illuminated by Kierkegaard and his successors, draws its acuteness only from its tense relation with thought or, rather, the feeling of a transcendence that surpasses it and in relation to which it is. Yet once again we are led to attempt to surpass these oppositions; for as soon as we have seen that the world is internal to us and at the same time external, we will say that transcendence is also internal and external to us.

In our relation with transcendence, poetry can again help us.

> A peine si je sais si je puis dire un nom
> Lorsque je vois briller juste sur ma limite
> Ce feu fait de reflets, ce réel fait de mythes,
> Et le caillou lancé ne renvoie aucun son.
>
> Mais je suis seulement dans mon rapport à Lui,
> Le niant, l'affirmant même quand je le nie,
> Me séparant de lui, vivant mon agonie.
> Un éclat d'outre-mort sur mes confins à lui.
>
> Quand la pensée échoue, elle dresse un drapeau
> Noir et flottant au vent qui vient des autres mondes.
> Mais le soleil bondit, une clarté l'inonde.
> Quand la pensée échoue elle éveille un écho.
>
> Miroitements, scintillements au bord suprême;
> Le silex innommé voit la flamme sans nom
> Sortir de lui, créant un ciel stable et profond,
> Et l'homme dans le noir reçoit un diadème.
>
> Nous sentons alors le sombre attrait
> De cet Autre inconnu qui n'est même pas être,
> Dont personne jamais ne fera le portrait
> Et sur lequel ne peut donner nulle fenêtre.
>
> C'est comme un noyau dur, sombre rayonnement
> Sans que rien du rayon puisse nous apparaître.
> C'est la limite extrême, la borne de notre pensée;
> C'est la transcendance,
> Et quand je peux l'atteindre il est un mur vivant.

Hardly do I know whether I can utter a name
When I see shining just on my horizon
That fire made of reflections, that reality made of myths,
And the stone cast returns no sound.

But I only am in my relation to It,
Denying it, affirming it even when I deny it,
Separating myself from it, living my agony.
A luster on my borders of the thither side of death.

When thought fails, it raises a black flag
That wafts in the wind and comes from other worlds.
But the sun springs up, a clarity floods it.
When thought fails it awakens an echo.

Shimmerings, sparklings at the utmost brink;
The unnamed flint sees the flame without name
Part from it, creating a stable and deep heaven,
And the man in the night receives a diadem.

We feel then the dark attraction
Of that unknown Other that is not even being,
Whose portrait no one will take
And onto which no window can open.

It is like a hard core, a dark radiation
In which no ray can appear to us.
It is the extreme limit, the boundary of our thought;
It is transcendence,
And when I am able to reach it, it is a living wall.

To the question: "Does this light that we perceive beyond ourselves come from ourselves or from something else," we cannot and doubtlessly even ought not to give a response.

It cannot, and truly even ought not to be resolved. If it were, whether in the one way or the other, it would make us accept either an immanence believing itself to be self-sufficient, or a dogmatic transcendence. Thus do we willingly say that it must remain in the state of a question, that what matters here is letting it vibrate in us without, strictly speaking, expecting an answer.

Univers mon immense frère,
Car je ne suis en toi ni de toi,
Et pourtant nous sommes liés
Par la commune destinée.
Je te parle, tu me réponds presque.

Je te vois à travers les brumes.
Nous roulons au but inconnu,
Nés du même père inconnu,
Univers frère mal connu.

Universe, my immense brother,
For I am neither in you nor of you,
And yet we are linked
By common destiny.
I speak to you, you answer me almost.
I see you through the mists.
We roll toward an unknown goal,
Born of the same unknown father,
Universe, brother not well known.

Can Transcendence Be Transcended?

From the moment in which we conceive and sense the idea of transcendence in us, we are able, under the very impulsion of this idea, to feel the need to transcend this very transcendence. The force of this idea can be such that it must surpass itself. Nietzsche was sensitive to this. Yet isn't transcending transcendence necessarily not falling back into immanence but rediscovering immanence? We reply that this immanence we will rediscover is that of nature as the first Greek sages conceived it. In this nature, there is a principle of self-surpassing.

Yet, by making transcendence immanent in this way, don't we risk losing something essential: the fact that man places beyond himself realities that he affirms as superior to him? The question is thus one of knowing whether, just as the nature of things is self-surpassing, the nature of man does not contain this possibility of placing beyond himself, through his very will, realities that he will welcome as superior to him, to whose value he will submit himself, thereby rendering them sacred through his sacrifice.

The Silences of the Dialectic

Our position in the world is such that we can doubtlessly describe it only by joining one of the antitheses to the other. Knowledge is at once distance and fusion. Everywhere we find such joinings of antitheses. We have noted this in the very evolution of science, as well as in the evolution of philosophical problems. But can this be explained otherwise than by the fact that we are attempting to describe something that presents itself to us as a problem? Our theory of knowledge will permit us to insist on the value of the immediate; if one wishes to oppose Hegelianism, then it is necessary to oppose it at its point of departure, at the moment in which it negates the immediate, at the moment in which it transfers the immediate into language and thus finds in it only empty generality. We will only understand the mediate in its relation to the immediate; and the dialectic is justified only insofar as we affirm the realities that precede it, on the one hand, and that surpass it, on the other.

In saying that the dialectic, as we conceive it, is not immanent, we thereby affirm that there is something besides dialectic that can be represented as its point of departure and that can be represented as its point of arrival. Hence the dialectic takes place between two nondialectical moments, between two silences of the dialectic. It is perhaps because he understood these silences of the dialectic that Plato is superior to Hegel. We said that we tried to transcend transcendence; and now we see that we transcend the dialectic. By the first movement we return to the world as it is given to us; by the second, we conceive it as the point of departure and the point of arrival for the movement of the dialectic.

The Levels of the Real

Contemporary philosophy's insistence on subjectivity and on becoming must not make us lose sight of the fact that becoming has rhythms and that subjectivity only makes sense in relation to the objectivities by which it navigates, even if this means also investigating whether it is possible to surpass these two ideas of subjectivity and objectivity at once.

Finally, that before which we would find ourselves would be the world as Plato describes it in the *Philebus*, a world made of essences that have come to be, of a becoming that goes toward essences and obtains them within itself, so to speak, through various sorts of condensations of its own turbulences, in objects that are no longer separate from subjects, in works, in things.

What we have just said indicates that a hierarchy of essences that have come to be will be possible. We do not know the profound reason for the order that is in nature; but there is an order, there is a hierarchy. As Pascal felt, we are situated in the midst. Placed in the midst of this universal given that is the world, opening our eyes onto it, we become aware that the faculty of receptivity and of reception that is in us must not be relegated to second place, even in relation to the creative faculties. "There are," said

Novalis, "many things to say in favor of passivity."[5] Wordsworth spoke of wise passiveness. Between the maxim of Novalis—"One does not make, but one makes possible that it can be made"[6]—and that of Lequier—"To make and in making to make oneself"[7]—we grasp a tension, a lived antinomy, a thesis and an antithesis, without synthesis, which man can encounter without being inserted into the schemas of logic or submitted to the yoke of the dialectic.

The Value of Value?

In classical philosophies, the theory of value was implicit; and this was one of the things that marked their greatness. For Plato, the Good has the greatest worth; yet this statement is not found in a part of Plato's theory that would be separated from his theory of the real. If the theories of value began to be developed above all in the nineteenth century, it is because this was a period in which reality was conceived as separate from value; the scientific view of the world, even the mechanization of the modern world, made philosophers feel the need to add a theory of value to the theory of reality; it was to recognize that reality ceased to have value in itself. It is in the moments in which the reality of value risks disappearing from humanity that the theory of value develops.

Just as knowledge is explained by something immediate that precedes it and is rooted in this immediate something, so is what we conventionally call value rooted in the lived feeling of value.

Each time we investigate the particular problems that arise for us, we will draw out what for us is of absolute worth. Contemporary reflection has brought to light the relation between the affirmation of values and sub-

---

5. [Perhaps Wahl is referring to a line from Fragment 88 of Novalis's *Das allgemeine Brouillon*. See Novalis, *Schriften: Die Werke Friedrich von Hardenbergs*, ed. Paul Kluckhorn and Richard Samuel, vol. 3, *Das philosophische Werk II*, ed. Richard Samuel in collaboration with Hans-Joachim Mähl and Gerhard Schulz (Stuttgart: Kohlhammer, 1960), 256: "Passivitaet ist nicht so verächtlich, als man glaubt." Novalis, *Notes for a Romantic Encyclopaedia: Das Allgemeine Brouillon*, trans. David W. Wood (Albany: State University of New York Press, 2007), 14: "Passivity is not as contemptible as one imagines."]

6. [Wahl cites Novalis's French sentence from Teplitz Fragment 77: ". . . Alle Construction ist also indirect. On ne fait pas, mais on fait, qu'il se puisse faire. . . ." See Novalis, *Schriften: Die Werke Friedrich von Hardenbergs*, vol. 2 (*Das philosophische Werk I*), 609.]

7. ["La formule de la science: FAIRE, non pas *devenir* mais faire, et en faisant SE FAIRE" ("The formula of science: TO MAKE, not to *become* but to make, and in making to MAKE ONESELF"). Jules Lequier, *La recherche d'une première vérité: Fragments posthumes*, ed. Charles Renouvier (Saint-Cloud: Mme Vve Belin, 1865), 92.]

jectivity. And each time we must grasp this subjectivity in its particularity. Even this particularity will only allow us to better enter into contact with what we grasp of the universal within us. Yet, conversely, what we said about the tiered levels of reality will make us understand that our decisions, even if they are ultimately based only on themselves, are framed by, and, so to speak, integrated within, hierarchical wholes.

Philosophy and Non-Philosophy

For us, philosophy is not a self-sufficient totality. It derives its value and its reality from something that comes before it, and also from something that comes after it. Each philosophical idea brings us back and leads us out toward what we would willingly call the non-idea; and philosophy doubly presupposes non-philosophy, which precedes and completes it.[8]

> **Philosophers of to-morrow**
> I see dimly the philosophers of to-morrow
> Anxious to be amid the breath and depth of things,
> Feeling space, time, feeling dense existence,
> Abrupt nextness and fusion of souls.
> They will not be satisfied with a shadowy knowledge,
> For their knowledge will be a sting and an obtuseness,
> A shout rich with silence.

> **Les philosophes de demain**
> Je devine les philosophes de demain
> Anxieux d'être au milieu du souffle et de la profondeur des choses,
> Sentant l'espace, le temps, sentant l'opaque existence,
> L'abrupte proximité et la fusion des âmes.
> Ils ne se satisferont pas d'un obscur savoir,
> Car leur savoir sera dard aigu et masse obtuse,
> Un cri riche de silence.

There are many forms of knowledge besides scientific knowledge. There is a knowledge that lets us commune with the density, with the enormous torpor of things.

> Les sens alors
> > Nous révèlent une vie sans vie, sourde, aveugle,
> > Et pourtant qui est vision, abîme, connaissance.

---

8. [In the original, the following poem is rendered first in English, then in French. As with many other of his poems, Wahl probably wrote it first in English, then included a French translation for its publication in the *Encyclopédie française*.]

Ils nous révèlent
>	Tout l'élément grondant, hérissé, étincelant,
Et il y a d'autres connaissances
>	Ma connaissance aiguë de moi inconnue
et qui nous mènent peut-être vers des expériences mystiques.
>	Et puis par delà
>	De nouvelles clartés cristallines
>	Comme au sortir des grottes
>	Comme au premier matin,
>	Déshabitué.

The senses, then,
>	Reveal to us a life without life, deaf, blind,
>	And yet one which is vision, abyss, knowledge.
They reveal to us
>	The whole growling, bristling, sparkling element,
And there are other knowledges
>	My acute knowledge of my unknown self
and they lead us perhaps toward mystical experiences.
>	And then beyond
>	New crystalline clarities
>	Like quitting caves
>	Like the first morning,
>	Unaccustomed.

To think is to return toward the origin of thought, it is to pass through the understanding in order to pass beyond it, it is to attempt to recapture an unconscious moment that cannot completely be recaptured. Let us recall the words of Heraclitus when he said that it is necessary to hope for what is hopeless, that it is necessary to find the treasure that cannot be found and to which no path will lead. We do not believe, as has been said, that being conceals itself; nor do we believe that it reveals itself; it is again to Heraclitus that we turn, when he tells us: "The prince neither conceals nor reveals himself, but rather signifies."[9]

>	Ainsi sur des béquilles s'avance ma philosophie.
>	Elle n'a pas tout le temps pour arriver

---

9. [Fragment 93 in the Diels/Kranz enumeration. Wahl's French rendition has been translated directly. Cf. Charles H. Kahn's version in *The Art and Thought of Heraclitus: An Edition of the Fragments with Translation and Commentary* (Cambridge: Cambridge University Press, 1979), Fragment 33, p. 43: "The lord whose oracle is in Delphi neither declares nor conceals, but gives a sign."]

Comme la sagesse de Dieu.
    Mais elle sait que là où elle s'asseoira elle sera aussi bien qu'ailleurs, les yeux bandés,
Voyant une route très longue devant elle et derrière elle, et pleurant sur sa tombe au seuil de Chanaan.

Thus upon crutches does my philosophy advance.
It does not have all the time in the world to arrive
Like the wisdom of God.
    But it knows that there where it sits down it will be as well as elsewhere, blindfolded,
Seeing before and behind it a very long path, and lamenting over its tomb at the threshold of Canaan.

Translated by Ian Alexander Moore

Acknowledgments

The editors gratefully acknowledge the following for permission to publish translations of the articles mentioned below.

Librairie Philosophique J. Vrin for permission to translate and publish Jean Wahl, "Préface," in *Vers le concret: Etudes d'histoire de la philosophie contemporaine (William James, Whitehead, Gabriel Marcel)*, 2nd ed. (Paris, 2004), 29–46; and Wahl, "Heidegger et Kierkegaard: Recherche des éléments originaux de la philosophie de Heidegger," *Recherches Philosophiques* 2 (1932–33): 349–70; reprinted in Wahl, *Études kierkegaardiennes* (Paris, 1938), 455–76, © Librairie Philosophique J. Vrin, Paris. http://www.vrin.fr.

Revue de Métaphysique et de Morale for permission to translate and publish Jean Wahl, "Commentaire sur un passage de la 'Phénoménologie de l'Esprit' de Hegel," *Revue de Métaphysique et de Morale* 34, no. 4 (October–December 1927): 441–71, and Wahl, "Le problème du choix: L'existence et la transcendance dans la philosophie de Jaspers," *Revue de Métaphysique et de Morale* 41, no. 3 (July 1934): 405–44.

Mohr Siebeck Tübingen for permission to translate and publish Jean Wahl, "Hegel et Kierkegaard," in *Verhandlungen des dritten Hegelkongresses vom 19. bis 23. April 1933 in Rom*, ed. B. Wigersma (Tübingen: J. C. B. Mohr [P. Siebeck], 1934), 235–49.

La Société Française de Philosophie for permission to translate and publish Jean Wahl, "Subjectivité et transcendance," plus discussion and letters that followed from the *Bulletin de la Société Française de Philosophie* 37, no. 5 (October–December 1937): 161–211.

Madame Béatrice Wahl, Arnulf Heidegger, and the Deutsches Literaturarchiv Marbach for permission to translate and publish Jean Wahl's letter to Martin Heidegger from December 12, 1937, and to update Heidegger's letter to Wahl from December 5, 1937, both housed at the Deutsches Literaturarchiv Marbach and available under access numbers 75.6908/2 and 75.6803.

Éditions de la Baconnière for permission to translate and publish Jean Wahl, "Poésie et métaphysique," in *Existence humaine et transcendance* (Neuchâtel: Éditions de la Baconnière, 1944), 78–97.

The Foundation Royaumont and Madame Béatrice Wahl for permission to translate and publish Jean Wahl, "Ordre et désordre dans la pensée de Nietzsche" and the discussion that followed in *Nietzsche: Cahiers du Royaumont* (Paris: Éditions de Minuit, 1967), 85–94.

La Société Nouvelle de l'Encyclopédie Française and Béatrice Wahl for permission to translate and publish J. Wahl, "Expérience et transcendance," in *L'Encyclopédie Française*, vol. 19 (Paris: Société Nouvelle de l'Encyclopédie Française, 1957), 19.12.9–19.12.14.

Anton Hügli, the Karl Jaspers Stiftung, and the Deutsches Literaturarchiv Marbach for permission to cite and translate from Karl Jaspers's unpublished letters to Jean Wahl, housed at the Deutsches Literaturarchiv Marbach and available under access number 75.9716.

We wish to also thank Bruce Baugh, Scott Davidson, Russell Ford, Anna Johnson, Leonard Lawlor, and Simone Rowen for donating their time and expertise in providing translations and introductions to some of these chapters. We would also like to thank Madame Barbara Wahl for providing us with the picture of her father that appears on the cover of this volume, the Mount Holyoke College Archives and Special Collections for providing a copy of the picture that appears on the frontispiece, and the staff at the Institut Mémoires de l'Édition Contemporaine (IMEC) for their assistance and access to the Fonds Jean Wahl.

Most of all, we wish to thank Madame Béatrice Wahl, the eldest daughter of Jean Wahl and the executor of his literary estate, for her support of this project and her assistance in securing the various permissions to translate and publish the work of her father.

A Bibliography of Works by Jean Wahl

Jean-François Revel once wrote that Jean Wahl's "oral as well as written prolixity made me think of that Greek author from the first century BCE, Didymus, whom his contemporaries had nicknamed Bibliolathas, 'Book-Forgetter,' because he could never recall the complete list of his own works, so many had he composed."[1] Wahl in fact published so much that compiling a complete list would amount to a book project in and of itself, to say nothing of the countless pages of Wahl's unpublished lectures, letters, notes, and poems written in French, English, Italian, and German.[2] We therefore content ourselves with citing his principal works, as well as his other texts and courses on German philosophy that we have used or think may be of interest to the Anglophone reader. We have also endeavored to include the majority of Wahl's works written or available in English. Omitted for the most part are Wahl's brief introductions to journals he edited, his translations appearing in journals, various published conversations in which Wahl took part, and the bulk of his innumerable reviews, such as in the *Nouvelle Revue Française* and *Recherches Philosophiques*.

---

1. Jean-François Revel, *Mémoires: Le voleur dans la maison vide* (Paris: Plon, 1997), 266. Reference found in Hélène Politis, *Kierkegaard en France au XXe siècle: Archéologie d'une réception* (Paris: Éditions Kimé, 2005), 126n72.

2. See Riccardo Piaggio, *Tra esistenza e pensiero: Saggio su Jean Wahl* (Genoa: Il Melangolo, 2007), 12–13.

Les philosophies pluralistes d'Angleterre et d'Amérique. Paris: Félix Alcan, 1920. English translation: *The Pluralist Philosophies of England and America*. Trans. Fred Rothwell. London: Open Court Company, 1925.

Du rôle de l'idée d'instant dans la philosophie de Descartes [The role of the idea of the moment in Descartes's philosophy]. Paris: Félix Alcan, 1920.

Étude sur le Parménide de Platon [A study of Plato's *Parmenides*]. Paris: Rieder, 1926.

Le malheur de la conscience dans la philosophie de Hegel [The unhappiness of consciousness in Hegel's philosophy]. Paris: Rieder, 1929. 2nd ed., Paris: Presses Universitaires de France, 1951.

Vers le concret: Études d'histoire de la philosophie contemporaine [Toward the concrete: Studies in the history of contemporary philosophy]. Paris: Vrin, 1932. 2nd, augmented ed., Paris: Vrin, 2004.

"Le Nietzsche de Jaspers" [Jaspers's Nietzsche]. *Recherches Philosophiques* 6 (1936–37): 346–62. Republished in *Poésie, pensée, perception* (1948).

"Sur l'idée de transcendance" [On the idea of transcendence]. In *Travaux du IXe Congrès International de Philosophie: Congrès Descartes,* 12 vols., 8:56–59. Paris: Hermann et Cie, 1937. Republished in *Existence humaine et transcendance* (1944).

Études kierkegaardiennes [Kierkegaardian studies]. Paris: Aubier, 1938.

Connaître sans connaître [Knowing without knowing]. Paris: G. L. M. [Guy Lévis Mano], 1938.

Existence humaine et transcendance. Neuchâtel: Éditions de la Baconnière, 1944. English translation: *Human Existence and Transcendence*. Trans. and ed. William C. Hackett. Notre Dame: University of Notre Dame Press, 2016.

Poèmes de circonstance, 1939–1941 [Occasional poems, 1939–1941]. Éditions de la revue "Confluences." Lyon: DIA, 1944.

Poèmes. Montreal: L'Arbre, 1945. Partially translated by Charles Guenther in *Voices in the Dark: Fifteen Poems of the Prison and the Camp*. Kirkwood, Mo.: The Printery, 1974. Partially reprinted in *Voices within the Ark: The Modern Jewish Poets*, ed. Howard Schwartz and Anthony Rudolf, 924–25. New York: Avon, 1980.

Tableau de la philosophie française [Portrait of French philosophy]. Paris: Fontaine, 1946.

"Introduction à la pensée de Heidegger" [Introduction to Heidegger's thought (course at the Sorbonne, spring semester, 1946)]. Paris: Centre de Documentation Universitaire, 1946. Republished as *Introduction à la pensée de Heidegger: Cours donnés en Sorbonne de janvier à juin 1946*. Paris: Librairie Générale Française, 1998.

"Les philosophies dans le monde d'aujourd'hui" [Philosophies in the world today]. In *Le choix, le monde, l'existence*, 11–36. Cahiers du Collège Philosophique. Grenoble: B. Arthaud, 1947.

"Note sur la métaphysique." *Revue de Métaphysique et de Morale* 52, nos. 3–4 (July–October 1947): 228–32. English translation: "Note on

Metaphysics." Trans. Hermine Priestman-Bréal. *Transition* 48, no. 1 (1948): 70–72.

Petite histoire de l'existentialisme, suivie de Kafka et Kierkegaard, commentaires. Paris: Club Maintenant, 1947. English translation (without the commentaries on Kafka and Kierkegaard): *A Short History of Existentialism.* Trans. Forrest Williams and Stanley Maron. New York: Philosophical Library, 1949. Republished in part in "The Roots of Existentialism: An Introduction by Jean Wahl." In Jean-Paul Sartre, *Essays in Existentialism*, edited by Wade Baskin, 3–28. New York: Citadel, 1993.

"Karl Jaspers en France" [Karl Jaspers in France (review of Michel Dufrenne and Paul Ricoeur, *Karl Jaspers et la Philosophie de l'Existence: Avec une préface de Karl Jaspers*)]. *Critique* 4, no. 25 (June 1948): 523–30.

The Philosopher's Way. New York: Oxford University Press, 1948.

Poésie, pensée, perception [Poetry, thought, perception]. Paris: Calmann-Lévy, 1948.

Jules Lequier, 1814–1862. Edited with an introduction by Jean Wahl. Geneva: Traits, 1948.

"Lettre-Préface" [Epistolary introduction]. In Karl Jaspers, *Nietzsche: Introduction à sa philosophie.* Trans. from the German by Henri Niel. i–vii. Paris: Gallimard, 1950.

"La théorie de la vérité dans la philosophie de Jaspers" [The theory of truth in Jaspers's philosophy (course at the Sorbonne)]. Paris: Centre de Documentation Universitaire, 1950.

"Sur l'introduction à *L'Être et le Néant*" [On the introduction to *Being and Nothingness*"]. In *Deucalion 3: Vérité et liberté*, 143–66. Neuchâtel: Éditions de la Baconnière, 1950.

La pensée de l'existence [The thought of existence]. Paris: Flammarion, 1951.

"1848–1948: Cent années de l'histoire de l'idée d'existence" [1848–1948: One hundred years of the history of the idea of existence (course at the Sorbonne, December 1, 1948, February 16, 1950)]. Vol. 1, Kierkegaard and Jaspers. Vol. 2, Heidegger. Paris: Centre de Documentation Universitaire, 1951.

"Esquisse pour un tableau des catégories de la philosophie de l'existence" [Sketch for a table of categories of the philosophy of existence (course at the Sorbonne)]. Paris: Centre de Documentation Universitaire, 1951.

"L'idée de d'être chez Heidegger" [The idea of being in Heidegger (course at the Sorbonne)]. Paris: Centre de Documentation Universitaire, 1951.

"Sur l'interpretation de l'histoire de la métaphysique d'après Heidegger" [On Heidegger's interpretation of the history of metaphysics (course at the Sorbonne)]. Paris: Centre de Documentation Universitaire, 1951.

Thomas Traherne: Poèmes de la félicité [Poems of felicity]. Trans. and commentary by Jean Wahl. Paris: Seuil, 1951.

"Notes sur le première partie de *Erfahrung und Urteil* de Husserl." *Revue de la Métaphysique et de Morale* 56, no. 1 (1951): 6–34. English translation: "Notes on the First Part of *Experience and Judgment.*" Trans. Laurence E.

Winters. In *Apriori and World: European Contributions to Husserlian Phenomenology*, edited by William McKenna, Robert M. Harlan, and Laurence E. Winters, 172–97. The Hague: Martinus Nijhoff, 1981.

"La pensée de Heidegger et la poésie de Hölderlin" [Heidegger's thought and Hölderlin's poetry (course at the Sorbonne, December 1951–March 1952)]. Paris: Centre de Documentation Universitaire, 1952.

"Note sur quelques aspects empiristes de la pensée de Husserl." *Revue de Métaphysique et de Morale* (January–March 1952): 17–45. Reprinted in *Phénoménologie, Existence*, a collection of essays devoted to Husserl and Heidegger by Henri Birault, H. L. Van Breda, Aron Gurwitsch, Emmanuel Levinas, Paul Ricoeur, and Jean Wahl. Paris: Librairie Armand Colin, 1953. English translation: "A Note on Some Empiricist Aspects of the Thought of Husserl." Trans. Laurence E. Winters. In *Apriori and World: European Contributions to Husserlian Phenomenology*, edited by William McKenna, Robert M. Harlan, and Laurence E. Winters, 202–25. The Hague: Martinus Nijhoff, 1981. This translation has been revised and edited by Ian Alexander Moore and Alan D. Schrift and is available at https://www.academia.edu/16712734/Jean_Wahl_A_Note_on_Some_Empiricist_Aspects_of_the_Thought_of_Husserl.

Traité de métaphysique. I. Le devenir, genèse des permanences, les essences qualitatives, vers l'homme. II. Les mondes ouverts à l'homme, immanence et transcendance. Cours professés à la Sorbonne [Metaphysical treatise. I. Becoming: The genesis of permanence, qualitative essences, toward man. II. Worlds open to man: Immanence and transcendence (courses delivered at the Sorbonne)]. Paris: Payot, 1953.

La philosophie de l'existence. Paris: Armand Colin, 1954. English translation: *Philosophies of Existence: An Introduction to the Basic Thought of Kierkegaard, Heidegger, Jaspers, Marcel, Sartre*. Trans. F. M. Lory. New York: Schocken Books, 1968.

"Les aspects qualitatifs du réel. I. Introduction, la philosophie de l'existence. II. Début d'une étude sur Husserl. III. La philosophie de la nature de N. Hartmann" [The qualitative aspects of the real. I. Introduction: The philosophy of existence. II: The beginning of a study on Husserl. III: The philosophy of nature in N. Hartmann (course at the Sorbonne, December 1953–May 1954)]. Paris: Centre de Documentation Universitaire, 1955.

Vers la fin de l'ontologie, étude sur "l'Introduction dans la métaphysique" par Heidegger [Toward the end of ontology: Study of Heidegger's *Introduction to Metaphysics*]. Paris: Société d'Édition d'Enseignement Supérieur, 1956.

"*L'introduction à la métaphysique* de M. Heidegger" [M. Heidegger's *Introduction to Metaphysics*]. *Revue de Métaphysique et de Morale* 61, no. 2 (April–June 1956): 113–30.

"Brève introduction aux philosophies françaises de l'existence" [Brief introduction to French philosophies of existence]. In *Encyclopédie Française*, vol. 19,

Philosophie Religion, 19.12-3–19.12-8. Paris: Société Nouvelle de l'Encyclopédie Française, 1957.

"Philosophie et poésie" [Philosophy and poetry]. In *Encyclopédie Française*, vol. 19, *Philosophie Religion*, 19.30-8–19.30-12. Paris: Société Nouvelle de l'Encyclopédie Française, 1957.

"Appendix: Hegel et Heidegger" In Angèle (Kremer-)Marietti, *La pensée de Hegel*, 185–95. Paris: Bordas, 1957.

"Notes on Some Relations of Jaspers to Kierkegaard and Heidegger." Trans. Forrest W. Williams. In *The Philosophy of Karl Jaspers*, ed. Paul Arthur Schilpp, 393–406. New York: Tudor, 1957.

"L'ouvrage posthume de Husserl: La Krisis; la crise des sciences européennes et la phénoménologie transcendantale" [Husserl's posthumous work: The *Krisis*; The crisis of the European sciences and transcendental phenomenology (course at the Sorbonne)]. Paris: Centre de Documentation Universitaire, 1957.

"Sur des écrits récents de Heidegger et de Fink" [On some recent writings by Heidegger and Fink]. *Revue de Métaphysique et de Morale* 63, no. 4 (October–December 1958): 474–89.

"Husserl" (course at the Sorbonne, January–April 1958). Paris: Centre de Documentation Universitaire, 1958.

"Commentaires de la logique de Hegel" [Commentaries on Hegel's logic (course at the Sorbonne, December 1958–February 1959)]. Paris: Centre de Documentation Universitaire, 1959.

"La pensée philosophique de Nietzsche des années 1885–1888" [Nietzsche's philosophical thought in the years 1885–1888 (course at the Sorbonne, January–March 1959)]. Paris: Centre de Documentation Universitaire, 1959.

"Husserl, la 'Philosophie première' 'Erste Philosophie'" [Husserl, "first philosophy" (course at the Sorbonne, April 1959–January 1960?)]. Paris: Centre de Documentation Universitaire, 1961.

"L'avant-dernière pensée de Nietzsche" [Nietzsche's penultimate thought (course at the Sorbonne, December 1959–January 1960)]. Paris: Centre de Documentation Universitaire, 1961.

"Mots, mythes et réalité dans la philosophie de Heidegger" [Words, myths, and reality in Heidegger's philosophy (course at the Sorbonne)]. Paris: Centre de Documentation Universitaire, 1961.

"Le Nietzsche de Fink" [Fink's Nietzsche]. *Revue de Métaphysique et de Morale* 67, no. 4 (October–December 1962): 475–89.

"Présentation" [Introduction]. In a reprint of *Nietzsche: Les plus belles pages*, vii–xiii. Chosen and translated into French by Henri Albert. Paris: Mercure de France, 1963. First published 1899.

Existence et pensée [Existence and thought]. Montreal: Cahiers AGEUM, 1963.

"Préface" [Introduction]. In Ludwig Wittgenstein, *Le Cahier bleu et le Cahier brun: Études préliminaires aux "Investigations Philosophiques,"* trans. Guy Durand, i–xix. Paris: Gallimard, 1965.

L'expérience métaphysique [Metaphysical experience]. Paris: Flammarion, 1964.

"La logique de Hegel comme phénoménologie" [Hegel's logic as phenomenology (course at the Sorbonne)]. Paris: Centre de Documentation Universitaire, 1965.

"Husserl" (course at the Sorbonne). Paris: Centre de Documentation Universitaire, 1966.

"Le mouvement des idées philosophiques depuis 1900" [The movement of philosophical ideas since 1900]. In *Dictionnaire des idées contemporaines*, edited by Michel Mourre, 15–33. Paris: Éditions Universitaires, 1966.

"Poèmes de Jean Wahl." *Revue de Métaphysique et de Morale* 80, no. 3 (July–September 1975): 289–315. Republished in part in an expanded version in *In'hui* 39: *Jean Wahl, le poète* (1992): 5–39.

Kierkegaard: L'Un devant l'Autre [Kierkegaard: The one before the other]. Ed. Vincent Delecroix and Frédéric Worms. Paris: Hachette Littératures, 1998.

La pensée du peintre: Sur la correspondance de Vincent Van Gogh [The thinking of painting: On the correspondence of Vincent Van Gogh]. Ed. Thibaud Trochu and Cyrille Habert. Chatou: Les Éditions de la Transparence, 2008.

And Marc Chagall. *Illustrations for the Bible*. Text by Jean Wahl, with an appreciation by Meyer Schapiro. New York: Harcourt, Brace, 1956.

Other Works by Jean Wahl in English or Available in English Translation

"Poèmes anglais" [English poems]. *Mesures* 3 (July 15, 1935): 111–21. Poems written in English with an accompanying French translation.

"On Poetry." *Chimera* 2, no. 3 (Winter–Spring 1944): 35–40. Republished in an expanded French version in *In'hui* 39: *Jean Wahl, le poète* (1992): 163–69.

"Realism, Dialectic, and the Transcendent." *Philosophy and Phenomenological Research* 4, no. 4 (June 1944): 496–506.

"Concerning Bergson's Relation to the Catholic Church." *Review of Religion* 9, no. 1 (November 1944): 45–50.

"Miss Stein's Battle." *New Republic* (March 19, 1945): 396–98. Review of *Wars I Have Seen*, by Gertrude Stein.

"Summa Contra Aquinatem." *New Republic* (May 21, 1945): 712–13. Review of *Basic Writings of Saint Thomas Aquinas*, edited by Anton C. Pegis. Republished (with additional footnotes) in French as "Note sur les *Basic Writings of Saint Thomas Aquinas*," in Wahl, *Poésie, pensée, perception* (1948).

"Mr. Ransom's Poetry." *New Republic* (August 13, 1945): 196–98. Review of *Selected Poems*, by John Crowe Ransom.

"Existentialism: A Preface." *New Republic* (October 1, 1945): 442–44. Republished in *The Development and Meaning of Twentieth-Century Existentialism*, edited by William L. McBride, 30–32. New York: Garland, 1997. Republished in a revised French version as "La vogue de l'existentialisme," in *Poésie, pensée, perception* (1948).

"A Question: On the Impossibility of Possibility, on the Unnecessariness of Necessity, and on the Reality of Reality." *Philosophy and Phenomenological Research* 7, no. 1 (September 1946): 159–60.

"Freedom and Existence in Some Recent Philosophies." *Philosophy and Phenomenological Research* 8, no. 4 (June 1948): 538–56. Republished in *The Development and Meaning of Twentieth-Century Existentialism*, edited by William L. McBride, 92–110. New York: Garland, 1997.

"Introduction to Leon Brunschvicg's 'The Toil towards Truth.'" Trans. Roger Senhouse. *Transition* 48, no. 3 (1948): 14–18.

"On Reading the Four Quartets." *Poetry* 73, no. 6 (March 1949): 317.

"The Present Situation and the Present Future of French Philosophy." In *Philosophic Thought in France and the United States: Essays Representing Major Trends in Contemporary French and American Philosophy*, edited by Marvin Farber, 35–54. Buffalo, N.Y.: University of Buffalo Publications in Philosophy, 1950.

"A Letter to Marvin Farber." *Philosophy and Phenomenological Research* 11, no. 3 (March 1951): 401–5.

"Interrogation of John Wahl: Conducted by Newton P. Stallknecht." In *Philosophical Interrogations: Interrogations of Martin Buber, John Wild, Jean Wahl, Brand Blanshard, Paul Weiss, Charles Hartshorne, Paul Tillich*, edited by Sydney and Beatrice Rome, 179–200. New York: Holt, Rinehart and Winston, 1964.

"Martin Buber and the Philosophies of Existence." Trans. Forest Williams. In *The Philosophy of Martin Buber*, edited by Paul Arthur Schilpp and Maurice Friedman, 475–510. La Salle, Ill.: Open Court, 1967. Buber's reply to Wahl can be found on 713–14 of the same volume.

"Four Anti-Quartets." *In'hui* 39: *Jean Wahl, le poète* (1992): 41–77. Originally written in English with an accompanying French translation by Jacques Darras.

"Poèmes à William Blake." *In'hui* 39: *Jean Wahl, le poète* (1992): 171–85. Poems in English with an accompanying French translation by Jacques Darras.

"Meditation, Negativity, and Separation." Trans. Christopher Fox and Leonard Lawlor. In *Hegel and Contemporary Continental Philosophy*, edited by Dennis King Keenan, 1–25. Albany: State University of New York Press, 2004. This is a chapter taken from the second edition of Jean Wahl, *Le malheur de la conscience dans la philosophie de Hegel*, 119–47. Paris: Presses Universitaires de France, 1951.

"The Problem of Choice: Existence and Transcendence in Jaspers's Philosophy." Trans. Scott Davidson. Ed. Alan D. Schrift and Ian Alexander Moore. *Journal of French and Francophone Philosophy* 24, no. 1 (forthcoming 2016). Partially translated as Chapter 6 in this volume.

Index of Names

Abraham, 69–70, 95, 160
Adorno, Theodor, 23n86, 102n20, 110n10
Albert the Great, 266
Alexander, Samuel, 37, 38n18, 44, 48, 226
Alquié, Ferdinand, 31
Ambrosino, Georges, 14n42, 216
Anaximander, 223
Aquinas. *See* Thomas Aquinas, Saint
Arendt, Hannah, 9
Aristotle, 40, 40n20, 46, 49, 120, 134, 163, 212, 222n9, 260
Aron, Raymond, 8n19, 9n26, 153, 155, 203–6
Axelos, Kostas, 25n99

Bachelard, Gaston, 220–21
Baeumler, Alfred, 102n20
Baring, Edward, 153–54
Barth, Karl, 52–53, 121, 154
Bastide, Georges, 206–10
Bataille, Georges, 1, 9n26, 14–16, 21, 92, 216–17, 242
Bauch, Bruno, 47
Baugh, Bruce, 21
Beaufret, Jean, 24, 237, 239, 251–53
Beauvoir, Simone de, 1, 6n14, 16, 24, 203n64

Beckett, Samuel, 30
Béguin, Albert, 222n9, 235n47
Bellmer, Hans, 220–21
Bénézé, Georges, 155n12
Benfey, Christopher, 8
Berdyaev, Nicolas, 153, 154n9, 179–81, 183–85, 198, 211
Berger, Gaston, 10
Bergson, Henri, 1, 3, 5, 10n26, 17, 20, 22, 22–23n83, 41, 43, 45–46, 50, 53, 108, 125n46, 126, 211, 214, 224n13, 233, 257–58, 266
Berkeley, George, 44, 261–62, 266
Berthelot, René, 174–79
Bertram, Ernst, 243
Bespaloff, Rachel, 6n13, 7, 8n20, 23n86, 200–1
Bianquis, Geneviève, 18
Birault, Henri, 239–40, 243, 255
Blake, William, 157, 166, 220–21, 225–26, 228, 230, 233n40, 236n50
Blanchot, Maurice, 13, 92, 155
Blin, Georges, 13
Blondel, Maurice, 210n70
Boehme, Jakob, 22, 52–53, 90, 166, 214, 228
Bonnefoy, Yves, 9n26

287

Borkman, Jean-Gabriel, 177
Bourgeois, Louise, 9
Bourget, Paul, 245
Boutang, Pierre, 6n13
Boutroux, Émile, 135n5
Bradley, F. H., 29, 38, 41, 47n32, 265
Brand, 176–77
Brandes, Georg, 175–76
Brémond, Henri, 222n9
Brunschvicg, Léon, 4n6, 23n83, 39n19, 152, 158n19, 165, 174, 185n40, 210n70, 260
Buber, Martin, 9n26, 16
Burman, Frans, 260
Butor, Michel, 1, 9n26

Cabanis, Pierre Jean Georges, 211
Caillois, Roger, 14, 216
Calvin, John, 177
Candide, 87
Canguilhem, Georges, 9n26, 17n53
Carcopino, Jérôme, 3–4n5
Carlyle, Thomas, 177
Cézanne, Paul, 37n12, 164, 231, 257, 267
Chagall, Marc, 9, 30
Chénier, André, 232
Christ. See Jesus
Claudel, Paul, 36, 37n12, 221, 226, 229, 257, 261
Cohen, Gustave, 7n18, 8
Comte, Auguste, 176, 247
Corbin, Henry, 154n10, 211n70
Corte, Marcel de, 222n9
Crane, Hart, 30

Dannecker, Theodor, 6
Darwin, Charles, 176
David, King, 69–70
Davy, Georges, 16n50
de Man, Paul, 9n26
Deguy, Michel, 19n68
Delacroix, Henri, 158n19
Deleuze, Gilles, 1, 9n26, 15, 17–19, 21, 34, 54, 57, 92, 237–38
Derrida, Jacques, 1, 9n26, 17, 19–21, 54, 57, 92
Descartes, René, 3, 39, 45, 90, 111, 155, 158n19, 189n45, 198, 210n70, 259–60

Desjardins, Paul, 8
Diderot, Denis, 211
Didymus (Chalcenterus), 279
Dilthey, Wilhelm, 36n11, 48n34, 51, 119–20
Dionysus, 182–83, 230
Dostoyevsky, Fyodor, 209
Dubief, Henri, 14

Eckhart, Meister, 22
El Greco (Doménikos Theotokópoulos), 231
Eliot, T. S., 30
Éluard, Paul, 220
Epictetus, 58–59
Estève, Claude-Louis, 222n9

Faulkner, William, 30n124
Faust, 87
Feuerbach, Ludwig, 56, 95
Fichte, Johann Gottlieb, 39, 52, 99, 176, 178
Fink, Eugen, 18, 238
Focillon, Henri, 7n18
Fondane, Benjamin, 23, 110n10
Foucault, Michel, 1, 19, 21, 92, 237
Freud, Sigmund, 48n36
Frost, Robert, 30

Gandillac, Maurice Patronnier de, 4n6, 6nn13–14, 16, 19
Gassendi, Pierre, 260
Gast, Peter (Heinrich Köselitz), 242, 246, 251
Gaudefroy-Demonbynes, Jean, 250–51
Geismar, Eduard, 93–94
Geroulanos, Stefanos, 11n30, 107
Gide, André, 157, 166, 242
Gilson, Étienne, 40n20
Girel, Matthias, 26
Glissant, Édouard, 1
Godwin, William, 43n25
Goethe, Johann Wolfgang von, 22, 174n31, 194, 202
Goldthorpe, Rhiannon, 16n48
Green, Elizabeth Alden, 3n4, 6
Guedenet, Pierre, 8
Guenther, Charles, 4n9

Gueroult, Martial, 237, 254–55
Gurvitch, Georges, 5n12, 8n18, 137n12
Guyon, Jeanne-Marie Bouvier de la Motte-, 242

Hadot, Pierre, 9n26
Hamann, Johann Georg, 39, 97, 100–1
Hamlet, 97
Hartmann, Nicolai, 24, 42, 47, 52n39, 184
Hartshorne, Charles, 28
Hegel, G. W. F., 2, 17n54, 21–24, 26, 29, 32–34, 36, 51–106, 108, 110n10, 111, 123, 126n50, 132, 136, 138, 142, 153n6, 158–59, 176, 180–81, 202n60, 209, 211, 222, 227, 231, 238–39, 253–54, 257, 262, 265–66, 271
Heidegger, Martin, 2, 4, 9n25, 11, 12n37, 15, 18–19, 23–27, 29, 33, 36n11, 40–41n21, 42n24, 47–48, 52, 91–92, 103, 107–31, 137n12, 145n41, 148, 153–54, 157–58, 161–65, 168, 170–72, 174, 177–82, 184–89, 192, 196–97, 199, 200n54, 201–2, 208, 213–15, 233, 238, 239n4, 242, 248–49, 251n27, 257–58, 264, 267
Heimsoeth, Heinz, 248, 255
Heinemann, Fritz, 108
Hemingway, Ernest, 30n124
Henry, Michel, 24
Heraclitus, 212, 217, 223, 234, 239, 254, 274
Hersch, Jeanne, 25n97, 198–200
Hesiod, 223
Hocking, William Ernest, 48, 53
Hölderlin, Friedrich, 4, 22, 165, 168, 222, 224, 227, 230–33, 235
Homer, 223
Hönigswald, Richard, 47
Horkheimer, Max, 23n86
Hügel, Friedrich von, 53
Hughes, Langston, 30
Hugo, Victor, 157n17, 224n14
Hume, David, 17, 39
Husserl, Edmund, 11, 14n41, 15, 19, 24, 26–27, 43, 161, 184, 257–58, 261–62, 267
Huxley, Thomas Henry, 176

Hyppolite, Jean, 1, 6n14, 9n26, 17n53, 21, 22n80, 24, 54, 57, 91

Ibsen, Henrik, 117, 176–77
Ionesco, Eugene, 9n26

Jacobi, Friedrich Heinrich, 82, 97
Jakobson, Roman, 8n18, 9
James, William, 20, 32–33, 36–42, 44–46, 49–50, 247n23, 257–58, 261, 266
Jankélévitch, Vladimir, 8n19, 9n26, 13, 53
Jaspers, Karl, 2, 18, 24, 26, 92, 102–6, 108, 121, 130n53, 131–54, 157–58, 161–65, 168, 177–82, 184, 186, 189–93, 196–202, 205, 207, 216–19, 238, 242
Jeanpierre, Laurent, 8n19, 9
Jesus, 66, 69–71, 76–77, 80–83, 84n129, 84n132, 86–88, 92, 95, 97, 100, 120, 230, 249, 254
Johnson, Alvin, 7n18

Kant, Immanuel, 39, 80n113, 99, 120, 144, 184, 190, 193, 198, 249, 255
Keats, John, 232
Kierkegaard, Søren, 2, 9n25, 14–15, 19, 22–24, 26, 36n11, 48, 52, 56, 90–131, 133, 135nn6,8, 136n11, 137n12, 138, 140nn22,24, 141n27, 142n30, 143nn34–35, 145–46, 148–50, 153–54, 156–63, 165, 169–71, 173–84, 186, 188, 190, 192–93, 196–98, 200n54, 201, 206, 209–10, 215, 217–18, 222, 225n21, 242, 249, 254, 257, 267–68
Klages, Ludwig, 195
Klossowski, Pierre, 14, 216–17, 242
Kojève, Alexandre, 9n26, 21, 54
Köselitz, Heinrich. *See* Gast, Peter
Koyré, Alexandre, 5n12, 8n18, 10n26, 11n30, 21, 33, 90–92, 132
Kramer, Franz, 193n51

Lacan, Jacques, 1, 10n26, 16, 57
Lachelier, Jules, 36
Lalande, André, 16n50
Lalo, Charles, 16n50

Index ■ *289*

Lamartine, Alphonse de, 224n15
Landsberg, Paul, 179, 181–83, 185
Langer, Susanne, 9
Laporte, Jean, 16n50
Laurent, Noël, 15
Lavelle, Louis, 155, 203, 206, 211n70
Lawrence, D. H., 42, 53, 157, 166, 228
Le Rider, Jacques, 6n14
Leconte de Lisle, Charles Marie René, 224n16
Leibniz, Gottfried Wilhelm, 145n41, 260
Lenoir, Raymond, 210–13
Lequier, Jules, 247, 272
Leroux, Emmanuel, 152
Lescure, Paul, 220–21
Levinas, Emmanuel, 1–2, 9n25, 10–14, 23–27, 56n5, 92, 109n6, 123, 153–55, 158n18, 186–89
Lévi-Strauss, Claude, 1, 5n12, 8n18, 9
Libra, Pierre, 14n42
Lichnerowicz, André, 10n26
Löwith, Karl, 5n12, 9, 201–2, 217, 237
Lucretius, 234
Luther, Martin, 88, 110n10

Maine de Biran, 43, 48n34, 198, 211
Mallarmé, Stéphane, 3, 221–22, 225, 229, 233
Marcel, Gabriel, 1–3, 9n25, 10n26, 13, 20, 24, 32–33, 36–39, 41–42, 44–50, 52–53, 132–33, 135n6, 136–41, 143–47, 149n50, 150n52, 153, 154n9, 155, 165–74, 179n36, 181, 183, 200n54, 211n70, 237
Marck, Siegfried, 128, 183–84, 211n70
Marcus Aurelius, 58–59
Marion, Jean-Luc, 25n99
Maritain, Jacques, 1, 7n18, 8, 24, 222n9
Massignon, Louis, 10n26
Masson, André, 4n9, 9, 14, 217, 257n2
Mayer, Julius Robert von, 251
Merleau-Ponty, Maurice, 10n26, 16, 25n97, 26–27, 33
Meyerson, Émile, 39n19
Mill, John Stuart, 39
Miller, Henry, 30n124
Monnerot, Jules, 14n42, 216
Montaigne, Michel de, 63, 65

Moore, Marianne, 9
Moré, Marcel, 6n14
Morin, Edgar, 25n99
Morris, Charles, 33
Moses, 69–70
Motherwell, Robert, 9
Moyn, Samuel, 11–12, 22, 153
Mozart, Wolfgang Amadeus, 243
Musset, Alfred de, 221, 224

Nadler, Käte, 101–2, 202, 211n70
Nerval, Gérard de, 222, 229–30, 235
Nietzsche, Elisabeth, 241
Nietzsche, Friedrich, 9n25, 14–15, 17–18, 23n86, 24, 26, 47, 108, 121, 125n48, 133, 138, 144, 148–50, 153, 158, 163–65, 167–68, 170, 172–73, 179–80, 182, 186, 192, 196–202, 213, 216–19, 224n16, 225, 228–30, 233, 237–55, 257, 261–62, 270
Novalis (Friedrich von Hardenberg), 22, 42–43, 60n28, 97, 175, 222, 224–25, 228–30, 232n37, 233–34, 257, 266, 272

Olsen, Regine, 96
Otto, Rudolf, 53
Overbeck, Franz, 241

Parmenides, 207, 223, 229
Parodi, Dominique, 16n50
Pascal, Blaise, 63, 65–66, 79, 111, 133, 149, 239n4, 242, 271
Patch, Helen Elizabeth, 8
Patmore, Coventry, 231
Paul, Saint, 118, 149n50, 175, 249
Perry, R. B., 50
Plato, 32, 34, 37, 40n20, 49, 53, 92, 105, 125, 128, 134, 159, 184, 190–91, 193, 212, 214, 221–25, 228–30, 231n34, 249, 251, 257–59, 263, 266, 271–72
Plotinus, 156, 212
Pöggeler, Otto, 25
Pollnow, Heinz, 189n45, 193–98, 211n70
Polybius, 149n50
Powys, John Cowper, 157, 166
Proust, Marcel, 258
Puech, Henri-Charles, 132

Queneau, Raymond, 10n26
Quinot, Armand, 18

Ravaisson, Félix, 211
Raymond, Marcel, 222n9
Reid, Thomas, 51
Reiner, Hans, 110n10
Rembrandt van Rijn, 231
Renéville, Rolland de, 222n9, 229
Reuter, Hans, 102n20
Revel, Jean-François, 279
Rickert, Heinrich, 249
Ricoeur, Paul, 9n25, 10n26, 13
Rilke, Ranier Maria, 232
Rimbaud, Arthur, 30, 153, 158, 164–65, 168, 170, 172–74, 185, 192, 196, 198–99, 204, 206, 222, 228n28, 233, 236n50
Robbe-Grillet, Alain, 10n26
Roland, Jacques, 13n37
Rollin, Jean, 217
Rougemont, Denis de, 202
Rousseau, Jean-Jacques, 179, 242n12
Russell, Bertrand, 45, 265
Ruttenbeck, Walter, 102n20
Ruyer, Raymond, 38n15, 129, 131n55

Salomé, Lou, 18, 238, 242
Santayana, George, 41
Sartre, Jean-Paul, 1, 6n14, 9n25, 10n26, 12, 15–16, 21, 23–24, 25n97, 26, 32–33, 54–55, 57, 108, 155, 203n64
Saurat, Denis, 43n26, 222n9
Saussure, Raymond de, 8
Schaeffner, André, 242
Scheler, Max, 42–43, 47, 48n34, 119–20
Schelling, Friedrich Wilhelm Joseph, 39, 166, 171, 176, 178–79, 222, 228, 233n43, 258
Schiller, Friedrich, 22
Schlechta, Karl, 242, 244–45
Schlegel, August Wilhelm, 175
Schlegel, Friedrich, 87, 175
Schleiermacher, Friedrich, 81–82
Schopenhauer, Arthur, 213, 244
Schrift, Alan D., 15n45, 245n18
Shakespeare, William, 4, 30n121, 232

Shelley, Percy Bysshe, 43n25, 221, 223–25, 227n25, 230–31
Shestov, Lev, 23n86, 200n54
Simmel, Georg, 51–52
Spaier, Albert, 132
Spencer, Herbert, 39, 170–71, 179, 184
Spengler, Oswald, 36n11, 41n21
Spinoza, Baruch, 78n104, 167n30, 211
Stein, Gertrude, 30n124
Steinbeck, John, 30n124
Stenzel, Julius, 125n47
Stevens, Wallace, 9, 30
Swinburne, Algernon Charles, 225

Taine, Hippolyte, 211
Tarasti, Eero, 155
Taubes, Jacob, 239, 254–55
Theophrastus, 223
Thibaudet, Albert, 229
Thomas Aquinas, Saint, 39–40
Tieck, Ludwig, 175, 230n32
Tolstoy, Leo, 202
Traherne, Thomas, 29–30, 226–27
Troeltsch, Ernst, 51

Valéry, Paul, 144, 222, 228–29, 257, 260
Van Gogh, Vincent, 30, 153, 158, 164–65, 170, 172–73, 192, 196, 198–99, 204, 206, 231, 257, 267, 284
Vattimo, Gianni, 237
Vigny, Alfred de, 224n16, 231
Voltaire (François-Marie Arouet), 242

Waelhens, Alphonse de, 28–29
Wagner, Richard, 227n25, 229, 245
Wahl, Marcelle (née Sicard), 9, 13, 30n121
Weil, Eric, 10n26
Weil, Simone, 1, 7n16
Whitehead, Alfred North, 10n26, 26, 29, 32–33, 36–50, 109, 110n9, 126, 221, 223–24, 257, 259–60
Whitman, Walt 222, 228–29, 233
Woolf, Virginia, 258
Wordsworth, William, 43n25, 221, 223–24, 230–31, 272

Zadkine, Ossip, 9
Zamberlin, Mary, 15n45, 16n48

Perspectives in Continental Philosophy
John D. Caputo, series editor

Recent titles

An Yountae, *The Decolonial Abyss: Mysticism and Cosmopolitics from the Ruins.*

Jean Wahl, *Transcendence and the Concrete: Selected Writings.* Edited and with an Introduction by Alan D. Schrift and Ian Alexander Moore.

Colby Dickinson, *Words Fail: Theology, Poetry, and the Challenge of Representation.*

Emmanuel Falque, *The Wedding Feast of the Lamb: Eros, the Body, and the Eucharist.* Translated by George Hughes.

Emmanuel Falque, *Crossing the Rubicon: The Borderlands of Philosophy and Theology.* Translated by Reuben Shank. Introduction by Matthew Farley.

Colby Dickinson and Stéphane Symons, eds., *Walter Benjamin and Theology.*

Don Ihde, *Husserl's Missing Technologies.*

William S. Allen, *Aesthetics of Negativity: Blanchot, Adorno, and Autonomy.*

Jeremy Biles and Kent L. Brintnall, eds., *Georges Bataille and the Study of Religion.*

Tarek R. Dika and W. Chris Hackett, *Quiet Powers of the Possible: Interviews in Contemporary French Phenomenology.* Foreword by Richard Kearney.

Richard Kearney and Brian Treanor, eds., *Carnal Hermeneutics.*

Aaron T. Looney, *Vladimir Jankélévitch: The Time of Forgiveness.*

Vanessa Lemm, ed., *Nietzsche and the Becoming of Life.*

Edward Baring and Peter E. Gordon, eds., *The Trace of God: Derrida and Religion.*

Jean-Louis Chrétien, *Under the Gaze of the Bible.* Translated by John Marson Dunaway.

Michael Naas, *The End of the World and Other Teachable Moments: Jacques Derrida's Final Seminar.*

Noëlle Vahanian, *The Rebellious No: Variations on a Secular Theology of Language.*

A complete list of titles is available at http://fordhampress.com.

www.ingramcontent.com/pod-product-compliance
Lightning Source LLC
Chambersburg PA
CBHW030435300426
44112CB00009B/1011